CHARLES DICKENS

THE YORKSHIRE SCHOOLMASTER AT THE SARACEN'S HEAD.

CHARLES DICKENS

Nicholas Nickleby

VOLUME I

WITH ILLUSTRATIONS BY

HABLÔT KNIGHT BROWNE ('PHIZ')

WALTER J. BLACK, INC.

NEW YORK

PRINTED IN THE UNITED STATES OF AMERICA

CONTENTS

CONTENTS

CONTENTS

ILLUSTRATIONS

LIFE AND ADVENTURES OF NICHOLAS NICKLEBY

CHAPTER I

INTRODUCES ALL THE REST

THERE once lived, in a sequestered part of the county of Devonshire, one Mr. Godfrey Nickleby: a worthy gentleman, who, taking it into his head rather late in life that he must get married, and not being young enough or rich enough to aspire to the hand of a lady of fortune, had wedded an old flame out of mere attachment, who in her turn had taken him for the same reason. Thus two people who cannot afford to play cards for money, sometimes sit down to a quiet game for love.

Some ill-conditioned persons who sneer at the life-matrimonial, may perhaps suggest, in this place, that the good couple would be better likened to two principals in a sparring match, who, when fortune is low and backers scarce, will chivalrously set to, for the mere pleasure of the buffeting; and in one respect indeed this comparison would hold good: for, as the adventurous pair of the Fives' Court will afterwards send round a hat, and trust to the bounty of the lookers-on for the means of regaling themselves, so Mr. Godfrey Nickleby and *his* partner, the honey-moon

being over, looked wistfully out into the world, rely-
ing in no inconsiderable degree upon chance for the
improvement of their means.   Mr. Nickleby's income,
at the period of his marriage, fluctuated between sixty
and eighty pounds *per annum*.

There are people enough in the world, Heaven
knows! and even in London (where Mr. Nickleby
dwelt in those days) but few complaints prevail, of
the population being scanty.   It is extraordinary how
long a man may look among the crowd without discovering the face of a friend, but it is no less true.
Mr. Nickleby looked, and looked, till his eyes became
sore as his heart, but no friend appeared; and when,
growing tired of the search, he turned his eyes homeward, he saw very little there, to relieve his weary
vision.   A painter who has gazed too long upon some
glaring colour, refreshes his dazzled sight by looking
upon a darker and more sombre tint; but everything
that met Mr. Nickleby's gaze wore so black and
gloomy a hue, that he would have been beyond description refreshed by the very reverse of the contrast.

At length, after five years, when Mrs. Nickleby had
presented her husband with a couple of sons, and that
embarrassed gentleman, impressed with the necessity
of making some provision for his family, was seriously
revolving in his mind a little commercial speculation
of insuring his life next quarter-day, and then falling
from the top of the Monument by accident, there
came, one morning, by the general post, a black-
bordered letter to inform him how his uncle, Mr.
Ralph Nickleby, was dead, and had left him the bulk
of his little property, amounting in all to five thousand pounds sterling.

As the deceased had taken no further notice of his
nephew in his lifetime, than sending to his eldest boy

(who had been christened after him, on desperate speculation) a silver spoon in a morocco case, which, as he had not too much to eat with it, seemed a kind of satire upon his having been born without that useful article of plate in his mouth, Mr. Godfrey Nickleby could, at first, scarcely believe the tidings thus conveyed to him. On examination, however, they turned out to be strictly correct. The amiable old gentleman, it seemed, had intended to leave the whole to the Royal Humane Society, and had indeed executed a will to that effect; but the Institution, having been unfortunate enough, a few months before, to save the life of a poor relation to whom he paid a weekly allowance of three shillings and sixpence, he had, in a fit of very natural exasperation, revoked the bequest in a codicil, and left it all to Mr. Godfrey Nickleby; with a special mention of his indignation, not only against the society for saving the poor relation's life, but against the poor relation also, for allowing himself to be saved.

With a portion of this property Mr. Godfrey Nickleby purchased a small farm, near Dawlish in Devonshire, whither he retired with his wife and two children, to live upon the best interest he could get for the rest of his money, and the little produce he could raise from his land. The two prospered so well together that, when he died, some fifteen years after this period, and some five after his wife, he was enabled to leave, to his eldest son, Ralph, three thousand pounds in cash, and to his youngest son, Nicholas, one thousand and the farm, which was as small a landed estate as one would desire to see.

These two brothers had been brought up together in a school at Exeter; and, being accustomed to go home once a week, had often heard, from their mother's lips, long accounts of their father's sufferings in his days of poverty, and of their deceased uncle's importance in his days of affluence: which recitals produced a very different impression on the two: for, while the younger, who was of a timid and retiring disposition, gleaned from thence nothing but forewarnings to shun the great world and attach himself to the quiet routine of a country life, Ralph, the elder, deduced from the often-repeated tale the two great morals that riches are the only true source of happiness and power, and that it is lawful and just to compass their acquisition by all means short of felony. 'And,' reasoned Ralph with himself, 'if no good came of my uncle's money when he was alive, a great deal of good came of it after he was dead, inasmuch as my father has got it now, and is saving it up for me, which is a highly virtuous purpose; and, going back to the old gentleman, good *did* come of it to him too, for he had the pleasure of thinking of it all his life long, and of being envied and courted by all his family besides.'   And Ralph always wound up these mental soliloquies by arriving at the conclusion, that there was nothing like money.

Not confining himself to theory, or permitting his faculties to rust, even at that early age, in mere abstract speculations, this promising lad commenced usurer on a limited scale at school; putting out at good interest a small capital of slate-pencil and marbles, and gradually extending his operations until they aspired to the copper coinage of this realm, in which he speculated to considerable advantage.   Nor did he trouble his borrowers with abstract calculations of fig. ures, or references to ready-reckoners; his simple rule of interest being all comprised in the one golden sentence, 'two-pence for every halfpenny,' which greatly simplified the accounts, and which, as a familiar precept, more easily acquired and retained in the memory than any known rule of arithmetic, cannot be too strongly recommended to the notice of capitalists, both large and small, and more especially of money-brokers and bill-discounters. Indeed, to do these gentlemen justice, many of them are to this day in the frequent habit of adopting it, with eminent success.

In like manner, did young Ralph Nickleby avoid all those minute and intricate calculations of odd days, which nobody who has worked sums in simple interest can fail to have found most embarrassing, by establishing the one general rule that all sums of principal and interest should be paid on pocket-money day, that is to say, on Saturday: and that whether a loan were contracted on the Monday, or on the Friday, the amount of interest should be, in both cases, the same. Indeed he argued, and with great show of reason, that it ought to be rather more for one day than for five, inasmuch as the borrower might in the former case be very fairly presumed to be in great extremity, otherwise he would not borrow at all with such odds against him. This fact is interesting, as illustrating the secret connection and sympathy which always exists between great minds. Though Master Ralph Nickleby was not at that time aware of it, the class of gentlemen before alluded to, proceed on just the same principle in all their transactions.

From what we have said of this young gentleman, and the natural admiration the reader will immediately conceive of his character, it may perhaps be inferred that he is to be the hero of the work which we shall presently begin. To set this point at rest, for once and for ever, we hasten to undeceive them, and stride to its commencement.

On the death of his father, Ralph Nickleby, who had been some time before placed in a mercantile house in London, applied himself passionately to his old pursuit of money-getting, in which he speedily became so buried and absorbed, that he quite forgot his brother for many years; and if, at times, a recollection of his old playfellow broke upon him through the haze in which he lived—for gold conjures up a mist about a man, more destructive of all his old senses and lulling to his feelings than the fumes of charcoal—it brought along with it a companion thought, that if they were intimate he would want to borrow money of him. So, Mr. Ralph Nickleby shrugged his shoulders, and said things were better as they were.

As for Nicholas, he lived a single man on the patrimonial estate until he grew tired of living alone, and then he took to wife the daughter of a neighbouring gentleman with a dower of one thousand pounds. This good lady bore him two children, a son and a daughter, and when the son was about nineteen, and the daughter fourteen, as near as we can guess—impartial records of young ladies' ages being, before the passing of the new act, nowhere preserved in the registries of this country—Mr. Nickleby looked about him for the means of repairing his capital, now sadly reduced by this increase in his family, and the expenses of their education.

'Speculate with it,' said Mrs. Nickleby.

'Spec—u—late, my dear?' said Mr. Nickleby, as though in doubt.

'Why not?' asked Mrs. Nickleby.

'Because, my dear, if we *should* lose it,' rejoined Mr. Nickleby, who was a slow and time-taking speaker, 'if we *should* lose it, we shall no longer be able to live, my dear.'

'Fiddle!' said Mrs. Nickleby.

'I am not altogether sure of that, my dear,' said Mr. Nickleby.

'There 's Nicholas,' pursued the lady, 'quite a young man—it 's time he was in the way of doing something for himself; and Kate too, poor girl, without a penny in the world. Think of your brother! Would he be what he is, if he hadn't speculated?'

'That 's true,' replied Mr. Nickleby. 'Very good my dear. Yes, I *will* speculate, my dear.'

Speculation is a round game; the players see little or nothing of their cards at first starting; gains *may* be great—and so may losses. The run of luck went against Mr. Nickleby. A mania prevailed, a bubble burst, four stock-brokers took villa residences at Florence, four hundred nobodies were ruined, and among them Mr. Nickleby.

'The very house I live in,' sighed the poor gentleman, 'may be taken from me to-morrow. Not an article of my old furniture, but will be sold to strangers!'

The last reflection hurt him so much, that he took at once to his bed; apparently resolved to keep that, at all events.

'Cheer up, sir!' said the apothecary.

'You mustn't let yourself be cast down, sir,' said the nurse.

'Such things happen every day,' remarked the lawyer.

'And it is very sinful to rebel against them,' whispered the clergyman.

'And what no man with a family ought to do,' added the neighbours.

Mr. Nickleby shook his head, and motioning them all out of the room, embraced his wife and children, and having pressed them by turns to his languidly beating heart, sunk exhausted on his pillow. They were concerned to find that his reason went astray after this; for he babbled, for a long time, about the generosity and goodness of his brother, and the merry old times when they were at school together. This fit of wandering past, he solemnly commended them to One who never deserted the widow or her father-less children, and, smiling gently on them, turned upon his face, and observed, that he thought he could fall asleep.

CHAPTER II

OF MR. RALPH NICKLEBY, AND HIS ESTABLISHMENT, AND HIS UNDERTAKINGS. AND OF A GREAT JOINT STOCK COMPANY OF VAST NATIONAL IMPORTANCE

MR. RALPH NICKLEBY was not, strictly speaking, what you would call a merchant, neither was he a banker, nor an attorney, nor a special pleader, nor a notary. He was certainly not a tradesman, and still less could he lay any claim to the title of a professional gentleman; for it would have been impossible to men-tion any recognised profession to which he belonged. Nevertheless, as he lived in a spacious house in Golden Square, which, in addition to a brass plate upon the street-door, had another brass plate two sizes and a half smaller upon the left hand door-post, surmount-ing a brass model of an infant's fist grasping a frag-ment of a skewer, and displaying the word 'Office,' it was clear that Mr. Ralph Nickleby did, or pre-tended to do, business of some kind; and the fact, if it required any further circumstantial evidence, was abundantly demonstrated, by the diurnal attendance, between the hours of half-past nine and five, of a sal-low-faced man in rusty brown, who sat upon an un-commonly hard stool in a species of butler's pantry at the end of the passage, and always had a pen behind his ear when he answered the bell.

Although a few members of the graver professions live about Golden Square, it is not exactly in anybody's way to or from anywhere. It is one of the squares that have been; a quarter of the town that has gone down in the world, and taken to letting lodgings. Many of its first and second floors are let, furnished, to single gentlemen; and it takes boarders besides. It is a great resort of foreigners. The dark-complexioned men who wear large rings, and heavy watchguards, and bushy whiskers, and who congregate under the Opera Colonnade, and about the box-office in the season, between four and five in the afternoon, when they give away the orders,—all live in Golden Square, or within a street of it. Two or three violins and a wind instrument from the Opera band reside within its precincts. Its boarding houses are musical, and the notes of pianos and harps float in the evening time round the head of the mournful statue, the guardian genius of a little wilderness of shrubs, in the centre of the square. On a summer's night, windows are thrown open, and groups of swarthy mustachioed men are seen by the passer-by, lounging at the casements, and smoking fearfully. Sounds of gruff voices practising vocal music invade the evening's silence; and the fumes of choice tobacco scent the air. There, snuff and cigars, and German pipes and flutes, and violins and violoncellos, divide the supremacy between them. It is the region of song and smoke. Street bands are on their mettle in Golden Square; and itinerant glee-singers quaver involuntarily as they raise their voices within its boundaries.

This would not seem a spot very well adapted to

the transaction of business; but Mr. Ralph Nickleby had lived there, notwithstanding, for many years, and uttered no complaint on that score. He knew nobody round about, and nobody knew him, although he enjoyed the reputation of being immensely rich. The tradesmen held that he was a sort of lawyer, and the other neighbours opined that he was a kind of general agent; both of which guesses were as correct and definite as guesses about other people's affairs usually are, or need to be.

Mr. Ralph Nickleby sat in his private office one morning, ready dressed to walk abroad. He wore a bottle-green spencer over a blue coat; a white waistcoat, grey mixture pantaloons, and Wellington boots drawn over them. The corner of a small-plaited shirt-frill struggled out, as if insisting to show itself, from between his chin and the top button of his spencer; and the latter garment was not made low enough to conceal a long gold watch-chain, composed of a series of plain rings, which had its beginning at the handle of a gold repeater in Mr. Nickleby's pocket, and its termination in two little keys: one belonging to the watch itself, and the other to some patent padlock. He wore a sprinkling of powder upon his head, as if to make himself look benevolent; but if that were his purpose, he would perhaps have done better to powder his countenance also, for there was something in its very wrinkles, and in his cold restless eye, which seemed to tell of cunning that would announce itself in spite of him. However this might be, there he was; and as he was all alone, neither the powder, nor the wrinkles, nor the eyes, had the smallest effect, good or bad, upon anybody just then, and are consequently no business of ours just now.

Mr. Nickleby closed an account-book which lay on his desk, and, throwing himself back on his chair, gazed with an air of abstraction through the dirty window. Some London houses have a melancholy little plot of ground behind them, usually fenced in by four high whitewashed walls, and frowned upon by stacks of chimneys: in which there withers on, from year to year, a crippled tree, that makes a show of putting forth a few leaves late in autumn when other trees shed theirs, and, drooping in the effort, lingers on, all crackled and smoke-dried, till the following season, when it repeats the same process, and perhaps, if the weather be particularly genial, even tempts some rheumatic sparrow to chirrup in its branches. People sometimes call these dark yards 'gardens'; it is not supposed that they were ever planted, but rather that they are pieces of unreclaimed land, with the withered vegetation of the original brick-field. No man thinks of walking in this desolate place, or of turning it to any account. A few hampers, half a dozen broken bottles, and such-like rubbish, may be thrown there, when the tenant first moves in, but nothing more; and there they remain until he goes away again: the damp straw taking just as long to moulder as it thinks proper; and mingling with the scanty box, and stunted everbrowns, and broken flower-pots, that are scattered mournfully about—a prey to 'blacks' and dirt.

It was into a place of this kind that Mr. Ralph Nickleby gazed, as he sat with his hands in his pockets looking out at window. He had fixed his eyes upon a distorted fir-tree, planted by some former tenant in a tub that had once been green, and left there, years before, to rot away piecemeal. There was nothing very inviting in the object, but Mr. Nickleby was wrapt in a brown study, and sat contemplating it with far greater attention than, in a more conscious mood, he would have deigned to bestow upon the rarest exotic. At length, his eyes wandered to a little dirty window on the left, through which the face of the clerk was dimly visible; that worthy chancing to look up, he beckoned him to attend.

In obedience to this summons the clerk got off the high stool (to which he had communicated a high polish by countless gettings off and on), and presented himself in Mr. Nickleby's room. He was a tall man of middle age, with two goggle eyes whereof one was a fixture, a rubicund nose, a cadaverous face, and a suit of clothes (if the term be allowable when they suited him not at all) much the worse for wear, very much too small, and placed upon such a short allowance of buttons that it was marvellous how he contrived to keep them on.

'Was that half-past twelve, Noggs?' said Mr. Nickleby, in a sharp and grating voice.

'Not more than five-and-twenty minutes by the—' Noggs was going to add public-house clock, but recollecting himself, substituted 'regular time.'

'My watch has stopped,' said Mr. Nickleby; 'I don't know from what cause.'

'Not wound up,' said Noggs.

'Yes it is,' said Mr. Nickleby.

'Over-wound then,' rejoined Noggs.

'That can't very well be,' observed Mr. Nickleby.

'Must be,' said Noggs.

'Well!' said Mr. Nickleby, putting the repeater back in his pocket; 'perhaps it is.'

Noggs gave a peculiar grunt, as was his custom at the end of all disputes with his master, to imply that he (Noggs) triumphed; and (as he rarely spoke to anybody unless somebody spoke to him) fell into a grim silence, and rubbed his hands slowly over each other: cracking the joints of his fingers, and squeezing them into all possible distortions. The incessant performance of this routine on every occasion, and the communication of a fixed and rigid look to his unaffected eye, so as to make it uniform with the other, and to render it impossible for anybody to determine where or at what he was looking, were two among the numerous peculiarities of Mr. Noggs, which struck an inexperienced observer at first sight.

'I am going to the London Tavern this morning,' said Mr. Nickleby.

'Public meeting?' inquired Noggs.

Mr. Nickleby nodded. 'I expect a letter from the solicitor respecting that mortgage of Ruddle's. If it comes at all, it will be here by the two o'clock delivery. I shall leave the City about that time and walk to Charing Cross on the left-hand side of the way; if there are any letters, come and meet me, and bring them with you.'

Noggs nodded; and as he nodded, there came a ring at the office-bell. The master looked up from his papers, and the clerk calmly remained in a stationary position.

'The bell,' said Noggs, as though in explanation. 'At home?'

'Yes.'

'To anybody?'

'Yes.'

'To the tax-gatherer?'

'No! Let him call again.'

Noggs gave vent to his usual grunt, as much as to say, 'I thought so!' and, the ring being repeated, went to the door, whence he presently returned, ushering in, by the name of Mr. Bonney, a pale gentleman in a violent hurry, who, with his hair standing up in great disorder all over his head, and a very narrow white cravat tied loosely round his throat, looked as if he had been knocked up in the night and had not dressed himself since.

'My dear Nickleby,' said the gentleman, taking off a white hat which was so full of papers that it would scarcely stick upon his head, 'there's not a moment to lose; I have a cab at the door. Sir Matthew Pupker takes the chair, and three members of Parliament are positively coming. I have seen two of them safely out of bed. The third, who was at Crockford's all night, has just gone home to put a clean shirt on, and take a bottle or two of soda water, and will certainly be with us, in time to address the meeting. He is a little excited by last night, but never mind that; he always speaks the stronger for it.'

'It seems to promise pretty well,' said Mr. Ralph Nickleby, whose deliberate manner was strongly opposed to the vivacity of the other man of business.

'Pretty well!' echoed Mr. Bonney. 'It's the finest idea that was ever started. "United Metropolitan Improved Hot Muffin and Crumpet Baking and Punctual Delivery Company. Capital five millions, in five hundred thousand shares of ten pounds each." Why, the very name will get the shares up to a premium in ten days.'

'And when they *are* at a premium,' said Mr. Ralph Nickleby, smiling.

'When they are, you know what to do with them as well as any man alive, and how to back quietly out at the right time,' said Mr. Bonney, slapping the capitalist familiarly on the shoulder. 'By the bye, what a *very* remarkable man that clerk of yours is.'

'Yes, poor devil!' replied Ralph, drawing on his gloves. 'Though Newman Noggs kept his horses and hounds once.'

'Aye, aye?' said the other carelessly.

'Yes,' continued Ralph, 'and not many years ago either; but he squandered his money, invested it anyhow, borrowed at interest, and in short made first a thorough fool of himself, and then a beggar. He took to drinking, and had a touch of paralysis, and then came here to borrow a pound, as in his better days I had—'

'Done business with him,' said Mr. Bonney with a meaning look.

'Just so,' replied Ralph; 'I couldn't lend it, you know.'

'Oh, of course not.'

'But as I wanted a clerk just then, to open the door and so forth, I took him out of charity, and he has remained with me ever since. He is a little mad, I think,' said Mr. Nickleby, calling up a charitable look, 'but he is useful enough, poor creature—useful enough.'

The kind-hearted gentleman omitted to add that Newman Noggs, being utterly destitute, served him for rather less than the usual wages of a boy of thirteen; and likewise failed to mention in his hasty chronicle, that his eccentric tactiturnity rendered him an especially valuable person in a place where much business was done, of which it was desirable no mention should be made out of doors. The other gentleman was plainly impatient to be gone, however, and as they hurried into the hackney cabriolet immediately afterwards, perhaps Mr. Nickleby forgot to mention circumstances so unimportant.

There was a great bustle in Bishopsgate Street Within, as they drew up, and (it being a windy day) half a dozen men were tacking across the road under a press of paper, bearing gigantic announcements that a Public Meeting would be holden at one o'clock precisely, to take into consideration the propriety of petitioning Parliament in favour of the United Metropolitan Improved Hot Muffin and Crumpet Baking and Punctual Delivery Company, capital five millions, in five hundred thousand shares of ten pounds each; which sums were duly set forth in fat black figures of considerable size. Mr. Bonney elbowed his way briskly upstairs, receiving in his progress many low bows from the waiters who stood on the landings to show the way, and, followed by Mr. Nickleby, dived into a suite of apartments behind the great public-room: in the second of which was a business-looking table, and several business-looking people.

'Hear!' cried a gentleman with a double chin, as Mr. Bonney presented himself. 'Chair, gentlemen, chair!'

The new-comers were received with universal approbation, and Mr. Bonney bustled up to the top of the table, took off his hat, ran his fingers through his hair, and knocked a hackney-coachman's knock on the table with a little hammer: whereat several gentlemen cried 'Hear!' and nodded slightly to each other, as much as to say what spirited conduct that was. Just at this moment, a waiter, feverish with agitation, tore into the room, and throwing the door open with a crash, shouted 'Sir Matthew Pupker!'

The committee stood up and clapped their hands for joy; and while they were clapping them, in came Sir Matthew Pupker, attended by two live members of Parliament, one Irish and one Scotch, all smiling and bowing, and looking so pleasant that it seemed a perfect marvel how any man could have the heart to vote against them. Sir Matthew Pupker especially, who had a little round head with a flaxen wig on the top of it, fell into such a paroxysm of bows, that the wig threatened to be jerked off, every instant. When these symptoms had in some degree subsided, the gentlemen who were on speaking terms with Sir Matthew Pupker, or the two other members, crowded round them in three little groups, near one or other of which the gentlemen who were *not* on speaking terms with Sir Matthew Pupker or the two other members, stood lingering, and smiling, and rubbing their hands, in the desperate hope of something turning up which might bring them into notice. All this time, Sir Matthew Pupker and the two other members were relating to their separate circles what the intentions of government were, about taking up the bill; with a full account of what the government had said in a whisper the last time they dined with it, and how the government had been observed to wink when it said so; from which premises they were at no loss to draw the conclusion, that if the government had one object more at heart than another, that one object was the welfare and advantage of the United Metropolitan Improved Hot Muffin and Crumpet Baking and Punctual Delivery Company.

Meanwhile, and pending the arrangements of the proceedings, and a fair division of the speechifying, the public in the large room were eyeing, by turns, the empty platform, and the ladies in the Music Gallery. In these amusements the greater portion of them had been occupied for a couple of hours before, and as the most agreeable diversions pall upon the taste on a too protracted enjoyment of them, the sterner spirits now began to hammer the floor with their boot-heels, and to express their dissatisfaction by various hoots and cries. These vocal exertions, emanating from the people who had been there longest, naturally proceeded from those who were nearest to the platform and furthest from the policemen in attendance, who having no great mind to fight their way through the crowd, but entertaining nevertheless a praiseworthy desire to do something to quell the disturbance, immediately began to drag forth, by the coat tails and collars, all the quiet people near the door; at the same time dealing out various smart and tingling blows with their truncheons, after the manner of that ingenious actor, Mr. Punch: whose brilliant example, both in the fashion of his weapons and their use, this branch of the executive occasionally follows.

Several very exciting skirmishes were in progress, when a loud shout attracted the attention even of the belligerents, and then there poured on to the platform, from a door at the side, a long line of gentlemen with their hats off, all looking behind them, and uttering vociferous cheers; the cause whereof was sufficiently explained when Sir Matthew Pupker and the two other real members of Parliament came to the front, amidst deafening shouts, and testified to each other in dumb motions that they had never seen such a glorious sight as that, in the whole course of their public career.

At length, and at last, the assembly left off shouting, but Sir Matthew Pupker being voted into the chair, they underwent a relapse which lasted five minutes. This over, Sir Matthew Pupker went on to say what must be his fellings on that great occasion, and what must be that occasion in the eyes of the world, and what must be the intelligence of his fellow-countrymen before him, and what must be the wealth and respectability of his honourable friends behind him, and lastly, what must be the importance to the wealth, the happiness, the comfort, the liberty, the very existence of a free and great people, of such an Institution as the United Metropolitan Improved Hot

Muffin and Crumpet Baking and Punctual Delivery Company!

Mr. Bonney then presented himself to move the first resolution; and having run his right hand through his hair, and planted his left, in an easy manner, in his ribs, he consigned his hat to the care of the gentleman with the double chin (who acted as a species of bottle-holder to the orators generally), and said he would read to them the first resolution—'That this meeting views with alarm and apprehension, the existing state of the Muffin Trade in the Metropolis and its neighbourhood; that it considers the Muffin Boys, as at present constituted, wholly undeserving the confidence of the public; and that it deems the whole Muffin system alike prejudicial to the health and morals of the people, and subversive of the best interests of a great commercial and mercantile community.' The honourable gentleman made a speech which drew tears from the eyes of the ladies, and awakened the liveliest emotions in every individual present. He had visited the houses of the poor in the various districts of London, and had found them destitute of the slightest vestige of a muffin, which there appeared too much reason to believe some of these indigent persons did not taste from year's end to year's end. He had found that among muffin-sellers there existed drunkenness, debauchery, and profligacy, which he attributed to the debasing nature of their employment as at present exercised; he had found the same vices among the poorer class of people who ought to be muffin consumers; and this he attributed to the despair engendered by their being placed beyond the reach of that nutritious article, which drove them to seek a false stimulant in intoxicating liquors. He would undertake to prove before a committee of the House of Commons, that there existed a combination to keep up the price of muffins, and to give the bellmen a monopoly; he would prove it by bellmen at the bar of that house; and he would also prove, that these men corresponded with each other by secret words and signs, as 'Snooks,' 'Walker,' 'Ferguson,' 'Is Murphy right?' and many others. It was this melancholy state of things that the Company proposed to correct; firstly, by prohibiting, under heavy penalties, all private muffin trading of every description; secondly, by themselves supplying the public generally, and the poor at their own homes, with muffins of first quality at reduced prices. It was with this object that a bill had been introduced into Parliament by their patriotic chairman Sir Matthew Pupker; it was this bill that they had met to support; it was the supporters of this bill who would confer undying brightness and splendour upon England, under the name of the United Metropolitan Improved Hot Muffin and Crumpet Baking and Punctual Delivery Company; he would add, with a capital of Five Millions, in five hundred thousand shares of ten pounds each.

Mr. Ralph Nickleby, seconded the resolution, and another gentleman having moved that it be amended by the insertion of the words 'and crumpet' after the word 'muffin,' whenever it occurred, it was carried triumphantly. Only one man in the crowd cried 'No!' and he was promptly taken into custody, and straightway borne off.

The second resolution, which recognised the expediency of immediately abolishing 'all muffin (or crumpet) sellers, all traders in muffins (or crumpets) of whatsoever description, whether male or female, boys or men, ringing hand-bells or otherwise,' was moved by a grievous gentleman of semi-clerical appearance, who went at once into such deep pathetics, that he knocked the first speaker clean out of the course in no time. You might have heard a pin fall —a pin! a feather—as he described the cruelties inflicted on muffin boys by their masters, which he very wisely urged were in themselves a sufficient reason for the establishment of that inestimable company. It seemed that the unhappy youths were nightly turned out into the wet streets at the most inclement periods of the year, to wander about, in darkness and rain—or it might be hail or snow—for hours together, without shelter, food, or warmth; and let the public never forget upon the latter point, that while the muffins were provided with warm clothing and blankets, the boys were wholly unprovided for, and left to their own miserable resources. (Shame!) The honourable gentleman related one case of a muffin boy, who having been exposed to this inhuman and barbarous system for no less than five years, at length fell a victim to a cold in the head, beneath which he gradually sunk until he fell into a perspiration and recovered; this he could vouch for, on his own authority, but he had heard (and he had no reason to doubt the fact) of a still more heart-rending and appalling circumstance. He had heard of the case of an orphan muffin boy, who, having been run over by a hackney carriage, had been removed to the hospital, had undergone the amputation of his leg below the knee, and was now actually pursuing his occupation on crutches. Fountain of justice, were these things to last!

This was the department of the subject that took the meeting, and this was the style of speaking to enlist their sympathies. The men shouted; the ladies wept into their pocket-handkerchiefs till they were moist, and waved them till they were dry; the excitement was tremendous; and Mr. Nickleby whispered his friend that the shares were thenceforth at a premium of five-and-twenty per cent.

The resolution was, of course, carried with loud acclamations, every man holding up both hands in favour of it, as he would in his enthusiasm have held up both legs also, if he could have conveniently accomplished it. This done, the draft of the proposed petition was read at length; and the petition said, as all petitions *do* say, that the petitioners were very humble, and the petitioned very honourable, and the object very virtuous; therefore (said the petition) the bill ought to be passed into a law at once, to the everlasting honour and glory of that most honourable and glorious Commons of England in Parliament assembled.

Then, the gentleman who had been at Crockford's all night, and who looked something the worse about the eyes in consequence, came forward to tell his fellow-countrymen what a speech he meant to make in favour of that petition whenever it should be presented, and how desperately he meant to taunt the Parliament if they rejected the bill; and to inform them also, that he regretted his honourable friends had not inserted a clause rendering the purchase of muffins and crumpets compulsory upon all classes of the community, which he—opposing all half-measures, and preferring to go the extreme animal—pledged himself to propose and divide upon, in committee. After announcing this determination, the honourable gentleman grew jocular; and as patent boots, lemon-coloured kid gloves, and a fur coat collar, assist jokes materially, there was immense laughter and much cheering, and moreover such a brilliant display of ladies' pocket-handkerchiefs, as threw the grievous gentleman quite into the shade.

And when the petition had been read and was about

to be adopted, there came forward the Irish member (who was a young gentleman of ardent temperament), with such a speech as only an Irish member can make, breathing the true soul and spirit of poetry, and poured forth with such fervour, that it made one warm to look at him; in the course whereof, he told them how he would demand the extension of that great boon to his native country; how he would claim for her equal rights in the muffin laws as in all other laws; and how he yet hoped to see the day when crumpets should be toasted in her lowly cabins, and muffin bells should ring in her rich green valleys. And, after him, came the Scotch member, with various pleasant allusions to the probable amount of profits, which increased the good humour that the poetry had awakened; and all the speeches put together did exactly what they were intended to do, and established in the hearers' minds that there was no speculation so promising, or at the same time so praiseworthy, as the United Metropolitan Improved Hot Muffin and Crumpet Baking and Punctual Delivery Company.

So, the petition in favour of the bill was agreed upon, and the meeting adjourned with acclamations, and Mr. Nickleby and the other directors went to the office to lunch, as they did every day at half-past one o'clock; and to remunerate themselves for which trouble (as the company was yet in its infancy), they only charged three guineas each man for every such attendance.

CHAPTER III

MR. RALPH NICKLEBY RECEIVES SAD TIDINGS OF HIS
BROTHER, BUT BEARS UP NOBLY AGAINST THE IN-
TELLIGENCE COMMUNICATED TO HIM.   THE READER
IS INFORMED HOW HE LIKED NICHOLAS, WHO IS
HEREIN INTRODUCED, AND HOW KINDLY HE PRO-
POSED TO MAKE HIS FORTUNE AT ONCE

HAVING rendered his zealous assistance towards des-
patching the lunch, with all that promptitude and
energy which are among the most important qualities
that men of business can possess, Mr. Ralph Nickleby,
took a cordial farewell of his fellow-speculators, and
bent his steps westward in unwonted good humour.
As he passed Saint Paul's he stepped aside into a
doorway to set his watch, and with his hand on the key
and his eye on the cathedral dial, was intent upon so
doing, when a man suddenly stopped before him.
It was Newman Noggs.

'Ah! Newman,' said Mr. Nickleby, looking up as
he pursued his occupation.   'The letter about the
mortgage has come, has it?   I thought it would.'

'Wrong,' replied Newman.

'What! and nobody called respecting it?' inquired
Mr. Nickleby, pausing.   Noggs shook his head.

'What *has* come, then?' inquired Mr. Nickleby.

'I have,' said Newman.

'What else?' demanded the master, sternly.

'This,' said Newman, drawing a sealed letter slowly
from his pocket.   'Post-mark, Strand, black wax,
black border, woman's hand, C. N. in the corner.'

'Black wax?' said Mr. Nickleby, glancing at the
letter.   'I know something of that hand, too.   New-

man, I shouldn't be surprised if my brother were dead.'

'I don't think you would,' said Newman, quietly.

'Why not, sir?' demanded Mr. Nickleby.

'You never are surprised,' replied Newman, 'that's all.'

Mr. Nickleby snatched the letter from his assistant, and fixing a cold look upon him, opened it, read it, put it in his pocket, and having now hit the time to a second, began winding up his watch.

'It is as I expected, Newman,' said Mr. Nickleby, while he was thus engaged. 'He *is* dead. Dear me! Well, that's a sudden thing. I shouldn't have thought it, really.' With these touching expressions of sorrow, Mr. Nickleby replaced his watch in his fob, and, fitting on his gloves to a nicety, turned upon his way, and walked slowly westward with his hands behind him.

'Children alive?' inquired Noggs, stepping up to him.

'Why, that's the very thing,' replied Mr. Nickleby, as though his thoughts were about them at that moment. 'They are both alive.'

'Both!' repeated Newman Noggs, in a low voice.

'And the widow, too,' added Mr. Nickleby, 'and all three in London, confound them; all three here, Newman.'

Newman fell a little behind his master, and his face was curiously twisted as by a spasm; but whether of paralysis, or grief, or inward laughter, nobody but himself could possibly explain. The expression of a man's face is commonly a help to his thoughts, or glossary on his speech; but the countenance of Newman Noggs, in his ordinary moods, was a problem which no stretch of ingenuity could solve.

'Go home!' said Mr. Nickleby, after they had walked a few paces: looking round at the clerk as if he were his dog. The words were scarcely uttered when Newman darted across the road, slunk among the crowd, and disappeared in an instant.

'Reasonable, certainly!' muttered Mr. Nickleby to himself, as he walked on, 'very reasonable! My brother never did anything for me, and I never expected it; the breath is no sooner out of his body than I am to be looked to, as the support of a great hearty woman, and a grown boy and girl. What are they to me! *I* never saw them.'

Full of these, and many other reflections of a similar kind, Mr. Nickleby made the best of his way to the Strand, and, referring to his letter as if to ascertain the number of the house he wanted, stopped at a private door about half-way down that crowded thoroughfare.

A miniature painter lived there, for there was a large gilt frame screwed upon the street-door, in which were displayed, upon a black velvet ground, two portraits of naval dress coats with faces looking out of them, and telescopes attached; one of a young gentleman in a very vermilion uniform, flourishing a sabre; and one of a literary character with a high forehead, a pen and ink, six books, and a curtain. There was, moreover, a touching representation of a young lady reading a manuscript in an unfathomable forest, and a charming whole length of a large-headed little boy, sitting on a stool with his legs foreshortened to the size of salt-spoons. Besides these works of art, there were a great many heads of old ladies and gentlemen smirking at each other out of blue and brown skies, and an elegantly-written card of terms with an embossed border.

Mr. Nickleby glanced at these frivolities with great

contempt, and gave a double knock, which, having been thrice repeated, was answered by a servant girl with an uncommonly dirty face.

'Is Mrs. Nickleby at home, girl?' demanded Ralph sharply.

'Her name ain't Nickleby,' said the girl, 'La Creevy, you mean.'

Mr. Nickleby looked very indignant at the handmaid on being thus corrected, and demanded with much asperity what she meant; which she was about to state, when a female voice, proceeding from a perpendicular staircase at the end of the passage, inquired who was wanted.

'Mrs. Nickleby,' said Ralph.

'It 's the second floor, Hannah,' said the same voice; 'what a stupid thing you are! Is the second floor at home?'

'Somebody went out just now, but I think it was the attic which had been a cleaning of himself,' replied the girl.

'You had better see,' said the invisible female. 'Show the gentleman where the bell is, and tell him he mustn't knock double knocks for the second floor; I can't allow a knock except when the bell's broke, and then it must be two single ones.'

'Here,' said Ralph, walking in without more parley. 'I beg your pardon; is that Mrs. La what 's-her-name?'

'Creevy—La Creevy,' replied the voice, as a yellow head-dress bobbed over the banisters.

'I 'll speak to you a moment, ma'am, with your leave,' said Ralph.

The voice replied that the gentleman was to walk up; but he had walked up before it spoke, and stepping into the first floor, was received by the wearer of the yellow head-dress, who had a gown to corre-

spond, and was of much the same colour herself.
Miss La Creevy was a mincing young lady of fifty,
and Miss La Creevy's apartment was the gilt frame
downstairs on a larger scale and something dirtier.

'Hem!' said Miss La Creevy, coughing delicately
behind her black silk mitten. 'A miniature, I presume. A very strongly-marked countenance for the
purpose, sir. Have you ever sat before?'

'You mistake my purpose, I see, ma'am,' replied
Mr. Nickleby, in his usual blunt fashion. 'I have no
money to throw away on miniatures, ma'am, and nobody to give one to (thank God) if I had. Seeing
you on the stairs, I wanted to ask a question of you,
about some lodgers here.'

Miss La Creevy coughed once more—this cough
was to conceal her disappointment—and said, 'Oh, indeed!'

'I infer from what you said to your servant, that the
floor above belongs to you, ma'am?' said Mr. Nickleby.

Yes it did, Miss La Creevy replied. The upper
part of the house belonged to her, and as she had no
necessity for the second-floor rooms just then, she was
in the habit of letting them. Indeed, there was a lady
from the country and her two children in them, at that
present speaking.

'A widow, ma'am?' said Ralph.

'Yes, she is a widow,' replied the lady.

'A *poor* widow, ma'am,' said Ralph, with a powerful emphasis on that little adjective which conveys so
much.

'Well, I am afraid she *is* poor,' rejoined Miss La
Creevy.

'I happen to know that she is, ma'am,' said Ralph.
'Now, what business has a poor widow in such a house
as this, ma'am?'

'Very true,' replied Miss La Creevy, not at all displeased with this implied compliment to the apartments. 'Exceedingly true.'

'I know her circumstances intimately, ma'am,' said Ralph; 'in fact, I am a relation of the family; and I should recommend you not to keep them here, ma'am.'

'I should hope, if there was any incompatibility to meet the pecuniary obligations,' said Miss La Creevy with another cough, 'that the lady's family would—'

'No they wouldn't, ma'am,' interrupted Ralph, hastily. 'Don't think it.'

'If I am to understand that,' said Miss La Creevy, 'the case wears a very different appearance.'

'You may understand it then, ma'am,' said Ralph, 'and make your arrangements accordingly. I am the family, ma'am—at least, I believe I am the only relation they have, and I think it right that you should know *I* can't support them in their extravagances. How long have they taken these lodgings for?'

'Only from week to week,' replied Miss La Creevy. 'Mrs. Nickleby paid the first week in advance.'

'Then you had better get them out at the end of it,' said Ralph. 'They can't do better than go back to the country, ma'am; they are in everybody's way here.'

'Certainly,' said Miss La Creevy, rubbing her hands, 'if Mrs. Nickleby took the apartments without the means of paying for them, it was very unbecoming a lady.'

'Of course it was, ma'am,' said Ralph.

'And naturally,' continued Miss La Creevy, 'I who am, *at present*—hem—an unprotected female, cannot afford to lose by the apartments.'

'Of course you can't, ma'am,' replied Ralph.

'Though at the same time,' added Miss La Creevy, who was plainly wavering between her good-nature and her interest, 'I have nothing whatever to say against the lady, who is extremely pleasant and affable, though, poor thing, she seems terribly low in her spirits; nor against the young people either, for nicer, or better-behaved young people cannot be.'

'Very well, ma'am,' said Ralph, turning to the door, for these encomiums on poverty irritated him; 'I have done my duty, and perhaps more than I ought: of course nobody will thank me for saying what I have.'

'I am sure *I* am very much obliged to you at least, sir,' said Miss La Creevy in a gracious manner. 'Would you do me the favour to look at a few specimens of my portrait painting?'

'You 're very good, ma'am,' said Mr. Nickleby, making off with great speed; 'but as I have a visit to pay upstairs, and my time is precious, I really can't.'

'At any other time when you are passing, I shall be most happy,' said Miss La Creevy. 'Perhaps you will have the kindness to take a card of terms with you? Thank you—good-morning!'

'Good-morning, ma'am,' said Ralph, shutting the door abruptly after him to prevent any further conversation. 'Now for my sister-in-law. Bah!'

Climbing up another perpendicular flight, composed with great mechanical ingenuity of nothing but corner stairs, Mr. Ralph Nickleby stopped to take breath on the landing, when he was overtaken by the handmaid, whom the politeness of Miss La Creevy had despatched to announce him, and who had apparently been making a variety of unsuccessful attempts since their last interview, to wipe her dirty face clean, upon an apron much dirtier.

'What name?' said the girl.

'Nickleby,' replied Ralph.

'Oh! Mrs. Nickleby,' said the girl, throwing open the door, 'here 's Mr. Nickleby.'

A lady in deep mourning rose as Mr. Ralph Nickleby entered, but appeared incapable of advancing to meet him, and leant upon the arm of a slight but very beautiful girl of about seventeen, who had been sitting by her. A youth, who appeared a a year or two older, stepped forward and saluted Ralph as his uncle.

'Oh,' growled Ralph, with an ill-favoured frown, 'you are Nicholas, I suppose?'

'That is my name, sir,' replied the youth.

'Put my hat down,' said Ralph, imperiously. 'Well, ma'am, how do you do? You must bear up against sorrow, ma'am; *I* always do.'

'Mine was no common loss!' said Mrs. Nickleby, applying her handkerchief to her eyes.

'It was no *un*common loss, ma'am,' returned Ralph, as he coolly unbuttoned his spencer. 'Husbands die every day, ma'am, and wives too.'

'And brothers also, sir,' said Nicholas, with a glance of indignation.

'Yes, sir, and puppies, and pug-dogs likewise,' replied his uncle taking a chair. 'You didn't mention in your letter what my brother's complaint was, ma'am.'

'The doctors could attribute it to no particular disease,' said Mrs. Nickleby, shedding tears. 'We have too much reason to fear that he died of a broken heart.'

'Pooh!' said Ralph, 'there's no such thing. I can understand a man's dying of a broken neck, or suffering from a broken arm, or a broken head, or a broken leg, or a broken nose; but a broken heart!— nonsense, it's the cant of the day. If a man can't pay his debts, he dies of a broken heart, and his widow's a martyr.'

'Some people, I believe, have no hearts to break,' observed Nicholas, quietly.

'How old is this boy, for God's sake?' inquired Ralph, wheeling back his chair, and surveying his nephew from head to foot with intense scorn.

'Nicholas is very nearly nineteen,' replied the widow.

'Nineteen, eh!' said Ralph, 'and what do you mean to do for your bread, sir?'

'Not to live upon my mother,' replied Nicholas, his heart swelling as he spoke.

'You 'd have little enough to live upon, if you did,' retorted the uncle, eyeing him contemptuously.

'Whatever it be,' said Nicholas, flushed with anger, 'I shall not look to you to make it more.'

'Nicholas, my dear, recollect yourself,' remonstrated Mrs. Nickleby.

'Dear Nicholas, pray,' urged the young lady.

'Hold your tongue, sir,' said Ralph. 'Upon my word! Fine beginnings, Mrs. Nickleby—fine beginnings!'

Mrs. Nickleby made no other reply than entreating Nicholas by a gesture to keep silent; and the uncle and nephew looked at each other for some seconds without speaking. The face of the old man was stern, hard-featured and forbidding; that of the young one, open, handsome, and ingenuous. The old man's eye was keen with the twinklings of avarice and cunning; the young man's, bright with the light of intelligence and spirit. His figure was somewhat slight, but manly and well-formed; and, apart from all the grace of youth and comeliness, there was an emanation from the warm young heart in his look and bearing which kept the old man down.

However striking such a contrast as this may be to lookers-on, none ever feel it with half the keenness or acuteness of perfection with which it strikes to the very soul of him whose inferiority it marks. It galled Ralph to the heart's core, and he hated Nicholas from that hour.

The mutual inspection was at length brought to a close by Ralph withdrawing his eyes, with a great show of disdain, and calling Nicholas 'a boy.' This word is much used as a term of reproach by elderly gentlemen towards their juniors: probably with the view of deluding society into the belief that if they could be young again, they wouldn't on any account.

'Well, ma'am,' said Ralph, impatiently, 'the creditors have administered, you tell me, and there's nothing left for you?'

'Nothing,' replied Mrs. Nickleby.

'And you spent what little money you had, in coming all the way to London, to see what I could do for you?' pursued Ralph.

'I hoped,' faltered Mrs. Nickleby, 'that you might have, an opportunity of doing something for your brother's children. It was his dying wish that I should appeal to you in their behalf.'

'I don't know how it is,' muttered Ralph, walking up and down the room, 'but whenever a man dies without any property of his own, he always seems to think he has a right to dispose of other people's. What is your daughter fit for, ma'am?'

'Kate has been well educated,' sobbed Mrs. Nickleby. 'Tell your uncle, my dear, how far you went in French and extras.'

The poor girl was about to murmur something, when her uncle stopped her, very unceremoniously.

'We must try and get you apprenticed at some boarding-school,' said Ralph. 'You have not been brought up too delicately for that, I hope?'

'No, indeed, uncle,' replied the weeping girl. 'I

will try to do anything that will gain me a home and
bread.'

'Well, well,' said Ralph, a little softened, either by
his niece's beauty or her distress (stretch a point, and
say the latter). 'You must try it, and if the life is
too hard, perhaps dress-making or tambour-work
will come lighter. Have *you* ever done anything,
sir?' (turning to his nephew).

'No,' replied Nicholas bluntly.

'No, I thought not!' said Ralph. 'This is the way
my brother brought up his children, ma'am.'

'Nicholas has not long completed such education
as his poor father could give him,' rejoined Mrs.
Nickleby, 'and he was thinking of—'

'Of making something of him some day,' said
Ralph. 'The old story; always thinking, and never
doing. If my brother had been a man of activity
and prudence, he might have left you a rich woman,
ma'am: and if he had turned his son into the world,
as my father turned me, when I wasn't as old as that
boy by a year and a half, he would have been in a
situation to help you, instead of being a burden upon
you, and increasing your distress. My brother was
a thoughtless, inconsiderate man, Mrs. Nickleby, and
nobody, I am sure, can have better reason to feel that,
than you.'

This appeal set the widow upon thinking that perhaps she might have made a more successful venture
with her one thousand pounds, and then she began
to reflect what a comfortable sum it would have been
just then; which dismal thoughts made her tears flow
faster, and in the excess of these griefs she (being a
well-meaning woman enough, but weak withal) fell
first to deploring her hard fate, and then to remarking,
with many sobs, that to be sure she had been a slave
to poor Nicholas, and had often told him she might

have married better (as indeed she had, very often), and that she never knew in his life-time how the money went, but that if he had confided in her they might all have been better off that day; with other bitter recollections common to most married ladies, either during their coverture, or afterwards, or at both periods. Mrs. Nickleby concluded by lamenting that the dear departed had never deigned to profit by her advice, save on one occasion: which was a strictly veracious statement, inasmuch as he had only acted upon it once, and had ruined himself in consequence.

Mr. Ralph Nickleby heard all this with a half-smile; and when the widow had finished, quietly took up the subject where it had been left before the above outbreak.

'Are you willing to work, sir?' he inquired, frowning on his nephew.

'Of course I am,' replied Nicholas haughtily.

'Then see here, sir,' said his uncle. 'This caught my eye this morning, and you may thank your stars for it.'

With this exordium, Mr. Ralph Nickleby took a newspaper from his pocket, and after unfolding it, and looking for a short time among the advertisements, read as follows:

' "EDUCATION.—At Mr. Wackford Squeers's Academy, Dotheboys Hall, at the delightful village of Dotheboys, near Greta Bridge in Yorkshire, Youth are boarded, clothed, booked, furnished with pocket-money, provided with all necessaries, instructed in all languages living and dead, mathematics, orthography, geometry, astronomy, trigonometry, the use of the globes, algebra, single stick (if required), writing, arithmetic, fortification, and every other branch of classical literature. Terms, twenty guineas per annum. No extras, no vacations, and diet unparalleled. Mr. Squeers is in town, and attends daily, from one till four, at the Saracen's Head, Snow Hill. N. B. An able assistant wanted. Annual salary £5. A Master of Arts would be preferred."

'There,' said Ralph, folding the paper again. 'Let him get that situation, and his fortune is made.'

'But he is not a Master of Arts,' said Mrs. Nickleby.

'That,' replied Ralph, 'that I think, can be got over.'

'But the salary is so small, and it is such a long way off, uncle!' faltered Kate.

'Hush, Kate my dear,' interposed Mrs. Nickleby; 'your uncle must know best.'

'I say,' repeated Ralph, tartly, 'let him get that situation, and his fortune is made. If he don't like that, let him get one for himself. Without friends, money, recommendation, or knowledge of business of any kind, let him find honest employment in London which will keep him in shoe leather, and I 'll give him a thousand pounds. At least,' said Mr. Ralph Nickleby, checking himself, 'I would if I had it.'

'Poor fellow!' said the young lady. 'Oh! uncle, must we be separated so soon!'

'Don't tease your uncle with questions when he is thinking only for our good, my love,' said Mrs. Nickleby. 'Nicholas, my dear, I wish you would say something.'

'Yes, mother, yes,' said Nicholas, who had hitherto remained silent and absorbed in thought. 'If I am fortunate enough to be appointed to this post, sir, for which I am so imperfectly qualified, what will become of those I leave behind?'

'Your mother and your sister, sir,' replied Ralph, 'will be provided for, in that case (not otherwise), by me, and placed in some sphere of life in which they will be able to be independent. That will be my immediate care; they will not remain as they are, one week after your departure, I will undertake.'

'Then,' said Nicholas, starting gaily up, and wringing his uncle's hand, 'I am ready to do anything you wish me. Let us try our fortune with Mr. Squeers at once; he can but refuse.'

'He won't do that,' said Ralph. 'He will be glad to have you on my recommendation. Make yourself of use to him, and you 'll rise to be a partner in the establishment in no time. Bless me, only think! if he were to die, why your fortune 's made at once.'

'To be sure, I see it all,' said poor Nicholas, delighted with a thousand visionary ideas, that his good spirits and his inexperience were conjuring up before him. 'Or suppose some young nobleman who is being educated at the Hall, were to take a fancy to me, and get his father to appoint me his travelling tutor when he left, and when we come back from the Continent, procured me some handsome appointment. Eh! uncle?'

'Ah, to be sure!' sneered Ralph.

'And who knows, but when he came to see me when I was settled (as he would of course), he might fall in love with Kate, who would be keeping my house, and—and—marry her, eh! uncle? Who knows?'

'Who, indeed!' snarled Ralph.

'How happy we should be!' cried Nicholas with enthusiasm. 'The pain of parting is nothing to the joy of meeting again. Kate will be a beautiful woman, and I so proud to hear them say so, and mother so happy to be with us once again, and all these sad times forgotten, and—' The picture was too bright a one to bear, and Nicholas, fairly overpowered by it, smiled faintly, and burst into tears.

This simple family, born and bred in retirement, and wholly unacquainted with what is called the world —a conventional phrase which, being interpreted, often signifieth all the rascals, in it—mingled their tears together at the thought of their first separation; and, this first gush of feeling over, were proceeding to dilate with all the buoyancy of untried hope on the bright prospects before them, when Mr. Ralph Nickleby suggested, that if they lost time, some more fortunate candidate might deprive Nicholas of the stepping-stone to fortune which the advertisement pointed out, and so undermine all their air-built castles.   This timely reminder effectually stopped the conversation. Nicholas, having carefully copied the address of Mr. Squeers, the uncle and nephew issued forth together in quest of that accomplished gentleman; Nicholas firmly persuading himself that he had done his relative great injustice in disliking him at first sight; and Mrs. Nickleby being at some pains to inform her daughter that she was sure he was a much more kindly disposed person than he seemed; which, Miss Nickleby dutifully remarked, he might very easily be.

To tell the truth, the good lady's opinion had been not a little influenced by her brother-in-law's appeal to her better understanding, and his implied compliment to her high deserts; and although she had dearly loved her husband, and still doted on her children, he had struck so successfully on one of those little jarring chords in the human heart (Ralph was well acquainted with its worst weaknesses, though he knew nothing of its best), that she had already begun seriously to consider herself the amiable and suffering victim of her late husband's imprudence.

CHAPTER IV

NICHOLAS AND HIS UNCLE (TO SECURE THE FORTUNE
WITHOUT LOSS OF TIME) WAIT UPON MR. WACK-
FORD SQUEERS, THE YORKSHIRE SCHOOLMASTER

SNOW HILL! What kind of place can the quiet townspeople who see the words emblazoned, in all the legibility of gilt letters and dark shading, on the north-country coaches, take Snow Hill to be? All people have some undefined and shadowy notion of a place whose name is frequently before their eyes, or often in their ears. What a vast number of random ideas there must be perpetually floating about, regarding this same Snow Hill. The name is such a good one. Snow Hill—Snow Hill too, coupled with a Saracen's Head: picturing to us by a double association of ideas, something stern and rugged! A bleak desolate tract of country, open to piercing blasts and fierce wintry storms—a dark, cold, gloomy heath, lonely by day, and scarcely to be thought of by honest folks at night—a place which solitary wayfarers shun, and where desperate robbers congregate;—this, or something like this, should be the prevalent notion of Snow Hill, in those remote and rustic parts, through which the Saracen's Head, like some grim apparition, rushes each day and night with mysterious and ghost-like punctuality; holding its swift and headlong course in all weathers, and seeming to bid defiance to the very elements themselves.

The reality is rather different, but by no means to be despised notwithstanding. There, at the very core of London, in the heart of its business and animation, in the midst of a whirl of noise and motion:

stemming as it were the giant currents of life that flow ceaselessly on from different quarters, and meet beneath its walls: stands Newgate; and in that crowded street on which it frowns so darkly—within a few feet of the squalid tottering houses—upon the very spot on which the vendors of soup and fish and damaged fruit are now plying their trades—scores of human beings, amidst a roar of sounds to which even the tumult of a great city is as nothing, four, six, or eight strong men at a time, have been hurried violently and swiftly from the world, when the scene has been rendered frightful with excess of human life; when curious eyes have glared from casement, and house-top, and wall and pillar; and when, in the mass of white and upturned faces, the dying wretch, in his all-comprehensive look of agony, has met not one—not one—that bore the impress of pity or compassion.

Near to the gaol, and by consequence near to Smithfield also, and the Compter, and the bustle and noise of the city; and just on that particular part of Snow Hill where omnibus horses going eastward seriously think of falling down on purpose, and where horses in hackney cabriolets going westward not unfrequently fall by accident, is the coach-yard of the Saracen's Head Inn; its portal guarded by two Saracens' heads and shoulders, which it was once the pride and glory of the choice spirits of this metropolis to pull down at night, but which have for some time remained in undisturbed tranquillity; possibly because this species of humour is now confined to Saint James's parish, where door knockers are preferred as being more portable, and bell-wires esteemed as convenient tooth-picks. Whether this be the reason or not, there they are, frowning upon you from each side of the gateway. The inn itself garnished with another Saracen's Head, frowns upon you from the top of the yard; while from the door of the hind boot of all the red coaches that are standing therein, there glares a small Saracen's Head, with a twin expression to the large Saracens' Heads below, so that the general appearance of the pile is decidedly of the Saracenic order.

When you walk up this yard, you will see the booking-office on your left, and the tower of Saint Sepulchre's church, darting abruptly up into the sky, on your right, and a gallery of bed-rooms on both sides. Just before you, you will observe a long window with the words 'coffee room' legibly painted above it; and looking out of that window, you would have seen in addition, if you had gone at the right time, Mr. Wackford Squeers with his hands in his pockets.

Mr. Squeers's appearance was not prepossessing. He had but one eye, and the popular prejudice runs in favour of two. The eye he had, was unquestionably useful, but decidedly not ornamental; being of a greenish grey, and in shape resembling the fanlight of a street-door. The blank side of his face was much wrinkled and puckered up, which gave him a very sinister appearance, especially when he smiled, at which times his expression bordered closely on the villainous. His hair was very flat and shiny, save at the ends, where it was brushed stiffly up from a low protruding forehead, which assorted well with his harsh voice and coarse manner. He was about two or three and fifty, and a trifle below the middle size; he wore a white neckerchief with long ends, and a suit of scholastic black; but his coat sleeves being a great deal too long, and his trousers a great deal too short, he appeared ill at ease in his clothes, and as if he were in a perpetual state of astonishment at finding himself so respectable.

Mr. Squeers was standing in a box by one of the coffee-room fireplaces, fitted with one such table as is usually seen in coffee-rooms, and two of extraordinary shapes and dimensions made to suit the angles of the partition. In a corner of the seat, was a very small deal trunk, tied round with a scanty piece of cord; and on the trunk was perched—his lace-up half-boots and corduroy trousers dangling in the air—a diminutive boy, with his shoulders drawn up to his ears and his hands planted on his knees, who glanced timidly at the schoolmaster, from time to time, with evident dread and apprehension.

'Half-past three,' muttered Mr. Squeers, turning from the window, and looking sulkily at the coffee-room clock. 'There will be nobody here to-day.'

Much vexed by this reflection, Mr. Squeers looked at the little boy to see whether he was doing anything he could beat him for. As he happened not to be doing anything at all, he merely boxed his ears, and told him not to do it again.

'At Midsummer,' muttered Mr. Squeers, resuming his complaint, 'I took down ten boys; ten twenties is two hundred pound. I go back at eight o'clock to-morrow morning, and have got only three—three oughts is an ought—three twos is six—sixty pound. What's come of all the boys? what's parents got in their heads? what does it all mean?'

Here the little boy on the top of the trunk gave a violent sneeze.

'Halloa, sir!' growled the schoolmaster, turning round. 'What's that, sir?'

'Nothing, please sir,' said the little boy.

'Nothing, sir!' exclaimed Mr. Squeers.

'Please sir, I sneezed,' rejoined the boy, trembling till the little trunk shook under him.

'Oh! sneezed, did you?' retorted Mr. Squeers. 'Then what did you say "nothing" for, sir?'

In default of a better answer to this question, the little boy screwed a couple of knuckles into each of his eyes and began to cry, wherefore Mr. Squeers knocked him off the trunk with a blow on one side of the face, and knocked him on again with a blow on the other.

'Wait till I get you down into Yorkshire, my young gentleman,' said Mr. Squeers, 'and then I'll give you the rest. Will you hold that noise, sir?'

'Ye—ye—yes,' sobbed the little boy, rubbing his face very hard with the Beggar's Petition in printed calico.

'Then do so at once, sir,' said Squeers. 'Do you hear?'

As this admonition was accompanied with a threatening gesture, and uttered with a savage aspect, the little boy rubbed his face harder, as if to keep the tears back; and, beyond alternately sniffing and choking, gave no further vent to his emotions.

'Mr. Squeers,' said the waiter, looking in at this juncture; 'here's a gentleman asking for you at the bar.'

'Show the gentleman in, Richard,' replied Mr. Squeers, in a soft voice. 'Put your handkerchief in your pocket, you little scoundrel, or I'll murder you when the gentleman goes.'

The schoolmaster had scarcely uttered these words in a fierce whisper, when the stranger entered. Affecting not to see him, Mr. Squeers feigned to be intent upon mending a pen, and offering benevolent advice to his youthful pupil.

'My dear child,' said Mr. Squeers, 'all people have their trials. This early trial of yours, that is fit to make your little heart burst, and your very eyes come out of your head with crying, what is it? Nothing; less than nothing. You are leaving your friends, but you will have a father in me, my dear, and a mother in Mrs. Squeers. At the delightful village of Dotheboys, near Greta Bridge in Yorkshire, where youth are boarded, clothed, booked, washed, furnished with pocket-money, provided with all necessaries—'

'It *is* the gentleman,' observed the stranger, stopping the schoolmaster in the rehearsal of his advertisement. 'Mr. Squeers, I believe, sir?'

'The same, sir,' said Mr. Squeers, with an assumption of extreme surprise.

'The gentleman,' said the stranger, 'that advertised in the Times newspaper?'

—'Morning Post, Chronicle, Herald, and Advertiser, regarding the Academy called Dotheboys Hall at the delightful village of Dotheboys, near Greta Bridge in Yorkshire,' added Mr. Squeers. 'You come on business, sir. I see by my young friends. How do you do, my little gentleman? and how do *you* do, sir?' With this salutation Mr. Squeers patted the heads of two hollow-eyed, small-boned little boys, whom the applicant had brought with him, and waited for further communications.

'I am in the oil and colour way. My name is Snawley, sir,' said the stranger.

Squeers inclined his head as much as to say, 'And a remarkably pretty name, too.'

The stranger continued. 'I have been thinking, Mr. Squeers, of placing my two boys at your school.'

'It is not for me to say so, sir,' replied Mr. Squeers,

but I don't think you could possibly do a better thing.'

'Hem!' said the other. 'Twenty pounds per annewum, I believe, Mr. Squeers?'

'Guineas,' rejoined the schoolmaster, with a persuasive smile.

'Pounds for two, I think, Mr. Squeers,' said Mr. Snawley, solemnly.

'I don't think it could be done, sir,' replied Squeers, as if he had never considered the proposition before. 'Let me see; four fives is twenty, double that, and deduct the—well, a pound either way shall not stand betwixt us. You must recommend me to your connection, sir, and make it up that way.'

'They are not great eaters,' said Mr. Snawley.

'Oh! that doesn't matter at all,' replied Squeers. 'We don't consider the boys' appetites at our establishment.' This was strictly true; they did not.

'Every wholesome luxury, sir, that Yorkshire can afford,' continued Squeers; 'every beautiful moral that Mrs. Squeers can instil; every—in short, every comfort of a home that a boy could wish for, will be theirs, Mr. Snawley.'

'I should wish their morals to be particularly attended to,' said Mr. Snawley.

'I am glad of that, sir,' replied the schoolmaster, drawing himself up. 'They have come to the right shop for morals, sir.'

'You are a moral man yourself,' said Mr. Snawley.

'I rather believe I am, sir,' replied Squeers.

'I have the satisfaction to know you are, sir,' said Mr. Snawley. 'I asked one of your references, and he said you were pious.'

'Well, sir, I hope I am a little in that line,' replied Squeers.

'I hope I am also,' rejoined the other. 'Could I say a few words with you in the next box?'

'By all means,' rejoined Squeers with a grin. 'My dears, will you speak to your new playfellow a minute or two? That is one of my boys, sir. Belling his name is,—a Taunton boy that, sir.'

'Is he, indeed?' rejoined Mr. Snawley, looking at the poor little urchin as if he were some extraordinary natural curiosity.

'He goes down with me to-morrow, sir,' said Squeers. 'That's his luggage that he is a sitting upon now. Each boy is required to bring, sir, two suits of clothes, six shirts, six pairs of stockings, two nightcaps, two pocket-handkerchiefs, two pairs of shoes, two hats, and a razor.'

'A razor!' exclaimed Mr. Snawley, as they walked into the next box. 'What for?'

'To shave with,' replied Squeers, in a slow and measured tone.

There was not much in these three words, but there must have been something in the manner in which they were said, to attract attention; for the schoolmaster and his companion looked steadily at each other for a few seconds, and then exchanged a very meaning smile. Snawley was a sleek, flat-nosed man, clad in sombre garments, and long black gaiters, and bearing in his countenance an expression of much mortification and sanctity; so, his smiling without any obvious reason was the more remarkable.

'Up to what age do you keep boys at your school then?' he asked at length.

'Just as long as their friends make the quarterly payments to my agent in town, or until such time as they run away,' replied Squeers. 'Let us understand each other; I see we may safely do so. What are these boys;—natural children?'

'No,' rejoined Snawley, meeting the gaze of the schoolmaster's one eye. 'They ain't.'

'I thought they might be,' said Squeers, coolly. 'We have a good many of them; that boy 's one.'

'Him in the next box?' said Snawley.

Squeers nodded in the affirmative; his companion took another peep at the little boy on the trunk, and turning round again, looked as if he were quite disappointed to see him so much like other boys, and said he should hardly have thought it.

'He is,' cried Squeers. 'But about these boys of yours; you wanted to speak to me?'

'Yes,' replied Snawley. 'The fact is, I am not their father, Mr. Squeers. I 'm only their father-in-law.'

'Oh! Is that it?' said the schoolmaster. 'That explains it at once. I was wondering what the devil you were going to send them to Yorkshire for. Ha! ha! Oh, I understand now.'

'You see I have married the mother,' pursued Snawley; 'it 's expensive keeping boys at home, and as she has a little money in her own right, I am afraid (woman are so very foolish, Mr. Squeers) that she might be led to squander it on them, which would be their ruin, you know.'

'*I* see,' returned Squeers, throwing himself back in his chair, and waving his hand.

'And this,' resumed Snawley, 'has made me anxious to put them to some school a good distance off, where there are no holidays—none of those ill-judged comings home twice a year that unsettle children's minds so—and where they may rough it a little—you comprehend?'

'The payments regular, and no questions asked,' said Squeers, nodding his head.

'That's it, exactly,' rejoined the other. 'Morals strictly attended to, though.'

'Strictly,' said Squeers.

'Not too much writing home allowed, I suppose?' said the father-in-law, hesitating.

'None, except a circular at Christmas, to say they never were so happy, and hope they may never be sent for,' rejoined Squeers.

'Nothing could be better,' said the father-in-law, rubbing his hands.

'Then, as we understand each other,' said Squeers, 'will you allow me to ask you whether you consider me a highly virtuous, exemplary, and well-conducted man in private life; and whether as a person whose business it is to take charge of youth, you place the strongest confidence in my unimpeachable integrity, liberality, religious principles and ability?'

'Certainly I do,' replied the father-in-law, reciprocating the schoolmaster's grin.

'Perhaps you won't object to say that, if I make you a reference?'

'Not the least in the world.'

'That's your sort!' said Squeers, taking up a pen; 'this is doing business, and that's what I like.'

Having entered Mr. Snawley's address, the schoolmaster had next to perform the still more agreeable office of entering the receipt of the first quarter's payment in advance, which he had scarcely completed, when another voice was heard inquiring for Mr. Squeers.

'Here he is,' replied the schoolmaster: 'what is it?'

'Only a matter of business, sir,' said Ralph Nickleby, presenting himself, closely followed by Nicholas. 'There was an advertisement of yours in the papers this morning?'

'There was, sir. This way, if you please,' said

Squeers, who had by this time got back to the box by the fire-place. 'Won't you be seated?'

'Why, I think I will,' replied Ralph, suiting the action to the word, and placing his hat on the table before him. 'This is my nephew, sir, Mr. Nicholas Nickleby.'

'How do you do, sir?' said Squeers.

Nicholas bowed, said he was very well, and seemed very much astonished at the outward appearance of the proprietor of Dotheboys Hall: as indeed he was.

'Perhaps you recollect me?' said Ralph, looking narrowly at the schoolmaster.

'You paid me a small account at each of my half-yearly visits to town, for some years, I think, sir,' replied Squeers.

'I did,' rejoined Ralph.

'For the parents of a boy named Dorker, who unfortunately—'

'—Unfortunately died at Dotheboys Hall,' said Ralph, finishing the sentence.

'I remember very well, sir,' rejoined Squeers. 'Ah! Mrs. Squeers, sir, was as partial to that lad as if he had been her own; the attention, sir, that was bestowed upon that boy in his illness! Dry toast and warm tea offered him every night and morning when he couldn't swallow anything—a candle in his bed-room on the very night he died—the best dictionary sent up for him to lay his head upon—I don't regret it though. It is a pleasant thing to reflect that one did one's duty by him.'

Ralph smiled, as if he meant anything but smiling, and looked round at the strangers present.

'These are only some pupils of mine,' said Wackford Squeers, pointing to the little boy on the trunk and the two little boys on the floor, who had been staring at each other without uttering a word, and writhing their bodies into most remarkable contortions, according to the custom of little boys when they first become acquainted. 'This gentleman, sir, is a parent who is kind enough to compliment me upon the course of education adopted at Dotheboys Hall, which is situated, sir, at the delightful village of Dotheboys, near Greta Bridge in Yorkshire, where youth are boarded, clothed, booked, washed, furnished with pocket-money—'

'Yes, we know all about that, sir,' interrupted Ralph, testily. 'It's in the advertisement.'

'You are very right, sir; it *is* in the advertisement,' replied Squeers.

'And in the matter of fact besides,' interrupted Mr. Snawley. 'I feel bound to assure you, sir, and I am proud to have this opportunity *of* assuring you, that I consider Mr. Squeers a gentleman highly virtuous, exemplary, well-conducted, and—'

'I make no doubt of it, sir,' interrupted Ralph, checking the torrent of recommendation; 'no doubt of it at all. Suppose we come to business?'

'With all my heart, sir,' rejoined Squeers. ' "Never postpone business," is the very first lesson we instil into our commercial pupils. Master Belling, my dear, always remember that; do you hear?'

'Yes, sir,' repeated Master Belling.

'He recollects what it is, does he?' said Ralph.

'Tell the gentleman,' said Squeers.

' "Never," ' repeated Master Belling.

'Very good,' said Squeers; 'go on.'

'Never,' repeated Master Belling again.

'Very good indeed,' said Squeers. 'Yes.'

'P,' suggested Nicholas, good-naturedly.

'Perform—business!' said Master Belling. 'Never —perform—business!'

'Very well, sir,' said Squeers, darting a withering

look at the culprit. 'You and I will perform a little business on our private account by and by.'

'And just now,' said Ralph, 'we had better transact our own, perhaps.'

'If you please,' said Squeers.

'Well,' resumed Ralph, 'it's brief enough; soon broached; and I hope easily concluded. You have advertised for an able assistant, sir?'

'Precisely so,' said Squeers.

'And you really want one?'

'Certainly,' answered Squeers.

'Here he is!' said Ralph. 'My nephew Nicholas, hot from school, with everything he learnt there, fermenting in his head, and nothing fermenting in his pocket, is just the man you want.'

'I am afraid,' said Squeers, perplexed with such an application from a youth of Nicholas's figure, 'I am afraid the young man won't suit me.'

'Yes, he will,' said Ralph; 'I know better. Don't be cast down, sir; you will be teaching all the young noblemen in Dotheboys Hall in less than a week's time, unless this gentleman is more obstinate than I take him to be.'

'I fear, sir,' said Nicholas, addressing Mr. Squeers, 'that you object to my youth, and to my not being a Master of Arts?'

'The absence of a college degree *is* an objection,' replied Squeers, looking as grave as he could, and considerably puzzled, no less by the contrast between the simplicity of the nephew and the worldly manner of the uncle, than by the incomprehensible allusion to the young noblemen under his tuition.

'Look here, sir,' said Ralph; 'I'll put this matter in its true light in two seconds.'

'If you'll have the goodness,' rejoined Squeers.

'This is a boy, or a youth, or a lad, or a young man,

or a hobbledehoy, or whatever you like to call him, of eighteen or nineteen, or thereabouts,' said Ralph.

'That I see,' observed the schoolmaster.

'So do I,' said Mr. Snawley, thinking it as well to back his new friend occasionally.

'His father is dead, he is wholly ignorant of the world, has no resources whatever, and wants something to do,' said Ralph. 'I recommend him to this splendid establishment of yours, as an opening which will lead him to fortune if he turns it to proper account. Do you see that?'

'Everybody must see that,' replied Squeers, half imitating the sneer with which the old gentleman was regarding his unconscious relative.

'I do, of course,' said Nicholas, eagerly.

'He does, of course, you observe,' said Ralph, in the same dry, hard manner. 'If any caprice of temper should induce him to cast aside this golden opportunity before he has brought it to perfection, I consider myself absolved from extending any assistance to his mother and sister. Look at him, and think of the use he may be to you in half a dozen ways! Now, the question is, whether, for some time to come at all events, he won't serve your purpose better than twenty of the kind of people you would get under ordinary circumstances. Isn't that a question for consideration?'

'Yes, it is,' said Squeers, answering a nod of Ralph's head with a nod of his own.

'Good,' rejoined Ralph. 'Let me have two words with you.'

The two words were had apart; in a couple of minutes Mr. Wackford Squeers announced that Mr. Nicholas Nickleby was, from that moment, thoroughly nominated to, and installed in, the office of first assistant master at Dotheboys Hall.

'Your uncle's recommendation has done it, Mr. Nickleby,' said Wackford Squeers.

Nicholas, overjoyed at his success, shook his uncle's hand warmly, and could almost have worshipped Squeers upon the spot.

'He is an odd-looking man,' thought Nicholas. 'What of that? Porson was an odd-looking man, and so was Doctor Johnson; all these bookworms are.'

'At eight o'clock to-morrow morning, Mr. Nickleby,' said Squeers, 'the coach starts. You must be here at a quarter before, as we take these boys with us.'

'Certainly, sir,' said Nicholas.

'And your fare down, I have paid,' growled Ralph. 'So, you'll have nothing to do but keep yourself warm.'

Here was another instance of his uncle's generosity! Nicholas felt his unexpected kindness so much, that he could scarcely find words to thank him; indeed, he had not found half enough, when they took leave of the schoolmaster, and emerged from the Saracen's Head gateway.

'I shall be here in the morning to see you fairly off,' said Ralph. 'No skulking!'

'Thank you, sir,' replied Nicholas; 'I never shall forget this kindness.'

'Take care you don't,' replied his uncle. 'You had better go home now, and pack up what you have got to pack. Do you think you could find your way to Golden Square first?'

'Certainly,' said Nicholas. 'I can easily inquire.'

'Leave these papers with my clerk, then,' said Ralph, producing a small parcel, 'and tell him to wait till I come home.'

Nicholas cheerfully undertook the errand, and bidding his worthy uncle an affectionate farewell, which that warm-hearted old gentleman acknowledged by a growl, hastened away to execute his commission.

He found Golden Square in due course; Mr. Noggs, who had stepped out for a minute or so to the public-house, was opening the door with a latch-key as he reached the steps.

'What's that?' inquired Noggs, pointing to the parcel.

'Papers from my uncle,' replied Nicholas; 'and you're to have the goodness to wait till he comes home, if you please.'

'Uncle!' cried Noggs.

'Mr. Nickleby,' said Nicholas in explanation.

'Come in,' said Newman.

Without another word he led Nicholas into the passage, and thence into the official pantry at the end of it, where he thrust him into a chair, and mounting upon his high stool, sat, with his arms hanging straight down by his sides, gazing fixedly upon him, as from a tower of observation.

'There is no answer,' said Nicholas, laying the parcel on a table beside him.

Newman said nothing, but folding his arms, and thrusting his head forward so as to obtain a nearer view of Nicholas's face, scanned his features closely.

'No answer,' said Nicholas, speaking very loud, under the impression that Newman Noggs was deaf.

Newman placed his hands upon his knees, and, without uttering a syllable, continued the same close scrutiny of his companion's face.

This was such a very singular proceeding on the part of an utter stranger, and his appearance was so extremely peculiar, that Nicholas, who had a sufficiently keen sense of the ridiculous, could not refrain from breaking into a smile as he inquired whether Mr. Noggs had any commands for him.

Noggs shook his head and sighed; upon which Nicholas rose, and remarking that he required no rest, bade him good morning.

It was a great exertion for Newman Noggs, and nobody knows to this day how he ever came to make it, the other party being wholly unknown to him, but he drew a long breath and actually said, out loud, without once stopping, that if the young gentleman did not object to tell, he should like to know what his uncle was going to do for him.

Nicholas had not the least objection in the world, but on the contrary was rather pleased to have an opportunity of talking on the subject which occupied his thoughts; so, he sat down again, and (his sanguine imagination warming as he spoke) entered into a fervent and glowing description of all the honours and advantages to be derived from his appointment at that seat of learning, Dotheboys Hall.

'But, what's the matter—are you ill?' said Nicholas suddenly breaking off, as his companion, after throwing himself into a variety of uncouth attitudes, thrust his hands under the stool, and cracked his finger-joints as if he were snapping all the bones in his hands.

Newman Noggs mads no reply, but went on shrugging his shoulders and cracking his finger-joints; smiling horribly all the time, and looking steadfastly at nothing, out of the tops of his eyes in a most ghastly manner.

At first, Nicholas thought the mysterious man was in a fit, but, on further consideration, decided that he was in liquor, under which circumstances he deemed it prudent to make off at once. He looked back when he had got the street-door open. Newman Noggs was still indulging in the same extraordinary gestures, and the cracking of his fingers sounded louder than ever.

CHAPTER V

NICHOLAS STARTS FOR YORKSHIRE.   OF HIS LEAVE-TAK-
ING AND HIS FELLOW TRAVELLERS, AND WHAT BEFEL
THEM ON THE ROAD

IF tears dropped into a trunk were charms to preserve its owner from sorrow and misfortune, Nicholas Nickleby would have commenced his expedition under most happy auspices. There was so much to be done, and so little time to do it in; so many kind words to be spoken, and such bitter pain in the hearts in which they rose to impede their utterance; that the little preparations for his journey were made mournfully indeed. A hundred things which the anxious care of his mother and sister deemed indispensable for his comfort, Nicholas insisted on leaving behind, as they might prove of some after use, or might be convertible into money if occasion required. A hundred affectionate contests on such points as these, took place on the sad night which preceded his departure; and, as the termination of every angerless dispute brought them nearer and nearer to the close of their slight preparations, Kate grew busier and busier, and wept more silently.

The box was packed at last, and then there came supper, with some little delicacy provided for the occasion, and as a set-off against the expense of which, Kate and her mother had feigned to dine when Nicholas was out. The poor lad nearly choked himself by attempting to partake of it, and almost suffocated himself in affecting a jest or two, and forcing a melancholy laugh. Thus, they lingered on till the hour of separating for the night was long past; and then they found that they might as well have given vent to their real feelings before, for they could not suppress them, do what they would. So, they let them have their way, and even that was a relief.

Nicholas slept well till six next morning; dreamed of home, or of what was home once—no matter which, for things that are changed or gone will come back as they used to be, thank God! in sleep—and rose quite brisk and gay. He wrote a few lines in pencil, to say the good bye which he was afraid to pronounce himself, and laying them, with half his scanty stock of money, at his sister's door, shouldered his box and crept softly downstairs.

'Is that you, Hannah?' cried a voice from Miss La Creevy's sitting room, whence shone the light of a feeble candle.

'It is I, Miss La Creevy,' said Nicholas, putting down the box and looking in.

'Bless us!' exclaimed Miss La Creevy, starting and putting her hand to her curl-papers; 'you 're up very early, Mr. Nickleby.'

'So are you,' replied Nicholas.

'It 's the fine arts that bring me out of bed, Mr. Nickleby,' returned the lady. 'I 'm waiting for the light to carry out an idea.'

Miss La Creevy had got up early to put a fancy nose into a miniature of an ugly little boy, destined for his grandmother in the country, who was expected to bequeath him property if he was like the family.

'To carry out an idea,' repeated Miss La Creevy; 'and that 's the great convenience of living in a thoroughfare like the Strand. When I want a nose or an eye for any particular sitter, I have only to look out of window and wait till I get one.'

'Does it take long to get a nose, now?' inquired Nicholas, smiling.

'Why, that depends in a great measure on the pattern,' replied Miss La Creevy. 'Snubs and romans are plentiful enough, and there are flats of all sorts and sizes when there's a meeting at Exeter Hall; but perfect aquilines, I am sorry to say, are scarce, and we generally use them for uniforms or public characters.'

'Indeed!' said Nicholas. 'If I should meet with any in my travels, I'll endeavour to sketch them for you.'

'You don't mean to say that you are really going all the way down into Yorkshire this cold winter's weather, Mr. Nickleby?' said Miss La Creevy. 'I heard something of it last night.'

'I do, indeed,' replied Nicholas. 'Needs must, you know, when somebody drives. Necessity is my driver, and that is only another name for the same gentleman.'

'Well, I am very sorry for it; that's all I can say,' said Miss La Creevy; 'as much on your mother's and sister's account as on yours. Your sister is a very pretty young lady, Mr. Nickleby, and that is an additional reason why she should have somebody to protect her. I persuaded her to give me a sitting or two, for the street-door case. Ah! she'll make a sweet miniature.' As Miss La Creevy spoke, she held up an ivory countenance intersected with very perceptible sky-blue veins, and regarded it with so much complacency, that Nicholas quite envied her.

'If you ever have an opportunity of showing Kate some little kindness,' said Nicholas, presenting his hand, 'I think you will.'

'Depend upon that,' said the good-natured minia-

ture painter; 'and God bless you, Mr. Nickleby; and
I wish you well.'

It was very little that Nicholas knew of the world,
but he guessed enough about its ways to think, that
if he gave Miss La Creevy one little kiss, perhaps
she might not be the less kindly disposed towards
those he was leaving behind. So, he gave her three
of four with a kind of jocose gallantry, and Miss La
Creevy evinced no greater symptoms of displeasure
than declaring, as she adjusted her yellow turban,
that she had never heard of such a thing, and couldn't
have believed it possible.

Having terminated the unexpected interview in
this satisfactory manner, Nicholas hastily withdrew
himself from the house. By the time he had found
a man to carry his box it was only seven o'clock, so he
walked slowly on, a little in advance of the porter, and
very probably with not half as light a heart in his
breast as the man had, although he had no waistcoat to cover it with, and had evidently, from the
appearance of his other garments, been spending the
night in a stable, and taking his breakfast at a pump.

Regarding, with no small curiosity and interest, all
the busy preparations for the coming day which every
street and almost every house displayed; and thinking, now and then, that it seemed rather hard that
so many people of all ranks and stations could earn
a livelihood in London, and that he should be compelled to journey so far in search of one; Nicholas
speedily arrived at the Saracen's Head, Snow Hill.
Having dismissed his attendant, and seen the box
safely deposited in the coach-office, he looked into the
coffee-room in search of Mr. Squeers.

He found that learned gentleman sitting at breakfast, with the three little boys before noticed, and

two others who had turned up by some lucky chance
since the interview of the previous day, ranged in a
row on the opposite seat. Mr. Squeers had before
him a small measure of coffee, a plate of hot toast,
and a cold round of beef; but he was at that moment
intent on preparing breakfast for the little boys.

'This is twopenn'orth of milk, is it, waiter?' said
Mr. Squeers, looking down into a large blue mug,
and slanting it gently, so as to get an accurate view
of the quantity of liquid contained in it.

'That's twopenn'orth, sir,' replied the waiter.

'What a rare article milk is, to be sure, in London!'
said Mr. Squeers with a sigh. 'Just fill that mug up
with lukewarm water, William, will you?'

'To the wery top, sir?' inquired the waiter. 'Why,
the milk will be drownded.'

'Never you mind that,' replied Mr. Squeers.
'Serve it right for being so dear. You ordered that
bread and butter for three, did you?'

'Coming directly, sir.'

'You needn't hurry yourself,' said Squeers; 'there's
plenty of time. Conquer your passions, boys, and
don't be eager after vittles.' As he uttered this moral
precept, Mr. Squeers took a large bite out of the
cold beef, and recognised Nicholas.

'Sit down, Mr. Nickleby,' said Squeers. 'Here
we are, a breakfasting you see!'

Nicholas did *not* see that anybody was breakfasting, except Mr. Squeers; but he bowed with all becoming reverence, and looked as cheerful as he could.

'Oh; that's the milk and water, is it, William?'
said Squeers. 'Very good; don't forget the bread
and butter presently.'

At this fresh mention of the bread and butter, the
five little boys looked very eager, and followed the

waiter out, with their eyes; meanwhile Mr. Squeers tasted the milk and water.

'Ah!' said that gentleman, smacking his lips, 'here's richness! Think of the many beggars and orphans in the streets that would be glad of this, little boys. A shocking thing hunger is, isn't it, Mr. Nickleby?'

'Very shocking, sir,' said Nicholas.

'When I say number one,' pursued Mr. Squeers, putting the mug before the children, 'the boy on the left hand nearest the window may take a drink; and when I say number two, the boy next him will go in, and so till we come to number five, which is the last boy. Are you ready?'

'Yes, sir,' cried all the little boys with great eagerness.

'That's right,' said Squeers, calmly getting on with his breakfast; 'keep ready till I tell you to begin. Subdue your appetites, my dears, and you've conquered human natur. This is the way we inculcate strength of mind, Mr. Nickleby,' said the schoolmaster, turning to Nicholas, and speaking with his mouth very full of beef and toast.

Nicholas murmured something—he knew not what —in reply; and the little boys, dividing their gaze between the mug, the bread and butter (which had by this time arrived), and every morsel which Mr. Squeers took into his mouth, remained with strained eyes in torments of expectation.

'Thank God for a good breakfast,' said Squeers when he had finished. 'Number one may take a drink.'

Number one seized the mug ravenously, and had just drunk enough to make him wish for more, when Mr. Squeers gave the signal for number two, who gave up at the same interesting moment to number three; and the process was repeated until the milk and water terminated with number five.

'And now,' said the schoolmaster, dividing the bread and butter for three into as many portions as there were children, 'you had better look sharp with your breakfast, for the horn will blow in a minute or two, and then every boy leaves off.'

Permission being thus given to fall to, the boys began to eat voraciously, and in desperate haste: while the schoolmaster (who was in high good humour after his meal) picked his teeth with a fork, and looked smilingly on. In a very short time, the horn was heard.

'I thought it wouldn't be long,' said Squeers, jumping up and producing a little basket from under the seat; 'put what you haven't had time to eat, in here, boys! You'll want it on the road!'

Nicholas was considerably startled by these very economical arrangements; but he had no time to reflect upon them, for the little boys had to be got up to the top of the coach, and their boxes had to be brought out and put in, and Mr. Squeers's luggage was to be seen carefully deposited in the boot, and all these offices were in his department. He was in the full heat and bustle of concluding these operations, when his uncle, Mr. Ralph Nickleby, accosted him.

'Oh! here you are, sir!' said Ralph. 'Here are your mother and sister, sir.'

'Where?' cried Nicholas, looking hastily around.

'Here!' replied his uncle. 'Having too much money and nothing at all to do with it, they were paying a hackney coach as I came up, sir.'

'We were afraid of being too late to see him before he went away from us,' said Mrs. Nickleby, embracing her son, heedless of the unconcerned lookers-on in the coach-yard.

'Very good, ma'am,' returned Ralph, 'you 're the best judge of course. I merely said that you were paying a hackney coach. I never pay a hackney coach, ma'am, I never hire one. I haven't been in a hackney coach of my own hiring, for thirty years, and I hope I shan't be for thirty more, if I live as long.'

'I should never have forgiven myself if I had not seen him,' said Mrs. Nickleby. 'Poor dear boy—going away without his breakfast too, because he feared to distress us!'

'Mighty fine, certainly,' said Ralph, with great testiness. 'When I first went to business, ma'am, I took a penny loaf and a ha-porth of milk for my breakfast as I walked to the City every morning; what do you say to that, ma'am? Breakfast! Bah!'

'Now, Nickleby,' said Squeers, coming up at the moment buttoning his great-coat; 'I think you 'd better get up behind. I 'm afraid of one of them boys falling off, and then there 's twenty pound a year gone.'

'Dear Nicholas,' whispered Kate, touching her brother's arm, 'who is that vulgar man?'

'Eh!' growled Ralph, whose quick ears had caught the inquiry. 'Do you wish to be introduced to Mr. Squeers, my dear?'

'That the schoolmaster! No, uncle. Oh no!' replied Kate, shrinking back.

'I 'm sure I heard you say as much, my dear,' retorted Ralph in his cold sarcastic manner. 'Mr. Squeers, here 's my niece: Nicholas's sister!'

'Very glad to make your acquaintance, miss,' said Squeers, raising his hat an inch or two. 'I wish Mrs. Squeers took gals, and we had you for a teacher. I don't know, though, whether she mightn't grow jealous if we had. Ha! ha! ha!'

If the proprietor of Dotheboys Hall could have known what was passing in his assistant's breast at that moment, he would have discovered, with some surprise, that he was as near being soundly pummelled as he had ever been in his life. Kate Nickleby, having a quicker perception of her brother's emotions, led him gently aside, and thus prevented Mr. Squeers from being impressed with the fact in a peculiarly disagreeable manner.

'My dear Nicholas,' said the young lady, 'who is this man? What kind of place can it be that you are going to?'

'I hardly know, Kate,' replied Nicholas, pressing his sister's hand. 'I suppose the Yorkshire folks are rather rough and uncultivated; that 's all.'

'But this person,' urged Kate.

'Is my employer, or master, or whatever the proper name may be,' replied Nicholas quickly, 'and I was an ass to take his coarseness ill. They are looking this way, and it is time I was in my place. Bless you love, and good bye! Mother; look forward to our meeting again some day! Uncle, farewell! Thank you heartily for all you have done and all you mean to do. Quite ready, sir!'

With these hasty adieux, Nicholas mounted nimbly to his seat, and waved his hand as gallantly as if his heart went with it.

At this moment, when the coachman and guard were comparing notes for the last time before starting, on the subject of the way-bill; when porters were screwing out the last reluctant sixpences, itinerant newsman making the last offer of a morning paper, and the horses giving the last impatient rattle to their harness; Nicholas felt somebody pulling softly at his leg. He looked down, and there stood Newman Noggs, who pushed up into his hand a dirty letter.

'What's this?' inquired Nicholas.

'Hush!' rejoined Noggs, pointing to Mr. Ralph Nickleby, who was saying a few earnest words to Squeers, a short distance off. 'Take it. Read it. Nobody knows. That's all.'

'Stop!' cried Nicholas.

'No,' replied Noggs.

Nicholas cried stop, again, but Newman Noggs was gone.

A minute's bustle, a banging of the coach doors, a swaying of the vehicle to one side, as the heavy coachman, and still heavier guard, climbed into their seats; a cry of all right, a few notes from the horn, a hasty glance of two sorrowful faces below, and the hard features of Mr. Ralph Nickleby—and the coach was gone too, and rattling over the stones of Smithfield.

The little boys' legs being too short to admit of their feet resting upon anything as they sat, and the little boys' bodies being consequently in imminent hazard of being jerked off the coach, Nicholas had enough to do, over the stones, to hold them on. Between the manual exertion and the mental anxiety attendant upon this task, he was not a little relieved when the coach stopped at the Peacock at Islington. He was still more relieved when a hearty-looking gentleman, with a very good-humoured face, and a very fresh colour, got up behind, and proposed to take the other corner of the seat.

'If we put some of these youngsters in the middle,' said the new comer, 'they'll be safer in case of their going to sleep; eh?'

'If you'll have the goodness, sir,' replied Squeers, 'that'll be the very thing. Mr. Nickleby, take three of them boys between you and the gentleman. Belling and the youngest Snawley can sit between me and the guard. 'Three children,' said Squeers, explaining to the stranger, 'books as two.'

'I have not the least objection, I am sure,' said the fresh-coloured gentleman; 'I have a brother who wouldn't object to book his six children as two at any butcher's or baker's in the kingdom, I dare say. Far from it.'

'Six children, sir?' exclaimed Squeers.

'Yes, and all boys,' replied the stranger.

'Mr. Nickleby,' said Squeers, in great haste, 'catch hold of that basket. Let me give you a card, sir, of an establishment where those six boys can be brought up in an enlightened, liberal, and moral manner, with no mistake at all about it, for twenty guineas a year each—twenty guineas, sir—or I'd take all the boys together upon a average right through, and say a hundred pound a year for the lot.'

'Oh!' said the gentleman, glancing at the card, 'you are the Mr. Squeers mentioned here, I presume?'

'Yes, I am, sir,' replied the worthy pedagogue; 'Mr. Wackford Squeers is my name, and I'm very far from being ashamed of it. These are some of my boys, sir! that's one of my assistants, sir—Mr. Nickleby, a gentleman's son, and a good scholar, mathematical, classical, and commercial. We don't do things by halves at our shop. All manner of learning my boys take down, sir; the expense is never thought of; and they get paternal treatment and washing in.'

'Upon my word,' said the gentleman, glancing at Nicholas with a half smile, and a more than half expression of surprise, 'these are advantages indeed.'

'You may say that, sir,' rejoined Squeers, thrusting his hands into his great-coat pockets. 'The most unexceptionable references are given and required. I wouldn't take a reference with any boy, that wasn't responsible for the payment of five pound five a quarter, no, not if you went down on your knees, and asked me, with the tears running down your face, to do it.'

'Highly considerate,' said the passenger.

'It's my great aim and end to be considerate, sir,' rejoined Squeers. 'Snawley, junior, if you don't leave off chattering your teeth, and shaking with the cold, I'll warm you with a severe thrashing in about half a minute's time.'

'Sit fast here, gentlemen,' said the guard as he clambered up.

'All right behind there, Dick?' cried the coachman.

'All right,' was the reply. 'Off she goes!' And off she did go,—if coaches be feminine—amidst a loud flourish from the guard's horn, and the calm approval of all the judges of coaches and coach-horses congregated at the Peacock, but more especially of the helpers, who stood, with the cloths over their arms, watching the coach till it disappeared, and then lounged admiringly stablewards, bestowing various gruff encomiums on the beauty of the turn-out.

When the guard (who was a stout old Yorkshireman) had blown himself quite out of breath, he put the horn into a little tunnel of a basket fastened to the coach-side for the purpose, and giving himself a plentiful shower of blows on the chest and shoulders, observed it was uncommon cold; after which, he demanded of every person separately whether he was going right through, and if not where he *was* going. Satisfactory replies being made to these queries, he surmised that the roads were pretty heavy arter that fall last night, and took the liberty of asking whether any of them gentlemen carried a snuff-box. It happening that nobody did, he remarked with a mysterious air that he had heard a medical gentleman as went down to Grantham last week, say how that snuff-taking was bad for the eyes; but for his part he had never found it so, and what he said was, that everybody should speak as they found. Nobody attempting to controvert this position, he took a small brown-paper parcel out of his hat, and putting on a pair of horn spectacles (the writing being crabbed) read the direction half a dozen times over; having done which, he consigned the parcel to its old place, put up his spectacles again, and stared at everybody in turn. After this, he took another blow at the horn by way of refreshment; and, having now exhausted his usual topics of conversation, folded his arms as well as he could in so many coats, and falling into a solemn silence, looked carelessly at the familiar objects which met his eye on every side as the coach rolled on; the only things he seemed to care for, being horses and droves of cattle, which he scrutinised with a critical air as they passed upon the road.

The weather was intensely and bitterly cold; a great deal of snow fell from time to time; and the wind was intolerably keen. Mr. Squeers got down at almost every stage—to stretch his legs as he said—and as he always came back from such excursions with a very red nose, and composed himself to sleep directly, there is reason to suppose that he derived great benefit from the process. The little pupils having been stimulated with the remains of their breakfast, and further invigorated by sundry small cups of a curious cordial carried by Mr. Squeers, which tasted very like toast-and-water put into a brandy bottle by mistake, went to sleep, woke, shivered, and cried, as their feelings prompted. Nicholas and the good-tempered man found so many things to talk about, that between conversing together, and cheering up the boys, the time passed with them as rapidly as it could, under such adverse circumstances.

So the day wore on. At Eton Slocomb there was a good coach dinner, of which the box, the four front outsides, the one inside, Nicholas, the good-tempered man, and Mr. Squeers, partook; while the five little boys were put to thaw by the fire, and regaled with sandwiches. A stage or two further on, the lamps were lighted, and a great to-do occasioned by the taking up, at a roadside inn, of a very fastidious lady with an infinite variety of cloaks and small parcels, who loudly lamented, for the behoof of the outsides, the non-arrival of her own carriage which was to have taken her on, and made the guard solemnly promise to stop every green chariot he saw coming; which, as it was a dark night and he was sitting with his face the other way, that officer undertook, with many fervent asseverations, to do. Lastly, the fastidious lady, finding there was a solitary gentleman inside, had a small lamp lighted which she carried in her reticule, and being after much trouble shut in, the horses were put into a brisk canter and the coach was once more in rapid motion.

The night and the snow came on together, and dismal enough they were. There was no sound to be heard but the howling of the wind; for the noise of the wheels, and the tread of the horses' feet, were rendered inaudible by the thick coating of snow which covered the ground, and very fast increasing every moment. The streets of Stamford were deserted as they passed through the town; and its old churches rose, frowning and dark, from the whitened ground. Twenty miles further on, two of the front outside passengers wisely availing themselves of their arrival at one of the best inns in England, turned in, for the night, at the George at Grantham. The remainder wrapped themselves more closely in their coats and cloaks, and leaving the light and warmth of the town behind them, pillowed themselves against the luggage, and prepared, with many half-suppressed moans, again to encounter the piercing blast which swept across the open country.

They were little more than a stage out of Grantham, or about half-way between it and Newark, when Nicholas, who had been asleep for a short time, was suddenly roused by a violent jerk which nearly threw him from his seat. Grasping the rail, he found that the coach had sunk greatly on one side, though it was still dragged forward by the horses; and while—confused by their plunging and the loud screams of the lady inside—he hesitated, for an instant, whether to jump off or not, the vehicle turned easily over, and relieved him from all further uncertainty by flinging him into the road.

CHAPTER VI

IN WHICH THE OCCURRENCE OF THE ACCIDENT MENTIONED IN THE LAST CHAPTER, AFFORDS AN OPPORTUNITY TO A COUPLE OF GENTLEMEN TO TELL STORIES AGAINST EACH OTHER.

'Wo ho!' cried the guard, on his legs in a minute, and running to the leaders' heads. 'Is there ony genelmen there as can len' a hond here? Keep quiet, dang ye! Wo ho!'

'What 's the matter?' demanded Nicholas, looking sleepily up.

'Matther mun, matther eneaf for one neight,' replied the guard; 'dang the wall-eyed bay, he 's gane mad wi' glory I think, carse t' coorch is over. Here, can't ye len' a hond? Dom it, I 'd ha' dean it if all my boans were brokken.'

'Here!' cried Nicholas, staggering to his feet. 'I'm ready. I'm only a little abroad, that's all.'

'Hoold 'em toight,' cried the guard, 'while ar coot treaces. Hang on tiv 'em sumhoo. Well deane, my lod. That's it. Let 'em goa noo. Dang 'em, they'll gang whoam fast eneaf!'

In truth, the animals were no sooner released than they trotted back, with much deliberation, to the stable they had just left, which was distant not a mile behind.

'Can you blo' a harn?' asked the guard, disengaging one of the coach-lamps.

'I dare say I can,' replied Nicholas.

'Then just blo' away into that 'un as lies on the gr'und, fit to wakken the deead, will 'ee,' said the man, 'while I stop sum o' this here squealing inside. Cumin', cumin'. Dean't make that noise, wooman.'

As the man spoke, he proceeded to wrench open the uppermost door of the coach, while Nicholas, seizing the horn, awoke the echoes far and wide with one of the most extraordinary performances on that instrument ever heard by mortal ears. It had its effect, however, not only in rousing such of the passengers as were recovering from the stunning effects of their fall, but in summoning assistance to their relief; for lights gleamed in the distance, and people were already astir.

In fact, a man on horseback galloped down, before the passengers were well collected together; and a careful investigation being instituted, it appeared that the lady inside had broken her lamp, and the gentleman his head; and the two front outsides had escaped with black eyes; the box with a bloody nose; the coachman with a contusion on the temple; Mr. Squeers with a portmanteau bruise on his back:

and the remaining passengers without any injury at all—thanks to the softness of the snow-drift in which they had been overturned. These facts were no sooner thoroughly ascertained, than the lady gave several indications of fainting, but being forewarned that if she did, she must be carried on some gentleman's shoulders to the nearest public-house, she prudently thought better of it, and walked back with the rest.

They found on reaching it, that it was a lonely place with no very great accommodation in the way of apartments—that portion of its resources being all comprised in one public room with a sanded floor, and a chair or two. However, a large faggot and a plentiful supply of coals being heaped upon the fire, the appearance of things was not long in mending; and, by the time they had washed off all effaceable marks of the late accident, the room was warm and light, which was a most agreeable exchange for the cold and darkness out of doors.

'Well, Mr. Nickleby,' said Squeers, insinuating himself into the warmest corner, 'you did very right to catch hold of them horses. I should have done it myself if I had come to in time, but I am very glad you did it. You did it very well; very well.'

'So well,' said the merry-faced gentleman, who did not seem to approve very much of the patronising tone adopted by Squeers, 'that if they had not been firmly checked when they were, you would most probably have had no brains left to teach with.'

This remark called up a discourse relative to the promptitude Nicholas had displayed, and he was overwhelmed with compliments and commendations.

'I am very glad to have escaped, of course,' observed Squeers; 'every man is glad when he escapes from danger; but if any one of my charges had been hurt—if I had been prevented from restoring any one of these little boys to his parents whole and sound as I received him—what would have been my feelings? Why, the wheel atop of my head would have been far preferable to it.'

'Are they all brothers, sir?' inquired the lady who had carried the 'Davy' or safety-lamp.

'In one sense they are, ma'am,' replied Squeers, diving into his great-coat pocket for cards. 'They are all under the same parental and affectionate treatment. Mrs. Squeers and myself are a mother and father to every one of 'em. Mr. Nickleby, hand the lady them cards, and offer these to the gentleman. Perhaps they might know of some parents that would be glad to avail themselves of the establishment.'

Expressing himself to this effect, Mr. Squeers, who lost no opportunity of advertising gratuitously, placed his hands upon his knees, and looked at the pupils with as much benignity as he could possibly affect, while Nicholas, blushing with shame, handed round the cards as directed.

'I hope you suffer no inconvenience from the overturn, ma'am?' said the merry-faced gentleman, addressing the fastidious lady, as though he were charitably desirous to change the subject.

'No bodily inconvenience,' replied the lady.

'No mental inconvenience, I hope?'

'The subject is a very painful one to my feelings, sir,' replied the lady with strong emotion; 'and I beg you as a gentleman, not to refer to it.'

'Dear me,' said the merry-faced gentleman, looking merrier still, 'I merely intended to inquire—'

'I hope no inquiries will be made,' said the lady, 'or I shall be compelled to throw myself on the protection of the other gentlemen. Landlord, pray di-

rect a boy to keep watch outside the door—and if a
green chariot passes in the direction of Grantham,
to stop it instantly.'

The people of the house were evidently overcome
by this request, and when the lady charged the boy
to remember, as a means of identifying the expected
green chariot, that it would have a coachman with
a gold-laced hat on the box, and a footman, most
probably in silk stockings, behind, the attentions of
the good woman of the inn were redoubled. Even
the box-passenger caught the infection, and growing
wonderfully deferential, immediately inquired
whether there was not very good society in that
neighbourhood, to which the lady replied yes, there
was: in a manner which sufficiently implied that she
moved at the very tiptop and summit of it all.

'As the guard has gone on horseback to Grantham
to get another coach,' said the good-tempered gentleman when they had been all sitting round the
fire, for some time, in silence, 'and as he must be
gone a couple of hours at the very least, I propose
a bowl of hot punch. What say you, sir?'

This question was addressed to the broken-headed
inside, who was a man of very genteel appearance,
dressed in mourning. He was not past the middle
age, but his hair was grey; it seemed to have been
prematurely turned by care or sorrow. He readily
acceded to the proposal, and appeared to be prepossessed by the frank good-nature of the individual
from whom it emanated.

This latter personage took upon himself the office of tapster when the punch was ready, and after
dispensing it all round, led the conversation to the
antiquities of York, with which both he and the grey-
haired gentleman appeared to be well acquainted.
When this topic flagged, he turned with a smile to

the grey-headed gentleman, and asked if he could sing.

'I cannot indeed,' replied the gentleman, smiling in his turn.

'That's a pity,' said the owner of the good-humoured countenance. 'Is there nobody here who can sing a song to lighten the time?'

The passengers, one and all, protested that they could not; that they wished they could; that they couldn't remember the words of anything without the book; and so forth.

'Perhaps the lady would not object,' said the president with great respect, and a merry twinkle in his eye. 'Some little Italian thing out of the last opera brought out in town, would be most acceptable, I am sure.'

As the lady condescended to make no reply, but tossed her head contemptuously, and murmured some further expression of surprise regarding the absence of the green chariot, one of two voices urged upon the president himself, the propriety of making an attempt for the general benefit.

'I would if I could,' said he of the good-tempered face; 'for I hold that in this, as in all other cases where people who are strangers to each other are thrown unexpectedly together, they should endeavour to render themselves as pleasant, for the joint sake of the little community, as possible.'

'I wish the maxim were more generally acted on, in all cases,' said the grey-headed gentleman.

'I'm glad to hear it,' returned the other. 'Perhaps, as you can't sing. you'll tell us a story?'

'Nay. I should ask you.'

'After you, I will, with pleasure.'

'Indeed!' said the grey-haired gentleman, smiling. 'Well, let it be so. I fear the turn of my thoughts

is not calculated to ligthen the time you must pass
here; but you have brought this upon yourselves,
and shall judge. We were speaking of York Minster just now. My story shall have some reference
to it. Let us call it

'THE FIVE SISTERS OF YORK'

After a murmur of approbation from the other
passengers, during which the fastidious lady drank
a glass of punch unobserved, the grey-headed gentleman thus went on:

'A great many years ago—for the fifteenth century was scarce two years old at the time, and King
Henry the Fourth sat upon the throne of England
—there dwelt, in the ancient city of York, five
maiden sisters, the subjects of my tale.

'These five sisters were all of surpassing beauty.
The eldest was in her twenty-third year, the second
a year younger, the third a year younger than the
second, and the fourth a year younger than the third.
They were tall stately figures, with dark flashing
eyes and hair of jet; dignity and grace were in
their every movement; and the fame of their great
beauty had spread through all the country round.

'But, if the four elder sisters were lovely, how
bautiful was the youngest, a fair creature of sixteen!
The blushing tints in the soft bloom on the fruit, or
the delicate painting on the flower, are not more exquisite than was the blending of the rose and lily
in her gentle face, or the deep blue of her eye. The
vine, in all its elegant luxuriance, is not more graceful than were the clusters of rich brown hair that
sported round her brow.

'If we all had hearts like those which beat so lightly
in the bosoms of the young and beautiful, what a
heaven this earth would be! If, while our bodies

grow old and withered, our hearts could but retain their early youth and freshness, of what avail would be our sorrows and sufferings! But the faint image of Eden which is stamped upon them in childhood, chafes and rubs in our rough struggles with the world, and soon wears away: too often to leave nothing but a mournful blank remaining.

'The heart of this fair girl bounded with joy and gladness. Devoted attachment to her sisters, and a fervent love of all beautiful things in nature, were its pure affections. Her gleesome voice and merry laugh were the sweetest music of their home. She was its very light and life. The brightest flowers in the garden were reared by her; the caged birds sang when they heard her voice, and pined when they missed its sweetness. Alice, dear Alice; what living thing within the sphere of her gentle witchery, could fail to love her!

'You may seek in vain, now, for the spot on which these sisters lived, for their very names have passed away, and dusty antiquaries tell of them as of a fable. But they dwelt in an old wooden house—old even in those days—with overhanging gables and balconies of rudely-carved oak, which stood within a pleasant orchard, and was surrounded by a rough stone wall, whence a stout archer might have winged an arrow to Saint Mary's abbey. The old abbey flourished then; and the five sisters, living on its fair domains, paid yearly dues to the black monks of Saint Benedict, to which fraternity it belonged.

'It was a bright and sunny morning in the pleasant time of summer, when one of those black monks emerged from the abbey portal, and bent his steps towards the house of the fair sisters. Heaven above was blue, and earth beneath was green; the river glistened like a path of diamonds in the sun; the birds poured forth their songs from the shady trees; the lark soared high above the waving corn; and the deep buzz of insects filled the air.   Everything looked gay and smiling; but the holy man walked gloomily on, with his eyes bent upon the ground. The beauty of the earth is but a breath, and man is but a shadow.   What sympathy should a holy preacher have with either?

'With eyes bent upon the ground, then, or only raised enough to prevent his stumbling over such obstacles as lay in his way, the religious man moved slowly forward until he reached a small postern in the wall of the sisters' orchard, through which he passed, closing it behind him.   The noise of soft voices in conversation, and of merry laughter, fell upon his ears ere he had advanced many paces; and raising his eyes higher than was his humble wont, he descried, at no great distance, the five sisters seated on the grass, with Alice in the centre: all busily plying their customary task of embroidering.

' "Save you, fair daughters!" said the friar; and fair in truth they were.   Even a monk might have loved them as choice master-pieces of his Maker's hand.

'The sisters saluted the holy man with becoming reverence, and the eldest motioned him to a mossy seat beside them.   But the good friar shook his head, and bumped himself down on a very hard stone,— at which, no doubt, approving angels were gratified.

' "Ye were merry, daughters," said the monk.

' "You know how light of heart sweet Alice is," replied the eldest sister, passing her fingers through the tresses of the smiling girl.

' "And what joy and cheerfulness it wakes up within us, to see all nature beaming in brightness and sunshine, father," added Alice, blushing beneath the stern look of the recluse.

'The monk answered not, save by a grave inclination of the head, and the sisters pursued their task in silence.

' "Still wasting the precious hours," said the monk at length, turning to the eldest sister as he spoke, "still wasting the precious hours, on this vain trifling. Alas, alas! that the few bubbles on the surface of eternity—all that Heaven wills we should see of that dark deep stream—should be so lightly scattered!"

' "Father," urged the maiden, pausing, as did each of the others, in her busy task, "we have prayed at matins, our daily alms have been distributed at the gate, the sick peasants have been tended,—all our morning tasks have been performed. I hope our occupation is a blameless one?"

' "See here," said the friar, taking the frame from her hand, "an intricate winding of gaudy colours, without purpose or object, unless it be that one day it is destined for some vain ornament, to minister to the pride of your frail and giddy sex. Day after day has been employed upon this senseless task, and yet it is not half accomplished. The shade of each departed day falls upon our graves, and the worm exults as he beholds it, to know that we are hastening thither. Daughters, is there no better way to pass the fleeting hours?"

'The four elder sisters cast down their eyes as if abashed by the holy man's reproof, but Alice raised hers, and bent them mildly on the friar.

' "Our dear mother," said the maiden: "Heaven rest her soul!"

' "Amen!" cried the friar in a deep voice.

' "Our dear mother," faltered the fair Alice, "was

living when these long tasks began, and bade us, when she should be no more, ply them in all discretion and cheerfulness, in our leisure hours; she said that if in harmless mirth and maidenly pursuits we passed those hours together, they would prove the happiest and most peaceful of our lives, and that if, in later times, we went forth into the world, and mingled with its cares and trials—if, allured by its temptations and dazzled by its glitter, we ever forgot that love and duty which should bind, in holy ties, the children of one loved parent—a glance at the old work of our common girlhood would awaken good thoughts of bygone days, and soften our hearts to affection and love."

' "Alice speaks truly, father," said the elder sister, somewhat proudly. And so saying she resumed her work, as did the others.

'It was a kind of sampler of large size, that each sister had before her; the device was of a complex and intricate description, and the pattern and colours of all five were the same. The sisters bent gracefully over their work; the monk, resting his chin upon his hands, looked from one to the other in silence.

' "How much better," he said at length, "to shun all such thoughts and chances, and, in the peaceful shelter of the church, devote your lives to Heaven! Infancy, childhood, the prime of life, and old age, wither as rapidly as they crowd upon each other. Think how human dust rolls onward to the tomb, and turning your faces steadily towards that goal, avoid the cloud which takes its rise among the pleasures of the world, and cheats the senses of their votaries. The veil, daughters, the veil!"

' "Never, sisters," cried Alice. "Barter not the light and air of heaven, and the freshness of earth and all the beautiful things which breathe upon it, for the cold cloister and the cell. Nature's own blessings are the proper goods of life, and we may share them sinlessly together. To die is our heavy portion, but, oh, let us die with life about us; when our cold hearts cease to beat, let warm hearts be beating near; let our last look be upon the bounds which God has set to his own bright skies, and not on stone walls and bars of iron! Dear sisters, let us live and die, if you list, in this green garden's compass; only shun the gloom and sadness of a cloister, and we shall be happy."

'The tears fell fast from the maiden's eyes as she closed her impassioned appeal, and hid her face in the bosom of her sister.

' "Take comfort, Alice," said the eldest, kissing her fair forehead. "The veil shall never cast its shadow on thy young brow. How say you, sisters? For yourselves you speak, and not for Alice, or for me."

'The sisters, as with one accord, cried that their lot was cast together, and that there were dwellings for peace and virtue beyond the convent's walls.

' "Father," said the eldest lady, rising with dignity, "you hear our final resolve. The same pious care which enriched the abbey of Saint Mary, and left us, orphans, to its holy guardianship, directed that no constraint should be imposed upon our inclinations, but that we should be free to live according to our choice. Let us hear no more of this, we pray you. Sisters, it is nearly noon. Let us take shelter until evening!" With a reverence to the friar, the lady rose and walked towards the house, hand in hand with Alice; the other sisters followed.

'The holy man, who had often urged the same point before, but had never met with so direct a repulse, walked some little distance behind, with his eyes bent upon the earth, and his lips moving *as if* in prayer. As the sisters reached the porch, he quickened his pace, and called upon them to stop.

' "Stay!" said the monk, raising his right hand in the air, and directing an angry glance by turns at Alice and the eldest sister, "Stay, and hear from me what these recollections are, which you would cherish above eternity, and awaken—if in mercy they slumbered—by means of idle toys. The memory of earthly things is charged, in after life, with bitter disappointment, affliction, death; with dreary change and wasting sorrow. The time will one day come, when a glance at those unmeaning baubles will tear open deep wounds in the hearts of some among you, and strike to your inmost souls. When that hour arrives—and, mark me, come it will—turn from the world to which you clung, to the refuge which you spurned. Find me the cell which shall be colder than the fire of mortals grows, when dimmed by calamity and trial, and there weep for the dreams of youth. These things are Heaven's will, not mine," said the friar, subduing his voice as he looked round upon the shrinking girls. "The Virgin's blessing be upon you, daughters!"

'With these words he disappeared through the postern; and the sisters hastening into the house were seen no more that day.

'But nature will smile though priests may frown, and next day the sun shone brightly, and on the next, and the next again. And in the morning's glare and the evening's soft repose, the five sisters still walked, or worked, or beguiled the time by cheerful conversation, in their quiet orchard.

'Time passed away as a tale that is told; faster indeed than many tales that are told, of which number

I fear this may be one. The house of the five sisters stood where it did, and the same trees cast their pleasant shade upon the orchard grass. The sisters too were there, and lovely as at first, but a change had come over their dwelling. Sometimes, there was the clash of armour, and the gleaming of the moon on caps of steel; and, at others, jaded coursers were spurred up to the gate, and a female form glided hurriedly forth, as if eager to demand tidings of the weary messenger. A goodly train of knights and ladies lodged one night within the abbey walls, and next day rode away, with two of the fair sisters among them. Then, horsemen began to come less frequently, and seemed to bring bad tidings when they did, and at length they ceased to come at all, and footsore peasants slunk to the gate after sunset, and did their errand there, by stealth. Once, a vassal was despatched in haste to the abbey at dead of night, and when morning came, there were sounds of woe and wailing in the sisters' house; and after this, a mournful silence fell upon it, and knight or lady, horse or armour, was seen about it no more.

'There was a sullen darkness in the sky, and the sun had gone angrily down, tinting the dull clouds with the last traces of his wrath, when the same black monk walked slowly on, with folded arms, within a stone's-throw of the abbey. A blight had fallen on the trees and shrubs; and the wind, at length beginning to break the unnatural stillness that had prevailed all day, sighed heavily from time to time, as though foretelling in grief the ravages of the coming storm. The bat skimmed in fantastic flights through the heavy air, and the ground was alive with crawling things, whose instinct brought them forth to swell and fatten in the rain.

'No longer were the friar's eyes directed to the

earth; they were cast abroad, and roamed from point to point, as if the gloom and desolation of the scene found a quick response in his own bosom. Again he paused near the sisters' house, and again he entered by the postern.

'But not again did his ear encounter the sound of laughter, or his eyes rest upon the beautiful figures of the five sisters. All was silent and deserted. The boughs of the trees were bent and broken, and the grass had grown long and rank. No light feet had pressed it for many, many, a day.

'With the indifference or abstraction of one well accustomed to the change, the monk glided into the house, and entered a low, dark room. Four sisters sat there. Their black garments made their pale faces whiter still, and time and sorrow had worked deep ravages. They were stately yet; but the flush and pride of beauty were gone.

'And Alice—where was she? In Heaven.

'The monk—even the monk—could bear with some grief here; for it was long since these sisters had met, and there were furrows in their blanched faces which years could never plough. He took his seat in silence, and motioned them to continue their speech.

' "They are here, sisters," said the elder lady in a trembling voice. "I have never borne to look upon them since, and now I blame myself for my weakness. What is there in her memory that we should dread? To call up our old days, shall be a solemn pleasure yet."

'She glanced at the monk as she spoke, and, opening a cabinet, brought forth the five frames of work, completed long before. Her step was firm, but her hand trembled as she produced the last one; and, when the feelings of the other sisters gushed forth at sight of it, her pent-up tears made way, and she sobbed "God bless her!"

'The monk rose and advanced towards them. "It was almost the last thing she touched in health," he said in a low voice.

' "It was," cried the elder lady, weeping bitterly.

'The monk turned to the second sister.

' "The gallant youth who looked into thine eyes, and hung upon thy very breath when first he saw thee intent upon this pastime, lies buried on a plain whereof the turf is red with blood. Rusty fragments of armour once brightly burnished, lie rotting on the ground, and are as little distinguishable for his, as are the bones that crumble in the mould!"

'The lady groaned, and wrung her hands.

' "The policy of courts," he continued, turning to the two other sisters, "drew ye from your peaceful home to scenes of revelry and splendour. The same policy, and the restless ambition of proud and fiery men, have sent ye back, widowed maidens, and humbled outcasts. Do I speak truly?"

'The sobs of the two sisters were their only reply.

' "There is little need," said the monk, with a meaning look, "to fritter away the time in gewgaws which shall raise up the pale ghosts of hopes of early years. Bury them, heap penance and mortification on their heads, keep them down, and let the convent be their grave!"

'The sisters asked for three days to deliberate; and felt, that night, as though the veil were indeed the fitting shroud for their dead joys. But, morning came again, and though the boughs of the orchard trees drooped and ran wild upon the ground, it was the same orchard still. The grass was coarse and high, but there was yet the spot on which they had so often sat together, when change and sorrow were but names. There was every walk and nook which Alice had made glad; and in the minster nave was one flat stone beneath which she slept in peace.

'And could they, remembering how her young heart had sickened at the thought of cloistered walls, look upon her grave, in garbs which would chill the very ashes within it? Could they bow down in prayer, and when all Heaven turned to hear them, bring the dark shade of sadness on one angel's face? No.

'They sent abroad, to artists of great celebrity in those times, and having obtained the church's sanction to their work of piety, caused to be executed, in five large compartments of richly stained glass, a faithful copy of their old embroidery work. These were fitted into a large window until that time bare of ornament; and when the sun shone brightly, as she had so well loved to see it, the familiar patterns were reflected in their original colours, and throwing a stream of brilliant light upon the pavement, fell warmly on the name of Alice.

'For many hours in every day, the sisters paced slowly up and down the nave, or knelt by the side of the flat broad stone. Only three were seen in the customary place, after many years; then but two, and, for a long time afterwards, but one solitary female bent with age. At length she came no more, and the stone bore five plain Christian names.

'That stone has worn away and been replaced by others, and many generations have come and gone since then. Time has softened down the colours, but the same stream of light still falls upon the forgotten tomb, of which no trace remains; and, to this day, the stranger is shown in York Cathedral, an old window called the Five Sisters.'

'That's a melancholy tale,' said the merry-faced gentleman, emptying his glass.

'It is a tale of life, and life is made up of such sorrows,' returned the other, courteously, but in a grave and sad tone of voice.

'There are shades in all good pictures, but there are lights too, if we choose to contemplate them,' said the gentleman with the merry face. 'The youngest sister in your tale was always light-hearted.'

'And died early,' said the other, gently.

'She would have died earlier, perhaps, had she been less happy,' said the first speaker, with much feeling. 'Do you think the sisters who loved her so well, would have grieved the less if her life had been one of gloom and sadness? If anything could soothe the first sharp pain of a heavy loss, it would be—with me—the reflection, that those I mourned, by being innocently happy here, and loving all about them, had prepared themselves for a purer and happier world. The sun does not shine upon this fair earth to meet frowning eyes, depend upon it.'

'I believe you are right,' said the gentleman who had told the story.

'Believe!' retorted the other, 'can anybody doubt it? Take any subject of sorrowful regret, and see with how much pleasure it is associated. The recollection of past pleasure may become pain—'

'It does,' interposed the other.

'Well; it does. To remember happiness which cannot be restored, is pain, but of a softened kind. Our recollections are unfortunately mingled with much that we deplore, and with many actions which we bitterly repent; still in the most chequered life I firmly think there are so many little rays of sunshine to look back upon, that I do not believe any mortal (unless he had put himself without the pale of hope) would

deliberately drain a goblet of the waters of Lethe, if
he had it in his power.'

'Possibly you are correct in that belief,' said the
grey-haired gentleman after a short reflection. 'I
am inclined to think you are.'

'Why, then,' replied the other, 'the good in this state
of existence preponderates over the bad, let mis-called
philosophers tell us what they will. If our affections
be tried, our affections are our consolation and comfort; and memory, however sad, is the best and purest
link between this world and a better. But come! I 'll
tell you a story of another kind.'

After a very brief silence, the merry-faced gentleman sent round the punch, and glancing slily at the
fastidious lady, who seemed desperately apprehensive
that he was going to relate something improper, began—

THE BARON OF GROGZWIG

'The Baron Von Koëldwethout, of Grogzwig in
Germany, was as likely a young baron as you would
wish to see. I needn't say that he lived in a castle, because that 's of course; neither need I say that he lived
in an old castle; for what German baron ever lived in
a new one? There were many strange circumstances
connected with this venerable building, among which,
not the least startling and mysterious were, that when
the wind blew, it rumbled in the chimneys, or even
howled among the trees in the neighbouring forest;
and that when the moon shone, she found her way
through certain small loopholes in the wall, and
actually made some parts of the wide halls and gal-
leries quite light, while she left others in gloomy
shadow. I believe that one of the baron's ancestors,
being short of money, had inserted a dagger in a gentleman who called one night to ask his way, and it *was*

supposed that these miraculous occurrences took place
in consequence. And yet I hardly know how that
could have been, either, because the baron's ancestor,
who was an amiable man, felt very sorry afterwards
for having been so rash, and laying violent hands
upon a quantity of stone and timber which belonged to a weaker baron, built a chapel as an apology, and so took a receipt from Heaven, in full of all
demands.

'Talking of the baron's ancestor puts me in mind of
the baron's great claims to respect, on the score of his
pedigree. I am afraid to say, I am sure, how many
ancestors the baron had; but I know that he had a
great many more than any other man of his time; and
I only wish that he had lived in these latter days, that
he might have had more. It is a very hard thing upon
the great men of past centuries, that they should have
come into the world so soon, because a man who was
born three or four hundred years ago, cannot reason-
ably be expected to have had as many relations before
him, as a man who is born now. The last man, whoever he is—and he may be a cobbler or some low
vulgar dog for aught we know—will have a longer
pedigree than the greatest nobleman now alive; and I
contend that this is not fair.

'Well, but the Baron Von Koëldwethout of
Grogzwig! He was a fine swarthy fellow, with dark
hair and large moustachios, who rode a-hunting in
clothes of Lincoln green, with russet boots on his feet,
and a bugle slung over his shoulder, like the guard of
a long stage. When he blew this bugle, four-and-
twenty other gentlemen of inferior rank, in Lincoln
green a little coarser, and russet boots with a little
thicker soles, turned out directly; and away galloped
the whole train, with spears in their hands like lack-
ered area railings, to hunt down the boars, or perhaps

encounter a bear: in which latter case the baron killed him first, and greased his whiskers with him afterwards.

'This was a merry life for the Baron of Grogzwig, and a merrier still for the baron's retainers, who drank Rhine wine every night till they fell under the table, and then had the bottles on the floor, and called for pipes. Never were such jolly, roystering, rollicking, merry-making blades, as the jovial crew of Grogzwig.

'But the pleasures of the table, or the pleasures of under the table, require a little variety; especially when the same five-and-twenty people sit daily down to the same board to discuss the same subjects, and tell the same stories. The baron grew weary, and wanted excitement. He took to quarrelling with his gentlemen, and tried kicking two or three of them every day after dinner. This was a pleasant change at first; but it became monotonous after a week or so, and the baron felt quite out of sorts, and cast about, in despair, for some new amusement.

'One night, after a day's sport in which he had outdone Nimrod or Gillingwater, and slaughtered "another fine bear," and brought him home in triumph, the Baron Von Koëldwethout sat moodily at the head of his table, eyeing the smoky roof of the hall with a discontented aspect. He swallowed huge bumpers of wine, but the more he swallowed, the more he frowned. The gentlemen who had been honoured with the dangerous distinction of sitting on his right and left, imitated him to a miracle in the drinking, and frowned at each other.

' "I will!" cried the baron suddenly, smiting the table with his right hand, and twirling his moustache with his left. "Fill to the Lady of Grogzwig!"

'The four-and-twenty Lincoln greens turned pale,

with the exception of their four-and-twenty noses, which were unchangeable.

' "I said to the Lady of Grogzwig," repeated the baron, looking round the board.

' "To the Lady of Grogzwig!" shouted the Lincoln greens; and down their four-and-twenty throats went four-and-twenty imperial pints of such rare old hock, that they smacked their eight-and-forty lips, and winked again.

' "The fair daughter of the Baron Von Swillen- hausen," said Koëldwethout, condescending to ex- plain. "We will demand her in marriage of her father, ere the sun goes down to-morrow. If he re- fuse our suit, we will cut off his nose."

'A hoarse murmur arose from the company; every man touched, first the hilt of his sword, and then the tip of his nose, with appalling significance.

'What a pleasant thing filial piety is, to contem- plate! If the daughter of the Baron Von Swillen- hausen had pleaded a pre-occupied heart, or fallen at her father's feet and corned them in salt tears, or only fainted away, and complimented the old gentleman in frantic ejaculations, the odds are a hundred to one, but Swillenhausen castle would have been turned out at window, or rather the baron turned out at window, and the castle demolished. The damsel held her peace, however, when an early messenger bore the re- quest of Von Koëldwethout next morning, and mod- estly retired to her chamber, from the casement of which she watched the coming of the suitor and his retinue. She was no sooner assured that the horse- man with the large moustachios was her proffered husband, than she hastened to her father's presence, and expressed her readiness to sacrifice herself to se- cure his peace. The venerable baron caught his child to his arms, and shed a wink of joy.

'There was great feasting at the castle, that day. The four-and-twenty Lincoln greens of Von Koëldwethout exchanged vows of eternal friendship with twelve Lincoln greens of Von Swillenhausen, and promised the old baron that they would drink his wine "Till all was blue"—meaning probably until their whole countenances had acquired the same tint as their noses. Everybody slapped everybody else's back, when the time for parting came; and the Baron Von Koëldwethout and his followers rode gaily home.

'For six mortal weeks, the bears and boars had a holiday. The houses of Koëldwethout and Swillenhausen were united; the spears rusted; and the baron's bugle grew hoarse for lack of blowing.

'Those were great times for the four-and-twenty; but, alas! their high and palmy days had taken boots to themselves, and were already walking off.

' "My dear," said the baroness.

' "My love," said the baron.

' "Those coarse, noisy men—"

' "Which, ma'am?" said the baron starting.

'The baroness pointed, from the window at which they stood, to the court-yard beneath, where the unconscious Lincoln greens were taking a copious stirrup-cup, preparatory to issuing forth after a boar or two.

' "My hunting train, ma'am," said the baron.

' "Disband them, love," murmured the baroness.

' "Disband them!" cried the baron, in amazement.

' "To please me, love," replied the baroness.

' "To please the devil, ma'am," answered the baron.

'Whereupon the baroness uttered a great cry, and swooned away at the baron's feet.

'What could the baron do? He called for the lady's maid, and roared for the doctor; and then, rushing into the yard, kicked the two Lincoln greens who were the most used to it, and cursing the others all round, bade them go———— but never mind where. I don't know the German for it, or I would put it delicately that way.

'It is not for me to say by what means or by what degrees, some wives manage to keep down some husbands as they do, although I may have my private opinion on the subject, and may think that no Member of Parliament ought to be married, inasmuch as three married members out of every four, must vote according to their wives' consciences (if there be such things), and not according to their own. All I need say, just now, is, that the Baroness Von Koëldwethout somehow or other acquired great control over the Baron Von Koëldwethout, and that, little by little, and bit by bit, and day by day, and year by year, the baron got the worst of some disputed question, or was slyly unhorsed from some old hobby; and that by the time he was a fat hearty fellow of forty-eight or thereabouts, he had no feasting, no revelry, no hunting train, and no hunting—nothing in short that he liked, or used to have; and that, although he was as fierce as a lion and as bold as brass, he was decidedly snubbed and put down, by his own lady, in his own castle of Grogzwig.

'Nor was this the whole extent of the baron's misfortunes. About a year after his nuptials, there came into the world a lusty young baron, in whose honour a great many fireworks were let off, and a great many dozens of wine drunk; but next year there came a young baroness, and next year another young baron, and so on, every year, either a baron or baroness (and one year both together), until the baron found himself the father of a small family of twelve. Upon every one of these anniversaries, the venerable Baroness Von Swillenhausen was nervously sensitive for the

well-being of her child the Baroness Von Koëldwethout; and although it was not found that the good
lady ever did anything material towards contributing
to her child's recovery, still she made it a point of duty
to be as nervous as possible at the castle at Grogzwig,
and to divide her time between moral observations on
the baron's housekeeping, and bewailing the hard lot
of her unhappy daughter. And if the Baron of
Grogzwig, a little hurt and irritated at this, took heart,
and ventured to suggest that his wife was at least no
worse off than the wives of other barons, the Baroness
Von Swillenhausen begged all persons to take notice,
that nobody but she, sympathised with her dear
daughter's sufferings; upon which, her relations and
friends remarked, that to be sure she did cry a great
deal more than her son-in-law, and that if there were
a hardhearted brute alive, it was that Baron of
Grogzwig.

'The poor baron bore it all, as long as he could,
and when he could bear it no longer lost his appetite
and his spirits, and sat himself gloomily and de-
jectedly down. But there were worse troubles yet in
store for him, and as they came on, his melancholy
and sadness increased. Times changed. He got
into debt. The Grogzwig coffers ran low, though
the Swillenhausen family had looked upon them as
inexhaustible; and just when the baroness was on the
point of making a thirteenth addition to the family
pedigree, Von Koëldwethout discovered that he had
no means of replenishing them.

' "I don't see what is to be done," said the baron.
"I think I 'll kill myself."

'This was a bright idea. The baron took an old
hunting-knife from a cupboard hard by, and having sharpened it on his boot, made what boys call
"an offer" at his throat.

' "Hem!" said the baron, stopping short. "Perhaps it 's not sharp enough."

'The baron sharpened it again, and made another offer, when his hand was arrested by a loud screaming among the young barons and baronesses, who had a nursery in an upstairs tower with iron bars outside the window, to prevent their tumbling out into the moat.

' "If I had been a bachelor," said the baron, sighing, "I might have done it fifty times over, without being interrupted. Hallo! Put a flask of wine and the largest pipe, in the little vaulted room behind the hall."

'One of the domestics, in a very kind manner, executed the baron's order in the course of half an hour or so, and Von Koëldwethout being apprised thereof, strode to the vaulted room, the walls of which, being of dark shining wood, gleamed in the light of the blazing logs which were piled upon the hearth. The bottle and pipe were ready, and, upon the whole, the place looked very comfortable.

' "Leave the lamp," said the baron.

' "Anything else, my lord?" inquired the domestic.

' "The room," replied the baron. The domestic obeyed, and the baron locked the door.

' "I 'll smoke a last pipe," said the baron, "and then I 'll be off." So, putting the knife upon the table till he wanted it, and tossing off a goodly measure of wine, the Lord of Grogzwig threw himself back in his chair, stretched his legs out before the fire, and puffed away.

'He thought about a great many things—about his present troubles and past days of bachelorship, and about the Lincoln greens, long since dispersed up and down the country, no one knew whither: with the exception of two who had been unfortunately beheaded, and four who had killed themselves with drinking. His mind was running upon bears and boars, when, in the process of draining his glass to the bottom, he raised his eyes, and saw, for the first time and with unbounded astonishment, that he was not alone.

'No, he was not; for, on the opposite side of the fire, there sat with folded arms a wrinkled hideous figure, with deeply sunk and bloodshot eyes, and an immensely long cadaverous face, shadowed by jagged and matted locks of coarse black hair. He wore a kind of tunic of a dull bluish colour, which, the baron observed, on regarding it attentively, was clasped or ornamented down the front, with coffin handles. His legs too, were encased in coffin plates as though in armour; and over his left shoulder he wore a short dusky cloak, which seemed made of a remnant of some pall. He took no notice of the baron, but was intently eyeing the fire.

' "Halloa!" said the baron, stamping his foot to attract attention.

' "Halloa!" replied the stranger, moving his eyes towards the baron, but not his face or himself. "What now?"

' "What now!" replied the baron, nothing daunted by his hollow voice and lustreless eyes, "*I* should ask that question. How did you get here?"

' "Through the door," replied the figure.

' "What are you?" says the baron.

' "A man," replied the figure.

' "I don't believe it," says the baron.

' "Disbelieve it then," says the figure.

' "I will," rejoined the baron.

'The figure looked at the bold Baron of Grogzwig for some time, and then said familiarly—

' "There's no coming over you, I see. I 'm not a man!"

' "What are you then?" asked the baron.

' "A genius," replied the figure.

' "You don't look much like one," returned the baron scornfully.

' "I am the Genius of Despair and Suicide," said the apparition. "Now you know me."

'With these words the apparition turned towards the baron, as if composing himself for a talk—and, what was very remarkable, was, that he threw his cloak aside, and displayed a stake, which was run through the centre of his body, pulled it out with a jerk, and laid it on the table as composedly as if it had been a walking-stick.

' "Now," said the figure, glancing at the hunting-knife, "are you ready for me?"

' "Not quite," rejoined the baron; "I must finish this pipe first."

' "Look sharp then," said the figure.

' "You seem in a hurry," said the baron.

' "Why, yes, I am," answered the figure; "they 're doing a pretty brisk business in my way, over in England and France just now, and my time is a good deal taken up."

' "Do you drink?" said the baron, touching the bottle with the bowl of his pipe.

' "Nine times out of ten, and then very hard," rejoined the figure, drily.

' "Never in moderation?" asked the baron.

' "Never," replied the figure, with a shudder, "that breeds cheerfulness."

'The baron took another look at his new friend, whom he thought an uncommonly queer customer, and at length inquired whether he took any active part in such little proceedings as that which he had in contemplation.

' "No," replied the figure evasively; "but I am always present."

' "Just to see fair, I suppose?" said the baron.

' "Just that," replied the figure, playing with the stake, and examining the ferule.

" 'Be as quick as you can, will you, for there's a young gentleman who is afflicted with too much money and leisure wanting me now, I find."

' "Going to kill himself because he has too much money!" exclaimed the baron, quite tickled; "Ha! ha! that's a good one." (This was the first time the baron had laughed for many a long day.)

' "I say," expostulated the figure, looking very much scared; "don't do that again."

' "Why not?" demanded the baron.

' "Because it gives me pain all over," replied the figure. "Sigh as much as you please; that does me good."

'The baron sighed mechanically, at the mention of the word; the figure, brightening up again, handed him the hunting-knife with the most winning politeness.

' "It's not a bad idea though," said the baron, feeling the edge of the weapon; "a man killing himself because he has too much money."

' "Pooh!" said the apparition, petulantly, "no better than a man's killing himself because he has none or little."

'Whether the genius unintentionally committed himself in saying this, or whether he thought the baron's mind was so thoroughly made up that it didn't matter what he said, I have no means of knowing. I only know that the baron stopped his hand, all of a sudden, opened his eyes wide, and looked as if quite a new light had come upon him for the first time.

' "Why, certainly," said Von Koëldwethout, "nothing is too bad to be retrieved."

' "Except empty coffers," cried the genius.

' "Well; but they may be one day filled again," said the baron.

' "Scolding wives," snarled the genius.

' "Oh! They may be made quiet," said the baron.

' "Thirteen children," shouted the genius.

' "Can't all go wrong, surely," said the baron.

'The genius was evidently growing very savage with the baron, for holding these opinions all at once; but he tried to laugh it off, and said if he would let him know when he had left off joking, he should feel obliged to him.

' "But I am not joking; I was never farther from it," remonstrated the baron.

' "Well, I am glad to hear that," said the genius, looking very grim, "because a joke, without any figure of speech, *is* the death of me. Come! Quit this dreary world at once.'

' "I don't know," said the baron, playing with the knife; "it's a dreary one certainly, but I don't think yours is much better, for you have not the appearance of being particularly comfortable. That puts me in mind—what security have I, that I shall be any the better for going out of the world after all!" he cried, starting up; "I never thought of that."

' "Dispatch," cried the figure, gnashing its teeth.

' "Keep off!" said the baron. "I 'll brood over miseries no longer, but put a good face on the matter, and try the fresh air and the bears again; and if that don't do, I 'll talk to the baroness soundly, and cut the Von Swillenhausens dead." With this the baron fell into his chair, and laughed so loud and boisterously, that the room rang with it.

'The figure fell back a pace or two, regarding the baron meanwhile with a look of intense terror, and when he had ceased, caught up the stake, plunged it violently into its body, uttered a frightful howl, and disappeared.

'Von Koëldwethout never saw it again. Having once made up his mind to action, he soon brought the baroness and the Von Swillenhausens to reason, and died many years afterwards: not a rich man that I am aware of, but certainly a happy one: leaving behind him a numerous family, who had been carefully educated in bear and boar hunting under his own personal eye. And my advice to all men is, that if ever they become hipped and melancholy from similar causes (as very many men do), they look at both sides of the question, applying a magnifying glass to the best one; and if they still feel tempted to retire without leave, that they smoke a large pipe and drink a full bottle first, and profit by the laudable example of the Baron of Grogzwig.'

'The fresh coach is ready, ladies and gentlemen, if you please,' said a new driver, looking in.

This intelligence caused the punch to be finished in a great hurry, and prevented any discussion relative to the last story. Mr. Squeers was observed to draw the grey-headed gentleman on one side, and to ask a question with great apparent interest; it bore reference to the Five Sisters of York, and was, in fact, an inquiry whether he could inform him how much per annum the Yorkshire convents got in those days with their boarders.

The journey was then resumed. Nicholas fell asleep towards morning, and, when he awoke, found, with great regret, that, during his nap, both the Baron of Grogzwig and the grey-haired gentleman had got down and were gone. The day dragged on uncomfortably enough. At about six o'clock that night, he and Mr. Squeers, and the little boys, and their united luggage, were all put down together at the George and New Inn, Greta Bridge.

CHAPTER VII

MR. AND MRS. SQUEERS AT HOME

MR. SQUEERS, being safely landed, left Nicholas and the boys standing with the luggage in the road, to amuse themselves by looking at the coach as it changed horses, while he ran into the tavern and went through the leg-stretching process at the bar. After some minutes, he returned with his legs thoroughly stretched, if the hue of his nose and a short hiccup afforded any criterion; and at the same time there came out of the yard a rusty pony-chaise, and a cart, driven by two labouring men.

'Put the boys and the boxes into the cart,' said Squeers, rubbing his hands; 'and this young man and me will go on in the chaise. Get in, Nickleby.'

Nicholas obeyed. Mr. Squeers with some difficulty inducing the pony to obey also, they started off, leaving the cartload of infant misery to follow at leisure.

'Are you cold, Nickleby?' inquired Squeers, after they had traveled some distance in silence.

'Rather, sir, I must say.'

'Well, I don't find fault with that,' said Squeers; 'it's a long journey this weather.'

'Is it much farther to Dotheboys Hall, sir?' asked Nicholas.

'About three miles from here,' replied Squeers. 'But you needn't call it a Hall down here.'

Nicholas coughed, as if he would like to know why.

'The fact is, it ain't a Hall,' observed Squeers drily.

'Oh, indeed!' said Nicholas, whom this piece of intelligence much astonished.

'No,' replied Squeers. 'We call it a Hall up in London, because it sounds better, but they don't know it by that name in these parts. A man may call his house an island if he likes; there's no act of Parliament against that, I believe?'

'I believe not, sir,' rejoined Nicholas.

Squeers eyed his companion slily, at the conclusion of this little dialogue, and finding that he had grown thoughtful and appeared in nowise disposed to volunteer any observations, contented himself with lashing the pony until they reached their journey's end.

'Jump out,' said Squeers. 'Hallo there! come and put this horse up. Be quick, will you!'

While the schoolmaster was uttering these and other impatient cries, Nicholas had time to observe that the school was a long, cold-looking house, one story high, with a few straggling outbuildings behind, and a barn and stable adjoining. After the lapse of a minute or two, the noise of somebody unlocking the yard-gate was heard, and presently a tall lean boy, with a lantern in his hand, issued forth.

'Is that you, Smike?' cried Squeers.

'Yes, sir,' replied the boy.

'Then why the devil didn't you come before?'

'Please sir, I fell asleep over the fire,' answered Smike, with humility.

'Fire! what fire?   Where's there a fire?' demanded the schoolmaster, sharply.

'Only in the kitchen, sir,' replied the boy.   'Missus said as I was sitting up, I might go in there for a warm.'

'Your missus is a fool,' retorted Squeers.   'You'd have been a deuced deal more wakeful in the cold, I'll engage.'

By this time Mr. Squeers had dismounted; and after ordering the boy to see to the pony, and to take care that he hadn't any more corn that night, he told Nicholas to wait at the front door a minute while he went round and let him in.

A host of unpleasant misgivings, which had been crowding upon Nicholas during the whole journey, thronged into his mind with redoubled force when he was left alone.   His great distance from home and the impossibility of reaching it, except on foot, should he feel ever so anxious to return, presented itself to him in most alarming colours; and as he looked up at the dreary house and dark windows, and upon the wild country round, covered with snow, he felt a depression of heart and spirit which he had never experienced before.

'Now then!' cried Squeers, poking his head out at the front door.   'Where are you, Nickleby?'

'Here, sir,' replied Nicholas.

'Come in, then,' said Squeers, 'the wind blows in, at this door, fit to knock a man off his legs.'

Nicholas sighed, and hurried in.   Mr. Squeers, having bolted the door to keep it shut, ushered him into a small parlour scantily furnished with a few chairs, a yellow map hung against the wall, and a couple of tables; one of which bore some preparations for supper; while, on the other, a tutor's assistant, a Murray's grammar, half a dozen cards of terms and a worn letter directed to Wackford Squeers, Esquire, were arranged in picturesque confusion.

They had not been in this apartment a couple of minutes, when a female bounced into the room, and seized Mr. Squeers by the throat, gave him two loud kisses: one close after the other, like a postman's knock. The lady, who was of a large raw-boned figure, was about half a head taller than Mr. Squeers, and was dressed in a dimity night-jacket; with her hair in paper; she had also a dirty nightcap on, relieved by a yellow cotton handkerchief which tied it under the chin.

'How is my Squeery?' said this lady in a playful manner, and a very hoarse voice.

'Quite well, my love,' replied Squeers. 'How's the cows?'

'All right, every one of 'em,' answered the lady.

'And the pigs?' said Squeers.

'As well as they were when you went away.'

'Come; that's a blessing,' said Squeers, pulling off his great-coat. 'The boys are all as they were, I suppose?'

'Oh, yes, they're well enough,' replied Mrs. Squeers, snappishly. 'That young Pitcher's had a fever.'

'No!' exclaimed Squeers. 'Damn that boy, he's always at something of that sort.'

'Never was such a boy, I do believe,' said Mrs. Squeers; 'whatever he has is always catching too. I say it's obstinacy, and nothing shall ever convince me that it isn't. I'd beat it out of him; and I told you that, six months ago.'

'So you did, my love,' rejoined Squeers. 'We'll try what can be done.'

Pending these little endearments, Nicholas had

stood, awkwardly enough, in the middle of the room: not very well knowing whether he was expected to retire into the passage, or to remain where he was. He was now relieved from his perplexity by Mr. Squeers.

'This is the new young man, my dear,' said that gentleman.

'Oh,' replied Mrs. Squeers, nodding her head at Nicholas, and eyeing him coldly from top to toe.

'He 'll take a meal with us to-night,' said Squeers, 'and go among the boys to-morrow morning. You can give him a shake-down here, to-night, can't you?'

'We must manage it somehow,' replied the lady. 'You don't much mind how you sleep, I suppose, sir?'

'No, indeed,' replied Nicholas, 'I am not particular.'

'That 's lucky,' said Mrs. Squeers. And as the lady's humour was considered to lie chiefly in retort, Mr. Squeers laughed heartily, and seemed to expect that Nicholas should do the same.

After some further conversation between the master and mistress relative to the success of Mr. Squeers's trip, and the people who had paid, and the people who had made default in payment, a young servant girl brought in a Yorkshire pie and some cold beef, which being set upon the table, the boy Smike appeared with a jug of ale.

Mr. Squeers was emptying his great-coat pockets of letters to different boys, and other small documents, which he had brought down in them. The boy glanced, with an anxious and timid expression, at the papers, as if with a sickly hope that one among them might relate to him. The look was a very painful one, and went to Nicholas's heart at once; for it told a long and very sad history.

It induced him to consider the boy more attentively, and he was surprised to observe the extraordinary mixture of garments which formed his dress. Although he could not have been less than eighteen or nineteen years old, and was tall for that age, he wore a skeleton suit, such as it usually put upon very little boys, and which, though most absurdly short in the arms and legs, was quite wide enough for his attenuated frame. In order that the lower part of his legs might be in perfect keeping with this singular dress, he had a very large pair of boots, originally made for tops, which might have been once worn by some stout farmer, but were now too patched and tattered for a beggar. Heaven knows how long he had been there, but he still wore the same linen which he had first taken down; for, round his neck, was a tattered child's frill, only half concealed by a coarse, man's neckerchief. He was lame; and as he feigned to be busy in arranging the table, glanced at the letters with a look so keen, and yet so dispirited and hopeless, that Nicholas could hardly bear to watch him.

'What are you bothering about there, Smike?' cried Mrs. Squeers; 'let the things alone, can't you.'

'Eh!' said Squeers, looking up. 'Oh! it's you, is it?'

'Yes, sir,' replied the youth, pressing his hands together, as though to control, by force, the nervous wandering of his fingers; 'Is there—'

'Well!' said Squeers.

'Have you—did anybody—has nothing been heard —about me?'

'Devil a bit,' replied Squeers testily.

The lad withdrew his eyes, and, putting his hand to his face, moved towards the door.

'Not a word,' resumed Squeers, 'and never will be. Now, this is a pretty sort of thing, isn't it, that you should have been left here, all these years, and no money paid after the first six—nor no notice taken, nor no clue to be got who you belong to? It's a pretty sort of thing that I should have to feed a great fellow like you, and never hope to get one penny for it, isn't it?'

The boy put his hand to his head as if he were making an effort to recollect something, and then, looking vacantly at his questioner, gradually broke into a smile, and limped away.

'I'll tell you what, Squeers,' remarked his wife as the door closed, 'I think that young chap's turning silly.'

'I hope not,' said the schoolmaster; 'for he's a handy fellow out of doors, and worth his meat and drink, anyway. I should think he'd have wit enough for us though, if he was. But come; let's have supper, for I am hungry and tired, and want to get to bed.'

This reminder brought in an exclusive steak for Mr. Squeers, who speedily proceeded to do it ample justice. Nicholas drew up his chair, but his appetite was effectually taken away.

'How's the steak, Squeers?' said Mrs. S.

'Tender as a lamb,' replied Squeers. 'Have a bit?'

'I couldn't eat a morsel,' replied his wife. 'What'll the young man take, my dear?'

'Whatever he likes that's present,' rejoined Squeers, in a most unusual burst of generosity.

'What do you say, Mr. Knuckleboy?' inquired Mrs. Squeers.

'I'll take a little of the pie, if you please,' replied Nicholas. 'A very little, for I'm not hungry.'

'Well, it's a pity to cut pie if you're not hungry, isn't it?' said Mrs. Squeers. 'Will you try a bit of the beef?'

'Whatever you please,' replied Nicholas, abstractedly; 'it's all the same to me.'

Mrs. Squeers looked vastly gracious on receiving this reply; and nodding to Squeers, as much as to say that she was glad to find the young man knew his station, assisted Nicholas to a slice of meat with her own fair hands.

'Ale, Squeery?' inquired the lady, winking and frowning to give him to understand that the question propounded was, whether Nicholas should have ale, and not whether he (Squeers) would take any.

'Certainly,' said Squeers, re-telegraphing in the same manner. 'A glassful.'

So Nicholas had a glassful, and, being occupied with his own reflections, drank it, in happy innocence of all the foregone proceedings.

'Uncommon juicy steak that,' said Squeers, as he laid down his knife and fork, after plying it, in silence, for some time.

'It's prime meat,' rejoined his lady. 'I bought a good large piece of it myself on purpose for—'

'For what!' exclaimed Squeers hastily. 'Not for the—'

'No, no; not for them,' rejoined Mrs. Squeers; 'on purpose for you against you came home. Lor! you didn't think I could have made such a mistake as that.'

'Upon my word, my dear, I didn't know what you were going to say,' said Squeers, who had turned pale.

'You needn't make yourself uncomfortable,' remarked his wife, laughing heartily. 'To think that I should be such a noddy! Well!'

This part of the conversation was rather unintelligible; but popular rumour in the neighborhood asserted that Mr. Squeers, being amiably opposed to cruelty to animals, not unfrequently purchased for boy consumption the bodies of horned cattle who had died a natural death; possibly he was apprehensive of having unintentionally devoured some choice morsel intended for the young gentlemen.

Supper being over, and removed by a small servant girl with a hungry eye, Mrs. Squeers retired to lock it up, and also to take into safe custody the clothes of the five boys who had just arrived, and who were half-way up the troublesome flight of steps which leads to death's door, in consequence of exposure to the cold. They were then regaled with a light supper of porridge, and stowed away, side by side, in a small bedstead, to warm each other, and dream of a substantial meal with something hot after it, if their fancies set that way: which it is not at all improbable they did.

Mr. Squeers treated himself to a stiff tumbler of brandy-and-water, made on the liberal half-and-half principle, allowing for the dissolution of the sugar; and his amiable helpmate mixed Nicholas the ghost of a small glassful of the same compound. This done, Mr. and Mrs. Squeers drew close up to the fire, and sitting with their feet on the fender, talked confidentially in whispers; while Nicholas, taking up the tutor's assistant, read the interesting legends in the miscellaneous questions, and all the figures into the bargain, with as much thought or consciousness of what he was doing, as if he had been in a magnetic slumber.

At length, Mr. Squeers yawned fearfully, and opined that it was high time to go to bed; upon which signal, Mrs. Squeers and the girl dragged in a small straw mattress and a couple of blankets, and arranged them into a couch for Nicholas.

'We'll put you into your regular bed-room tomorrow, Nickleby,' said Squeers. 'Let me see! Who sleeps in Brooks's bed, my dear?'

'In Brooks's,' said Mrs. Squeers, pondering. 'There's Jennings, little Bolder, Graymarsh, and what's his name.'

'So there is,' rejoined Squeers. 'Yes! Brooks is full.'

'Full!' thought Nicholas. 'I should think he was.'

'There's a place somewhere, I know,' said Squeers; 'but I can't at this moment call to mind where it is. However, we'll have that all settled to-morrow. Good night, Nickleby.   Seven o'clock in the morning, mind.'

'I shall be ready, sir,' replied Nicholas. 'Good-night.'

'I'll come in myself and show you where the well is,' said Squeers. 'You'll always find a little bit of soap in the kitchen window; that belongs to you.'

Nicholas opened his eyes, but not his mouth; and Squeers was again going away, when he once more turned back.

'I don't know, I am sure,' he said, 'whose towel to put you on; but if you'll make shift with something to-morrow morning, Mrs. Squeers will arrange that, in the course of the day.   My dear, don't forget.'

'I'll take care,' replied Mrs. Squeers; 'and mind *you* take care, young man, and get first wash.   The teacher ought always to have it; but they get the better of him if they can.'

Mr. Squeers then nudged Mrs. Squeers to bring away the brandy bottle, lest Nicholas should help himself in the night; and the lady having seized it with great precipitation, they retired together.

Nicholas, being left alone, took half a dozen turns up and down the room in a condition of much agitation and excitement; but, growing gradually calmer, sat himself down in a chair, and mentally resolved that, come what come might, he would endeavour, for

a time, to bear whatever wretchedness might be in
store for him, and that remembering the helplessness
of his mother and sister, he would give his uncle no
plea for deserting them in their need. Good re-
solutions seldom fail of producing some good effect
in the mind from which they spring. He grew less
desponding, and—so sanguine and buoyant is youth
—even hoped that affairs at Dotheboys Hall might
yet prove better than they promised.

He was preparing for bed, with something like renewed cheerfulness, when a sealed letter fell from
his coat pocket. In the hurry of leaving London,
it had escaped his attention, and had not occurred to
him since, but it at once brought back to him the
recollection of the mysterious behaviour of Newman
Noggs.

'Dear me!' said Nicholas; 'what an extraordinary
hand!'

It was directed to himself, was written upon very
dirty paper, and in such cramped and crippled writing as to be almost illegible. After great difficulty
and much puzzling, he contrived to read as follows:—

'MY DEAR YOUNG MAN,
              'I know the world. Your father did not,
or he would not have done me a kindness when there
was no hope of return. You do not, or you would
not be bound on such a journey.

'If ever you want a shelter in London (don't be
angry at this, *I* once thought I never should), they
know where I live, at the sign of the Crown, in Silver
Street, Golden Square. It is at the corner of Silver
Street and James Street, with a bar door both ways.
You can come at night. Once, nobody was ashamed
—never mind that. It's all over.

'Excuse errors. I should forget how to wear ɔ

whole coat now. I have forgotten all my old ways. My spelling may have gone with them.

'NEWMAN NOGGS.

'*P.S.* If you should go near Barnard Castle, there is good ale at the King's Head. Say you know me, and I am sure they will not charge you for it. You may say *Mr.* Noggs there, for I was a gentleman then. I was indeed.'

It may be a very undignified circumstance to record, but after he had folded this letter and placed it in his pocket-book, Nicholas Nickleby's eyes were dimmed with a moisture that might have been taken for tears.

CHAPTTR VIII

OF THE INTERNAL ECONOMY OF DOTHEBOYS HALL

A RIDE of two hundred and odd miles in severe weather, is one of the best softeners of a hard bed that ingenuity can devise. Perhaps it is even a sweetener of dreams, for those which hovered over the rough couch of Nicholas, and whispered their airy nothings in his ear, were of an agreeable and happy kind. He was making his fortune very fast indeed, when the faint glimmer of an expiring candle shone before his eyes, and a voice he had no difficulty in recognising as part and parcel of Mr. Squeers, admonished him that it was time to rise.

'Past seven, Nickleby,' said Mr. Squeers.

'Has morning come already?' asked Nicholas, sitting up in bed.

'Ah! that has it,' replied Squeers, 'and ready iced too. Now, Nickleby, come; tumble up, will you?'

Nicholas needed no further admonition, but 'tumbled up' at once, and proceeded to dress himself by the light of the taper, which Mr. Squeers carried in his hand.

'Here's a pretty go,' said that gentleman; 'the pump's froze.'

'Indeed!' said Nicholas, not much interested in the intelligence.

'Yes,' replied Squeers. 'You can't wash yourself this morning.'

'Not wash myself!' exclaimed Nicholas.

'No, not a bit of it,' rejoined Squeers tartly. 'So you must be content with giving yourself a dry polish till we break the ice in the well, and can get a bucket-ful out for the boys. Don't stand staring at me, but do look sharp, will you?'

Offering no further observation, Nicholas huddled on his clothes. Squeers, meanwhile, opened the shutters and blew the candle out; when the voice of his amiable consort was heard in the passage, demanding admittance.

'Come in, my love,' said Squeers.

Mrs. Squeers came in, still habited in the primitive night-jacket which had displayed the symmetry of her figure on the previous night, and further ornamented with a beaver bonnet of some antiquity, which she wore, with much ease and lightness, on the top of the nightcap before mentioned.

'Drat the things,' said the lady, opening the cupboard; 'I can't find the school spoon anywhere.'

'Never mind it, my dear,' observed Squeers in a soothing manner; 'it's of no consequence.'

'No consequence, why how you talk!' retorted Mrs. Squeers sharply; 'isn't it brimstone morning?'

'I forgot, my dear,' rejoined Squeers; 'yes, it certainly is. We purify the boys' bloods now and then, Nickleby.'

'Purify fiddlesticks' ends,' said his lady. 'Don't think, young man, that we go to the expense of flower of brimstone and molasses, just to purify them; because if you think we carry on the business in that way, you 'll find yourself mistaken, and so I tell you plainly.'

'My dear,' said Squeers frowning. 'Hem!'

'Oh! nonsense,' rejoined Mrs. Squeers. 'If the young man comes to be a teacher here, let him understand, at once, that we don't want any foolery about the boys. They have the brimstone and treacle, partly because if they hadn't something or other in the way of medicine they 'd be always ailing and giving a world of trouble, and partly because it spoils their appetites and comes cheaper than breakfast and dinner. So, it does them good and us good at the same time, and that 's fair enough, I 'm sure.'

Having given this explanation, Mrs. Squeers put her hand into the closet and instituted a stricter search after the spoon, in which Mr. Squeers assisted. A few words passed between them while they were thus engaged, but as their voices were partially stifled by the cupboard, all that Nicholas could distinguish was, that Mr. Squeers said what Mrs. Squeers had said was injudicious, and that Mrs. Squeers said what Mr. Squeers said was 'stuff.'

A vast deal of searching and rummaging ensued, and it proving fruitless, Smike was called in, and pushed by Mrs. Squeers, and boxed by Mr. Squeers; which course of treatment brightening his intellects, enabled him to suggest that possibly Mrs. Squeers might have the spoon in her pocket, as indeed turned out to be the case. As Mrs. Squeers had previously protested, however, that she was quite certain she had not got it, Smike received another box on the ear for presuming to contradict his mistress, together with a promise of a sound thrashing if he were not more respectful in future; so that he took nothing very advantageous by his motion.

'A most invaluable woman, that, Nickleby,' said Squeers when his consort had hurried away, pushing the drudge before her.

'Indeed, sir!' observed Nicholas.

'I don't know her equal,' said Squeers; 'I do not know her equal. That woman, Nickleby, is always the same—always the same bustling, lively, active, saving creetur that you see her now.'

Nicholas sighed involuntarily at the thought of the agreeable domestic prospect thus opened to him; but Squeers was, fortunately, too much occupied with his own reflections to perceive it.

'It's my way to say, when I am up in London,' continued Squeers, 'that to them boys she is a mother. But she is more than a mother to them; ten times more. She does things for them boys, Nickleby, that I don't believe half the mothers going, would do for their own sons.'

'I should think they would not, sir,' answered Nicholas.

Now, the fact was, that both Mr. and Mrs. Squeers viewed the boys in the light of their proper and natural enemies; or, in other words, they held and considered that their business and profession was to get as much from every boy as could by possibility be screwed out of him. On this point they were both agreed, and behaved in unison accordingly. The only difference between them was, that Mrs. Squeers waged war against the enemy openly and fearlessly, and that Squeers covered his rascality, even at home,

with a spice of his habitual deceit; as if he really had
a notion of some day or other being able to take himself in, and persuade his own mind that he was a very
good fellow.

'But come,' said Squeers, interrupting the progress
of some thoughts to this effect in the mind of his
usher; 'let's go to the school-room; and lend me a
hand with my school coat, will you?'

Nicholas assisted his master to put on an old fustian
shooting-jacket, which he took down from a peg in
the passage; and Squeers, arming himself with his
cane, led the way across a yard, to a door in the rear
of the house.

'There,' said the schoolmaster as they stepped in
together; 'this is our shop, Nickleby!'

It was such a crowded scene, and there were so
many objects to attract attention, that, at first, Nicholas stared about him, really without seeing anything at all. By degrees, however, the place resolved
itself into a bare and dirty room, with a couple of
windows, whereof a tenth part might be of glass, the
remainder being stopped up with old copybooks and
paper. There were a couple of long old rickety
desks, cut and notched, and inked, and damaged, in
every possible way; two or three forms; a detached
desk for Squeers; and another for his assistant. The
ceiling was supported, like that of a barn, by cross
beams and rafters; and the walls were so stained and
discoloured, that it was impossible to tell whether they
had ever been touched with paint or whitewash.

But the pupils—the young noblemen! How the
last faint traces of hope, the remotest glimmering of
any good to be derived from his efforts in this den,
faded from the mind of Nicholas as he looked in dismay around! Pale and haggard faces, lank and
bony figures, children with the countenances of old

men, deformities with irons upon their limbs, boys of
stunted growth, and others whose long meagre legs
would hardly bear their stooping bodies, all crowded
on the view together; there were the bleared eye, the
hare-lip, the crooked foot, and every ugliness or dis-
tortion that told of unnatural aversion conceived by
parents for their offspring, or of young lives which,
from the earliest dawn of infancy, had been one horrible endurance of cruelty and neglect. There were
little faces which should have been handsome, darkened with the scowl of sullen, dogged suffering; there
was childhood with the light of its eye quenched, its
beauty gone, and its helplessness alone remaining;
there were vicious-faced boys, brooding, with leaden
eyes, like malefactors in a jail; and there were young
creatures on whom the sins of their frail parents had
descended, weeping even for the mercenary nurses
they had known, and lonesome even in their loneli-
ness. With every kindly sympathy and affection
blasted in its birth, with every young and healthy feeling flogged and starved down, with every revengeful
passion that can fester in swollen hearts, eating its
evil way to their core in silence, what an incipient Hell
was breeding here!

And yet this scene, painful as it was, had its grotesque features, which, in a less interested observer
than Nicholas, might have provoked a smile. Mrs.
Squeers stood at one of the desks, presiding over an
immense basin of brimstone and treacle, of which
delicious compound she administered a large instalment to each boy in succession: using for the purpose
a common wooden spoon, which might have been
originally manufactured for some gigantic top, and
which widened every young gentleman's mouth considerably: they being all obliged, under heavy corporal
penalties, to take in the whole of the bowl at a gasp.

In another corner, huddled together for companion-ship, were the little boys who had arrived on the pre-ceding night, three of them in very large leather breeches, and two in old trousers, a something tighter fit than drawers are usually worn; at no great dis-tance from these was seated the juvenile son and heir of Mr. Squeers—a striking likeness of his father—kicking, with great vigour, under the hands of Smike, who was fitting upon him a pair of new boots that bore a most suspicious resemblance to those which the least of the little boys had worn on the journey down —as the little boy himself seemed to think, for he was regarding the appropriation with a look of most rue-ful amazement.   Besides these, there was a long row of boys waiting, with countenances of no pleasant anticipation, to be treacled; and another file, who had just escaped from the infliction, making a variety of wry mouths indicative of anything but satisfaction. The whole were attired in such motley, ill-assorted, extraordinary garments, as would have been irresisti-bly ridiculous, but for the foul appearance of dirt, disorder, and disease, with which they were associated.

'Now,' said Squeers, giving the desk a great rap with his cane, which made half the little boys nearly jump out of their boots, 'is that physicking over?'

'Just over,' said Mrs. Squeers, choking the last boy in her hurry, and tapping the crown of his head with the wooden spoon to restore him.   'Here, you Smike; take away now.   Look sharp!'

Smike shuffled out with the basin, and Mrs. Squeers having called up a little boy with a curly head, and wiped her hands upon it, hurried out after him into a species of wash-house, where there was a small fire and a large kettle, together with a number of little wooden bowls which were arranged upon a board.

Into these bowls, Mrs. Squeers, assisted by the

hungry servant, poured a brown composition, which looked like diluted pincushions without the covers, and was called porridge. A minute wedge of brown bread was inserted in each bowl, and when they had eaten their porridge by means of the bread, the boys ate the bread itself, and had finished their breakfast; whereupon Mr. Squeers said in a solemn voice, 'For what we have received, may the Lord make us truly thankful!'—and went away to his own.

Nicholas distended his stomach with a bowl of porridge, for much the same reason which induces some savages to swallow earth—lest they should be inconveniently hungry when there is nothing to eat. Having further disposed of a slice of bread and butter, allotted to him in virtue of his office, he sat himself down, to wait for school-time.

He could not but observe how silent and sad the boys all seemed to be. There was none of the noise and clamour of a school-room; none of its boisterous play, or hearty mirth. The children sat crouching and shivering together, and seemed to lack the spirit to move about. The only pupil who evinced the slightest tendency towards locomotion or playfulness was Master Squeers, and as his chief amusement was to tread upon the other boys' toes in his new boots, his flow of spirits was rather disagreeable than otherwise.

After some half-hour's delay, Mr. Squeers reappeared, and the boys took their places and their books, of which latter commodity the average might be about one to eight learners. A few minutes having elapsed, during which Mr. Squeers looked very profound, as if he had a perfect apprehension of what was inside all the books, and could say every word of their contents by heart if he only chose to take the trouble, that gentleman called up the first class.

Obedient to this summons there ranged themselves

in front of the schoolmaster's desk, half a dozen scarecrows, out at knees and elbows, one of whom placed a torn and filthy book beneath his learned eye.

'This is the first class in English spelling and philosophy, Nickleby,' said Squeers, beckoning Nicholas to stand beside him. 'We'll get up a Latin one, and hand that over to you. Now, then, where's the first boy?'

'Please, sir, he's cleaning the back parlour window,' said the temporary head of the philosophical class.

'So he is, to be sure,' rejoined Squeers. 'We go upon the practical mode of teaching, Nickleby; the regular education system. C-l-e-a-n, clean, verb active, to make bright, to scour. W-i-n, win, d-e-r, winder, a casement. When the boy knows this out of book, he goes and does it. It's just the same principle as the use of the globes. Where's the second boy?'

'Please, sir, he's weeding the garden,' replied a small voice.

'To be sure,' said Squeers, by no means disconcerted. 'So he is. B-o-t, bot, t-i-n, bottin, n-e-y, ney, bottinney, noun substantive, a knowledge of plants. When he has learned that bottinney means a knowledge of plants, he goes and knows 'em. That's our system, Nickleby; what do you think of it?'

'It's a very useful one, at any rate,' answered Nicholas.

'I believe you,' rejoined Squeers, not remarking the emphasis of his usher. 'Third boy, what's a horse?'

'A beast, sir,' replied the boy.

'So it is,' said Squeers. 'Ain't it, Nickleby?'

'I believe there is no doubt of that, sir,' answered Nicholas

'Of course there isn't,' said Squeers. 'A horse is a quadruped, and quadruped's Latin for beast, as everybody that's gone through the grammar, knows, or else where's the use of having grammars at all?'

'Where, indeed!' said Nicholas abstractedly.

'As you're perfect in that,' resumed Squeers, turning to the boy, 'go and look after *my* horse, and rub him down well, or I'll rub you down. The rest of the class go and draw water up, till somebody tells you to leave off, for it's washing-day to-morrow, and they want the coppers filled.'

So saying, he dismissed the first class to their experiments in practical philosophy, and eyed Nicholas with a look, half cunning and half doubtful, as if he were not altogether certain what he might think of him by this time.

'That's the way we do it, Nickleby,' he said, after a pause.

Nicholas shrugged his shoulders in a manner that was scarcely perceptible, and said he saw it was.

'And a very good way it is, too,' said Squeers. 'Now, just take them fourteen little boys and hear them some reading, because, you know, you must begin to be useful. Idling about here, won't do.'

Mr. Squeers said this, as if it had suddenly occurred to him, either that he must not say too much to his assistant, or that his assistant did not say enough to him in praise of the establishment. The children were arranged in a semi-circle round the new master, and he was soon listening to their dull, drawling, hesitating recital of those stories of engrossing interest which are to be found in the more antiquated spelling books.

In this exciting occupation, the morning lagged heavily on. At one o'clock, the boys, having previously had their appetites thoroughly taken away by stir-about and potatoes, sat down in the kitchen to some hard salt beef, of which Nicholas was graciously permitted to take his portion to his own solitary desk, to eat it there in peace. After this, there was another hour of crouching in the school-room and shivering with cold, and then school began again.

It was Mr. Squeers's custom to call the boys together, and make a sort of report, after every half-yearly visit to the metropolis, regarding the relations and friends he had seen, the news he had heard, the letters he had brought down, the bills which had been paid, the accounts which had been left unpaid, and so forth. This solemn proceeding always took place in the afternoon of the day succeeding his return; perhaps, because the boys acquired strength of mind from the suspense of the morning, or, possibly, because Mr. Squeers himself acquired greater sternness and inflexibility from certain warm potations in which he was wont to indulge after his early dinner. Be this as it may, the boys were recalled from house-window, garden, stable, and cow-yard, and the school were assembled in full conclave, when Mr. Squeers, with a small bundle of papers in his hand, and Mrs. S. following with a pair of canes, entered the room and proclaimed silence.

'Let any boy speak a word without leave,' said Mr. Squeers, mildly, 'and I 'll take the skin off his back.'

This special proclamation had the desired effect, and a deathlike silence immediately prevailed, in the midst of which Mr. Squeers went on to say—

'Boys, I 've been to London, and have returned to my family and you, as strong and well as ever.'

According to half-yearly custom, the boys gave three feeble cheers at this refreshing intelligence. Such cheers! Sighs of extra strength with the chill on.

'I have seen the parents of some boys,' continued

Squeers, turning over his papers, 'and they 're so glad to hear how their sons are getting on, that there 's no prospect at all of their going away, which of course is a very pleasant thing to reflect upon, for all parties.'

Two or three hands went to two or three eyes when Squeers said this, but the greater part of the young gentlemen having no particular parents to speak of, were wholly uninterested in the thing one way or other.

'I have had disappointments to contend against,' said Squeers, looking very grim; 'Bolder's father was two pound ten short. Where is Bolder?'

'Here he is, please, sir,' rejoined twenty officious voices. Boys are very like men, to be sure.

'Come here, Bolder,' said Squeers.

An unhealthy-looking boy, with warts all over his hands, stepped from his place to the master's desk, and raised his eyes imploringly to Squeers's face; his own, quite white from the rapid beating of his heart.

'Bolder,' said Squeers, speaking very slowly, for he was considering, as the saying goes, where to have him. 'Bolder, if your father thinks that because—why, what 's this, sir?'

As Squeers spoke, he caught up the boy's hand by the cuff of his jacket, and surveyed it with an edifying aspect of horror and disgust.

'What do you call this, sir?' demanded the schoolmaster, administering a cut with the cane to expedite the reply.

'I can't help it, indeed, sir,' rejoined the boy, crying. 'They will come; it 's the dirty work I think, sir—at least I don't know what it is, sir, but it 's not my fault.'

'Bolder,' said Squeers, tucking up his wristbands, and moistening the palm of his right hand to get a good grip of the cane, 'you are an incorrigible young scoundrel, and as the last thrashing did you no good, we must see what another will do towards beating it out of you.'

With this, and wholly disregarding a piteous cry for mercy, Mr. Squeers fell upon the boy and caned him soundly: not leaving off indeed, until his arm was tired out.

'There,' said Squeers, when he had quite done; 'rub away as hard as you like, you won't rub that off in a hurry. Oh! you won't hold that noise, won't you? Put him out, Smike.'

The drudge knew better from long experience, than to hesitate about obeying, so he bundled the victim out by a side door, and Mr. Squeers perched himself again on his own stool, supported by Mrs. Squeers, who occupied another at his side.

'Now let us see,' said Squeers. 'A letter for Cobbey. Stand up, Cobbey.'

Another boy stood up, and eyed the letter very hard while Squeers made a mental abstract of the same.

'Oh!' said Squeers: 'Cobbey's grandmother is dead, and his uncle John has took to drinking, which is all the news his sister sends, except eighteenpence, which will just pay for that broken square of glass. Mrs. Squeers, my dear, will you take the money?'

The worthy lady pocketed the eighteenpence with a most business-like air, and Squeers passed on to the next boy, as coolly as possible.

'Graymarsh,' said Squeers, 'he's the next. Stand up, Graymarsh.'

Another boy stood up, and the schoolmaster looked over the letter as before.

'Graymarsh's maternal aunt,' said Squeers, when he had possessed himself of the contents, 'is very glad to hear he's so well and happy, and sends her respectful compliments to Mrs. Squeers, and thinks she must be an angel. She likewise thinks Mr. Squeers is too good for this world; but hopes he may long be spared to carry on the business. Would have sent the two pair of stockings as desired, but is short of money, so forwards a tract instead, and hopes Graymarsh will put his trust in Providence. Hopes, above all, that he will study in everything to please Mr. and Mrs. Squeers, and look upon them as his only friends; and that he will love Master Squeers; and not object to sleeping five in a bed, which no Christian should. Ah!' said Squeers, folding it up, 'a delightful letter. Very affecting indeed.'

It was affecting in one sense, for Graymarsh's maternal aunt was strongly supposed, by her more intimate friends, to be no other than his maternal parent; Squeers, however, without alluding to this part of the story (which would have sounded immoral before boys), proceeded with the business by calling out 'Mobbs,' whereupon another boy rose, and Graymarsh resumed his seat.

'Mobbs's mother-in-law,' said Squeers, 'took to her bed on hearing that he wouldn't eat fat, and has been very ill ever since. She wishes to know, by an early post, where he expects to go to, if he quarrels with his vittles; and with what feelings he could turn up his nose at the cow's liver broth, after his good master had asked a blessing on it. This was told her in the London newspapers—not by Mr. Squeers, for he is too kind and too good to set anybody against anybody— and it has vexed her so much, Mobbs can't think. She is sorry to find he is discontented, which is sinful and horrid, and hopes Mr. Squeers will flog him into a happier state of mind; with this view, she has also stopped his halfpenny a week pocket-money, and given a double-bladed knife with a corkscrew in it to the Missionaries, which she had bought on purpose for him.'

'A sulky state of feeling,' said Squeers, after a terrible pause, during which he had moistened the palm of his right hand again, 'won't do. Cheerfulness and contentment must be kept up. Mobbs, come to me!'

Mobbs moved slowly towards the desk, rubbing his eyes in anticipation of good cause for doing so; and he soon afterwards retired by the side door, with as good cause as a boy need have.

Mr. Squeers then proceeded to open a miscellaneous collection of letters; some enclosing money, which Mrs. Squeers 'took care of"; and others referring to small articles of apparel, as caps and so forth, all of which the same lady stated to be too large, or too small, and calculated for nobody but young Squeers, who would appear indeed to have had most accommodating limbs, since everything that came into the school fitted him to a nicety. His head, in particular, must have been singularly elastic, for hats and caps of all dimensions were alike to him.

This business despatched, a few slovenly lessons were performed, and Squeers retired to his fireside, leaving Nicholas to take care of the boys in the schoolroom, which was very cold, and where a meal of bread and cheese was served out shortly after dark.

There was a small stove at that corner of the room which was nearest to the master's desk, and by it Nicholas sat down, so depressed and self-degraded by the consciousness of his position, that if death could have come upon him at that time, he would have been almost happy to meet it. The cruelty of which he had been an unwilling witness, the coarse and ruffianly behaviour of Squeers even in his best moods, the filthy place, the sights and sounds about him, all contributed to this state of feeling; but when he recollected that, being there as an assistant, he actually seemed—no matter what unhappy train of circumstances had brought him to that pass—to be the aider and abettor of a system which filled him with honest disgust and indignation, he loathed himself, and felt, for the moment, as though the mere consciousness of his present situation must, through all time to come, prevent his raising his head again.

But, for the present, his resolve was taken, and the resolution he had formed on the preceding night remained undisturbed. He had written to his mother and sister, announcing the safe conclusion of his journey, and saying as little about Dotheboys Hall, and saying that little as cheerfully, as he possibly could. He hoped that by remaining where he was, he might do some good, even there; at all events, others depended too much on his uncle's favour, to admit of his awakening his wrath just then.

One reflection disturbed him far more than any selfish considerations arising out of his own position. This was the probable destination of his sister Kate. His uncle had deceived him, and might he not consign her to some miserable place where her youth and beauty would prove a far greater curse than ugliness and decrepitude? To a caged man, bound hand and foot, this was a terrible idea;—but no, he thought, his mother was by; there was the portrait-painter, too— simple enough, but still living in the world, and of it. He was willing to believe that Ralph Nickleby had conceived a personal dislike to himself. Having pretty good reason, by this time, to reciprocate it, he had no great difficulty in arriving at this conclusion, and tried to persuade himself that the feeling extended no farther than between them.

As he was absorbed in these meditations, he all at once encountered the upturned face of Smike, who

was on his knees before the stove, picking a few stray
cinders from the hearth and planting them on the fire.
He had paused to steal a look at Nicholas, and when
he saw that he was observed, shrunk back, as if expecting a blow.

'You need not fear me,' said Nicholas kindly. 'Are
you cold?'

'N-n-o.'

'You are shivering.'

'I am not cold,' replied Smike quickly. 'I am used
to it.'

There was such an obvious fear of giving offence in
his manner, and he was such a timid, broken-spirited
creature, that Nicholas could not help exclaiming,
'Poor fellow!'

If he had struck the drudge, he would have slunk
away without a word. But, now, he burst into tears.

'Oh dear, oh dear!' he cried, covering his face with
his cracked and horny hands. 'My heart will break.
It will, it will.'

'Hush!' said Nicholas, laying his hands upon his
shoulder. 'Be a man; you are nearly one by years,
God help you.'

'By years!' cried Smike. 'Oh dear, dear, how many
of them! How many of them since I was a little
child, younger than any that are here now! Where
are they all?'

'Whom do you speak of?' inquired Nicholas, wishing to rouse the poor half-witted creature to reason.
'Tell me.'

'My friends,' he replied, 'myself—my—oh! what
sufferings mine have been!'

'There is always hope,' said Nicholas; he knew not
what to say.

'No,' rejoined the other, 'no; none for me. Do you
remember the boy that died here?'

'I was not here, you know,' said Nicholas gently; 'but what of him?'

'Why,' replied the youth, drawing closer to his questioner's side, 'I was with him at night, and when it was all silent he cried no more for friends he wished to come and sit with him, but began to see faces round his bed that came from home; he said they smiled, and talked to him; and he died at last lifting his head to kiss them. Do you hear?'

'Yes, yes,' rejoined Nicholas.

'What faces will smile on me when I die?' cried his companion, shivering. 'Who will talk to me in those long nights? They cannot come from home; they would frighten me, if they did, for I don't know what it is, and shouldn't know them. Pain and fear, pain and fear for me, alive or dead. No hope, no hope!'

The bell rang to bed: and the boy, subsiding at the sound into his usual listless state, crept away as if anxious to avoid notice. It was with a heavy heart that Nicholas soon afterwards—no, not retired; there was no retirement there—followed—to his dirty and crowded dormitory.

CHAPTER IX

OF MISS SQUEERS, MRS. SQUEERS, MASTER SQUEERS, AND MR. SQUEERS; AND OF VARIOUS MATTERS AND PERSONS CONNECTED NO LESS WITH THE SQUEERSES THAN WITH NICHOLAS NICKLEBY

WHEN Mr. Squeers left the school-room for the night, he betook himself, as has been before remarked, to his own fireside, which was situated—not in the room in which Nicholas had supped on the night of his arrival, but in a smaller apartment in the rear of the premises, where his lady wife, his amiable son, and accomplished daughter, were in the full enjoyment of each other's society; Mrs. Squeers being engaged in the matronly pursuit of stocking-darning; and the young lady and gentleman being occupied in the adjustment of some youthful differences, by means of a pugilistic contest across the table, which, on the approach of their honoured parent, subsided into a noiseless exchange of kicks beneath it.

And, in this place, it may be as well to apprise the reader, that Miss Fanny Squeers was in her three-and-twentieth year. If there be any one grace or loveliness inseparable from that particular period of life, Miss Squeers may be presumed to have been possessed of it, as there is no reason to suppose that she was a solitary exception to a universal rule. She was not tall like her mother, but short like her father; from the former she inherited a voice of harsh quality; from the latter a remarkable expression of the right eye, something akin to having none at all.

Miss Squeers had been spending a few days with a neighbouring friend, and had only just returned to the parental roof. To this circumstance may be referred, her having heard nothing of Nicholas, until Mr. Squeers himself now made him the subject of conversation.

'Well, my dear,' said Squeers, drawing up his chair, 'what do you think of him by this time?'

'Think of who?' inquired Mrs. Squeers; who (as she often remarked) was no grammarian, thank Heaven.

'Of the young man—the new teacher—who else could I mean?'

'Oh! that Knuckleboy,' said Mrs. Squeers impatiently. 'I hate him.'

'What do you hate him for, my dear?' asked Squeers.

'What's that to you?' retorted Mrs. Squeers. 'If I hate him, that's enough, ain't it?'

'Quite enough for him, my dear, and a great deal too much, I dare say, if he knew it,' replied Squeers in a pacific tone. 'I only asked from curiosity, my dear.'

'Well then, if you want to know,' rejoined Mrs. Squeers, 'I'll tell you. Because he's a proud, haughty, consequential, turned-up-nosed peacock.'

Mrs. Squeers, when excited, was accustomed to use strong language, and, moreover, to make use of a plurality of epithets, some of which were of a figurative kind, as the word peacock, and furthermore the allusion to Nicholas's nose, which was not intended to be taken in its literal sense, but rather to bear a latitude of construction according to the fancy of the hearers.

Neither were they meant to bear reference to each other, so much as to the object on whom they were bestowed, as will be seen in the present case: a peacock with a turned-up nose being a novelty in ornithology, and a thing not commonly seen.

'Hem!' said Squeers, as if in mild deprecation of this outbreak. 'He is cheap, my dear; the young man is very cheap.'

'Not a bit of it,' retorted Mrs. Squeers.

'Five pound a year,' said Squeers.

'What of that; it's dear if you don't want him, isn't it?' replied his wife.

'But we *do* want him,' urged Squeers.

'I don't see that you want him any more than the dead,' said Mrs. Squeers. 'Don't tell me. You can put on the cards and in the advertisements, "Educa-

tion by Mr. Wackford Squeers and able assistants,"
without having any assistants, can't you? Isn't it
done every day by all the masters about? I 've no
patience with you.'

'Haven't you!' said Squeers, sternly. 'Now I 'll
tell you what, Mrs. Squeers. In this matter of having a teacher, I 'll take my own way, if you please.
A slave driver in the West Indies is allowed a man
under him, to see that his blacks don't run away, or
get up a rebellion; and I 'll have a man under me to
do the same with *our* blacks, till such time as little
Wackford is able to take charge of the school.'

'Am I to take care of the school when I grow up
a man, father?' said Wackford junior, suspending,
in the excess of his delight, a vicious kick which he
was administering to his sister.

'You are, my son,' replied Mr. Squeers, in a
sentimental voice.

'Oh my eye, won't I give it to the boys!' exclaimed
the interesting child, grasping his father's cane.
'Oh, father, won't I make 'em squeak again!'

It was a proud moment in Mr. Squeers's life, when
he witnessed that burst of enthusiasm in his young
child's mind, and saw in it a foreshadowing of his
future eminence. He pressed a penny into his hand,
and gave vent to his feelings (as did his exemplary
wife also), in a shout of approving laughter. The
infantine appeal to their common sympathies, at once
restored cheerfulness to the conversation, and harmony to the company.

'He 's a nasty stuck-up monkey, that 's what I consider him,' said Mrs. Squeers, reverting to Nicholas.

'Supposing he is,' said Squeers, 'he is as well stuck
up in our school-room as anywhere else, isn't he?—
especially as he don't like it.'

'Well,' observed Mrs. Squeers, 'there 's something

in that. I hope it'll bring his pride down, and it shall be no fault of mine if it don't.'

Now, a proud usher in a Yorkshire school was such a very extraordinary and unaccountable thing to hear of,—any usher at all being a novelty; but a proud one, a being of whose existence the wildest imagination could never have dreamed—that Miss Squeers, who seldom troubled herself with scholastic matters, inquired with much curiosity who this Knuckleboy was, that gave himself such airs.

'Nickleby,' said Squeers, spelling the name according to some eccentric system which prevailed in his own mind; 'your mother always calls things and people by their wrong names.'

'No matter for that,' said Mrs. Squeers, 'I see them with right eyes, and that's quite enough for me. I watched him when you were laying on to little Bolder this afternoon. He looked as black as thunder, all the while, and, one time started up as if he had more than got it in his mind to make a rush at you. *I* saw him, though he thought I didn't.'

'Never mind, that, father,' said Miss Squeers, as the head of the family was about to reply. 'Who is the man?'

'Why, your father has got some nonsense in his head that he's the son of a poor gentleman that died the other day,' said Mrs. Squeers.

'The son of a gentleman!'

'Yes; but I don't believe a word of it. If he's a gentleman's son at all, he's a fondling, that's my opinion.'

Mrs. Squeers intended to say 'foundling,' but, as she frequently remarked when she made any such mistake, it would be all the same a hundred years hence; with which axiom of philosophy, indeed, she was in the constant habit of consoling the boys when they laboured under more than ordinary ill usage.

'He 's nothing of the kind,' said Squeers, in answer to the above remark, 'for his father was married to his mother, years before he was born, and she is alive now.   If he was, it would be no business of ours, for we make a very good friend by having him here; and if he likes to learn the boys anything besides minding them, I have no objection I am sure.'

'I say again, I hate him worse than poison,' said Mrs. Squeers, vehemently.

'If you dislike him, my dear,' returned Squeers, 'I don't know anybody who can show dislike better than you, and of course there 's no occasion, with him, to take the trouble to hide it.'

'I don't intend to, I assure you,' interposed Mrs. S.

'That 's right,' said Squeers; 'and if he has a touch of pride about him, as I think he has, I don't believe there 's a woman in all England that can bring anybody's spirit down, as quick as you can, my love.'

Mrs. Squeers chuckled vastly on the receipt of these flattering compliments, and said, she hoped she had tamed a high spirit or two, in her day.   It is but due to her character to say, that in conjunction with her estimable husband, she had broken many and many a one.

Miss Fanny Squeers carefully treasured up this, and much more conversation on the same subject, until she retired for the night, when she questioned the hungry servant, minutely, regarding the outward appearance and demeanour of Nicholas; to which queries the girl returned such enthusiastic replies, coupled with so many laudatory remarks touching his beautiful dark eyes, and his sweet smile, and his straight legs—upon which last-named articles she laid particular stress; the general run of legs at Dotheboys Hall being crooked—that Miss Squeers was not long in arriving at the conclusion that the new usher must be a very remarkable person, or, as she herself significantly phrased it, 'something quite out of the common.' And so Miss Squeers made up her mind that she would take a personal observation of Nicholas the very next day.

In pursuance of this design, the young lady watched the opportunity of her mother being engaged, and her father absent, and went accidentally into the school-room to get a pen mended: where, seeing nobody but Nicholas presiding over the boys, she blushed very deeply, and exhibited great confusion.

'I beg your pardon,' faltered Miss Squeers; 'I thought my father was—or might be—dear me, how very awkward!'

'Mr. Squeers is out,' said Nicholas, by no means overcome by the apparition, unexpected though it was.

'Do you know will he be long, sir?' asked Miss Squeers, with bashful hesitation.

'He said about an hour,' replied Nicholas—politely of course, but without any indication of being stricken to the heart by Miss Squeers's charms.

'I never knew anything happen so cross,' exclaimed the young lady. 'Thank you! I am very sorry I intruded, I am sure. If I hadn't thought my father was here, I wouldn't upon any account have—it is very provoking—must look so very strange,' murmured Miss Squeers, blushing once more, and glancing, from the pen in her hand, to Nicholas at his desk, and back again.

'If that is all you want,' said Nicholas, pointing to the pen, and smiling, in spite of himself, at the affected embarrassment of the schoolmaster's daughter, 'perhaps I can supply his place.'

Miss Squeers glanced at the door, as if dubious

of the propriety of advancing any nearer to an utter stranger; then round the school-room, as though in some measure reassured by the presence of forty boys; and finally sidled up to Nicholas and delivered the pen into his hand, with a most winning mixture of reserve and condescension.

'Shall it be a hard or a soft nib?' inquired Nicholas, smiling to prevent himself from laughing outright.

'He *has* a beautiful smile,' thought Miss Squeers.

'Which did you say?' asked Nicholas.

'Dear me, I was thinking of something else for the moment, I declare,' replied Miss Squeers—'Oh! as soft as possible, if you please.' With which words, Miss Squeers sighed. It might be, to give Nicholas to understand that her heart was soft, and that the pen was wanted to match.

Upon these instructions Nicholas made the pen; when he gave it to Miss Squeers, Miss Squeers dropped it; and when he stooped to pick it up; Miss Squeers stooped also, and they knocked their heads together; whereat five-and-twenty little boys laughed aloud: being positively for the first and only time that half-year.

'Very awkward of me,' said Nicholas, opening the door for the young lady's retreat.

'Not at all, sir,' replied Miss Squeers; 'it was my fault. It was all my foolish—a—a—good morning!'

'Good bye,' said Nicholas. 'The next I make for you, I hope will be made less clumsily. Take care! You are biting the nib off now.'

'Really,' said Miss Squeers; 'so embarrassing that I scarcely know what I—very sorry to give you so much trouble.'

'Not the least trouble in the world,' replied Nicholas, closing the school-room door.

'I never saw such legs in the whole course of my life!' said Miss Squeers, as she walked away.

In fact, Miss Squeers was in love with Nicholas Nickleby.

To account for the rapidity with which this young lady had conceived a passion for Nicholas, it may be necessary to state, that the friend from whom she had so recently returned, was a miller's daughter of only eighteen, who had contracted herself unto the son of a small corn-factor, resident in the nearest market town.   Miss Squeers and the miller's daughter, being fast friends, had covenanted together some two years before, according to a custom prevalent among young ladies, that whoever was first engaged to be married, should straightway confide the mighty secret to the bosom of the other, before communicating it to any living soul, and bespeak her as bridesmaid without loss of time; in fulfilment of which pledge the miller's daughter, when her engagement was formed, came out express, at eleven o'clock at night as the corn-factor's son made an offer of his hand and heart at twenty-five minutes past ten by the Dutch clock in the kitchen, and rushed into Miss Squeers's bedroom with the gratifying intelligence.   Now, Miss Squeers being five years older, and out of her teens (which is also a great matter), had, since, been more than commonly anxious to return the compliment, and possess her friend with a similar secret; but, either in consequence of finding it hard to please herself, or harder still to please anybody else, had never had an opportunity so to do, inasmuch as she had no such secret to disclose.   The little interview with Nicholas had no sooner passed, as above described, however, than Miss Squeers, putting on her bonnet, made her way, with great precipitation, to her friend's house, and, upon

a solemn renewal of divers old vows of secrecy, re-
vealed how that she was—not exactly engaged, but
going to be—to a gentleman's son—(none of your
corn-factors, but a gentleman's son of high decent)
—who had come down as teacher to Dotheboys Hall,
under most mysterious and remarkable circumstances
—indeed, as Miss Squeers more than once hinted she
had good reason to believe, induced, by the fame of
her many charms, to seek her out, and woo and win
her.

'Isn't it an extraordinary thing?' said Miss Squeers,
emphasising the adjective strongly.

'Most extraordinary,' replied the friend. 'But
what has he said to you?'

'Don't ask me what he said, my dear,' rejoined
Miss Squeers. 'If you had only seen his looks and
smiles! I never was so overcome in all my life.'

'Did he look in this way?' inquired the miller's
daughter, counterfeiting, as nearly as she could, a
favourite leer of the corn-factor.

'Very like that—only more genteel,' replied Miss
Squeers.

'Ah!' said the friend, 'then he means something,
depend on it.'

Miss Squeers, having slight misgivings on the subject, was by no means ill pleased to be confirmed by
a competent authority; and, discovering, on further
conversation and comparison of notes, a great many
points of resemblance between the behaviour of
Nicholas, and that of the corn-factor, grew so exceedingly confidential, that she intrusted her friend
with a vast number of things Nicholas had *not* said,
which were all so very complimentary as to be quite
conclusive. Then, she dilated on the fearful hardship
of having a father and mother strenuously opposed
to her intended husband; on which unhappy circum-

stance she dwelt at great length; for the friend's father and mother were quite agreeable to her being married, and the whole courtship was in consequence as flat and common-place an affair as it was possible to imagine.

'How I should like to see him!' exclaimed the friend.

'So you shall, 'Tilda,' replied Miss Squeers. 'I should consider myself one of the most ungrateful creatures alive, if I denied you. I think mother's going away for two days to fetch some boys; and when she does, I'll ask you and John up to tea, and have him to meet you.'

This was a charming idea, and having fully discussed it, the friends parted.

It so fell out, that Mrs. Squeers's journey, to some distance, to fetch three new boys, and dun the relations of two old ones for the balance of a small account, was fixed, that very afternoon, for the next day but one; and on the next day but one, Mrs. Squeers got up outside the coach, as it stopped to change at Greta Bridge, taking with her a small bundle containing something in a bottle, and some sandwiches, and carrying besides a large white top coat to wear in the night-time; with which baggage she went her way.

Whenever such opportunities as these occurred, it was Squeers's custom to drive over to the market town, every evening, on pretence of urgent business, and stop till ten or eleven o'clock at a tavern he much affected. As the party was not in his way, therefore, but rather afforded a means of compromise with Miss Squeers, he readily yielded his full assent thereunto, and willingly communicated to Nicholas that he was expected to take his tea in the parlour that evening, at five o'clock.

To be sure Miss Squeers was in a desperate flutter

as the time approached, and to be sure she was dressed
out to the best advantage: with her hair—it had more
than a tinge of red, and she wore it in a crop—curled
in five distinct rows, up to the very top of her head,
and arranged dexterously over the doubtful eye; to say
nothing of the blue sash which floated down her back,
or the worked apron, or the long gloves, or the green
gauze scarf, worn over one shoulder and under the
other; or any of the numerous devices which were to
be as so many arrows to the heart of Nicholas. She
had scarcely completed these arrangements to her entire satisfaction, when the friend arrived with a whitey-
brown parcel—flat and three-cornered—containing
sundry small adornments which were to be put on upstairs, and which the friend put on, talking incessantly.
When Miss Squeers had 'done' the friend's hair, the
friend 'did' Miss Squeers's hair, throwing in some
striking improvements in the way of ringlets down the
neck; and then, when they were both touched up to
their entire satisfaction, they went downstairs in full
state with the long gloves on, all ready for company.

'Where 's John, 'Tilda?' said Miss Squeers.

'Only gone home to clean himself,' replied the
friend. 'He will be here by the time the tea 's drawn.'

'I do so palpitate,' observed Miss Squeers.

'Ah! I know what it is,' replied the friend.

'I have not been used to it, you know, 'Tilda,' said
Miss Squeers, applying her hand to the left side of
her sash.

'You 'll soon get the better of it, dear,' rejoined
the friend. While they were talking thus, the hungry
servant brought in the tea things, and, soon afterwards, somebody tapped at the room door.

'There he is!' cried Miss Squeers. 'Oh, 'Tilda!'

'Hush!' said 'Tilda. 'Hem! Say, come in.'

'Come in,' cried Miss Squeers faintly. And in walked Nicholas.

'Good evening,' said that young gentleman, all unconscious of his conquest. 'I understood from Mr. Squeers that—'

'Oh yes; it's all right,' interposed Miss Squeers. 'Father don't tea with us, but you won't mind that, I dare say.' (This was said archly.)

Nicholas opened his eyes at this, but he turned the matter off very coolly—not caring, particularly, about anything just then—and went through the ceremony of introduction to the miller's daughter, with so much grace, that that young lady was lost in admiration.

'We are only waiting for one more gentleman,' said Miss Squeers, taking off the tea-pot lid, and looking in, to see how the tea was getting on.

It was matter of equal moment to Nicholas whether they were waiting for one gentleman or twenty, so he received the intelligence with perfect unconcern; and, being out of spirits, and not seeing any especial reason why he should make himself agreeable, looked out of the window and sighed involuntarily.

As luck would have it, Miss Squeers's friend was of a playful turn, and hearing Nicholas sigh, she took it into her head to rally the lovers on their lowness of spirits.

'But if it's caused by my being here,' said the young lady, 'don't mind me a bit, for I'm quite as bad. You may go on just as you would if you were alone.'

'Tilda,' said Miss Squeers, colouring up to the top row of curls, 'I am ashamed of you'; and here the two friends burst into a variety of giggles, and glanced, from time to time over the tops of their pocket-handkerchiefs, at Nicholas, who from a state of unmixed astonishment, gradually fell into one of irrepressible laughter—occasioned, partly by the bare notion of his being in love with Miss Squeers, and partly by the preposterous appearance and behaviour of the two girls. These two causes of merriment, taken together, struck him as being so keenly ridiculous, that, despite his miserable condition, he laughed till he was thoroughly exhausted.

'Well,' thought Nicholas, 'as I am here, and seem expected, for some reason or other, to be amiable, it 's of no use looking like a goose. I may as well accommodate myself to the company.'

We blush to tell it; but his youthful spirits and vivacity, getting, for a time, the better of his sad thoughts, he no sooner formed this resolution than he saluted Miss Squeers and the friend, with great gallantry, and drawing a chair to the tea-table, began to make himself more at home than in all probability an usher has ever done in his employer's house since ushers were first invented.

The ladies were in the full delight of this altered behaviour on the part of Mr. Nickleby, when the expected swain arrived, with his hair very damp from recent washing, and a clean shirt, whereof the collar might have belonged to some giant ancestor, forming, together with a white waistcoat of simlar dimensions the chief ornament of his person.

'Well, John,' said Miss Matilda Price (which, by the bye, was the name of the miller's daughter).

'Weel,' said John, with a grin that even the collar could not conceal.

'I beg your pardon,' interposed Miss Squeers, hastening to do the honours, 'Mr. Nickleby—Mr. John Browdie.'

'Servant, sir,' said John, who was something over six feet high, with a face and body rather above the due proportion than below it.

'Yours to command, sir,' replied Nicholas, making fearful ravages on the bread and butter.

Mr. Browdie was not a gentleman of great conversational powers, so he grinned twice more, and having now bestowed his customary mark of recognition on every person in company, grinned at nothing particular, and helped himself to food.

'Old wooman awa', bean't she?' said Mr. Browdie, with his mouth full.

Miss Squeers nodded assent.

Mr. Browdie gave a grin of special width, as if he thought that really was something to laugh at, and went to work at the bread and butter with increased vigour. It was quite a sight to behold how he and Nicholas emptied the plate between them.

'Ye wean't get bread and butther ev'ry neight, I expect, mun,' said Mr. Browdie, after he had sat staring at Nicholas a long time over the empty plate.

Nicholas bit his lip, and coloured, but affected not to hear the remark.

'Ecod,' said Mr. Browdie, laughing boisterously, 'they dean't put too much intiv'em. Ye'll be nowt but skeen and boans if you stop here long eneaf. Ho! ho! ho!'

'You are facetious, sir,' said Nicholas, scornfully.

'Na; I dean't know,' replied Mr. Browdie, 'but t'oother teacher, 'cod he wur a learn 'un, he wur.' The recollection of the last teacher's leanness seemed to afford Mr. Browdie the most exquisite delight, for he laughed until he found it necessary to apply his coat-cuffs to his eyes.

'I don't know whether your perceptions are quite keen enough, Mr. Browdie, to enable you to understand that your remarks are offensive,' said Nicholas in a towering passion, 'but if they are, have the goodness to—'

'If you say another word, John,' shrieked Miss Price, stopping her admirer's mouth as he was about to interrupt, 'only half a word, I'll never forgive you, or speak to you again.'

'Weel, my lass, I dean't care aboot 'un,' said the corn-factor, bestowing a hearty kiss on Miss Matilda; 'let 'un gang on, let 'un gang on.'

It now became Miss Squeers's turn to intercede with Nicholas, which she did with many symptoms of alarm and horror; the effect of the double intercession, was, that he and John Browdie shook hands across the table with much gravity; and such was the imposing nature of the ceremonial, that Miss Squeers was overcome and shed tears.

'What's the matter, Fanny?' said Miss Price.

'Nothing, 'Tilda,' replied Miss Squeers, sobbing.

'There never was any danger,' said Miss Price, 'was there, Mr. Nickleby?'

'None at all,' replied Nicholas. 'Absurd.'

'That's right,' whispered Miss Price, 'say something kind to her, and she'll soon come round. Here! Shall John and I go into the little kitchen, and come back presently?'

'Not on any account,' rejoined Nicholas, quite alarmed at the proposition. 'What on earth should you do that for?'

'Well,' said Miss Price, beckoning him aside, and speaking with some degree of contempt—'you *are* a one to keep company.'

'What do you mean?' said Nicholas; 'I am not a one to keep company at all—here at all events. I can't make this out.'

'No, nor I neither,' rejoined Miss Price; 'but men are always fickle, and always were, and always will be; that I can make out, very easily.'

'Fickle!' cried Nicholas; 'what do you suppose? You don't mean to say that you think—'

'Oh no, I think nothing at all,' retorted Miss Price, pettishly. 'Look at her, dressed so beautiful and looking so well—really *almost* handsome. I am ashamed at you.'

'My dear girl, what have I got to do with her dressing beautifully or looking well?' inquired Nicholas.

'Come, don't call me a dear girl,' said Miss Price— smiling a little though, for she was pretty, and a coquette too in her small way, and Nicholas was good-looking, and she supposed him the property of somebody else, which were all reasons why she should be gratified to think she had made an impression on him, —'or Fanny will be saying it's my fault. Come; we're going to have a game of cards.' Pronouncing these last words aloud, she tripped away and rejoined the big Yorkshireman.

This was wholly unintelligible to Nicholas, who had no other distinct impression on his mind at the moment, than that Miss Squeers was an ordinary-looking girl, and her friend Miss Price a pretty one; but he had not time to enlighten himself by reflection, for the hearth being by this time swept up, and the candle snuffed, they sat down to play speculation.

'There are only four of us, 'Tilda,' said Miss Squeers, looking slyly at Nicholas; 'so we had better go partners, two against two.'

'What do you say, Mr. Nickleby?' inquired Miss Price.

'With all the pleasure in life,' replied Nicholas. And so saying, quite unconscious of his heinous offence, he amalgamated into one common heap those portions of a Dotheboys Hall card of terms, which represented his own counters, and those allotted to Miss Price, respectively.

'Mr. Browdie,' said Miss Squeers hysterically, 'shall we make a bank against them?'

The Yorkshireman assented—apparently quite overwhelmed by the new usher's impudence—and Miss Squeers darted a spiteful look at her friend, and giggled convulsively.

The deal fell to Nicholas, and the hand prospered.

'We intend to win everything,' said he.

''Tilda *has* won something she didn't expect, I think, haven't you, dear?' said Miss Squeers, maliciously.

'Only a dozen and eight, love,' replied Miss Price, affecting to take the question in a literal sense.

'How dull you are to-night!' sneered Miss Squeers.

'No, indeed,' replied Miss Price, 'I am in excellent spirits. I was thinking *you* seemed out of sorts.'

'Me!' cried Miss Squeers, biting her lips, and trembling with very jealousy; 'Oh no!'

'That's well,' remarked Miss Price. 'Your hair's coming out of curl, dear.'

'Never mind me,' tittered Miss Squeers; 'you had better attend to your partner.'

'Thank you for reminding her,' said Nicholas. 'So she had.'

The Yorkshireman flattened his nose, once or twice, with his clenched fist, as if to keep his hand in, till he had an opportunity of exercising it upon the features of some other gentleman; and Miss Squeers tossed her head with such indignation, that the gust of wind raised by the multitudinous curls in motion, nearly blew the candle out.

'I never had such luck, really,' exclaimed coquettish Miss Price, after another hand or two. 'It's all along of you, Mr. Nickleby, I think. I should like to have you for a partner always.'

'I wish you had.'

'You 'll have a bad wife, though, if you always win at cards,' said Miss Price.

'Not if your wish is gratified,' replied Nicholas. 'I am sure I shall have a good one in that case.'

To see how Miss Squeers tossed her head, and the corn-factor flattened his nose, while this conversation was carrying on! It would have been worth a small annuity to have beheld that; let alone Miss Price's evident joy at making them jealous, and Nicholas Nickleby's happy unconsciousness of making anybody uncomfortable.

'We have all the talking to ourselves, it seems,' said Nicholas, looking good-humouredly round the table as he took up the cards for a fresh deal.

'You do it so well,' tittered Miss Squeers, 'that it would be a pity to interrupt, wouldn't it, Mr. Browdie? He! he! he!'

'Nay,' said Nicholas, 'we do it in default of having anybody else to talk to.'

'We 'll talk to you, you know, if you 'll say anything,' said Miss Price.

'Thank you, 'Tilda, dear,' retorted Miss Squeers, majestically.

'Or you can talk to each other, if you don't choose to talk to us,' said Miss Price, rallying her dear friend. 'John, why don't you say something?'

'Say summat?' repeated the Yorkshireman.

'Ay, and not sit there so silent and glum.'

'Weel, then!' said the Yorkshireman, striking the table heavily with his fist, 'what I say 's this—Dang my boans and boddy, if I stan' this ony longer. Do ye gang whoam wi' me, and do yon loight an' toight young whipster, look sharp out for a brokken head, next time he cums under my hond.'

'Mercy on us, what's all this?' cried Miss Price, in affected astonishment.

'Cum whoam, tell'e, cum whoam,' replied the Yorkshireman, sternly. And as he delivered the reply, Miss Squeers burst into a shower of tears; arising in part from desperate vexation, and in part from an impotent desire to lacerate somebody's countenance with her fair finger-nails.

This state of things had been brought about, by divers means and workings. Miss Squeers had brought it about, by aspiring to the high state and condition of being matrimonially engaged, without good grounds for so doing; Miss Price had brought it about, by indulging in three motives of action: first, a desire to punish her friend for laying claim to a rivalship in dignity, having no good title: secondly, the gratification of her own vanity, in receiving the compliments of a smart young man: and thirdly, a wish to convince the corn-factor of the great danger he ran, in deferring the celebration of their expected nuptials; while Nicholas had brought it about, by half an hour's gaiety and thoughtlessness, and a very sincere desire to avoid the imputation of inclining at all to Miss Squeers. So the means employed, and the end produced, were alike the most natural in the world; for young ladies will look forward to being married, and will jostle each other in the race to the altar, and will avail themselves of all opportunities of displaying their own attractions to the best advantage, down to the very end of time, as they have done from its beginning.

'Why, and here's Fanny in tears now!' exclaimed Miss Price, as if in fresh amazement. 'What can be the matter?'

'Oh! you don't know, miss, of course you don't

know. Pray don't trouble yourself to inquire,' said Miss Squeers, producing that change of countenance which children call, making a face.

'Well, I 'm sure!' exclaimed Miss Price.

'And who cares whether you are sure or not, ma'am?' retorted Miss Squeers, making another face.

'You are monstrous polite, ma'am,' said Miss Price.

'I shall not come to you to take lessons in the art, ma'am!' retorted Miss Squeers.

'You needn't take the trouble to make yourself plainer than you are, ma'am, however,' rejoined Miss Price, 'because that 's quite unnecessary.'

Miss Squeers, in reply, turned very red, and thanked God that she hadn't got the bold faces of some people. Miss Price, in rejoinder, congratulated herself upon not being possessed of the envious feeling of other people; whereupon Miss Squeers made some general remark touching the danger of associating with low persons; in which Miss Price entirely coincided: observing that it was very true indeed, and she had thought so a long time.

''Tilda,' exclaimed Miss Squeers with dignity, 'I hate you.'

'Ah! There 's no love lost between us, I assure you,' said Miss Price, tying her bonnet strings with a jerk. 'You 'll cry your eyes out, when I 'm gone; you know you will.'

'I scorn your words, minx,' said Miss Squeers.

'You pay me a great compliment when you say so,' answered the miller's daughter, curtseying very low. 'Wish you a very good night, ma'am, and pleasant dreams attend your sleep!'

With this parting benediction, Miss Price swept from the room, followed by the huge Yorkshireman, who exchanged with Nicholas, at parting, that peculiarly expressive scowl with which the cut-and-thrust counts, in melodramatic performances, inform each other they will meet again.

They were no sooner gone, than Miss Squeers fulfilled the prediction of her quondam friend by giving vent to a most copious burst of tears, and uttering various dismal lamentations and incoherent words. Nicholas stood looking on for a few seconds, rather doubtful what to do, but feeling uncertain whether the fit would end in his being embraced, or scratched, and considering that either infliction would be equally agreeable, he walked off very quietly while Miss Squeers was moaning in her pocket-handkerchief.

'This is one consequence,' thought Nicholas, when he had groped his way to the dark sleeping-room, 'of my cursed readiness to adapt myself to any society in which chance carries me. If I had sat mute and motionless, as I might have done, this would not have happened.'

He listened for a few minutes, but all was quiet.

'I was glad,' he murmured, 'to grasp at any relief from the sight of this dreadful place, or the presence of its vile master. I have set these people by the ears, and made two new enemies, where, Heaven knows, I needed none. Well, it is a just punishment for having forgotten, even for an hour, what is around me now!'

So saying, he felt his way among the throng of weary-hearted sleepers, and crept into his poor bed.

CHAPTER X

HOW MR. RALPH NICKLEBY PROVIDED FOR HIS NIECE
AND SISTER-IN-LAW

On the second morning after the departure of Nicholas for Yorkshire, Kate Nickleby sat in a very faded chair raised upon a very dusty throne in Miss La Creevy's room, giving that lady a sitting for the portrait upon which she was engaged; and towards the full perfection of which, Miss La Creevy had had the street-door case brought upstairs, in order that she might be the better able to infuse into the counterfeit countenance of Miss Nickleby, a bright salmon flesh-tint which she had originally hit upon while executing the miniature of a young officer therein contained, and which bright salmon flesh-tint was considered by Miss La Creevy's chief friends and patrons, to be quite a novelty in art: as indeed it was.

'I think I have caught it now,' said Miss La Creevy. 'The very shade! This will be the sweetest portrait I have ever done, certainly.'

'It will be your genius that makes it so, then, I am sure,' replied Kate, smiling.

'No, no, I won't allow that, my dear,' rejoined Miss La Creevy. 'It's a very nice subject—a very nice subject, indeed—though of course, something depends upon the mode of treatment.'

'And not a little,' observed Kate.

'Why, my dear, you are right there,' said Miss La Creevy, 'in the main you are right there; though I don't allow that it is of such very great importance in the present case. Ah! The difficulties of Art, my dear, are great.'

'They must be, I have no doubt,' said Kate, humouring her good-natured little friend.

'They are beyond anything you can form the faintest conception of,' replied Miss La Creevy. 'What with bringing out eyes with all one's power, and keeping down noses with all one's force, and adding to heads, and taking away teeth altogether, you have no idea of the trouble one little miniature is.'

'The remuneration can scarcely repay you,' said Kate.

'Why, it does not, and that's the trurth,' answered Miss La Creevy; 'and then people are so dissatisfied and unreasonable, that, nine times out of ten, there's no pleasure in painting them. Sometimes they say, "Oh, how very serious you have made me look, Miss La Creevy!" and at others, "La, Miss La Creevy, how very smirking!" when the very essence of a good portrait is, that it must be either serious or smirking, or it's no portrait at all.'

'Indeed!' said Kate, laughing.

'Certainly, my dear; because the sitters are always either the one or the other,' replied Miss La Creevy. 'Look at the Royal Academy! All those beautiful shiny portraits of gentlemen in black velvet waistcoats, with their fists doubled up on round tables, or marble slabs, are serious, you know; and all the ladies who are playing with little parasols, or little dogs, or little children—it's the same rule in art, only varying the objects—are smirking. In fact,' said Miss La Creevy, sinking her voice to a confidential whisper, 'there are only two styles of portrait painting; the serious and the smirk; and we always use the serious for professional people (except actors sometimes), and the smirk for private ladies and gentlemen who don't care so much about looking clever.'

Kate seemed highly amused by this information, and Miss La Creevy went on painting and talking, with immovable complacency.

'What a number of officers you seem to paint!' said Kate, availing herself of a pause in the discourse, and glancing round the room.

'Number of what, child?' inquired Miss La Creevy, looking up from her work. 'Character portraits, oh yes—they 're not real military men, you know.'

'No!'

'Bless your heart, of course not; only clerks and that, who hire a uniform coat to be painted in and send it here in a carpet bag. Some artists,' said Miss La Creevy, 'keep a red coat, and charge seven-and-sixpence extra for hire and carmine; but I don't do that myself, for I don't consider it legitimate.'

Drawing herself up, as though she plumed herself greatly upon not resorting to these lures to catch sitters, Miss La Creevy applied herself, more intently, to her task: only raising her head occasionally, to look with unspeakable satisfaction at some touch she had just put in: and now and then giving Miss Nickleby to understand what particular feature she was at work upon, at the moment; 'not,' she expressly observed, 'that you should make it up for painting, my dear, but because it 's our custom some-times, to tell sitters what part we are upon, in order that if there 's any particular expression they want introduced, they may throw it in, at the time, you know.'

'And when,' said Miss La Creevy, after a long silence, to wit, an interval of full a minute and a half, 'when do you expect to see your uncle again?'

'I scarcely know; I had expected to have seen him before now,' replied Kate. 'Soon, I hope, for this state of uncertainty is worse than anything.'

'I suppose he has money, hasn't he?' inquired Miss La Creevy.

'He is very rich, I have heard,' rejoined Kate. 'I don't know that he is, but I believe so.'

'Ah, you may depend upon it he is, or he wouldn't be so surly,' remarked Miss La Creevy, who was an odd little mixture of shrewdness and simplicity. 'When a man's a bear, he is generally pretty independent.'

'His manner is rough,' said Kate.

'Rough!' cried Miss La Creevy, 'a porcupine's a featherbed to him! I never met with such a cross-grained old savage.'

'It is only his manner, I believe,' observed Kate, timidly: 'he was disappointed in early life, I think I have heard, or has had his temper soured by some calamity. I should be sorry to think ill of him until I knew he deserved it.'

'Well; that's very right and proper,' observed the miniature-painter, 'and Heaven forbid that I should be the cause of your doing so! But, now, mightn't he, without feeling it himself, make you and your mamma some nice little allowance that would keep you both comfortable until you were well married, and be a little fortune to her afterwards? What would a hundred a year, for instance, be to him?'

'I don't know what it would be to him,' said Kate, with energy, 'but it would be that to me I would rather die than take.'

'Heyday!' cried Miss La Creevy.

'A dependence upon him,' said Kate, 'would embitter my whole life. I should feel begging a far less degradation.'

'Well!' exclaimed Miss La Creevy. 'This of a relation whom you will not hear an indifferent person

speak ill of, my dear, sounds oddly enough, I confess.'

'I dare say it does,' replied Kate, speaking more
gently, 'indeed, I am sure it must. I—I—only mean
that with the feelings and recollection of better times
upon me, I could not bear to live on anybody's bounty
—not his particularly, but anybody's.'

Miss La Creevy looked slyly at her companion, as
if she doubted whether Ralph himself were not the
subject of dislike, but seeing that her young friend
was distressed, made no remark.

'I only ask of him,' continued Kate, whose tears
fell while she spoke, 'that he will move so little out
of his way, in my behalf, as to enable me by his recommendation—only by his recommendation—to
earn, literally my bread and remain with my mother.
Whether we shall ever taste happiness again, depends
upon the fortunes of my dear brother; but if he will
do this, and Nicholas only tells us that he is well and
cheerful, I shall be contented.'

As she ceased to speak, there was a rustling behind
the screen which stood between her and the door,
and some person knocked at the wainscot.

'Come in, whoever it is!' cried Miss La Creevy.

The person complied, and, coming forward at once,
gave to view the form and features of no less an individual than Mr. Ralph Nickleby himself.

'Your servant, ladies,' said Ralph, looking sharply
at them by turns. 'You were talking so loud, that
I was unable to make you hear.'

When the man of business had a more than commonly vicious snarl lurking at his heart, he had a trick
of almost concealing his eyes under their thick and
protruding brows, for an instant, and then displaying them in their full keenness. As he did so now,

and tried to keep down the smile which parted his thin compressed lips, and puckered up the bad lines about his mouth, they both felt certain that some part, if not the whole, of their recent conversation, had been overheard.

'I called in, on my way upstairs, more than half expecting to find you here,' said Ralph, addressing his niece, and looking contemptuously at the portrait. 'Is that my niece's portrait, ma'am?'

'Yes it is, Mr. Nickleby,' said Miss La Creevy, with a very sprightly air, 'and between you and me and the post, sir, it will be a very nice portrait too, though I say it who am the painter.'

'Don't trouble yourself to show it to me, ma'am,' cried Ralph, moving away, 'I have no eye for likenesses. Is it nearly finished?'

'Why, yes,' replied Miss La Creevy, considering with the pencil end of her brush in her mouth. 'Two sittings more will—'

'Have them at once, ma'am,' said Ralph. 'She 'll have no time to idle over fooleries after to-morrow. Work, ma'am, work; we must all work. Have you let your lodgings, ma'am?'

'I have not put a bill up yet, sir.'

'Put it up at once, ma'am; they won't want the rooms after this week, or if they do, can't pay for them. Now, my dear, if you 're ready, we 'll lose no more time.'

With an assumption of kindness which sat worse upon him, even than his usual manner, Mr. Ralph Nickleby motioned to the young lady to precede him, and bowing gravely to Miss La Creevy, closed the door and followed upstairs, where Mrs. Nickleby received him with many expressions of regard. Stopping them somewhat abruptly, Ralph waved his hand with an impatient gesture, and proceeded to the object of his visit.

'I have found a situation for your daughter, ma'am,' said Ralph.

'Well,' replied Mrs. Nickleby. 'Now, I will say that that is only just what I have expected of you. "Depend upon it," I said to Kate, only yesterday morning at breakfast, "that after your uncle has provided, in that most ready manner, for Nicholas, he will not leave us until he has done at least the same for you." These were my very words, as near as I remember. Kate, my dear, why don't you thank your—'

'Let me proceed, ma'am, pray,' said Ralph, interrupting his sister-in-law in the full torrent of her discourse.

'Kate, my love, let your uncle proceed,' said Mrs. Nickleby.

'I am most anxious that he should, mamma,' rejoined Kate.

'Well, my dear, if you are anxious that he should, you had better allow your uncle to say what he has to say, without interruption,' observed Mrs. Nickleby, with many small nods and frowns. 'Your uncle's time is very valuable, my dear; and however desirous you may be—and naturally desirous, as I am sure any affectionate relations who have seen so little of your uncle as we have, must naturally be—to protract the pleasure of having him among us, still we are bound not to be selfish, but to take into consideration the important nature of his occupations in the City.'

'I am very much obliged to you, ma'am,' said Ralph with a scarcely perceptible sneer. 'An absence of business habits in this family leads, apparently, to a great waste of words before business—when it does come under consideration—is arrived at, at all.'

'I fear it is so indeed,' replied Mrs. Nickleby with a sigh. 'Your poor brother—'

'My poor brother, ma'am,' interposed Ralph tartly, 'had no idea what business was—was unacquainted, I verily believe, with the very meaning of the word.'

'I fear he was,' said Mrs. Nickleby, with her handkerchief to her eyes. 'If it hadn't been for me, I don't know what would have become of him.'

What strange creatures we are! The slight bait so skilfully thrown out by Ralph, on their first interview, was dangling on the hook yet. At every small deprivation or discomfort which presented itself in the course of the four-and-twenty hours to remind her of her straitened and altered circumstances, peevish visions of her dower of one thousand pounds had arisen before Mrs. Nickleby's mind, until, at last, she had come to persuade herself that of all her late husband's creditors she was the worst used and the most to be pitied. And yet, she had loved him dearly for many years, and had no greater share of selfishness than is the usual lot of mortals. Such is the irritability of sudden poverty. A decent annuity would have restored her thoughts to their old train, at once.

'Repining is of no use, ma'am,' said Ralph. 'Of all fruitless errands, sending a tear to look after a day that is gone, is the most fruitless.'

'So it is,' sobbed Mrs. Nickleby. 'So it is.'

'As you feel so keenly, in your own purse and person, the consequences of inattention to business, ma'am,' said Ralph, 'I am sure you will impress upon your children the necessity of attaching themselves to it, early in life.'

'Of course I must see that,' rejoined Mrs. Nickleby. 'Sad experience, you know, brother-in-law— Kate, my dear, put that down in the next letter to Nicholas, or remind me to do it if I write.'

Ralph paused, for a few moments, and seeing that he had now made pretty sure of the mother, in case the daughter objected to his proposition, went on to say—

'The situation that I have made interest to procure, ma'am, is with—with a milliner and dressmaker, in short.'

'A milliner!' cried Mrs. Nickleby.

'A milliner and dressmaker, ma'am,' replied Ralph. 'Dressmakers in London, as I need not remind you, ma'am, who are so well acquainted with all matters in the ordinary routine of life, make large fortunes, keep equipages, and become persons of great wealth and fortune.'

Now, the first ideas called up in Mrs. Nickleby's mind by the words milliner and dressmaker were connected with certain wicker baskets lined with black oilskin, which she remembered to have seen carried to and fro in the streets; but, as Ralph proceeded, these disappeared, and were replaced by visions of large houses at the West End, neat private carriages, and a banker's book; all of which images succeeded each other, with such rapidity, that he had no sooner finished speaking, then she nodded her head and said, 'Very true,' with great appearance of satisfaction.

'What your uncle says, is very true, Kate, my dear,' said Mrs. Nickleby. 'I recollect when your poor papa and I came to town after we were married, that a young lady brought me home a chip cottage-bonnet, with white and green trimming, and green persian lining, in her own carriage, which drove up to the door full gallop;—at least, I am not quite certain whether it was her own carriage or a hackney chariot, but I remember very well that the horse dropped down dead as he was turning round, and that your poor papa said he hadn't had any corn for a fortnight.'

This anecdote, so strikingly illustrative of the opulence of milliners, was not received with any great demonstration of feeling, inasmuch as Kate hung down her head while it was relating, and Ralph manifested very intelligible symptoms of extreme impatience.

'The lady's name,' said Ralph, hastily striking in, 'is Mantalini—Madame Mantalini. I know her. She lives near Cavendish Square. If your daughter is disposed to try after the situation, I'll take her there, directly.'

'Have you nothing to say to your uncle, my love?' inquired Mrs. Nickleby.

'A great deal,' replied Kate; 'but not now. I would rather speak to him when we are alone;—it will save his time if I thank him and say what I wish to say to him, as we walk along.'

With these words, Kate hurried away, to hide the traces of emotion that were stealing down her face, and to prepare herself for the walk, while Mrs. Nickleby amused her brother-in-law by giving him, with many tears, a detailed account of the dimensions of a rosewood cabinet piano they had possessed in their early days of affluence, together with a minute description of eight drawing-room chairs, with turned legs and green chintz squabs to match the curtains, which had cost two pounds fifteen shillings a-piece and had gone at the sale for a mere nothing.

These reminiscences were at length cut short by Kate's return in her walking dress, when Ralph, who had been fretting and fuming during the whole time of her absence, lost no time, and used very little ceremony, in descending into the street.

'Now,' he said, taking her arm, 'walk as fast as you

can, and you 'll get into the step that you 'll have to walk to business with, every morning.'   So saying, he led Kate off, at a good round pace, towards Cavendish Square.

'I am very much obliged to you, uncle,' said the young lady, after they had hurried on in silence for some time; 'very.'

'I am glad to hear it,' said Ralph.   'I hope you 'll do your duty.'

'I will try to please, uncle,' replied Kate; 'indeed I—'

'Don't begin to cry,' growled Ralph; 'I hate crying.'

'It is very foolish, I know, uncle,' began poor Kate.

'It is,' replied Ralph, stopping her short, 'and very affected besides.   Let me see no more of it.'

Perhaps this was not the best way to dry the tears of a young and sensitive female, about to make the first entry on an entirely new scene of life, among cold and uninterested strangers; but it had its effect notwithstanding.   Kate coloured deeply, breathed quickly for a few moments, and then walked on with a firmer and more determined step.

It was a curious contrast to see how the timid country girl shrunk through the crowd that hurried up and down the streets, giving way to the press of people, and clinging closely to Ralph as though she feared to lose him in the throng; and how the stern and hard-featured man of business went doggedly on, elbowing the passengers aside, and now and then exchanging a gruff salutation with some passing acquaintance, who turned to look back upon his pretty charge, with looks expressive of surprise, and seemed to wonder at the ill-assorted companionship.   But, it would have been a stranger contrast still, to have read the hearts that were beating side by side; to have laid bare the gentle innocence of the one, and the rugged villainy of the other; to have hung upon the guileless thoughts of the affectionate girl, and been amazed that, among all the wily plots and calculations of the old man, there should not be one word or figure denoting thought of death or of the grave. But so it was; and stranger still—though this is a thing of every day—the warm young heart palpitated with a thousand anxieties and apprehensions, while that of the old worldly man lay rusting in its cell, beating only as a piece of cunning mechanism, and yielding no one throb of hope, or fear, or love, or care, for any living thing.

'Uncle,' said Kate, when she judged they must be near their destination, 'I must ask one question of you. I am to live at home?'

'At home!' replied Ralph; 'where's that?'

'I mean with my mother—*the widow*,' said Kate emphatically.

'You will live, to all intents and purposes, here,' rejoined Ralph; 'for here you will take your meals, and here you will be from morning till night—occasionally perhaps till morning again.'

'But at night, I mean,' said Kate; 'I cannot leave her, uncle. I must have some place that I can call a home; it will be wherever she is, you know, and may be a very humble one.'

'May be!' said Ralph, walking faster, in the impatience provoked by the remark, 'must be, you mean. May be a humble one! Is the girl mad?'

'The word slipped from my lips, I did not mean it indeed,' urged Kate.

'I hope not,' said Ralph.

'But my question, uncle; you have not answered it.'

'Why, I anticipated something of the kind,' said Ralph; 'and—though I object very strongly, mind—have provided against it.   I spoke of you as an out-of-door worker; so you will go to this home that may be humble, every night.'

There was comfort in this.   Kate poured forth many thanks for her uncle's consideration, which Ralph received as if he had deserved them all, and they arrived without any further conversation at the dressmaker's door, which displayed a very large plate, with Madame Mantalini's name and occupation, and was approached by a handsome flight of steps. There was a shop to the house, but it was let off to an importer of otto of roses.   Madame Mantalini's show-rooms were on the first floor: a fact which was notified to the nobility and gentry, by the casual exhibition, near the handsomely curtained windows, of two or three elegant bonnets of the newest fashion, and some costly garments in the most approved taste.

A liveried footman opened the door, and in reply to Ralph's inquiry whether Madame Mantalini was at home, ushered them, through a handsome hall and up a spacious staircase, into the show saloon, which comprised two spacious drawing-rooms, and exhibited an immense variety of superb dresses and materials for dresses: some arranged on stands, others laid carelessly on sofas, and others again, scattered over the carpet, hanging on the cheval glasses, or mingling, in some other way, with the rich furniture of various descriptions, which was profusely displayed.

They waited here, a much longer time than was agreeable to Mr. Ralph Nickleby, who eyed the gaudy frippery about with very little concern, and was at length about to pull the bell, when a gentleman suddenly popped his head into the room, and, seeing somebody there, as suddenly popped it out again.

'Here. Hollo!' cried Ralph. 'Who's that?'

At the sound of Ralph's voice, the head reappeared, and the mouth, displayed a very long row of very white teeth, uttered in a mincing tone the words, 'Demmit. What, Nickleby! oh, demmit!' Having uttered which ejaculations, the gentleman advanced, and shook hands with Ralph, with great warmth. He was dressed in a gorgeous morning gown, with a waistcoat and Turkish trousers of the same pattern, a pink silk neckerchief, and bright green slippers, and had a very copious watch-chain wound round his body. Moreover, he had whiskers and a mustache, both dyed black and gracefully curled.

'Demmit, you don't mean to say you want me, do you, demmit?' said this gentleman, smiting Ralph on the shoulder.

'Not yet,' said Ralph, sarcastically.

'Ha! ha! demmit,' cried the gentleman; when, wheeling round to laugh with greater elegance, he encountered Kate Nickleby, who was standing near.

'My niece,' said Ralph.

'I remember,' said the gentleman, striking his nose with the knuckle of his fore finger as a chastening for his forgetfulness. 'Demmit, I remember what you come for. Step this way, Nickleby; my dear, will you follow me? Ha! ha! They all follow me, Nickleby; always did, demmit, always.'

Giving loose to the playfulness of his imagination, after this fashion, the gentleman led the way to a private sitting-room on the second floor, scarcely less elegantly furnished than the apartment below, where the presence of a silver coffee-pot, an egg-shell, and sloppy china for one, seemed to show that he had just breakfasted.

'Sit down, my dear,' said the gentleman: first staring Miss Nickleby out of countenance, and then grinning in delight at the achievement. 'This cursed high room takes one's breath away. These infernal sky parlours—I 'm afraid I must move, Nickleby.'

'I would, by all means,' replied Ralph, looking bitterly round.

'What a demd rum fellow you are, Nickleby,' said the gentleman, 'the demdest, longest-headed, queerest-tempered old coiner of gold and silver ever was—demmit.'

Having complimented Ralph to this effect, the gentleman rang the bell, and stared at Miss Nickleby until it was answered, when he left off to bid the man desire his mistress to come directly; after which, he began again, and left off no more until Madame Mantalini appeared.

The dressmaker was a buxom person, handsomely dressed and rather good-looking, but much older than the gentleman in the Turkish trousers, whom she had wedded some six months before. His name was originally Muntle; but it had been converted, by an easy transition, into Mantalini: the lady rightly considering that an English appellation would be of serious injury to the business. He had married on his whiskers; upon which property he had previously subsisted, in a genteel manner, for some years; and which he had recently improved, after patient cultivation, by the addition of a moustache, which promised to secure him an easy independence: his share in the labours of the business being at present confined to spending the money, and occasionally, when that ran short, driving to Mr. Ralph Nickleby to procure discount—at a percentage—for the customers' bills.

'My life,' said Mr. Mantalini, 'what a demd devil of a time you have been!'

'I didn't even know Mr. Nickleby was here, my love,' said Madame Mantalini.

'Then what a doubly demd infernal rascal that footman must be, my soul,' remonstrated Mr. Mantalini.

'My dear,' said Madame, 'that is entirely your fault.'

'My fault, my heart's joy?'

'Certainly,' returned the lady; 'what can you expect, dearest, if you will not correct the man?'

'Correct the man, my soul's delight!'

'Yes; I am sure he wants speaking to, badly enough,' said Madame, pouting.

'Then do not vex itself,' said Mr. Mantalini; 'he shall be horse-whipped till he cries out demnebly.' With this promise Mr. Mantalini kissed Madame Mantalini, and, after that performance, Madame Mantalini pulled Mr. Mantalini playfully by the ear: which done, they descended to business.

'Now, ma'am,' said Ralph, who had looked on, at all this, with such scorn as few men can express in looks, 'this is my niece.'

'Just so, Mr. Nickleby,' replied Madame Mantalini, surveying Kate from head to foot, and back again. 'Can you speak French, child?'

'Yes, ma'am,' replied Kate, not daring to look up; for she felt that the eyes of the odious man in the dressing-gown were directed towards her.

'Like a demd native?' asked the husband.

Miss Nickleby offered no reply to this inquiry, but turned her back upon the questioner, as if addressing herself to make answer to what his wife might demand.

'We keep twenty young women constantly employed in the establishment,' said Madame.

'Indeed, ma'am!' replied Kate, timidly.

'Yes; and some of 'em demd handsome, too,' said the master.

'Mantalini!' exclaimed his wife, in an awful voice.

'My senses' idol!' said Mantalini.

'Do you wish to break my heart?'

'Not for twenty thousand hemispheres populated with—with—with little ballet-dancers,' replied Mantalini in a poetical strain.

'Then you will, if you persevere in that mode of speaking,' said his wife. 'What can Mr. Nickleby think when he hears you?'

'Oh! Nothing, ma'am, nothing,' replied Ralph. 'I know his amiable nature, and yours,—mere little remarks that give a zest to your daily intercourse—lovers' quarrels that add sweetness to those domestic joys which promise to last so long—that's all; that's all.'

If an iron door could be supposed to quarrel with its hinges, and to make a firm resolution to open with slow obstinacy, and grind them to powder in the process, it would emit a pleasanter sound in so doing, than did these words in the rough and bitter voice in which they were uttered by Ralph. Even Mr. Mantalini felt their influence, and turning affrighted round, exclaimed: 'What a demd horrid croaking!'

'You will pay no attention, if you please, to what Mr. Mantalini says,' observed his wife, addressing Miss Nickleby.

'I do not, ma'am,' said Kate, with quiet contempt.

'Mr. Mantalini knows nothing whatever about any of the young women,' continued Madame, looking at her husband, and speaking to Kate. 'If he has seen any of them, he must have seen them in the street, going to, or returning from, their work, and not here. He was never even in the room. I do not allow it. What hours of work have you been accustomed to?'

'I have never yet been accustomed to work at all, ma'am,' replied Kate, in a low voice.

'For which reason she'll work all the better now,' said Ralph, putting in a word, lest this confession should injure the negotiation.

'I hope so,' returned Madame Mantalini; 'our hours are from nine to nine, with extra work when we're very full of business, for which I allow payment as over-time.'

Kate bowed her head, to intimate that she heard, and was satisfied.

'Your meals,' continued Madame Mantalini, 'that is, dinner and tea, you will take here. I should think your wages would average from five to seven shillings a week; but I can't give you any certain information on that point, until I see what you can do.'

Kate bowed her head again.

'If you're ready to come,' said Madame Mantalini, 'you had better begin on Monday morning at nine exactly, and Miss Knag the forewoman shall then have directions to try you with some easy work at first. Is there anything more, Mr. Nickleby?'

'Nothing more, ma'am,' replied Ralph, rising.

'Then I believe that's all,' said the lady. Having arrived at this natural conclusion, she looked at the door, as if she wished to be gone, but hesitated notwithstanding, as though unwilling to leave to Mr. Mantalini the sole honour of showing them downstairs. Ralph relieved her from her perplexity by taking his departure without delay: Madame Mantalini making many gracious inquiries why he never came to see them; and Mr. Mantalini anathematising the stairs with great volubility as he followed them down, in the hope of inducing Kate to look round,— a hope, however, which was destined to remain ungratified.

'There!' said Ralph when they got into the street; 'now you're provided for.'

Kate was about to thank him again, but he stopped her.

'I had some idea,' he said, 'of providing for your mother in a pleasant part of the country—(he had a presentation to some almshouses on the borders of Cornwall, which had occurred to him more than once) —but as you want to be together, I must do something else for her. She has a little money?'

'A very little,' replied Kate.

'A little will go a long way if it's used sparingly,' said Ralph. 'She must see how long she can make it last, living rent free. You leave your lodgings on Saturday?'

'You told us to do so, uncle.'

'Yes; there is a house empty that belongs to me, which I can put you into, till it is let, and then, if nothing else turns up, perhaps I shall have another. You must live there.'

'Is it far from here, sir?' inquired Kate.

'Pretty well,' said Ralph: 'in another quarter of the town—at the East End; but I'll send my clerk down to you, at five o'clock on Saturday, to take you there. Good-bye. You know your way? Straight on.'

Coldly shaking his niece's hand, Ralph left her at the top of Regent Street, and turned down a bye thoroughfare, intent on schemes of money-getting. Kate walked sadly back, to their lodgings in the Strand.

CHAPTER XI

NEWMAN NOGGS INDUCTS MRS. AND MISS NICKLEBY
INTO THEIR NEW DWELLING IN THE CITY

Miss NICKLEBY's reflections, as she wended her way homewards, were of that desponding nature which the occurrences of the morning had been sufficiently calculated to awaken. Her uncle's was not a manner likely to dispel any doubts or apprehensions she might have formed, in the outset, neither was the glimpse she had had of Madame Mantalini's establishment, by any means encouraging. It was with many gloomy forebodings and misgivings, therefore, that she looked forward, with a heavy heart, to the opening of her new career.

If her mother's consolations could have restored her to a pleasanter and more enviable state of mind, there were abundance of them to produce the effect. By the time Kate reached home, the good lady had called to mind two authentic cases of milliners who had been possessed of considerable property, though whether they had acquired it all in business, or had had a capital to start with, or had been lucky and married to advantage, she could not exactly remember. However, as she very logically remarked, there must have been *some* young person in that way of business who had made a fortune without having anything to begin with, and that being taken for granted, why should not Kate do the same? Miss La Creevy, who was a member of the little council, ventured to insinuate some doubts relative to the probability of Miss Nickleby's arriving at this happy consummation in the compass of an ordinary lifetime; but the good lady set that question entirely at rest, by in-

forming them that she had a presentiment on the subject—a species of second-sight with which she had
been in the habit of clenching every argument with
the deceased Mr. Nickleby, and, in nine cases and
three-quarters out of every ten, determining it the
wrong way.

'I am afraid it is an unhealthy occupation,' said
Miss La Creevy. 'I recollect getting three young
milliners to sit to me, when I first began to paint,
and I remember that they were all very pale and
sickly.'

'Oh! that's not a general rule by any means,' observed Mrs. Nickleby; 'for I remember, as well as if
it was only yesterday, employing one that I was particularly recommended to, to make me a scarlet cloak
at the time when scarlet cloaks were fashionable, and
she had a very red face—a very red face, indeed.'

'Perhaps she drank,' suggested Miss La Creevy.

'I don't know how that may have been,' returned
Mrs. Nickleby: 'but I know she had a very red face,
so your argument goes for nothing.'

In this manner, and with like powerful reasoning, did the worthy matron meet every little objection that presented itself to the new scheme of the
morning. Happy Mrs. Nickleby! A project had
but to be new, and it came home to her mind, brightly varnished and gilded as a glittering toy.

This question disposed of, Kate communicated her
uncle's desire about the empty house, to which Mrs.
Nickleby assented with equal readiness, characteristi-
cally remarking, that, on the fine evenings, it would
be a pleasant amusement for her to walk to the West
End to fetch her daughter home; and no less char-
acteristically forgetting, that there were such things
as wet nights and bad weather to be encountered in
almost every week of the year.

'I shall be sorry—truly sorry to leave you, my kind friend,' said Kate, on whom the good feeling of the poor miniature-painter had made a deep impression.

'You shall not shake me off, for all that,' replied Miss La Creevy, with as much sprightliness as she could assume. 'I shall see you very often, and come and hear how you get on; and if, in all London, or all the wide world besides, there is no other heart that takes an interest in your welfare, there will be one little lonely woman that prays for it night and day.'

With this, the poor soul, who had a heart big enough for Gog, the guardian genius of London, and enough to spare for Magog to boot, after making a great many extraordinary faces which would have secured her an ample fortune, could she have transferred them to ivory or canvass, sat down in a corner, and had what she termed 'a real good cry.'

But no crying, or talking, or hoping, or fearing, could keep off the dreaded Saturday afternoon, or Newman Noggs either; who, punctual to his time, limped up to the door, and breathed a whiff of cordial gin through the keyhole, exactly as such of the church clocks in the neighbourhood as agreed among themselves about the time, struck five. Newman waited for the last stroke, and then knocked.

'From Mr. Ralph Nickleby,' said Newman, announcing his errand, when he got upstairs, with all possible brevity.

'We shall be ready directly,' said Kate. 'We have not much to carry, but I fear we must have a coach.'

'I 'll get one,' replied Newman.

'Indeed you shall not trouble yourself,' said Mrs. Nickleby.

'I will,' said Newman.

'I can't suffer you to think of such a thing,' said Mrs. Nickleby.

'You can't help it,' said Newman.

'Not help it!'

'No; I thought of it as I came along; but didn't get one, thinking you mightn't be ready. I think of a great many things. Nobody can prevent that.'

'Oh yes, I understand you, Mr. Noggs,' said Mrs. Nickleby. 'Our thoughts are free, of course. Everybody's thoughts are their own, clearly.'

'They wouldn't be, if some people had their way,' muttered Newman.

'Well, no more they would, Mr. Noggs, and that's very true,' rejoined Mrs. Nickleby. 'Some people to be sure are such—how's your master?'

Newman darted a meaning glance at Kate, and replied with a strong emphasis on the last word of his answer, that Mr. Ralph Nickleby was well, and sent his *love*.

'I am sure we are very much obliged to him,' observed Mrs. Nickleby.

'Very,' said Newman. 'I'll tell him so.'

It was no very easy matter to mistake Newman Noggs, after having once seen him, and as Kate, attracted by the singularity of his manner (in which on this occasion, however, there was something respectful and even delicate, notwithstanding the abruptness of his speech), looked at him more closely, she recollected having caught a passing glimpse of that strange figure before.

'Excuse my curiosity,' she said, 'but did I not see you in the coachyard, on the morning my brother went away to Yorkshire?'

Newman cast a wistful glance on Mrs. Nickleby, and said 'No,' most unblushingly.

'No!' exclaimed Kate, 'I should have said so anywhere.'

'You'd have said wrong,' rejoined Newman. 'It's

the first time I 've been out for three weeks. I 've had the gout.'

Newman was very, very far from having the appearance of a gouty subject, and so Kate could not help thinking; but the conference was cut short by Mrs. Nickleby's insisting on having the door shut, lest Mr. Noggs should take cold, and further persisting in sending the servant girl for a coach, for fear he should bring on another attack of his disorder. To both conditions, Newman was compelled to yield. Presently, the coach came; and, after many sorrowful farewells, and a great deal of running backwards and forwards across the pavement on the part of Miss La Creevy, in the course of which the yellow turban came into violent contact with sundry foot-passengers, it (that is to say the coach, not the turban) went away again, with the two ladies and their luggage inside; and Newman, despite all Mrs. Nickleby's assurances that it would be his death—on the box beside the driver.

They went into the City, turning down by the river side; and, after a long and very slow drive, the streets being crowded at that hour with vehicles of every kind, stopped in front of a large old dingy house in Thames Street: the door and windows of which were so bespattered with mud, that it would have appeared to have been uninhabited for years.

The door of this deserted mansion Newman opened with a key which he took out of his hat—in which, by the bye, in consequence of the dilapidated state of his pockets, he deposited everything, and would most likely have carried his money if he had had any —and the coach being discharged, he led the way into the interior of the mansion.

Old, and gloomy, and black, in truth it was, and

sullen and dark were the rooms, once so bustling with life and enterprise. There was a wharf behind, opening on the Thames. An empty dog-kennel, some bones of animals, fragments of iron hoops, and staves of old casks, lay strewn about, but no life was stirring there. It was a picture of cold, silent decay.

'This house depresses and chills one,' said Kate, 'and seems as if some blight had fallen on it. If I were superstitious, I should be almost inclined to believe that some dreadful crime had been perpetrated within these old walls, and that the place had never prospered since. How frowning and how dark it looks!'

'Lord, my dear,' replied Mrs. Nickleby, 'don't talk in that way, or you'll frighten me to death.'

'It is only my foolish fancy, mamma,' said Kate, forcing a smile.

'Well, then, my love, I wish you would keep your foolish fancy to yourself, and not wake up *my* foolish fancy to keep it company,' retorted Mrs. Nickleby. 'Why didn't you think of all this before—you are so careless—we might have asked Miss Le Creevy to keep us company, or borrowed a dog, or a thousand things—but it always was the way, and was just the same with your poor dear father. Unless I thought of everything—' This was Mrs. Nickleby's usual commencement of a general lamentation, running through a dozen or so of complicated sentences addressed to nobody in particular, and into which she now launched until her breath was exhausted.

Newman appeared not to hear these remarks, but preceded them to a couple of rooms on the first floor, which some kind of attempt had been made to render habitable. In one, were a few chairs, a table, an old hearth-rug, and some faded baize; and a fire was ready laid in the grate. In the other, stood an old tent bedstead, and a few scanty articles of chamber furniture.

'Well, my dear,' said Mrs. Nickleby, trying to be pleased, 'now isn't this thoughtful and considerate of your uncle? Why, we should not have had anything but the bed we bought yesterday, to lie down upon, if it hadn't been for his thoughtfulness!'

'Very kind, indeed,' replied Kate, looking round.

Newman Noggs did not say that he had hunted up the old furniture they saw, from attic and cellar; or that he had taken in the halfpennyworth of milk for tea that stood upon a shelf, or filled the rusty kettle on the hob, or collected the wood-chips from the wharf, or begged the coals. But the notion of Ralph Nickleby having directed it to be done, tickled his fancy so much, that he could not refrain from cracking all his ten fingers in succession: at which performance Mrs. Nickleby was rather startled at first, but supposing it to be in some remote manner connected with the gout, did not remark upon.

'We need retain you no longer, I think,' said Kate.

'Is there nothing I can do?' asked Newman.

'Nothing, thank you,' rejoined Miss Nickleby.

'Perhaps, my dear, Mr. Noggs would like to drink our healths,' said Mrs. Nickleby, fumbling in her reticule for some small coin.

'I think, mamma,' said Kate, hesitating, and remarking Newman's averted face, 'you would hurt his feelings if you offered it.'

Newman Noggs, bowing to the young lady more like a gentleman than the miserable wretch he seemed, placed his hand upon his breast, and, pausing for a moment, with the air of a man who struggles to speak but is uncertain what to say, quitted the room.

As the jarring echoes of the heavy house-door, clos-

NEWMAN NOGGS LEAVES THE LADIES IN THE EMPTY HOUSE.

ing on its latch, reverberated dismally through the building, Kate felt half tempted to call him back, and beg him to remain a little while; but she was ashamed to own her fears. and Newman Noggs was on his road homewards.

CHAPTER XII

WHEREBY THE READER WILL BE ENABLED TO TRACE THE FURTHER COURSE OF MISS FANNY SQUEERS'S LOVE, AND TO ASCERTAIN WHETHER IT RAN SMOOTH OR OTHERWISE

IT was a fortunate circumstance for Miss Fanny Squeers that when her worthy papa returned home on the night of the small tea-party, he was what the initiated term 'too far gone' to observe the numerous tokens of extreme vexation of spirit which were plainly visible in her countenance. Being, however, of a rather violent and quarrelsome mood in his cups, it is not impossible that he might have fallen out with her, either on this or some imaginary topic, if the young lady had not, with a foresight and prudence highly commendable, kept a boy up, on purpose, to bear the first brunt of the good gentleman's anger; which, having vented itself in a variety of kicks and cuffs, subsided sufficiently to admit of his being persuaded to go to bed. Which he did with his boots on, and an umbrella under his arm.

The hungry servant attended Miss Squeers in her own room according to custom, to curl her hair, perform the other little offices of her toilet, and administer as much flattery as she could get up, for the purpose; for Miss Squeers was quite lazy enough (and sufficiently vain and frivolous withal) to have been a fine lady; and it was only the arbitrary distinctions of rank and station which prevented her from being one.

'How lovely your hair do curl to-night, miss!' said the handmaiden. 'I declare if it isn't a pity and a shame to brush it out!'

'Hold your tongue!' replied Miss Squeers wrathfully.

Some considerable experience prevented the girl from being at all surprised at any outbreak of ill-temper on the part of Miss Squeers. Having a half perception of what had occurred in the course of the evening, she changed her mode of making herself agreeable, and proceeded on the indirect tack.

'Well, I couldn't help saying, miss, if you was to kill me for it,' said the attendant, 'that I never see nobody look so vulgar as Miss Price this night.'

Miss Squeers sighed, and composed herself to listen.

'I know it's very wrong in me to say so, miss,' continued the girl, delighted to see the impression she was making, 'Miss Price being a friend of your'n, and all; but she do dress herself out so, and go on in such a manner to get noticed, that—oh—well, if people only saw themselves!'

'What do you mean, Phib?' asked Miss Squeers, looking in her own little glass, where, like most of us, she saw—not herself, but the reflection of some pleasant image in her own brain. 'How you talk!'

'Talk, miss! It's enough to make a Tom cat talk French grammar, only to see how she tosses her head,' replied the handmaid.

'She *does* toss her head,' observed Miss Squeers, with an air of abstraction.

'So vain, and so very—very plain,' said the girl.

'Poor 'Tilda!' sighed Miss Squeers, compassionately.

'And always laying herself out so, to get to be admired,' pursued the servant. 'Oh, dear! It 's positive indelicate.'

'I can't allow you to talk in that way, Phib,' said Miss Squeers. ''Tilda's friends are low people, and if she don't know any better, it 's their fault, and not hers.'

'Well, but you know, miss,' said Phœbe, for which name 'Phib' was used as a patronising abbreviation, 'if she was only to take copy by a friend—oh! if she only knew how wrong she was, and would but set herself right by you, what a nice young woman she might be in time!'

'Phib,' rejoined Miss Squeers, with a stately air, 'it 's not proper for me to hear these comparisons drawn; they make 'Tilda look a coarse improper sort of person, and it seems unfriendly in me to listen to them. I would rather you dropped the subject, Phib; at the same time, I must say, that if 'Tilda Price would take pattern by somebody—not me particularly—'

'Oh yes; you, miss,' interposed Phib.

'Well, me, Phib, if you will have it so,' said Miss Squeers. 'I must say, that if she would, she would be all the better for it.'

'So somebody else thinks, or I am much mistaken,' said the girl mysteriously.

'What do you mean?' demanded Miss Squeers.

'Never mind, miss,' replied the girl; '*I* know what I know; that 's all.'

'Phib,' said Miss Squeers dramatically, 'I insist upon your explaining yourself. What is this dark mystery? Speak.'

'Why, if you will have it, miss, it's this,' said the servant girl. 'Mr. John Browdie thinks as you think; and if he wasn't too far gone to do it creditable, he'd be very glad to be off with Miss Price, and on with Miss Squeers.'

'Gracious Heavens!' exclaimed Miss Squeers, clasping her hands with great dignity. 'What is this?'

'Truth, ma'am, and nothing but truth,' replied the artful Phib.

'What a situation!' cried Miss Squeers; 'on the brink of unconsciously destroying the peace and happiness of my own 'Tilda. What is the reason that men fall in love with me, whether I like it or not, and desert their chosen intendeds for my sake?'

'Because they can't help it, miss,' replied the girl; 'the reason's plain.' (If Miss Squeers were the rea· son, it was very plain.)

'Never let me hear of it again,' retorted Miss Squeers. 'Never! Do you hear? 'Tilda Price has faults—many faults—but I wish her well, and above all I wish her married; for I think it highly desirable —most desirable from the very nature of her failings —that she should be married as soon as possible. No, Phib. Let her have Mr. Browdie. I may pity *him,* poor fellow; but I have a great regard for 'Tilda, and only hope she may make a better wife than I think she will.'

With this effusion of feeling, Miss Squeers went to bed.

Spite is a little word; but it represents as strange a jumble of feelings, and compound of discords, as any polysyllable in the language. Miss Squeers knew as well in her heart of hearts, that what the miserable serving girl had said was sheer, coarse, lying flattery, as did the girl herself; yet the mere opportunity of venting a little ill-nature against the offending Miss

Price, and affecting to compassionate her weaknesses and foibles, though only in the presence of a solitary dependant, was almost as great a relief to her spleen as if the whole had been gospel truth. Nay, more. We have such extraordinary powers of persuasion when they are exerted over ourselves, that Miss Squeers felt quite high-minded and great after her noble renunciation of John Browdie's hand, and looked down upon her rival with a kind of holy calmness and tranquillity, that had a mighty effect in soothing her ruffled feelings.

This happy state of mind had some influence in bringing about a reconciliation; for, when a knock came at the front door next day, and the miller's daughter was announced, Miss Squeers betook herself to the parlour in a Christian frame of spirit, perfectly beautiful to behold.

'Well, Fanny,' said the miller's daughter, 'you see I have come to see you, although we *had* some words last night.'

'I pity your bad passions, 'Tilda,' replied Miss Squeers; 'but I bear no malice. I am above it.'

'Don't be cross, Fanny,' said Miss Price. 'I have come to tell you something that I know will please you.'

'What may that be, 'Tilda?' demanded Miss Squeers; screwing up her lips, and looking as if nothing in earth, air, fire, or water, could afford her the slightest gleam of satisfaction.

'This,' rejoined Miss Price. 'After we left here last night, John and I had a dreadful quarrel.'

'That doesn't please me,' said Miss Squeers—relaxing into a smile, though.

'Lor! I wouldn't think so bad of you as to suppose it did,' rejoined her companion. 'That's not it.'

'Oh!' said Miss Squeers, relapsing into melancholy. 'Go on.'

'After a great deal of wrangling, and saying we would never see each other any more,' continued Miss Price, 'we made it up, and this morning John went and wrote our names down to be put up, for the first time, next Sunday, so we shall be married in three weeks, and I give you notice to get your frock made.'

There was mingled gall and honey in this intelligence. The prospect of the friend's being married so soon, was the gall, and the certainty of her not entertaining serious designs upon Nicholas was the honey. Upon the whole, the sweet greatly preponderated over the bitter, so Miss Squeers said she would get the frock made, and that she hoped 'Tilda might be happy, though at the same time she didn't know, and would not have her build too much upon it, for men were strange creatures, and a great many married women were very miserable, and wished themselves single again with all their hearts; to which condolences Miss Squeers added others equally calculated to raise her friend's spirits and promote her cheerfulness of mind.

'But come now, Fanny,' said Miss Price. 'I want to have a word or two with you about young Mr. Nickleby.'

'He is nothing to me,' interrupted Miss Squeers, with hysterical symptoms. 'I despise him too much!'

'Oh, you don't mean that, I am sure?' replied her friend. 'Confess, Fanny; don't you like him now?'

Without returning any direct reply, Miss Squeers, all at once, fell into a paroxysm of spiteful tears, and exclaimed that she was a wretched, neglected, miserable, castaway.

'I hate everybody,' said Miss Squeers, 'and I wish that everybody was dead—that I do.'

'Dear, dear,' said Miss Price, quite moved by this avowal of misanthropical sentiments. 'You are not serious, I am sure.'

'Yes, I am,' rejoined Miss Squeers, tying tight knots in her pocket-handkerchief, and clenching her teeth. 'And I wish *I* was dead too. There!'

'Oh! you 'll think very differently in another five minutes,' said Matilda. 'How much better to take him into favour again, than to hurt yourself by going on in that way. Wouldn't it be much nicer, now, to have him all to yourself on good terms, in a company-keeping, love-making, pleasant sort of manner?'

'I don't know but what it would,' sobbed Miss Squeers. 'Oh! 'Tilda, how could you have acted so mean and dishonourable? I wouldn't have believed it of you, if anybody had told me.'

'Heyday!' exclaimed Miss Price, giggling. 'One would suppose I had been murdering somebody at least.'

'Very nigh as bad,' said Miss Squeers passionately.

'And all this, because I happen to have enough of good looks to make people civil to me,' cried Miss Price. 'Persons don't make their own faces, and it 's no more my fault if mine is a good one than it is other people's fault if theirs is a bad one.'

'Hold your tongue,' shrieked Miss Squeers, in her shrillest tone; 'or you 'll make me slap you, ''Tilda, and afterwards I should be sorry for it!'

It is needless to say, that, by this time, the temper of each young lady was in some slight degree affected by the tone of her conversation, and that a dash of personality was infused into the altercation, in consequence. Indeed, the quarrel, from slight beginnings, rose to a considerable height, and was assuming a very violent complexion, when both parties.

falling into a great passion of tears, exclaimed simultaneously, that they had never thought of being spoken to in that way: which exclamation, leading to a remonstrance, gradually brought on an explanation: and the upshot was, that they fell into each other's arms and vowed eternal friendship; the occasion in question, making the fifty-second time of repeating the same impressive ceremony within a twelvemonth.

Perfect amicability being thus restored, a dialogue naturally ensued upon the number and nature of the garments which would be indispensable for Miss Price's entrance into the holy state of matrimony, when Miss Squeers clearly showed that a great many more than the miller could, or would, afford, were absolutely necessary, and could not decently be dispensed with. The young lady then, by an easy digression, led the discourse to her own wardrobe, and after recounting its principle beauties, at some length, took her friend upstairs to make inspection thereof. The treasures of two drawers and a closet having been displayed, and all the smaller articles tried on, it was time for Miss Price to return home; and as she had been in raptures with all the frocks, and had been stricken quite dumb with admiration of a new pink scarf, Miss Squeers said in high good humour, that she would walk part of the way with her, for the pleasure of her company; and off they went together: Miss Squeers dilating, as they walked along, upon her father's accomplishments: and multiplying his income by ten, to give her friend some faint notion of the vast importance and superiority of her family.

It happened that that particular time, comprising the short daily interval which was suffered to elapse between what was pleasantly called the dinner, of Mr. Squeers's pupils, and their return to the pursuit of useful knowledge, was precisely the hour when

Nicholas was accustomed to issue forth for a melancholy walk, and to brood, as he sauntered listlessly through the village, upon his miserable lot. Miss Squeers knew this, perfectly well, but had perhaps forgotten it, for when she caught sight of that young gentleman advancing towards them, she evinced many symptoms of surprise and consternation, and assured her friend that she 'felt fit to drop into the earth.'

'Shall we turn back, or run into a cottage?' asked Miss Price. 'He don't see us yet.'

'No, 'Tilda,' replied Miss Squeers, 'it is my duty to go through with it, and I will!'

As Miss Squeers said this, in the tone of one who has made a high moral resolution, and was, besides, taken with one or two chokes and catchings of breath, indicative of feelings at a high pressure, her friend made no farther remark, and they bore straight down upon Nicholas, who, walking with his eyes bent upon the ground, was not aware of their approach until they were close upon him; otherwise he might, perhaps, have taken shelter himself.

'Good morning,' said Nicholas, bowing and passing by.

'He is going,' murmured Miss Squeers. 'I shall choke, 'Tilda.'

'Come back, Mr. Nickleby, do!' cried Miss Price, affecting alarm at her friend's threat, but really actuated by a malicious wish to hear what Nicholas would say; 'come back, Mr. Nickleby.'

Mr. Nickleby came back, and looked as confused as might be, as he inquired whether the ladies had any commands for him.

'Don't stop to talk,' urged Miss Price, hastily: 'but support her on the other side. How do you feel now, dear?'

'Better,' sighed Miss Squeers, laying a beaver bonnet of a reddish brown with a green veil attached, on Mr. Nickleby's shoulder. 'This foolish faintness!'

'Don't call it foolish, dear,' said Miss Price: her bright eye dancing with merriment as she saw the perplexity of Nicholas; 'you have no reason to be ashamed of it. It's those who are too proud to come round again, without all this to-do, that ought to be ashamed.'

'You are resolved to fix it upon me, I see,' said Nicholas, smiling, 'although I told you, last night, it was not my fault.'

'There; he says it was not his fault, my dear,' remarked the wicked Miss Price. 'Perhaps you were too jealous, or too hasty with him? He says it was not his fault. You hear; I think that's apology enough.'

'You will not understand me,' said Nicholas. 'Pray dispense with this jesting, for I have no time, and really no inclination, to be the subject or promoter of mirth just now.'

'What do you mean?' asked Miss Price, affecting amazement.

'Don't ask him, 'Tilda,' cried Miss Squeers: 'I forgive him.'

'Dear me,' said Nicholas, as the brown bonnet went down on his shoulder again, 'this is more serious than I supposed. Allow me! Will you have the goodness to hear me speak?'

Here he raised up the brown bonnet, and regarding with most unfeigned astonishment a look of tender reproach from Miss Squeers, shrunk back a few paces to be out of the reach of the fair burden, and went on to say:

'I am very sorry—truly and sincerely sorry—for having been the cause of any difference among you, last night. I reproach myself, most bitterly, for having been so unfortunate as to cause the dissension that occurred, although I did so, I assure you, most unwittingly and heedlessly.'

'Well; that's not all you have got to say surely,' exclaimed Miss Price as Nicholas paused.

'I fear there is something more,' stammered Nicholas with a half smile, and looking towards Miss Squeers, 'it is a most awkward thing to say—but—the very mention of such a supposition makes one look like a puppy—still—may I ask if that lady supposes that I entertain any—in short, does she think that I am in love with her?'

'Delightful embarrassment,' thought Miss Squeers, 'I have brought him to it, at last. Answer for me, dear,' she whispered to her friend.

'Does she think so?' rejoined Miss Price; 'of course she does.'

'She does!' exclaimed Nicholas with such energy of utterance as might have been, for the moment, mistaken for rapture.

'Certainly,' replied Miss Price.

'If Mr. Nickleby has doubted that, 'Tilda,' said the blushing Miss Squeers in soft accents, 'he may set his mind at rest. His sentiments are recipro—'

'Stop,' cried Nicholas hurriedly; 'pray hear me. This is the grossest and wildest delusion, the completest and most signal mistake, that ever human being laboured under, or committed. I have scarcely seen the young lady half a dozen times, but if I had seen her sixty times, or am destined to see her sixty thousand, it would be, and will be, precisely the same. I have not one thought, wish, or hope, connected with her, unless it be—and I say this, not to hurt her feelings, but to impress her with the real state of my own —unless it be the one object, dear to my heart as life

itself, of being one day able to turn my back upon
this accursed place, never to set foot in it again, or
to think of it—even think of it—but with loathing
and disgust.'

With this particularly plain and straight-forward
declaration, which he made with all the vehemence
that his indignant and excited feelings could bring to
bear upon it, Nicholas, waiting to hear no more, re-
treated.

But poor Miss Squeers!   Her anger, rage, and
vexation; the rapid succession of bitter and passion-
ate feelings that whirled through her mind; are not
to be described. Refused! refused by a teacher,
picked up by advertisement, at an annual salary of
five pounds payable at indefinite periods, and 'found'
in food and lodging like the very boys themselves;
and this too in the presence of a little chit of a miller's
daughter of eighteen, who was going to be married,
in three weeks' time, to a man who had gone down
on his very knees to ask her!   She could have choked
in right good earnest, at the thought of being so
humbled.

But there was one thing clear in the midst of her
mortification; and that was, that she hated and detested Nicholas with all the narrowness of mind and
littleness of purpose worthy a descendant of the house
of Squeers.   And there was one comfort too; and
that was, that every hour in every day she could
wound his pride, and goad him with the infliction of
some slight, or insult, or deprivation, which could not
but have some effect on the most insensible person,
and must be acutely felt by one so sensitive as Nicholas.   With these two reflections uppermost in her
mind, Miss Squeers made the best of the matter to
her friend, by observing that Mr. Nickleby was such
an odd creature, and of such a violent temper, that

she feared she should be obliged to give him up; and parted from her.

And here it may be remarked, that Miss Squeers, having bestowed her affections (or whatever it might be that, in the absence of anything better, represented them) on Nicholas Nickleby, had never once seriously contemplated the possibility of his being of a different opinion from herself in the business. Miss Squeers reasoned that she was prepossessing and beautiful, and that her father was master, and Nicholas man, and that her father had saved money, and Nicholas had none, all of which seemed to her conclusive arguments why the young man should feel only too much honoured by her preference. She had not failed to recollect, either, how much more agreeable she could render his situation if she were his friend, and how much more disagreeable if she were his enemy; and, doubtless, many less scrupulous young gentlemen than Nicholas would have encouraged her extravagance had it been only for this very obvious and intelligible reason. However, he had thought proper to do otherwise, and Miss Squeers was outrageous.

'Let him see,' said the irritated young lady, when she had regained her own room, and eased her mind by committing an assault on Phib, 'if I don't set mother against him a little more when she comes back!'

It was scarcely necessary to do this, but Miss Squeers was as good as her word; and poor Nicholas, in addition to bad food, dirty lodging, and the being compelled to witness one dull unvarying round of squalid misery, was treated with every special indignity that malice could suggest, or the most grasping cupidity put upon him.

Nor was this all. There was another and deeper

system of annoyance which made his heart sink, and nearly drove him wild, by its injustice and cruelty.

The wretched creature, Smike, since the night Nicholas had spoken kindly to him in the school-room, had followed him to and fro, with an ever-restless desire to serve or help him; anticipating such little wants as his humble ability could supply, and content only to be near him. He would sit beside him for hours, looking patiently into his face; and a word would brighten up his careworn visage, and call into it a passing gleam, even of happiness. He was an altered being; he had an object now; and that object was, to show his attachment to the only person—that person a stranger—who had treated him, not to say with kindness, but like a human creature.

Upon this poor being, all the spleen and ill-humour that could not be vented on Nicholas were unceasingly bestowed. Drudgery would have been nothing— Smike was well used to that. Buffetings inflicted without cause, would have been equally a matter of course; for to them also, he had served a long and weary apprenticeship; but it was no sooner observed that he had become attached to Nicholas, than stripes and blows, stripes and blows, morning, noon, and night, were his only portion. Squeers was jealous of the influence which his man had so soon acquired, and his family hated him, and Smike paid for both. Nicholas saw it, and ground his teeth at every repetition of the savage and cowardly attack.

He had arranged a few regular lessons for the boys; and one night as he paced up and down the dismal school-room, his swollen heart almost bursting to think that his protection and countenance should have increased the misery of the wretched being whose peculiar destitution had awakened his pity, he paused mechanically in a dark corner where sat the object of his thoughts.

The poor soul was pouring hard over a tattered book, with the traces of recent tears still upon his face; vainly endeavouring to master some task which a child of nine years old, possessed of ordinary powers, could have conquered with ease, but which, to the addled brain of the crushed boy of nineteen, was a sealed and hopeless mystery. Yet there he sat, patiently conning the page again and again, stimulated by no boyish ambition, for he was the common jest and scoff even of the uncouth objects that congregated about him, but inspired by the one eager desire to please his solitary friend.

Nicholas laid his hand upon his shoulder.

'I can't do it,' said the dejected creature, looking up with bitter disappointment in every feature. 'No, no.'

'Do not try,' replied Nicholas.

The boy shook his head, and closing the book with a sigh, looked vacantly round, and laid his head upon his arm. He was weeping.

'Do not for God's sake,' said Nicholas, in an agitated voice; 'I cannot bear to see you.'

'They are more hard with me than ever,' sobbed the boy.

'I know it,' rejoined Nicholas. 'They are.'

'But for you,' said the outcast, 'I should die. They would kill me; they would; I know they would.'

'You will do better, poor fellow,' replied Nicholas, shaking his head mournfully, 'when I am gone.'

'Gone!' cried the other, looking intently in his face.

'Softly!' rejoined Nicholas. 'Yes.'

'Are you going?' demanded the boy, in an earnest whisper.

'I cannot say,' replied Nicholas. 'I was speaking more to my own thoughts than to you.'

'Tell me,' said the boy imploringly, 'Oh, do tell me, *will* you go—*will* you?'

'I shall be driven to that at last!' said Nicholas. 'The world is before me, after all.'

'Tell me,' urged Smike, 'is the world as bad and dismal as this place?'

'Heaven forbid,' replied Nicholas, pursuing the train of his own thoughts, 'its hardest, coarsest toil, were happiness to this.'

'Should I ever meet you there?' demanded the boy, speaking with unusual wildness and volubility.

'Yes,' replied Nicholas, willing to soothe him.

'No, no!' said the other, clasping him by the hand. 'Should I—should I—tell me that again. Say I should be sure to find you.'

'You would,' replied Nicholas, with the same humane intention, 'and I would help and aid you, and not bring fresh sorrow on you as I have done here.'

The boy caught both the young man's hands passionately in his, and hugging them to his breast, uttered a few broken sounds which were unintelligible. Squeers entered, at the moment, and he shrunk back into his old corner.

CHAPTER XIII

NICHOLAS VARIES THE MONOTONY OF DOTHEBOYS HALL BY A MOST VIGOROUS AND REMARKABLE PROCEEDING, WHICH LEADS TO CONSEQUENCES OF SOME IMPORTANCE

THE cold, feeble, dawn of a January morning was stealing in at the windows of the common sleeping-room, when Nicholas, raising himself on his arm, looked among the prostrate forms which on every side surrounded him, as though in search of some particular object.

It needed a quick eye to detect, from among the huddled mass of sleepers, the form of any given individual. As they lay closely packed together, for warmth's sake, with their patched and ragged clothes, little could be distinguished but the sharp outlines of pale faces, over which the sombre light shed the same dull heavy colour; with, here and there, a gaunt arm thrust forth: its thinness hidden by no covering, but fully exposed to view, in all its shrunken ugliness. There were some who, lying on their backs with upturned faces and clenched hands, just visible in the leaden light, bore more the aspect of dead bodies than of living creatures; and there were others coiled up into strange and fantastic postures, such as might have been taken for the uneasy efforts of pain to gain some temporary relief, rather than the freaks of slumber. A few—and these were among the youngest of the children—slept peacefully on, with smiles upon their faces, dreaming perhaps of hope; but ever and again a deep and heavy sigh, breaking the stillness of the room, announced that some new sleeper had awakened to the misery of another day; and, as morning took the place of night, the smiles gradually faded away, with the friendly darkness which had given them birth.

Dreams are the bright creatures of poem and legend, who sport on earth in the night season, and melt away in the first beam of the sun, which lights grim care and stern reality on their daily pilgrimage through the world.

Nicholas looked upon the sleepers; at first, with the air of one who gazes upon a scene which, though familiar to him, has lost none of its sorrowful effect in consequence; and, afterwards, with a more intense and searching scrutiny, as a man would, who missed something his eye was accustomed to meet, and had expected to rest upon. He was still occupied in this search, and had half risen from his bed in the eagerness of his quest, when the voice of Squeers was heard, calling from the bottom of the stairs.

'Now then,' cried that gentleman, 'are you going to sleep all day, up there—'

'You lazy hounds?' added Mrs. Squeers, finishing the sentence, and producing, at the same time, a sharp sound, like that which is occasioned by the lacing of stays.

'We shall be down directly, sir,' replied Nicholas.

'Down directly!' said Squeers. 'Ah! you had better be down directly, or I'll be down upon some of you in less. Where's that Smike?'

Nicholas looked hurriedly round again, but made no answer.

'Smike!' shouted Squeers.

'Do you want your head broke in a fresh place, Smike?' demanded his amiable lady in the same key.

Still there was no reply, and still Nicholas stared about him, as did the greater part of the boys, who were by this time roused.

'Confound his impudence!' muttered Squeers, rapping the stair-rail impatiently with his cane. 'Nickleby!'

'Well, sir.'

'Send that obstinate scoundrel down; don't you hear me calling?'

'He is not here, sir,' replied Nicholas.

'Don't tell me a lie,' retorted the schoolmaster. 'He is.'

'He is not,' retorted Nicholas angrily, 'don't tell me one.'

'We shall soon see that,' said Mr. Squeers, rushing upstairs. 'I 'll find him, I warrant you.'

With which assurance Mr. Squeers bounced into the dormitory, and, swinging his cane in the air ready for a blow, darted into the corner where the lean body of the drudge was usually stretched at night. The cane descended harmlessly upon the ground. There was nobody there.

'What does this mean?' said Squeers, turning round with a very pale face. 'Where have you hid him?'

'I have seen nothing of him, since last night,' replied Nicholas.

'Come,' said Squeers, evidently frightened, though he endeavoured to look otherwise, 'you won't save him this way. Where is he?'

'At the bottom of the nearest pond for aught I know,' rejoined Nicholas in a low voice, and fixing his eyes full on the master's face.

'D—n you, what do you mean by that?' retorted Squeers in great perturbation. Without waiting for a reply, he inquired of the boys whether any one among them knew anything of their missing schoolmate.

There was a general hum of anxious denial, in the midst of which, one shrill voice was heard to say (as, indeed, everybody thought) —

'Please, sir, I think Smike's run away, sir.'

'Ha!' cried Squeers, turning sharp round; 'Who said that?'

'Tompkins, please, sir,' rejoined a chorus of voices. Mr. Squeers made a plunge into the crowd, and at one dive, caught a very little boy, habited still in his night-gear, and the perplexed expression of whose countenance as he was brought forward, seemed to intimate that he was as yet uncertain whether he was about to be punished or rewarded for the suggestion. He was not long in doubt.

'You think he has run away, do you, sir?' demanded Squeers.

'Yes, please sir,' replied the little boy.

'And what, sir,' said Squeers, catching the little boy suddenly by the arms and whisking up his drapery in a most dexterous manner, 'what reason have you to suppose that any boy would want to run away from this establishment? Eh, sir?'

The child raised a dismal cry, by way of answer, and Mr. Squeers, throwing himself into the most favourable attitude for exercising his strength, beat him until the little urchin in his writhings actually rolled out of his hands, when he mercifully allowed him to roll away, as he best could.

'There,' said Squeers. 'Now if any other boy thinks Smike has run away, I should be glad to have a talk with him.'

There was, of course, a profound silence, during which Nicholas showed his disgust as plainly as looks could show it.

'Well, Nickleby,' said Squeers, eyeing him maliciously. '*You* think he has run away, I suppose?'

'I think it extremely likely,' replied Nicholas, in a quiet manner.

'Oh, you do, do you?' sneered Squeers. 'Maybe you know he has?'

'I know nothing of the kind.'

'He didn't tell you he was going, I suppose, did he?' sneered Squeers.

'He did not,' replied Nicholas; 'I am very glad he did not, for it would then have been my duty to have warned you, in time.'

'Which no doubt you would have been devilish sorry to do,' said Squeers, in a taunting fashion.

'I should indeed,' replied Nicholas. 'You interpret my feelings with great accuracy.'

Mrs. Squeers had listened to this conversation, from the bottom of the stairs; but, now losing all patience, she hastily assumed her night-jacket, and made her way to the scene of action.

'What's all this here to-do?' said the lady, as the boys fell off right and left, to save her the trouble of clearing a passage with her brawny arms. 'What on earth are you a talking to him for, Squeery?'

'Why, my dear,' said Squeers, 'the fact is, that Smike is not to be found.'

'Well, I know that,' said the lady, 'and where's the wonder? If you get a parcel of proud-stomached teachers that set the young dogs a rebelling, what else can you look for? Now, young man, you just have the kindness to take yourself off to the school-room, and take the boys off with you, and don't you stir out of there till you have leave given you, or you and I may fall out in a way that'll spoil your beauty, handsome as you think yourself, and so I tell you.'

'Indeed!' said Nicholas.

'Yes; and indeed and indeed again, Mister Jacka-napes,' said the excited lady; 'and I wouldn't keep such as you in the house, another hour, if I had my way.'

'Nor would you if I had mine,' replied Nicholas. 'Now, boys!'

'Ah! Now, boys,' said Mrs. Squeers, mimicking, as nearly as she could, the voice and manner of the usher. 'Follow your leader, boys, and take pattern by Smike if you dare. See what he'll get for him-self. when he is brought back; and, mind! I tell you that you shall have as bad, and twice as bad, if you so much as open your mouths about him.'

'If I catch him,' said Squeers, 'I 'll only stop short of flaying him alive. I give you notice, boys.'

'*If* you catch him,' retorted Mrs. Squeers, contemptuously, 'you are sure to; you can't help it, if you go the right way to work. Come. Away with you!'

With these words, Mrs. Squeers dismissed the boys, and after a little light skirmishing with those in the rear who were pressing forward to get out of the way, but were detained for a few moments by the throng in front, succeeded in clearing the room, when she confronted her spouse alone.

'He is off,' said Mrs. Squeers. 'The cow-house and stable are locked up, so he can't be there; and he 's not downstairs anywhere, for the girl has looked. He must have gone York way, and by a public road too.'

'Why must he?' inquired Squeers.

'Stupid!' said Mrs. Squeers angrily. 'He hadn't any money, had he?'

'Never had a penny of his own in his whole life, that I know of,' replied Squeers.

'To be sure,' rejoined Mrs. Squeers, 'and he didn't take anything to eat with him; that I 'll answer for. Ha! ha! ha!'

'Ha! ha! ha!' laughed Squeers.

'Then, of course,' said Mrs. S., 'he must beg his way, and he could do that, nowhere, but on the public road.'

'That 's true,' exclaimed Squeers, clapping his hands.

'True! Yes; but you would never have thought of it, for all that, if I hadn't said so,' replied his wife. 'Now, if you take the chaise and go one road, and I borrow Swallow's chaise, and go the other, what with keeping our eyes open, and asking questions, one or other of us is pretty certain to lay hold of him.'

The worthy lady's plan was adopted and put in execution without a moment's delay. After a very hasty breakfast, and the prosecution of some inquiries in the village, the result of which seemed to show that he was on the right track, Squeers started forth in the pony-chaise, intent upon discovery and vengeance. Shortly afterwards, Mrs. Squeers, arrayed in the white top-coat, and tied up in various shawls and handkerchiefs, issued forth in another chaise and another direction, taking with her a good-sized bludgeon, several odd pieces of strong cord, and a stout labouring man: all provided and carried upon the expedition, with the sole object of assisting in the capture, and (once caught) insuring the safe custody of the unfortunate Smike.

Nicholas remained behind, in a tumult of feeling, sensible that whatever might be the upshot of the boy's flight, nothing but painful and deplorable consequences were likely to ensue from it. Death, from want and exposure to the weather, was the best that could be expected from the protracted wandering of so poor and helpless a creature, alone and unfriended, through a country of which he was wholly ignorant. There was little, perhaps, to choose between this fate and a return to the tender mercies of the Yorkshire school; but the unhappy being had established a hold upon his sympathy and compassion, which made his heart ache at the prospect of the suffering he was destined to undergo. He lingered on, in restless anxiety, picturing a thousand possibilities, until the evening of next day, when Squeers returned, alone and unsuccessful.

'No news of the scamp!' said the schoolmaster, who

had evidently been stretching his legs, on the old principle, not a few times during the journey. 'I'll have consolation for this out of somebody, Nickleby, if Mrs. Squeers don't hunt him down; so I give you warning.'

'It is not in my power to console you, sir,' said Nicholas. 'It is nothing to me.'

'Isn't it?' said Squeers in a threatening manner. 'We shall see!'

'We shall,' rejoined Nicholas.

'Here's the pony run right off his legs, and me obliged to come home with a hack cob, that'll cost fifteen shillings besides other expenses,' said Squeers; 'who's to pay for that, do you hear?'

Nicholas shrugged his shoulders and remained silent.

'I'll have it out of somebody, I tell you,' said Squeers, his usual harsh crafty manner changed to open bullying. 'None of your whining vapourings here, Mr. Puppy, but be off to your kennel, for it's past your bed-time! Come! Get out!'

Nicholas bit his lip and knit his hands involuntarily, for his finger-ends tingled to avenge the insult; but remembering that the man was drunk, and that it could come to little but a noisy brawl, he contented himself with darting a contemptuous look at the tyrant, and walked, as majestically as he could, upstairs: not a little nettled, however, to observe that Miss Squeers and Master Squeers, and the servant girl, were enjoying the scene from a snug corner; the two former, indulging in many edifying remarks about the presumption of poor upstarts, which occasioned a vast deal of laughter, in which even the most miserable of all miserable servant girls joined: while Nicholas, stung to the quick, drew over his head such bed-clothes as he had, and sternly resolved that the outstanding account between himself and Mr. Squeers should be settled rather more speedily than the latter anticipated.

Another day came, and Nicholas was scarcely awake when he heard the wheels of a chaise approaching the house. It stopped. The voice of Mrs. Squeers was heard, and in exultation, ordering a glass of spirits for somebody, which was in itself a sufficient sign that something extraordinary had happened. Nicholas hardly dared to look out of the window; but he did so, and the very first object that met his eyes was the wretched Smike: so bedabbled with mud and rain, so haggard and worn, and wild, that, but for his garments being such as no scarecrow was ever seen to wear, he might have been doubtful, even then, of his identity.

'Lift him out,' said Squeers, after he had literally feasted his eyes, in silence, upon the culprit. 'Bring him in; bring him in!'

'Take care,' cried Mrs. Squeers, as her husband proffered his assistance. 'We tied his legs under the apron and made em' fast to the chaise, to prevent his giving us the slip again.'

With hands trembling with delight, Squeers unloosened the cord; and Smike, to all appearance more dead than alive, was brought into the house and securely locked up in a cellar, until such time as Mr. Squeers should deem it expedient to operate upon him, in presence of the assembled school.

Upon a hasty consideration of the circumstances, it may be matter of surprise to some persons, that Mr. and Mrs. Squeers should have taken so much trouble to repossess themselves of an incumbrance of which it was their wont to complain so loudly; but their surprise will cease when they are informed that the manifold services of the drudge, if performed by anybody else, would have cost the establishment some ten or twelve shillings per week in the shape of wages; and furthermore, that all runaways were, as a matter of policy, made severe examples of, at Dotheboys Hall, inasmuch as, in consequence of the limited extent of its attractions, there was but little inducement, beyond the powerful impulse of fear, for any pupil, provided with the usual number of legs and the power of using them, to remain.

The news that Smike had been caught and brought back in triumph, ran like wild-fire through the hungry community, and expectation was on tiptoe all the morning. On tiptoe it was destined to remain, however, until afternoon; when Squeers, having refreshed himself with his dinner, and further strengthened himself by an extra libation or so, made his appearance (accompanied by his amiable partner) with a countenance of portentous import, and a fearful instrument of flagellation, strong, supple, wax-ended, and new—in short, purchased that morning, expressly for the occasion.

'Is every boy here?' asked Squeers, in a tremendous voice.

Every boy was there, but every boy was afraid to speak; so, Squeers glared along the lines to assure himself; and every eye drooped, and every head cowered down, as he did so.

'Each boy keep his place,' said Squeers, administering his favourite blow to the desk, and regarding with gloomy satisfaction the universal start which it never failed to occasion. 'Nickleby! to your desk, sir.'

It was remarked by more than one small observer, that there was a very curious and unusual expression in the usher's face; but he took his seat, without opening his lips in reply. Squeers, casting a triumphant glance at his assistant and a look of most comprehensive despotism on the boys, left the room, and shortly afterwards returned, dragging Smike by the collar—or rather by that fragment of his jacket which was nearest the place where his collar would have been, had he boasted such a decoration.

In any other place, the appearance of the wretched, jaded, spiritless object would have occasioned a murmur of compassion and remonstrance. It had some effect, even there; for the lookers-on moved uneasily in their seats; and a few of the boldest ventured to steal looks at each other, expressive of indignation and pity.

They were lost on Squeers, however, whose gaze was fastened on the luckless Smike, as he inquired, according to custom in such cases, whether he had anything to say for himself.

'Nothing, I suppose?' said Squeers, with a diabolical grin.

Smike glanced round, and his eye rested, for an instant, on Nicholas, as if he had expected him to intercede; but his look was riveted on his desk.

'Have you anything to say?' demanded Squeers again: giving his right arm two or three flourishes to try its power and suppleness. 'Stand a little out of the way, Mrs. Squeers, my dear; I've hardly got room enough.'

'Spare me, sir!' cried Smike.

'Oh! that's all, is it?' said Squeers. 'Yes, I'll flog you within an inch of your life, and spare you that.'

'Ha, ha, ha,' laughed Mrs. Squeers, 'that's a good 'un!'

'I was driven to do it,' said Smike faintly; and casting another imploring look about him.

'Driven to do it, were you?' said Squeers. 'Oh! it wasn't your fault; it was mine, I suppose—eh?'

'A nasty, ungrateful, pig-headed, brutish, obstinate, sneaking dog,' exclaimed Mrs. Squeers, taking Smike's head under her arm, and administering a cuff at every epithet; 'what does he mean by that?'

'Stand aside, my dear,' replied Squeers. 'We'll try and find out.'

Mrs. Squeers being out of breath with her exertions, complied. Squeers caught the boy firmly in his grip; one desperate cut had fallen on his body—he was wincing from the lash and uttering a scream of pain—it was raised again, and again about to fall—when Nicholas Nickleby suddenly starting up, cried 'Stop!' in a voice that made the rafters ring.

'Who cried stop?' said Squeers, turning savagely round.

'I,' said Nicholas, stepping forward. 'This must not go on.'

'Must not go on!' cried Squeers, almost in a shriek.

'No!' thundered Nicholas.

Aghast and stupefied by the boldness of the interference, Squeers released his hold of Smike, and, falling back a pace or two, gazed upon Nicholas with looks that were positively frightful.

'I say must not,' repeated Nicholas, nothing daunted; 'shall not. I will prevent it.'

Squeers continued to gaze upon him, with his eyes starting out of his head; but astonishment had actually, for the moment, bereft him of speech.

'You have disregarded all my quiet interference in the miserable lad's behalf,' said Nicholas; 'you have returned no answer to the letter in which I begged forgiveness for him, and offered to be responsible that he would remain quietly here. Don't blame me for this public interference. You have brought it upon yourself; not I.'

'Sit down, beggar!' screamed Squeers, almost be-

NICHOLAS ASTONISHES MR. SQUEERS AND FAMILY.

side himself with rage, and seizing Smike as he spoke.

'Wretch,' rejoined Nicholas, fiercely, 'touch him at your peril! I will not stand by, and see it done. My blood is up, and I have the strength of ten such men as you. Look to yourself, for by Heaven I will not spare you, if you drive me on!'

'Stand back,' cried Squeers, brandishing his weapon.

'J have a long series of insults to avenge,' said Nicholas, flushed with passion; 'and my indignation is aggravated by the dastardly cruelties practised on helpless infancy in this foul den. Have a care; for if you do raise the devil within me, the consequences shall fall heavily upon your own head!'

He had scarcely spoken, when Squeers, in a violent outbreak of wrath, and with a cry like the howl of a wild beast, spat upon him, and struck him a blow across the face with his instrument of torture, which raised up a bar of livid flesh as it was inflicted. Smarting with the agony of the blow, and concentrating into that one moment all his feelings of rage, scorn, and indignation, Nicholas sprang upon him, wrested the weapon from his hand, and pinning him by the throat, beat the ruffian till he roared for mercy.

The boys—with the exception of Master Squeers, who, coming to his father's assistance, harassed the enemy in the rear—moved not, hand or foot; but Mrs. Squeers, with many shrieks for aid, hung on to the tail of her partner's coat, and endeavoured to drag him from his infuriated adversary; while Miss Squeers, who had been peeping through the key-hole in expectation of a very different scene, darted in at the very beginning of the attack, and after launching a shower of ink-stands at the usher's head, beat Nicholas to her heart's content: animating herself, at every blow, with the recollection of his having refused her proffered love, and thus imparting additional strength to an arm which (as she took after her mother in this respect) was, at no time, one of the weakest.

Nicholas, in the full torrent of his violence, felt the blows no more than if they had been dealt with feathers; but, becoming tired of the noise and uproar, and feeling that his arm grew weak besides, he threw all his remaining strength into half a dozen finishing cuts, and flung Squeers from him, with all the force he could muster. The violence of his fall precipitated Mrs. Squeers completely over an adjacent form; and Squeers striking his head against it in his descent, lay at his full length on the ground, stunned and motionless.

Having brought affairs to this happy termination, and ascertained, to his thorough satisfaction, that Squeers was only stunned, and not dead (upon which point he had had some unpleasant doubts at first), Nicholas left his family to restore him, and retired to consider what course he had better adopt. He looked anxiously round for Smike, as he left the room, but he was nowhere to be seen.

After a brief consideration, he packed up a few clothes in a small leather valise, and, finding that nobody offered to oppose his progress, marched boldly out by the front door, and shortly afterwards, struck into the road which led to Greta Bridge.

When he had cooled, sufficiently to be enabled to give his present circumstances some little reflection, they did not appear in a very encouraging light; he had only four shillings and a few pence in his pocket, and was something more than two hundred and fifty miles from London, whither he resolved to direct his steps, that he might ascertain among other things, what account of the morning's proceeding Mr. Squeers transmitted to his most affectionate uncle.

Lifting up his eyes, as he arrived at the conclusion that there was no remedy for this unfortunate state of things, he beheld a horseman coming towards him, whom, on nearer approach, he discovered, to his infinite chagrin, to be no other than Mr. John Browdie, who, clad in cords and leather leggings, was urging his animal forward by means of a thick ash stick, which seemed to have been recently cut from some stout sapling.

'I am in no mood for more noise and riot,' thought Nicholas, 'and yet, do what I will, I shall have an altercation with this honest blockhead, and perhaps a blow or two from yonder staff.'

In truth, there appeared some reason to expect that such a result would follow from the encounter, for John Browdie no sooner saw Nicholas advancing, than he reined in his horse by the footpath, and waited until such time as he should come up; looking meanwhile, very sternly between the horses ears, at Nicholas, as he came on at his leisure.

'Servant, young genelman,' said John.

'Yours,' said Nicholas.

'Weel; we ha' met at last,' observed John, making the stirrup ring under a smart touch of the ash stick.

'Yes,' replied Nicholas, hesitating. 'Come!' he said, frankly, after a moment's pause, 'we parted on no very good terms the last time we met; it was my fault, I believe; but I had no intention of offending you, and no idea that I was doing so. I was very sorry for it, afterwards. Will you shake hands?'

'Shake honds!' cried the good-humoured Yorkshireman; 'ah! that I weel'; at the same time, he bent down from the saddle, and gave Nicholas's fist a huge wrench; 'but wa'at be the matther wi' thy feace, mun? it be all brokken loike.'

'It is a cut,' said Nicholas, turning scarlet as he

spoke,—'a blow; but I returned it to the giver, and with good interest too.'

'Noa, did 'ee, though?' exclaimed John Browdie. 'Well deane! I loike 'un for thot!'

'The fact is,' said Nicholas, not very well knowing how to make the avowal, 'the fact is, that I have been ill treated.'

'Noa!' interposed John Browdie, in a tone of compassion; for he was a giant in strength and stature, and Nicholas, very likely, in his eyes, seemed a mere dwarf; 'dean't say thot.'

'Yes, I have,' replied Nicholas, 'by that man Squeers, and I have beaten him soundly, and am leaving this place in consequence.'

'What!' cried John Browdie, with such an ecstatic shout, that the horse quite shied at it. 'Beatten the schoolmeasther! Ho! ho! ho! Beatten the schoolmeasther! who ever heard o' the loike o' that noo! Giv' us thee hond agean, yoongster. Beatten the schoolmeasther! Dang it, I loove thee for 't.'

With these expressions of delight, John Browdie laughed and laughed again—so loud that the echoes, far and wide, sent back nothing but jovial peals of merriment—and shook Nicholas by the hand meanwhile, no less heartily. When his mirth had subsided, he inquired what Nicholas meant to do; on his informing him, to go straight to London, he shook his head doubtfully, and inquired if he knew how much the coaches charged, to carry passengers so far.

'No, I do not,' said Nicholas; 'but it is of no great consequence to me, for I intend walking.'

'Gang awa' to Lunnun afoot!' cried John, in amazement.

'Every step of the way,' replied Nicholas. 'I should be many steps further on by this time, and so good-bye!'

'Nay noo,' replied the honest countryman, reining in his impatient horse, 'stan' still, tell'ee. Hoo much cash hast thee gotten?'

'Not much,' said Nicholas, colouring, 'but I can make it enough. Where there's a will, there's a way, you know.'

John Browdie made no verbal answer to this remark, but putting his hand in his pocket, pulled out an old purse of soiled leather, and insisted that Nicholas should borrow from him whatever he required for his present necessities.

'Dean't be afeard, mun,' he said; 'tak' eneaf to carry thee whoam. Thee 'lt pay me yan day, a' warrant.'

Nicholas could by no means be prevailed upon to borrow more than a sovereign, with which loan Mr. Browdie, after many entreaties that he would accept of more (observing, with a touch of Yorkshire caution, that if he didn't spend it all, he could put the surplus by, till he had an opportunity of remitting it carriage free), was fain to content himself.

'Tak' that bit o' timber to help thee on wi', mun,' he added, pressing his stick on Nicholas, and giving his hand another squeeze; 'keep a good heart, and bless thee. Beatten the schoolmeasther! 'Cod, it's the best thing a 've heerd this twonty year!'

So saying, and indulging, with more delicacy than might have been expected from him, in another series of loud laughs, for the purpose of avoiding the thanks which Nicholas poured forth, John Browdie set spurs to his horse, and went off at a smart canter: looking back, from time to time, as Nicholas stood gazing after him, and waving his hand cheerily, as if to encourage him on his way. Nicholas watched the horse and rider until they disappeared over the brow of a distant hill, and then set forward on his journey.

He did not travel far, that afternoon, for by this time it was nearly dark, and there had been a heavy fall of snow, which not only rendered the way toilsome, but the track uncertain and difficult to find, after daylight, save by experienced wayfarers. He lay, that night, at a cottage, where beds were let at a cheap rate to the more humble class of travellers; and, rising betimes next morning, made his way before night to Boroughbridge. Passing through that town in search of some cheap resting-place, he stumbled upon an empty barn within a couple of hundred yards of the roadside; in a warm corner of which, he stretched his weary limbs, and soon fell asleep.

When he awoke next morning, and tried to recollect his dreams, which had been all connected with his recent sojourn at Dotheboys Hall, he sat up, rubbed his eyes, and stared—not with the most composed countenance possible—at some motionless object which seemed to be stationed within a few yards in front of him.

'Strange!' cried Nicholas; 'can this be some lingering creation of the visions that have scarcely left me? It cannot be real—and yet I—I am awake! Smike!'

The form moved, rose, advanced, and dropped upon its knees at his feet. It was Smike indeed.

'Why do you kneel to me?' said Nicholas, hastily raising him.

'To go with you—anywhere—everywhere—to the world's end—to the churchyard grave,' replied Smike, clinging to his hand. 'Let me, oh do let me. You are my home—my kind friend—take me with you, pray.'

'I am a friend who can do little for you,' said Nicholas, kindly. 'How came you here?'

He had followed him, it seemed; had never lost sight of him all the way; had watched while he slept, and when he halted for refreshment; and had feared to appear, before, lest he should be sent back. He had not intended to appear now, but Nicholas had awakened more suddenly than he looked for, and he had had no time to conceal himself.

'Poor fellow!' said Nicholas, 'your hard fate denies you any friend but one, and he is nearly as poor and helpless as yourself.'

'May I—may I go with you?' asked Smike, timidly. 'I will be your faithful, hard-working servant, I will, indeed. I want no clothes,' added the poor creature, drawing his rags together; 'these will do very well. I only want to be near you.'

'And you shall,' cried Nicholas. 'And the world shall deal by you as it does by me, till one or both of us shall quit it for a better. Come!'

With these words, he strapped his burden on his shoulders, and, taking his stick in one hand, extended the other to his delighted charge; and so they passed out of the old barn together.

CHAPTER XIV

HAVING THE MISFORTUNE TO TREAT OF NONE BUT COMMON PEOPLE, IS NECESSARILY OF A MEAN AND VULGAR CHARACTER

IN that quarter of London in which Golden Square is situated, there is a bygone, faded, tumble-down street, with two irregular rows of tall meagre houses, which seem to have stared each other out of countenance, years ago. The very chimneys appear to have grown dismal and melancholy, from having had nothing better to look at, than the chimneys over the way. Their tops are battered, and broken, and blackened with smoke; and, here and there, some taller stack than the rest, inclining heavily to one side, and toppling over the roof, seems to meditate taking revenge for half a century's neglect, by crushing the inhabitants of the garrets beneath.

The fowls who peck about the kennels, jerking their bodies hither and thither with a gait which none but town fowls are ever seen to adopt, and which any country cock or hen would be puzzled to understand, are perfectly in keeping with the crazy habitations of their owners. Dingy, ill-plumed drowsy flutterers, sent, like many of the neighbouring children, to get a livelihood in the streets, they hop, from stone to stone, in forlorn search of some hidden eatable in the mud, and can scarcely raise a crow among them. The only one with anything approaching to a voice, is an aged bantam at the baker's; and even he is hoarse, in consequence of bad living in his last place.

To judge from the size of the houses, they have been, at one time, tenanted by persons of better condition than their present occupants; but they are now let off, by the week, in floors or rooms, and every door has almost as many plates or bell-handles as there are apartments within. The windows are, for the same reason, sufficiently diversified in appearance, being ornamented with every variety of common blind and curtain that can easily be imagined; while every doorway is blocked up, and rendered nearly impassable, by a motely collection of children and porter pots of all sizes, from the baby in arms and the half-pint pot, to the full-grown girl and half-gallon can.

In the parlour of one of these houses, which was perhaps a thought dirtier than any of its neighbours; which exhibited more bell-handles, children, and porter pots, and caught in all its freshness the first gust of the thick black smoke that poured forth, night and day, from a large brewery hard by; hung a bill, announcing that there was yet one room to let within its walls, though on what story the vacant room could be—regard being had to the outward tokens of many lodgers which the whole front displayed, from the mangle in the kitchen window to the flower-pots on the parapet— it would have been beyond the power of a calculating boy to discover.

The common stairs of this mansion were bare and carpetless; but a curious visitor who had to climb his way to the top, might have observed that there were not wanting indications of the progressive poverty of the inmates, although their rooms were shut. Thus, the first-floor lodgers, being flush of furniture, kept an old mahogany table—real mahogany—on the landing-place outside, which was only taken in, when occasion required. On the second story, the spare furniture dwindled down to a couple of old deal chairs, of which one, belonging to the back-room, was shorn of a leg, and bottomless. The story above, boasted no greater excess than a worm-eaten wash-tub; and the garret landing-place displayed no costlier articles than two crippled pitchers, and some broken blacking-bottles.

It was on this garret landing-place that a hard-featured square-faced man, elderly and shabby, stopped to unlock the door of the front attic, into which, having surmounted the task of turning the rusty key in its still more rusty wards, he walked with the air of legal owner.

This person wore a wig of short, coarse, red hair, which he took off with his hat, and hung upon a nail. Having adopted in its place a dirty cotton nightcap, and groped about in the dark till he found a remnant of candle, he knocked at the partition which divided the two garrets, and inquired, in a loud voice, whether Mr. Noggs had a light.

The sounds that came back, were stifled by the lath and plaster, and it seemed moreover as though the speaker had uttered them from the interior of a mug or other drinking vessel; but they were in the voice of Newman, and conveyed a reply in the affirmative.

'A nasty night, Mr. Noggs!' said the man in the nightcap, stepping in to light his candle.

'Does it rain?' asked Newman.

'Does it?' replied the other pettishly. 'I am wet through.'

'It doesn't take much to wet you and me through, Mr. Crowl,' said Newman, laying his hand upon the lappel of his threadbare coat.

'Well; and that makes it the more vexatious,' observed Mr. Crowl, in the same pettish tone.

Uttering a low querulous growl, the speaker, whose harsh countenance was the very epitome of selfishness, raked the scanty fire nearly out of the grate, and, emptying the glass which Noggs had pushed towards him, inquired where he kept his coals.

Newman Noggs pointed to the bottom of a cupboard, and Mr. Crowl, seizing the shovel, threw on half the stock: which Noggs very deliberately took off again, without saying a word.

'You have not turned saving, at this time of day, I hope?' said Crowl.

Newman pointed to the empty glass, as though it were a sufficient refutation of the charge, and briefly said that he was going downstairs to supper.

'To the Kenwigses?' asked Crowl.

Newman nodded assent.

'Think of that now!' said Crowl. 'If I didn't—thinking that you were certain not to go, because you said you wouldn't—tell Kenwigs I couldn't come, and make up my mind to spend the evening with you!'

'I was obliged to go,' said Newman. 'They would have me.'

'Well; but what's to become of me?' urged the selfish man, who never thought of anybody else. 'It's all your fault. I'll tell you what—I'll sit by your fire till you come back again.'

Newman cast a despairing glance at his small store of fuel, but, not having the courage to say no—a word which in all his life he never had said at the right time, either to himself or any one else—gave way to the proposed arrangement. Mr. Crowl immediately went about making himself as comfortable, with Newman Nogg's means, as circumstances would admit of his being made.

The lodgers to whom Crowl had made allusion under the designation of 'the Kenwigses,' were the wife and olive branches of one Mr. Kenwigs, a turner in ivory, who was looked upon as a person of some consideration on the premises, inasmuch as he occupied the whole of the first floor, comprising a suite of two rooms. Mrs. Kenwigs, too, was quite a lady in her manners, and of a very genteel family, having an uncle who collected a water-rate; besides which distinction, the two eldest of her little girls went twice a week to a dancing-school in the neighbourhood, and had flaxen hair, tied with blue ribands, hanging in luxuriant pigtails down their backs; and wore little white trousers with frills round the ankles—for all of which reasons, and many more equally valid but too numerous to mention, Mrs. Kenwigs was considered a very desirable person to know, and was the constant theme of all the gossips in the street, and even three or four doors round the corner at both ends.

It was the anniversary of that happy day on which

the Church of England as by law established, had bestowed Mrs. Kenwigs upon Mr. Kenwigs; and in grateful commemoration of the same, Mrs. Kenwigs had invited a few select friends to cards and a supper in the first floor, and had put on a new gown to receive them in; which gown, being of a flaming colour and made upon a juvenile principle, was so successful that Mr. Kenwigs said the eight years of matrimony and the five children seemed all a dream, and Mrs. Kenwigs younger and more blooming than on the very first Sunday he had kept company with her.

Beautiful as Mrs. Kenwigs looked when she was dressed though, and so stately that you would have supposed she had a cook and housemaid at least, and nothing to do but order them about, she had a world of trouble with the preparations; more, indeed, than she, being of a delicate and genteel constitution, could have sustained, had not the pride of housewifery upheld her. At last, however, all the things that had to be got together were got together, and all the things that had to be got out of the way were got out of the way, and everything was ready, and the collector himself having promised to come, fortune smiled upon the occasion.

The party was admirably selected. There were, first of all, Mr. Kenwigs and Mrs. Kenwigs, and four olive Kenwigses who sat up to supper; firstly, because it was but right that they should have a treat on such a day; and secondly, because their going to bed, in presence of the company, would have been inconvenient, not to say improper. Then, there was a young lady who had made Mrs. Kenwigs's dress, and who—it was the most convenient thing in the world —living in the two-pair back, gave up her bed to the baby, and got a little girl to watch it. Then, to match this young lady, was a young man, who had known Mr. Kenwigs when he was a bachelor, and was much esteemed by the ladies, as bearing the reputation of a rake. To these, were added a newly-married couple, who had visited Mr. and Mrs. Kenwigs in their courtship; and a sister of Mrs. Kenwigs's, who was quite a beauty; besides whom, there was another young man, supposed to entertain honourable designs upon the lady last mentioned; and Mr. Noggs, who was a genteel person to ask, because he had been a gentleman once. There were also an elderly lady from the back-parlour, and one more young lady, who, next to the collector, perhaps was the great lion of the party, being the daughter of a theatrical fireman, who 'went on' in the pantomime, and had the greatest turn for the stage that was ever known, being able to sing and recite in a manner that brought the tears into Mrs. Kenwigs's eyes. There was only one drawback upon the pleasure of seeing such friends, and that was, that the lady in the back-parlour, who was very fat, and turned of sixty, came in a low book-muslin dress and short kid gloves, which so exasperated Mrs. Kenwigs, that that lady assured her visitors, in private, that if it hadn't happened that the supper was cooking at the back-parlour grate at that moment, she certainly would have requested its representative to withdraw.

'My dear,' said Mr. Kenwigs, 'wouldn't it be better to begin a round game?'

'Kenwigs, my dear,' returned his wife, 'I am surprised at you. Would you begin without my uncle?'

'I forgot the collector,' said Kenwigs; 'oh no, that would never do.'

'He's so particular,' said Mrs. Kenwigs, turning to the other married lady, 'that if we began without him, I should be out of his will for ever.'

'Dear!' cried the married lady.

'You've no idea what he is,' replied Mrs. Kenwigs; 'and yet as good a creature as ever breathed.'

'The kindest-hearted man as ever was,' said Kenwigs.

'It goes to his heart, I believe, to be forced to cut the water off, when the people don't pay,' observed the bachelor friend, intending a joke.

'George,' said Mr. Kenwigs, solemnly, 'none of that, if you please.'

'It was only my joke,' said the friend, abashed.

'George,' rejoined Mr. Kenwigs, 'a joke is a wery good thing—a wery good thing—but when that joke is made at the expense of Mrs. Kenwigs's feelings, I set my face against it. A man in public life expects to be sneered at—it is the fault of his elewated sitiwation, and not of himself. Mrs. Kenwigs's relation is a public man, and that he knows, George, and that he can bear; but putting Mrs. Kenwigs out of the question (if I *could* put Mrs. Kenwigs out of the question on such an occasion as this), I have the honour to be connected with the collector by marriage; and I cannot allow these remarks in my—' Mr. Kenwigs was going to say 'house,' but he rounded the sentence with 'apartments.'

At the conclusion of these observations, which drew forth evidences of acute feeling from Mrs. Kenwigs, and had the intended effect of impressing the company with a deep sense of the collector's dignity, a ring was heard at the bell.

'That's him,' whispered Mr. Kenwigs, greatly excited. 'Morleena, my dear, run down and let your uncle in, and kiss him directly you get the door open. Hem! Let's be talking.'

Adopting Mr. Kenwigs's suggestion, the company spoke very loudly, to look easy and unembarrassed; and almost as soon as they had begun to do so, a short old gentleman in drabs and gaiters, with a face that might have been carved out of *lignum vitæ,* for anything that appeared to the contrary, was led playfully in by Miss Morleena Kenwigs, regarding whose uncommon Christian name it may be here remarked that it had been invented and composed by Mrs. Kenwigs previous to her first lying-in, for the special distinction of her eldest child, in case it should prove a daughter.

'Oh uncle, I am *so* glad to see you,' said Mrs. Kenwigs, kissing the collector affectionately on both cheeks. 'So glad!'

'Many happy returns of the day, my dear,' replied the collector, returning the compliment.

Now, this was an interesting thing. Here was a collector of water-rates, without his book, without his pen and ink, without his double knock, without his intimidation, kissing—actually kissing—an agreeable female, and leaving taxes, summonses, notices that he had called, or announcements that he would never call again, for two quarters' due, wholly out of the question. It was pleasant to see how the company looked on, quite absorbed in the sight, and to behold the nods and winks with which they expressed their gratification at finding so much humanity in a tax-gatherer.

'Where will you sit, uncle?' said Mrs. Kenwigs, in the full glow of family pride, which the appearance of her distinguished relation occasioned.

'Anywheres, my dear,' said the collector, 'I am not particular.'

Not particular! What a meek collector. If he had been an author, who knew his place, he couldn't have been more humble.

'Mr. Lillyvick,' said Kenwigs, addressing the collector, 'some friends here, sir, are very anxious for the honour of—thank you—Mr. and Mrs. Cutler, Mr. Lillyvick.'

'Proud to know you, sir,' said Mr. Cutler, 'I 've heerd of you very often.' These were not mere words of ceremony; for, Mr. Cutler, having kept house in Mr. Lillyvick's parish, had heard of him very often indeed. His attention in calling had been quite extraordinary.

'George, you know, I think, Mr. Lillyvick,' said Kenwigs; 'lady from downstairs—Mr. Lillyvick. Mr. Snewkes—Mr. Lillyvick. Miss Green—Mr. Lillyvick. Mr. Lillyvick—Miss Petowker of the Theatre Royal, Drury Lane. Very glad to make two public characters acquainted! Mrs. Kenwigs, my dear, will you sort the counters?'

Mrs. Kenwigs, with the assistance of Newman Noggs, (who, as he performed sundry little acts of kindness for the children, at all times and seasons, was humoured in his request to be taken no notice of, and was merely spoken about, in a whisper, as the decayed gentleman), did as she was desired; and the greater part of the guests sat down to speculation, while Newman himself, Mrs. Kenwigs, and Miss Petowker of the Theatre Royal, Drury Lane, looked after the supper-table.

While the ladies were thus busying themselves, Mr. Lillyvick was intent upon the game in progress, and as all should be fish that comes to a water-collector's net, the dear old gentleman was by no means scrupulous in appropriating to himself the property of his neighbours, which, on the contrary, he abstracted whenever an opportunity presented itself, smiling good-humouredly all the while, and making so many condescending speeches to the owners, that they were delighted with his amiability, and thought in their hearts that he deserved to be Chancellor of the Exchequer at least.

After a great deal of trouble, and the administration of many slaps on the head to the infant Kenwigses, whereof two of the most rebellious were summarily banished, the cloth was laid with much elegance, and a pair of boiled fowls, a large piece of pork, apple-pie, potatoes and greens, were served; at sight of which, the worthy Mr. Lillyvick vented a great many witticisms, and plucked up amazingly: to the immense delight and satisfaction of the whole body of admirers.

Very well and very fast the supper went off; no more serious difficulties occurring, than those which arose from the incessant demand for clean knives and forks: which made poor Mrs. Kenwigs wish, more than once, that private society adopted the principle of schools, and required that every guest should bring his own knife, fork, and spoon; which doubtless would be a great accommodation in many cases, and to no one more so than to the lady and gentleman of the house, especially if the school principle were carried out to the full extent, and the articles were expected, as a matter of delicacy, not to be taken away again.

Everybody having eaten everything, the table was cleared in a most alarming hurry, and with great noise; and the spirits, whereat the eyes of Newman Noggs glistened, being arranged in order, with water both hot and cold, the party composed themselves for conviviality; Mr. Lillyvick being stationed in a large arm-chair by the fireside, and the four little Kenwigses disposed on a small form in front of the company with their flaxen tails towards them, and their faces to the fire; an arrangement which was no sooner perfected, than Mrs. Kenwigs was overpowered by the feelings of a mother, and fell upon the left shoulder of Mr. Kenwigs dissolved in tears.

'They are so beautiful!' said Mrs. Kenwigs, sobbing.

'Oh, dear,' said all the ladies, 'so they are! it's very natural you should feel proud of that; but don't give way, don't.'

'I can—not help it, and it don't signify,' sobbed Mrs. Kenwigs; 'oh! they're too beautiful to live, much too beautiful!'

On hearing this alarming presentiment of their being doomed to an early death in the flower of their infancy, all four little girls raised a hideous cry, and burying their heads in their mother's lap simultaneously, screamed until the eight flaxen tails vibrated again; Mrs. Kenwigs meanwhile clasping them alternately to her bosom, with attitudes expressive of distraction, which Miss Petowker herself might have copied.

At length, the anxious mother permitted herself to be soothed into a more tranquil state, and the little Kenwigses, being also composed, were distributed among the company, to prevent the possibility of Mrs. Kenwigs being again overcome by the blaze of their combined beauty. This done, the ladies and gentlemen united in prophesying that they would live for many, many years, and that there was no occasion at all for Mrs. Kenwigs to distress herself: which, in good truth, there did not appear to be; the loveliness of the children by no means justifying her apprehensions.

'This day eight year,' said Mr. Kenwigs after a pause. 'Dear me—ah!'

This reflection was echoed by all present, who said 'Ah!' first, and 'dear me,' afterwards.

'I was younger then,' tittered Mrs. Kenwigs.

'No,' said the collector.

'Certainly not,' added everybody.

'I remember my niece,' said Mr. Lillyvick, surveying his audience with a grave air; 'I remember her, on that very afternoon, when she first acknowledged to her mother a partiality for Kenwigs. "Mother," she says, "I love him."'

' "Adore him," I said, uncle,' interposed Mrs. Kenwigs.

' "Love him," I think, my dear,' said the collector, firmly.

'Perhaps you are right, uncle,' replied Mrs. Kenwigs, submissively. 'I thought it was "adore."'

' "Love," my dear,' retorted Mr. Lillyvick. ' "Mother," she says, "I love him!" "What do I hear?" cries her mother; and instantly falls into strong conwulsions.'

A general exclamation of astonishment burst from the company.

'Into strong conwulsions,' repeated Mr. Lillyvick, regarding them with a rigid look. 'Kenwigs will excuse my saying, in the presence of friends, that there was a very great objection to him, on the ground that he was beneath the family, and would disgrace it. You remember, Kenwigs?'

'Certainly,' replied that gentleman, in no way displeased at the reminiscence, inasmuch as it proved, beyond all doubt, what a high family Mrs. Kenwigs came of.

'I shared in that feeling,' said Mr. Lillyvick: 'perhaps it was natural; perhaps it wasn't.'

A gentle murmur seemed to say, that, in one of Mr. Lillyvick's station, the objection was not only natural, but highly praiseworthy.

'I came round to him in time,' said Mr. Lillyvick.

'After they were married, and there was no help for it, I was one of the first to say that Kenwigs must be taken notice of. The family *did* take notice of him, in consequence, and on my representation; and I am bound to say—and proud to say—that I have always found him a very honest, well-behaved, upright, respectable sort of man. Kenwigs, shake hands.'

'I am proud to do it, sir,' said Mr. Kenwigs.

'So am I, Kenwigs,' rejoined Mr. Lillyvick.

'A very happy life I have led with your niece, sir,' said Kenwigs.

'It would have been your own fault if you had not, sir,' remarked Mr. Lillyvick.

'Morleena Kenwigs,' cried her mother, at this crisis, much affected, 'kiss your dear uncle!'

The young lady did as she was requested, and the three other little girls were successively hoisted up to the collector's countenance, and subjected to the same process, which was afterwards repeated on them by the majority of those present.

'Oh dear, Mrs. Kenwigs,' said Miss Petowker, 'while Mr. Noggs is making that punch to drink happy returns in, do let Morleena go through that figure dance before Mr. Lillyvick.'

'No, no, my dear,' replied Mrs. Kenwigs, 'it will only worry my uncle.'

'It can't worry him, I am sure,' said Miss Petowker. 'You will be very much pleased, won't you, sir?'

'That I am sure I shall,' replied the collector, glancing at the punch-mixer.

'Well then, I'll tell you what,' said Mrs. Kenwigs, 'Morleena shall do the steps, if uncle can persuade Miss Petowker to recite us the Blood-Drinker's Burial, afterwards.'

There was a great clapping of hands and stamping

of feet, at this proposition; the subject whereof, gently inclined her head several times, in acknowledgment of the reception.

'You know,' said Miss Petowker, reproachfully, 'that I dislike doing anything professional in private parties.'

'Oh, but not here!' said Mrs. Kenwigs. 'We are all so very friendly and pleasant, that you might as well be going through it in your own room; besides, the occasion—'

'I can't resist that,' interrupted Miss Petowker; 'anything in my humble power I shall be delighted to do.'

Mrs. Kenwigs and Miss Petowker had arranged a small *programme* of the entertainments between them, of which this was the prescribed order, but they had settled to have a little pressing on both sides, because it looked more natural. The company being all ready, Miss Petowker hummed a tune, and Morleena danced a dance; having previously had the soles of her shoes chalked, with as much care as if she were going on the tight-rope. It was a very beautiful figure, comprising a great deal of work for the arms, and was received with unbounded applause.

'If I was blessed with a—a child—' said Miss Petowker, blushing, 'of such genius as that, I would have her out at the Opera instantly.'

Mrs. Kenwigs sighed, and looked at Mr. Kenwigs, who shook his head, and observed that he was doubtful about it.

'Kenwigs is afraid,' said Mrs. K.

'What of?' inquired Miss Petowker, 'not of her failing?'

'Oh no,' replied Mrs. Kenwigs, 'but if she grew up what she is now,—only think of the young dukes and marquises.'

'Very right,' said the collector.

'Still,' submitted Miss Petowker, 'if she took a proper pride in herself, you know—'

'There's a good deal in that,' observed Mrs. Kenwigs, looking at her husband.

'I only know—' faltered Miss Petowker,—'it may be no rule to be sure—but I have never found any inconvenience or unpleasantness of that sort.'

Mr. Kenwigs, with becoming gallantry, said that settled the question at once, and that he would take the subject into his serious consideration. This being resolved upon, Miss Petowker was entreated to begin the Blood-Drinker's Burial; to which end, that young lady let down her back hair, and taking up her position at the other end of the room, with the bachelor friend posted in a corner, to rush out at the cue 'in death expire,' and catch her in his arms when she died raving mad, went through the performance with extraordinary spirit, and to the great terror of the little Kenwigses, who were all but frightened into fits.

The ecstasies consequent upon the effort had not yet subsided, and Newman (who had not been thoroughly sober at so late an hour for a long time,) had not yet been able to put in a word of announcement, that the punch was ready, when a hasty knock was heard at the room-door, which elicited a shriek from Mrs. Kenwigs, who immediately divined that the baby had fallen out of bed.

'Who is that?' demanded Mr. Kenwigs, sharply.

'Don't be alarmed, it's only me,' said Crowl, looking in, in his nightcap. 'The baby is very comfortable, for I peeped into the room as I came down, and it's fast asleep, and so is the girl; and I don't think the candle will set fire to the bed-curtain, unless a draught was to get into the room—it's **Mr. Noggs** that's wanted.'

'Me!' cried Newman, much astonished.

'Why, it *is* a queer hour, isn't it?' replied Crowl, who was not best pleased at the prospect of losing his fire; 'and they are queer-looking people, too, all covered with rain and mud. Shall I tell them to go away?'

'No,' said Newman, rising. 'People? How many?'

'Two,' rejoined Crowl.

'Want me? By name?' asked Newman.

'By name,' replied Crowl. 'Mr. Newman Noggs, as pat as need be.'

Newman reflected for a few seconds, and then hurried away, muttering that he would be back directly. He was as good as his word; for, in an exceedingly short time, he burst into the room, and seizing, without a word of apology or explanation, a lighted candle and tumbler of hot punch from the table, darted away like a madman.

'What the deuce is the matter with him?' exclaimed Crowl, throwing the door open. 'Hark! Is there any noise above?'

The guests rose in great confusion, and, looking in each other's faces with much perplexity and some fear, stretched their necks forward, and listened attentively.

CHAPTER XV

ACQUAINTS THE READER WITH THE CAUSE AND ORIGIN
OF THE INTERRUPTION DESCRIBED IN THE LAST
CHAPTER, AND WITH SOME OTHER MATTERS NECES-
SARY TO BE KNOWN

NEWMAN NOGGS scrambled in violent haste upstairs
with the steaming beverage, which he had so unceremoniously snatched from the table of Mr. Kenwigs, and indeed from the very grasp of the water-
rate collector, who was eyeing the contents of the
tumbler, at the moment of its unexpected abstraction,
with lively marks of pleasure visible in his countenance. He bore his prize straight to his own back-
garret, where, footsore and nearly shoeless, wet,
dirty, jaded, and disfigured with every mark of
fatiguing travel, sat Nicholas, and Smike, at once
the cause and partner of his toil: both perfectly worn
out, by their unwonted and protracted exertion.

Newman's first act was to compel Nicholas, with
gentle force, to swallow half of the punch at a breath,
nearly boiling as it was; and his next, to pour the remainder down the throat of Smike, who, never having tasted anything stronger than aperient medicine
in his whole life, exhibited various odd manifesta-
tions of surprise and delight, during the passage
of the liquor down his throat, and turned up his eyes
most emphatically when it was all gone.

'You are wet through,' said Newman, passing his
hand hastily over the coat which Nicholas had thrown
off; 'and I—I—haven't even a change,' he added,
with a wistful glance at the shabby clothes he wore
himself.

'I have dry clothes, or at least such as will serve

my turn well, in my bundle,' replied Nicholas. 'If you look so distressed to see me, you will add to the pain I feel already, at being compelled, for one night, to cast myself upon your slender means for aid and shelter.'

Newman did not look the least distressed to hear Nicholas talking in this strain; but, upon his young friend grasping him heartily by the hand, and assuring him that nothing but implicit confidence in the sincerity of his professions, and kindness of feeling towards himself, would have induced him, on any consideration, even to have made him acquainted with his arrival in London, Mr. Noggs brightened up again, and went about making such arrangements as were in his power for the comfort of his visitors, with extreme alacrity.

These were simple enough; poor Newman's means halting at a very considerable distance short for his inclinations; but, slight as they were, they were not made without much bustling and running about. As Nicholas had husbanded his scanty stock of money, so well that it was not yet quite expended, a supper of bread and cheese, with some cold beef from the cook's shop, was soon placed upon the table; and these viands being flanked by a bottle of spirits and a pot of porter, there was no ground for apprehension on the score of hunger or thirst, at all events. Such preparations as Newman had it in his power to make, for the accommodation of his guests during the night, occupied no very great time in completing; and as he had insisted, as an express preliminary, that Nicholas should change his clothes, and that Smike should invest himself in his solitary coat (which no entreaties would dissuade him from stripping off for the purpose), the travellers partook of their frugal fare, with more satisfaction than one of them at least had derived from many a better meal.

They then drew near the fire, which Newman Noggs had made up as well as he could, after the inroads of Crowl upon the fuel; and Nicholas, who had hitherto been restrained by the extreme anxiety of his friend that he should refresh himself after his journey, now pressed him with earnest questions concerning his mother and sister.

'Well'; replied Newman, with his accustomed taciturnity; 'both well.'

'They are living in the City still?' inquired Nicholas.

'They are,' said Newman.

'And my sister'—added Nicholas. 'Is she still engaged in the business which she wrote to tell me she thought she would like so much?'

Newman opened his eyes rather wider than usual, but merely replied by a gasp, which, according to the action of the head that accompanied it, was interpreted by his friend as meaning yes or no. In the present instance, the pantomime consisted of a nod, and not a shake; so Nicholas took the answer as a favorable one.

'Now listen to me,' said Nicholas, laying his hand on Newman's shoulder. 'Before I would make an effort to see them, I deemed it expedient to come to you, lest, by gratifying my own selfish desire, I should inflict an injury upon them which I can never repair. What has my uncle heard from Yorkshire?'

Newman opened and shut his mouth, several times, as though he were trying his utmost to speak, but could make nothing of it, and finally fixed his eyes on Nicholas with a grim and ghastly stare.

'What has he heard?' urged Nicholas, colouring. 'You see that I am prepared to hear the very worst that malice can have suggested. Why should you conceal it from me? I must know it sooner or later; and what purpose can be gained by trifling with the matter for a few minutes, when half the time would put me in possession of all that has occurred? Tell me at once, pray.'

'To-morrow morning,' said Newman; 'hear it to-morrow.'

'What purpose would that answer?' urged Nicholas.

'You would sleep the better,' replied Newman.

'I should sleep the worse,' answered Nicholas impatiently. 'Sleep! Exhausted as I am, and standing in no common need of rest, I cannot hope to close my eyes all night, unless you tell me everything.'

'And if I should tell you everything,' said Newman, hesitating.

'Why, then you may rouse my indignation or wound my pride,' rejoined Nicholas; 'but you will not break my rest; for if the scene were acted over again, I could take no other part than I have taken; and whatever consequences may accrue to myself from it, I shall never regret doing as I have done— never, if I starve or beg in consequence. What is a little poverty or suffering, to the disgrace of the basest and most inhuman cowardice! I tell you, if I had stood by, tamely and passively, I should have hated myself, and merited the contempt of every man in existence. The black-hearted scoundrel!'

With this gentle allusion to the absent Mr. Squeers, Nicholas repressed his rising wrath, and relating to Newman exactly what had passed at Dotheboys Hall, entreated him to speak out without more pressing. Thus adjured, Mr. Noggs took, from an old trunk, a sheet of paper, which appeared to have been scrawled over in great haste; and after sundry extraordinary demonstrations of reluctance, delivered himself in the following terms.

'My dear young man, you mustn't give way to
—this sort of thing will never do, you know—as to
getting on in the world, if you take everybody's part
that's ill-treated—Damn it, I am proud to hear of
it; and would have done it myself!'

Newman accompanied this very unusual outbreak
with a violent blow upon the table, as if, in the heat
of the moment, he had mistaken it for the chest or
ribs of Mr. Wackford Squeers. Having, by this
open declaration of his feelings, quite precluded himself from offering Nicholas any cautious worldly
advice (which had been his first intention), Mr.
Noggs went straight to the point.

'The day before yesterday,' said Newman, 'your
uncle received this letter. I took a hasty copy of
it, while he was out. Shall I read it?'

'If you please,' replied Nicholas. Newman
Noggs accordingly read as follows:—

Dotheboys Hall,
'SIR,   *'Thursday Morning.*

'My pa requests me to write to you, the doctors considering it doubtful whether he will ever
recuvver the use of his legs which prevents his holding a pen.

'We are in a state of mind beyond everything, and
my pa is one mask of brooses both blue and green
likewise two forms are steepled in his Goar. We
were kimpelled to have him carried down into the
kitchen where he now lays. You will judge from
this that he has been brought very low.

'When your nevew that you recommended for a
teacher had done this to my pa and jumped upon
his body with his feet and also langwedge which I
will not pollewt my pen with describing, he assaulted my ma with dreadful violence, dashed her

to the earth, and drove her back comb several inches into her head. A very little more and it must have entered her skull. We have a medical certifiket that if it had, the tortershell would have affected the brain.

'Me and my brother were then the victims of his feury since which we have suffered very much which leads us to the arrowing belief that we have received some injury in our insides, especially as no marks of violence are visible externally. I am screaming out loud all the time I write and so is my brother which takes off my attention rather and I hope will excuse mistakes.

'The monster having sasiated his thirst for blood ran away, taking with him a boy of desperate character that he had excited to rebellyon, and a garnet ring belonging to my ma, and not having been apprehended by the constables is supposed to have been took up by some stage-coach. My pa begs that if he comes to you the ring may be returned, and that you will let the thief and assassin go, as if we prosecuted him he would only be transported, and if he is let go he is sure to be hung before long which will save us trouble and be much more satisfactory. Hoping to hear from you when convenient

'I remain
'Yours and cetrer
'FANNY SQUEERS.

'*P.S.* I pity his ignorance and despise him.'

A profound silence succeeded to the reading of this choice epistle, during which Newman Noggs, as he folded it up, gazed with a kind of grotesque pity at the boy of desperate character therein re-

ferred to; who, having no more distinct preception of
the matter in hand, than that he had been the unfortunate cause of heaping trouble and falsehood
upon Nicholas, sat mute and dispirited, with a most
woebegone and heart-stricken look.

'Mr. Noggs,' said Nicholas, after a few moments'
reflection, 'I must go out at once.'

'Go out!' cried Newman.

'Yes,' said Nicholas, 'to Golden Square. Nobody
who knows me would believe this story of the ring;
but it may suit the purpose, or gratify the hatred
of Mr. Ralph Nickleby to feign to attach credence
to it. It is due—not to him, but to myself—that
I should state the truth; and moreover, I have a word
or two to exchange with him, which will not keep
cool.'

'They must,' said Newman.

'They must not, indeed,' rejoined Nicholas firmly,
as he prepared to leave the house.

'Hear me speak,' said Newman, planting himself
before his impetuous young friend. 'He is not
there. He is away from town. He will not be back
for three days; and I know that letter will not be
answered before he returns.'

'Are you sure of this?' asked Nicholas, chafing
violently, and pacing the narrow room with rapid
strides.

'Quite,' rejoined Newman. 'He had hardly read
it when he was called away. Its contents are known
to nobody but himself and us.'

'Are you certain?' demanded Nicholas, precipi-
tately; 'not even to my mother or sister? If I thought
that they—I will go there—I must see them.
Which is the way? Where is it?'

'Now, be advised by me,' said Newman, speaking
for the moment, in his earnestness, like any other

man—'make no effort to see even them, till he comes
home. I know the man. Do not seem to have been
tampering with anybody. When he returns, go
straight to him, and speak as boldly as you like.
Guessing at the real truth, he knows it as well as you
or I. Trust him for that.'

'You mean well to me, and should know him better than I can,' replied Nicholas, after some consideration. 'Well; let it be so.'

Newman, who had stood during the foregoing conversation with his back planted against the door,
ready to oppose any egress from the apartment by
force, if necessary, resumed his seat with much satisfaction; and as the water in the kettle was by this
time boiling, made a glassful of spirits and water for
Nicholas, and a cracked mugful for the joint accommodation of himself and Smike, of which the
two partook in great harmony, while Nicholas, leaning his head upon his hand, remained buried in
melancholy meditation.

Meanwhile, the company below stairs, after listening attentively and not hearing any noise which
would justify them in interfering for the gratification of their curiosity, returned to the chamber of
the Kenwigses, and employed themselves in hazard-
ing a great variety of conjectures relative to the
cause of Mr. Noggs's sudden disappearance and de-
tention.

'Lor, I'll tell you what,' said Mrs. Kenwigs.
'Suppose it should be an express sent up to say that
his property has all come back again!'

'Dear me,' said Mr. Kenwigs; 'it's not impossible.
Perhaps, in that case, we'd better send up and ask if
he won't take a little more punch.'

'Kenwigs!' said Mr. Lillyvick, in a loud voice,
'I'm surprised at you.'

'What's the matter, sir?' asked Mr. Kenwigs, with becoming submission to the collector of water-rates.

'Making such a remark as that, sir,' replied Mr. Lillyvick, angrily. 'He has had punch already, has he not, sir? I consider the way in which that punch was cut off, if I may use the expression, highly disrespectful to this company; scandalous, perfectly scandalous. It may be the custom to allow such things in this house, but it's not the kind of behaviour that I've been used to see displayed, and so I don't mind telling you, Kenwigs. A gentleman has a glass of punch before him to which he is just about to set his lips, when another gentleman comes and collars that glass of punch, without a "with your leave," or "by your leave," and carries that glass of punch away. This may be good manners—I dare say it is—but I don't understand it, that's all; and what's more, I don't care if I never do. It's my way to speak my mind, Kenwigs, and that is my mind; and if you don't like it, it's past my regular time for going to bed, and I can find my way home without making it later.'

Here was an untoward event! The collector had sat swelling and fuming in offended dignity for some minutes, and had now fairly burst out. The great man—the rich relation—the unmarried uncle—who had it in his power to make Morleena an heiress, and the very baby a legatee—was offended. Gracious Powers, where was this to end?

'I am very sorry, sir,' said Mr. Kenwigs, humbly.

'Don't tell me you're sorry,' retorted Mr. Lillyvick, with much sharpness. 'You should have prevented it, then.'

The company were quite paralysed by this domestic crash. The back-parlour sat with her mouth wide open, staring vacantly at the collector, in a stupor of dismay; the other guests were scarcely less overpowered by the great man's irritation. Mr. Kenwigs, not being skilful in such matters, only fanned the flame in attempting to extinguish it.

'I didn't think of it, I am sure, sir,' said that gentleman. 'I didn't suppose that such a little thing as a glass of punch would have put you out of temper.'

'Out of temper! What the devil do you mean by that piece of impertinence, Mr. Kenwigs?' said the collector. 'Morleena, child—give me my hat.'

'Oh, you 're not going, Mr. Lillyvick, sir,' interposed Miss Petowker, with her most bewitching smile.

But still Mr. Lillyvick, regardless of the siren, cried obdurately, 'Morleena, my hat!' upon the fourth repetition of which demand, Mrs. Kenwigs sunk back in her chair, with a cry that might have softened a water-butt, not to say a water-collector; while the four little girls (privately instructed to that effect) clasped their uncle's drab shorts in their arms, and prayed him, in imperfect English, to remain.

'Why should I stop here, my dears?' said Mr. Lillyvick; 'I 'm not wanted here.'

'Oh, do not speak so cruelly, uncle,' sobbed Mrs. Kenwigs, 'unless you wish to kill me.'

'I shouldn't wonder if some people were to say I did,' replied Mr. Lillyvick, glancing angrily at Kenwigs. 'Out of temper!'

'Oh! I cannot bear to see him look so, at my husband,' cried Mrs. Kenwigs. 'It 's so dreadful in families. Oh!'

'Mr. Lillyvick,' said Kenwigs, 'I hope, for the sake of your niece, that you won't object to be reconciled.'

The collector's features relaxed, as the company added their entreaties to those of his nephew-in-law. He gave up his hat, and held out his hand.

'There, Kenwigs,' said Mr. Lillyvick; 'and let me tell you, at the same time, to show you how much out of temper I was, that if I had gone away without another word, it would have made no difference respecting that pound or two which I shall leave among your children when I die.'

'Morleena Kenwigs,' cried her mother, in a torrent of affection, 'Go down upon your knees to your dear uncle, and beg him to love you all his life through, for he's more a angel than a man, and I've always said so.'

Miss Morleena approaching to do homage, in compliance with this injunction, was summarily caught up and kissed by Mr. Lillyvick; and thereupon Mrs. Kenwigs darted forward and kissed the collector, and an irrepressible murmur of applause broke from the company who had witnessed his magnanimity.

The worthy gentleman then became once more the life and soul of the society; being again reinstated in his old post of lion, from which high station the temporary distraction of their thoughts had for a moment dispossessed him. Quadruped lions are said to be savage, only when they are hungry; biped lions are rarely sulky longer than when their appetite for distinction remains unappeased. Mr. Lillyvick stood higher than ever; for he had shown his power; hinted at his property and testamentary intentions; gained great credit for disinterestedness and virtue; and, in addition to all, was finally accommodated with a much larger tumbler of punch than that which Newman Noggs had so feloniously made off with.

'I say! I beg everybody's pardon for intruding again,' said Crowl, looking in at this happy juncture; 'but what queer business this is, isn't it? Noggs has lived in this house, now going on for five years, and nobody has ever been to see him before, within the memory of the oldest inhabitant.'

'It's a strange time of night to be called away, sir, certainly,' said the collector; 'and the behaviour of Mr. Noggs himself, is, to say the least of it, mysterious.'

'Well, so it is,' rejoined Crowl; 'and I 'll tell you what 's more—I think these two geniuses, whoever they are, have run away from somewhere.'

'What makes you think that, sir?' demanded the collector, who seemed, by a tacit understanding, to have been chosen and elected mouthpiece to the company. 'You have no reason to suppose that they have run away from anywhere without paying the rates and taxes due, I hope?'

Mr. Crowl, with a look of some contempt, was about to enter a general protest against the payment of rates or taxes, under any circumstances, when he was checked by a timely whisper from Kenwigs, and several frowns and winks from Mrs. K., which providentially stopped him.

'Why the fact is,' said Crowl, who had been listening at Newman's door, with all his might and main; 'the fact is, that they have been talking so loud, that they quite disturbed me in my room, and so I couldn't help catching a word here, and a word there; and all I heard, certainly seemed to refer to their having bolted from some place or other. I don't wish to alarm Mrs. Kenwig; but I hope they haven't come from any gaol or hospital, and brought away a fever or some unpleasantness of that sort, which might be catching for the children.'

Mrs. Kenwigs was so overpowered by this supposition, that it needed all the tender attentions of Miss Petowker, of the Theatre Royal, Drury Lane, to restore her to anything like a state of calmness; not to mention the assiduity of Mr. Kenwigs, who held a fat smelling-bottle to his lady's nose, until it became matter of some doubt whether the tears which coursed down her face, were the result of feelings or *sal volatile.*

The ladies, having expressed their sympathy, singly and separately, fell, according to custom, into a little chorus of soothing expressions, among which, such condolences as 'Poor dear!'—'I should feel just the same, if I was her'—'To be sure, it's a very trying thing'—and 'Nobody but a mother knows what a mother's feelings is,' were among the most prominent, and most frequently repeated. In short, the opinion of the company was so clearly manifested, that Mr. Kenwigs was on the point of repairing to Mr. Noggs's room, to demand an explanation, and had indeed swallowed a preparatory glass of punch, with great inflexibility and steadiness of purpose, when the attention of all present was diverted by a new and terrible surprise.

This was nothing less than the sudden pouring forth of a rapid succession of the shrillest and most piercing screams, from an upper story; and to all appearance from the very two-pair back, in which the infant Kenwigs was at that moment enshrined. They were no sooner audible, than Mrs. Kenwigs, opining that a strange cat had come in, and sucked the baby's breath while the girl was asleep, made for the door, wringing her hands, and shrieking dismally; to the great consternation and confusion of the company.

'Mr. Kenwigs, see what it is; make haste!' cried the sister, laying violent hands upon Mrs. Kenwigs, and holding her back by force. 'Oh don't twist about so, dear, or I can never hold you.'

'My baby, my blessed, blessed, blessed, blessed

baby!' screamed Mrs. Kenwigs, making every blessed louder than the last. 'My own darling, sweet, innocent Lillyvick—Oh let me go to him. Let me go-o-o-o!'

Pending the utterance of these frantic cries, and the wails and lamentations of the four little girls, Mr. Kenwigs rushed upstairs to the room whence the sounds proceeded; at the door of which, he encountered Nicholas, with the child in his arms, who darted out with such violence, that the anxious father was thrown down six stairs, and alighted on the nearest landing-place, before he had found time to open his mouth to ask what was the matter.

'Don't be alarmed,' cried Nicholas, running down; 'here it is; it's all out, it's all over; pray compose yourselves; there's no harm done'; and with these, and a thousand other assurances, he delivered the baby (whom, in his hurry, he had carried upside down), to Mrs. Kenwigs, and ran back to assist Mr. Kenwigs, who was rubbing his head very hard, and looking much bewildered by his tumble.

Reassured by this cheering intelligence, the company in some degree recovered from their fears, which had been productive of some most singular instances of a total want of presence of mind; thus, the bachelor friend had, for a long time, supported in his arms Mrs. Kenwigs's sister, instead of Mrs. Kenwigs; and the worthy Mr. Lillyvick had been actually seen, in the perturbation of his spirits, to kiss Miss Petowker several times, behind the room-door, as calmly as if nothing distressing were going forward.

'It is a mere nothing,' said Nicholas, returning to Mrs. Kenwigs; 'the little girl, who was watching the child, being tired I suppose, fell asleep, and set her hair on fire.'

'Oh you malicious little wretch!' cried Mrs. Kenwigs, impressively shaking her forefinger at the small unfortunate, who might be thirteen years old, and was looking on with a singed head and a frightened face.

'I heard her cries,' continued Nicholas, 'and ran down, in time to prevent her setting fire to anything else. You may depend upon it that the child it not hurt; for I took it off the bed myself, and brought it here to convince you.'

This brief explanation over, the infant, who, as he was christened after the collector, rejoiced in the names of Lillyvick Kenwigs, was partially suffocated under the caresses of the audience, and squeezed to his mother's bosom, until he roared again. The attention of the company was then directed, by a natural transition, to the little girl who had had the audacity to burn her hair off, and who, after receiving sundry small slaps and pushes from the more energetic of the ladies, was mercifully sent home; the ninepence, with which she was to have been rewarded, being escheated to the Kenwigs family.

'And whatever we are to say to you, sir,' exclaimed Mrs. Kenwigs, addressing young Lillyvick's deliverer, 'I am sure I don't know.'

'You need say nothing at all,' replied Nicholas. 'I have done nothing to found any very strong claim upon your eloquence, I am sure.'

'He might have been burnt to death, if it hadn't been for you, sir,' simpered Miss Petowker.

'Not very likely, I think,' replied Nicholas; 'for there was abundance of assistance here, which must have reached him before he had been in any danger.'

'You will let us drink your health, anyvays, sir!' said Mr. Kenwigs, motioning towards the table.

'—In my absence, by all means,' rejoined Nicholas, with a smile. 'I have had a very fatiguing journey, and should be most indifferent company—a far greater check upon your merriment, than a promoter of it, even if I kept awake, which I think very doubtful. If you will allow me, I'll return to my friend, Mr. Noggs, who went upstairs again, when he found nothing serious had occurred. Good night.'

Excusing himself, in these terms, from joining in the festivities, Nicholas took a most winning farewell of Mrs. Kenwigs and the other ladies, and retired, after making a very extraordinary impression upon the company.

'What a delightful young man!' cried Mrs. Kenwigs.

'Uncommon gentlemanly, really,' said Mr. Kenwigs. 'Don't you think so, Mr. Lillyvick?'

'Yes,' said the collector, with a dubious shrug of his shoulders. 'He *is* gentlemanly, very gentlemanly—in appearance.'

'I hope you don't see anything against him, uncle?' inquired Mrs. Kenwigs.

'No, my dear,' replied the collector, 'no. I trust he may not turn out—well—no matter—my love to you, my dear, and long life to the baby!'

'Your namesake,' said Mrs. Kenwigs, with a sweet smile.

"And I hope a worthy namesake,' observed Mr. Kenwigs, willing to propitiate the collector. 'I hope a baby as will never disgrace his godfather, and as may be considered, in arter years, of a piece with the Lillyvicks whose name he bears. I do say—and Mrs. Kenwigs is of the same sentiment, and feels it as strong as I do—that I consider his being called Lillyvick one of the greatest blessings and *h*onours of my existence.'

'*The* greatest blessing, Kenwigs,' murmured his lady.

'*The* greatest blessing,' said Mr. Kenwigs, correcting himself. 'A blessing that I hope, one of these days, I may be able to deserve.'

This was a politic stroke of the Kenwigses, because it made Mr. Lillyvick the great head and fountain of the baby's importance. The good gentleman felt the delicacy and dexterity of the touch, and at once proposed the health of the gentleman, name unknown, who had signalised himself, that night, by his coolness and alacrity.

'Who, I don't mind saying,' observed Mr. Lillyvick, as a great concession, 'is a good-looking young man enough, with manners that I hope his character may be equal to.'

'He has a very nice face and style, really,' said Mrs. Kenwigs.

'He certainly has,' added Miss Petowker. 'There's something in his appearance quite—dear, dear, what's that word again?'

'What word?' inquired Mr. Lillyvick.

'Why—dear me, how stupid I am,' replied Miss Petowker, hesitating. 'What do you call it, when lords break off door-knockers and beat policemen, and play at coaches with other people's money, and all that sort of thing?'

'Aristocratic?' suggested the collector.

'Ah! aristocratic,' replied Miss Petowker; 'something very aristocratic about him, isn't there?'

The gentlemen held their peace, and smiled at each other, as who should say, 'Well! there's no accounting for tastes': but the ladies resolved unanimously that Nicholas had an aristocratic air; and nobody caring to dispute the position, it was established, triumphantly.

The punch being, by this time, drunk out, and the little Kenwigses (who had for some time previously

held their little eyes open with their little forefingers)
becoming fractious, and requesting rather urgently
to be put to bed, the collector made a move by pulling out his watch, and acquainting the company that
it was nigh two o'clock; whereat some of the guests
were surprised and others shocked, and hats and bonnets being groped for under the tables, and in course
of time found, their owners went away, after a vast
deal of shaking of hands, and many remarks how they
had never spent such a delightful evening, and how
they marvelled to find it so late, expecting to have
heard that it was half-past ten at the very latest, and
how they wished that Mr. and Mrs. Kenwigs had a
wedding-day once a week, and how they wondered by
what hidden agency Mrs. Kenwigs could possibly have
managed so well; and a great deal more of the same
kind.   To all of which flattering expressions, Mr. and
Mrs. Kenwigs replied, by thanking every lady and
gentleman, *seriatim,* for the favour of their company,
and hoping they might have enjoyed themselves only
half as well as they said they had.

As to Nicholas, quite unconscious of the impression
he had produced, he had long since fallen asleep, leaving Mr. Newman Noggs and Smike to empty the
spirit bottle between them; and this office they performed with such extreme good-will, that Newman
was equally at a loss to determine whether he himself was quite sober, and whether he had ever seen
any gentleman so heavily, drowsily, and completely in-
toxicated, as his new acquaintance.

CHAPTER XVI

NICHOLAS SEEKS TO EMPLOY HIMSELF IN A NEW
CAPACITY, AND BEING UNSUCCESSFUL, ACCEPTS AN
ENGAGEMENT AS TUTOR IN A PRIVATE FAMILY

THE first care of Nicholas, next morning was, to look
after some room in which, until better times dawned
upon him, he could contrive to exist, without trench-
ing upon the hospitality of Newman Noggs, who
would have slept upon the stairs with pleasure, so
that his young friend was accommodated.

The vacant apartment to which the bill in the parlour window bore reference, appeared, on inquiry, to
be a small back-room on the second floor, reclaimed
from the leads, and overlooking a soot-bespeckled
prospect of tiles and chimney-pots. For the letting
of this portion of the house from week to week, on
reasonable terms, the parlour lodger was empowered
to treat; he being deputed by the landlord to dispose
of the rooms as they became vacant, and to keep a
sharp look-out that the lodgers didn't run away. As
a means of securing the punctual discharge of which
last service he was permitted to live rent-free, lest he
should at any time be tempted to run away himself.

Of this chamber, Nicholas became the tenant; and
having hired a few common articles of furniture from
a neighbouring broker, and paid the first week's hire
in advance, out of a small fund raised by the conver-
sion of some spare clothes into ready money, he sat
himself down to ruminate upon his prospects, which,
like the prospect outside his window, were sufficiently
confined and dingy. As they by no means improved
on better acquaintance, and as familiarity breeds contempt, he resolved to banish them from his thoughts

by dint of hard walking. So, taking up his hat, and leaving poor Smike to arrange and re-arrange the room with as much delight as if it had been the costliest palace, he betook himself to the streets, and mingled with the crowd which thronged them.

Although a man may lose a sense of his own importance when he is a mere unit among a busy throng, all utterly regardless of him, it by no means follows that he can dispossess himself, with equal facility, of a very strong sense of the importance and magnitude of his cares. The unhappy state of his own affairs was the one idea which occupied the brain of Nicholas, walk as fast as he would; and when he tried to dislodge it by speculating on the situation and prospects of the people who surrounded him, he caught himself, in a few seconds, contrasting their condition with his own, and gliding almost imperceptibly back into his own train of thoughts again.

Occupied in these reflections, as he was making his way along one of the great public thoroughfares of London, he chanced to raise his eyes to a blue board, whereon was inscribed, in characters of gold, 'General Agency Office; for places and situations of all kinds inquire within.' It was a shop-front, fitted up with a gauze blind and an inner door; and in the window hung a long and tempting array of written placards, announcing vacant places of every grade, from a secretary's to a footboy's.

Nicholas halted, instinctively, before this temple of promise, and ran his eye over the capital-text openings in life which were so profusely displayed. When he had completed his survey he walked on a little way, and then back, and then on again; at length, after pausing irresolutely several times before the door of the General Agency Office, he made up his mind, and stepped in.

He found himself in a little floor-clothed room, with a high desk railed off in one corner, behind which sat a lean youth with cunning eyes and a protruding chin, whose performances in capital-text darkened the window. He had a thick ledger lying open before him, and with the fingers of his right hand inserted between the leaves, and his eyes fixed on a very fat old lady in a mob-cap—evidently the proprietress of the establishment—who was airing herself at the fire, seemed to be only waiting her directions to refer to some entries contained within its rusty clasps.

As there was a board outside, which acquainted the public that servants-of-all-work were perpetually in waiting to be hired from ten till four, Nicholas knew at once that some half-dozen strong young women, each with pattens and an umbrella, who were sitting upon a form in one corner, were in attendance for that purpose: especially as the poor things looked anxious and weary. He was not quite so certain of the callings and stations of two smart young ladies who were in conversation with the fat lady before the fire, until —having sat himself down in a corner, and remarked that he would wait until the other customers had been served—the fat lady resumed the dialogue which his entrance had interrupted.

'Cook, Tom,' said the fat lady, still airing herself as aforesaid.

'Cook,' said Tom, turning over some leaves of the ledger, 'Well!'

'Read out an easy place or two,' said the fat lady.

'Pick out very light ones, if you please, young man,' interposed a genteel female, in shepherd's-plaid boots, who appeared to be the client.

' "Mrs. Marker," ' said Tom, reading, ' "Russell Place, Russell Square; offers eighteen guineas; tea and sugar found. Two in family, and see very little company. Five servants kept. No man. No followers." '

'Oh Lor!' tittered the client. '*That* won't do. Read another, young man, will you?'

' "Mrs. Wrymug," ' said Tom, ' "Pleasant Place, Finsbury. Wages, twelve guineas. No tea, no sugar. Serious family—" '

'Ah! you needn't mind reading that,' interrupted the client.

' "Three serious footmen," ' said Tom, impressively.

'Three? did you say?' asked the client in an altered tone.

'Three serious footmen,' replied Tom. ' "Cook, housemaid, and nursemaid; each female servant required to join the Little Bethel Congregation three times every Sunday—with a serious footman. If the cook is more serious than the footman, she will be expected to improve the footman; if the footman is more serious than the cook, he will be expected to improve the cook." '

'I 'll take the address of that place,' said the client; 'I don't know but what it mightn't suit me pretty well.'

'Here 's another,' remarked Tom, turning over the leaves; ' "Family of Mr. Gallanbile, M.P. Fifteen guineas, tea and sugar, and servants allowed to see male cousins, if godly. Note. Cold dinner in the kitchen on the Sabbath, Mr. Gallanbile being devoted to the Observance question. No victuals whatever, cooked on the Lord's Day, with the exception of dinner for Mr. and Mrs. Gallanbile, which, being a work of piety and necessity, is exempted. Mr. Gallanbile dines late on the day of rest, in order to prevent the sinfulness of the cook's dressing herself." '

'I don't think that 'll answer as well as the other,' said the client, after a little whispering with her friend. 'I 'll take the other direction, if you please, young man. I can but come back again, if it don't do.'

Tom made out the address, as requested, and the genteel client, having satisfied the fat lady with a small fee, meanwhile, went away, accompanied by her friend.

As Nicholas opened his mouth, to request the young man to turn to letter S, and let him know what secretaryships remained undisposed of, there came into the office an applicant, in whose favour he immediately retired, and whose appearance both surprised and interested him.

This was a young lady who could be scarcely eighteen, of very slight and delicate figure, but exquisitely shaped, who, walking timidly up to the desk, made an inquiry, in a very low tone of voice, relative to some situation as governess, or companion to a lady. She raised her veil, for an instant, while she preferred the inquiry, and disclosed a countenance of most uncommon beauty, though shaded by a cloud of sadness, which, in one so young, was doubly remarkable. Having received a card of reference to some person on the books, she made the usual acknowledgment, and glided away.

She was neatly, but very quietly attired; so much so, indeed, that it seemed as though her dress, if it had been worn by one who imparted fewer graces of her own to it, might have looked poor and shabby. Her attendant—for she had one—was a red-faced, round-eyed, slovenly girl, who, from a certain roughness about the bare arms that peeped from under her draggled shawl, and the half-washed-out traces of smut and blacklead which tattooed her countenance, was clearly of a kin with the servants-of-all-work on the form: between whom and herself there had passed various grins and glances, indicative of the freemasonry of the craft.

This girl followed her mistress; and, before Nicholas had recovered from the first effects of his surprise and admiration, the young lady was gone. It is not a matter of such complete and utter improbability as some sober people may think, that he would have followed them out, had he not been restrained by what passed between the fat lady and her book-keeper.

'When is she coming again, Tom?' asked the fat lady.

'To-morrow morning,' replied Tom, mending his pen.

'Where have you sent her to?' asked the fat lady.

'Mrs. Clark's,' replied Tom.

'She 'll have a nice life of it, if she goes there,' observed the fat lady, taking a pinch of snuff from a tin box.

Tom made no other reply than thrusting his tongue into his cheek, and pointing the feather of his pen towards Nicholas—reminders which elicited from the fat lady an inquiry, of, 'Now, sir, what can we do for *you?*'

Nicholas briefly replied, that he wanted to know whether there was any such post to be had, as secretary or amanuensis to a gentleman.

'Any such!' rejoined the mistress; 'a dozen such. An't there, Tom?'

'*I* should think so,' answered that young gentleman; and as he said it, he winked towards Nicholas, with a degree of familiarity which he, no doubt, intended for a rather flattering compliment, but with which Nicholas was most ungratefully disgusted.

Upon reference to the book, it appeared that the dozen secretaryships had dwindled down to one. Mr. Gregsbury, the great member of Parliament, of Manchester Buildings, Westminster, wanted a young man, to keep his papers and correspondence in order; and Nicholas was exactly the sort of young man that Mr. Gregsbury wanted.

'I don't know what the terms are, as he said he'd settle them himself with the party,' observed the fat lady; 'but they must be pretty good ones, because he's a member of Parliament.'

Inexperienced as he was, Nicholas did not feel quite assured of the force of this reasoning, or the justice of this conclusion; but without troubling himself to question it, he took down the address, and resolved to wait upon Mr. Gregsbury, without delay.

'I don't know what the number is,' said Tom; 'but Manchester Buildings isn't a large place; and if the worst comes to the worst, it won't take you very long to knock at all the doors on both sides of the way till you find him out. I say, what a good-looking gal that was, wasn't she?'

'What girl?' demanded Nicholas, sternly.

'Oh yes. I know—what gal, eh?' whispered Tom, shutting one eye, and cocking his chin in the air. 'You didn't see her, you didn't—I say, don't you wish you was me, when she comes to-morrow morning?'

Nicholas looked at the ugly clerk, as if he had a mind to reward his admiration of the young lady by beating the ledger about his ears, but he refrained, and strode haughtily out of the office; setting at defiance, in his indignation, those ancient laws of chivalry, which not only made it proper and lawful for all good knights to hear the praise of the ladies to whom they were devoted, but rendered it incumbent upon them to roam about the world, and knock on the head all such matter-of-fact and unpoetical characters, as declined to exalt, above all the earth, damsels whom they had never chanced to look upon or hear of—as if that were any excuse!

Thinking no longer of his own misfortunes, but wondering what could be those of the beautiful girl he had seen, Nicholas, with many wrong turns, and many inquiries, and almost as many misdirections, bent his steps towards the place whither he had been directed.

Within the precincts of the ancient city of Westminster, and within half a quarter of a mile of its ancient sanctuary, is a narrow and dirty region, the sanctuary of the smaller members of Parliament in modern days. It is all comprised in one street of gloomy lodging-houses, from whose windows, in vacation-time, there frown long melancholy rows of bills, which say, as plainly as did the countenances of their occupiers, ranged on ministerial and opposition benches in the session which slumbers with its fathers, 'To Let,' 'To Let.' In busier periods of the year these bills disappear, and the houses swarm with legislators. There are legislators in the parlours, in the first floor, in the second, in the third, in the garrets; the small apartments reek with the breath of deputations and delegates. In damp weather, the place is rendered close, by the steams of moist acts of Parliament and frowsy petitions; general postmen grow faint as they enter its infected limits, and shabby figures in quest of franks, flit restlessly to and fro like the troubled ghosts of Complete Letter-writers departed. This is Manchester Buildings; and here, at all hours of the night, may be heard the rattling of latchkeys in their respective keyholes: with now and then—when a gust of wind sweeping across the water which washes the Buildings' feet, impels the sound towards its entrance—the weak, shrill voice of some young member practising to-morrow's speech. All the livelong day, there is a grinding of organs and clashing and clanging of little boxes of music; for Manchester Buildings is an eel-pot, which has no outlet but its awkward mouth —a case-bottle which has no thoroughfare, and a short and narrow neck—and in this respect it may be typical of the fate of some few among its more adventurous residents, who, after wriggling themselves into Parliament by violent efforts and contortions, find that it, too, is no thoroughfare for them; that, like Manchester Buildings, it leads to nothing beyond itself; and that they are fain at last to back out, no wiser, no richer, not one whit more famous than they went in.

Into Manchester Buildings Nicholas turned, with the address of the great Mr. Gregsbury in his hand. As there was a stream of people pouring into a shabby house not far from the entrance, he waited until they had made their way in, and then making up to the servant, ventured to inquire if he knew where Mr. Gregsbury lived.

The servant was a very pale, shabby boy, who looked as if he had slept underground from his infancy, as very likely he had. 'Mr. Gregsbury?' said he; 'Mr. Gregsbury lodges here. It's all right. Come in!'

Nicholas thought he might as well get in while he could, so in he walked; and he had no sooner done so, than the boy shut the door, and made off.

This was odd enough; but what was more embarrassing was, that all along the passage, and all along the narrow stairs, blocking up the window and making the dark entry darker still, was a confused crowd of persons with great importance depicted in their looks; who were, to all appearance, waiting in silent expectation of some coming event. From time to

time, one man would whisper to his neighbour, or a
little group would whisper together, and then the
whisperers would nod fiercely to each other, or give
their heads a relentless shake, as if they were bent
upon doing something very desperate, and were determined not to be put off, whatever happened.

As a few minutes elapsed without anything occurring to explain this phenomenon, and as he felt his
own position a peculiarly uncomfortable one, Nicholas was on the point of seeking some information
from the man next him, when a sudden move was
visible on the stairs, and a voice was heard to cry,
'Now, gentlemen, have the goodness to walk up!'

So far from walking up, the gentlemen on the stairs
began to walk down with great alacrity, and to entreat, with extraordinary politeness, that the gentleman nearest the street would go first; the gentleman
nearest the street retorted, with equal courtesy, that
they couldn't think of such a thing on any account;
but they did it, without thinking of it, inasmuch as
the other gentlemen pressing some half-dozen (among
whom was Nicholas) forward, and closing up behind,
pushed them, not merely up the stairs, but into the
very sitting-room of Mr. Gregsbury, which they were
thus compelled to enter with most unseemly precipitation, and without the means of retreat; the press behind them, more than filling the apartment.

'Gentlemen,' said Mr. Gregsbury, 'you are welcome
I am rejoiced to see you.'

For a gentleman who was rejoiced to see a body
of visitors, Mr. Gregsbury looked as uncomfortable
as might be; but perhaps this was occasioned by sena-
torial gravity, and a statesmanlike habit of keeping
his feelings under control. He was a tough, burly,
thick-headed gentleman, with a loud voice, a pompous

manner, a tolerable command of sentences with no meaning in them, and, in short, every requisite for a very good member indeed.

'Now, gentlemen,' said Mr. Gregsbury, tossing a great bundle of papers into a wicker basket at his feet, and throwing himself back in his chair with his arms over the elbows, 'you are dissatisfied with my conduct, I see by the newspapers.'

'Yes, Mr. Gregsbury, we are,' said a plump old gentleman in a violent heat, bursting out of the throng, and planting himself in the front.

'Do my eyes deceive me,' said Mr. Gregsbury, looking towards the speaker, 'or is that my old friend Pugstyles?'

'I am that man, and no other, sir,' replied the plump old gentleman.

'Give me your hand, my worthy friend,' said Mr. Gregsbury. 'Pugstyles, my dear friend, I am very sorry to see you here.'

'I am very sorry to be here, sir,' said Mr. Pugstyles; 'but your conduct, Mr. Gregsbury, has rendered this deputation from your constituents, imperatively necessary.'

'My conduct, Pugstyles,' said Mr. Gregsbury, looking round upon the deputation with gracious magnanimity—'My conduct has been, and ever will be, regulated by a sincere regard for the true and real interests of this great and happy country. Whether I look at home, or abroad; whether I behold the peaceful industrious communities of our island home: her rivers covered with steamboats, her roads with locomotives, her streets with cabs, her skies with balloons of a power and magnitude hitherto unknown in the history of aëronautics in this or any other nation—I say, whether I look merely at home, or, stretching my eyes farther, contemplate the boundless prospect of conquest and possession—achieved by British perseverance and British valour—which is outspread before me, I clasp my hands, and turning my eyes to the broad expanse above my head, exclaim, "Thank Heaven, I am a Briton!"'

The time had been, when this burst of enthusiasm would have been cheered to the very echo; but now, the deputation received it with chilling coldness. The general impression seemed to be, that as an explanation of Mr. Gregsbury's political conduct, it did not enter quite enough into detail; and one gentleman in the rear did not scruple to remark aloud, that, for his purpose, it savoured rather too much of a 'gammon' tendency.

'The meaning of that term—gammon,' said Mr. Gregsbury, 'is unknown to me. If it means that I grow a little too fervid, or perhaps even hyperbolical, in extolling my native land, I admit the full justice of the remark. I *am* proud of this free and happy country. My form dilates, my eye glistens, my breast heaves, my heart swells, my bosom burns, when I call to mind her greatness and her glory.'

'We wish, sir,' remarked Mr. Pugstyles, calmly, 'to ask you a few questions.'

'If you please, gentlemen; my time is yours—and my country's—and my country's—' said Mr. Gregsbury.

This permission being conceded, Mr. Pugstyles put on his spectacles, and referred to a written paper which he drew from his pocket; whereupon nearly every other member of the deputation pulled a written paper from *his* pocket, to check Mr. Pugstyles off, as he read the questions.

This done, Mr. Pugstyles proceeded to business.

'Question number one.—Whether, sir, you did not give a voluntary pledge previous to your election, that in event of your being returned, you would immediately put down the practice of coughing and groaning in the House of Commons? And whether you did not submit to be coughed and groaned down in the very first debate of the session, and have since made no effort to effect a reform in this respect? Whether you did not also pledge yourself to astonish the government, and make them shrink in their shoes? And whether you have astonished them, and made them shrink in their shoes, or not?'

'Go on to the next one, my dear Pugstyles,' said Mr. Gregsbury.

'Have you any explanation to offer with reference to that question, sir?' asked Mr. Pugstyles.

'Certainly not,' said Mr. Gregsbury.

The members of the deputation looked fiercely at each other, and afterwards at the member. 'Dear Pugstyles' having taken a very long stare at Mr. Gregsbury over the tops of his spectacles, resumed his list of inquiries.

'Question number two.—Whether, sir, you did not likewise give a voluntary pledge that you would support your colleague on every occasion; and whether you did not, the night before last, desert him and vote upon the other side, because the wife of a leader on that other side had invited Mrs. Gregsbury to an evening party?'

'Go on,' said Mr. Gregsbury.

'Nothing to say on that, either, sir?' asked the spokesman.

'Nothing whatever,' replied Mr. Gregsbury. The deputation, who had only seen him at canvassing or election time, were struck dumb by his coolness. He didn't appear like the same man; then he was all milk and honey; now he was all starch and vinegar. But men *are* so different at different times!

'Question number three—and last—' said Mr. Pugstyles, emphatically. 'Whether, sir, you did not state upon the hustings, that it was your firm and determined intention to oppose everything proposed; to divide the house upon every question, to move for returns on every subject, to place a motion on the books every day, and, in short, in your own memorable words, to play the very devil with everything and everybody?' With this comprehensive inquiry, Mr. Pugstyles folded up his list of questions, as did all his backers.

Mr. Gregsbury reflected, blew his nose, threw himself further back in his chair, came forward again, leaning his elbows on the table, made a triangle with his two thumbs and his two forefingers, and tapping his nose with the apex thereof, replied (smiling as he said it), 'I deny everything.'

At this unexpected answer, a hoarse murmur arose from the deputation; and the same gentleman who had expressed an opinion relative to the gammoning nature of the introductory speech, again made a monosyllabic demonstration, by growling out 'Resign!' Which growl being taken up by his fellows, swelled into a very earnest and general remonstrance.

'I am requested, sir, to express a hope,' said Mr. Pugstyles, with a distant bow, 'that on receiving a requisition to that effect from a great majority of your constituents, you will not object at once to resign your seat in favour of some candidate whom they think they can better trust.'

To this, Mr. Gregsbury read the following reply, which, anticipating the request, he had composed in the form of a letter, whereof copies had been made to send round to the newspapers.

'MY DEAR MR. PUGSTYLES,

'Next to the welfare of our beloved island—this great and free and happy country, whose powers and resources are, I sincerely believe, illimitable—I value that noble independence which is an Englishman's proudest boast, and which I fondly hope to bequeath to my children, untarnished and unsullied. Actuated by no personal motives, but moved only by high and great constitutional considerations; which I will not attempt to explain, for they are really beneath the comprehension of those who have not made themselves masters, as I have, of the intricate and arduous study of politics; I would rather keep my seat, and intend doing so.

'Will you do me the favour to present my compliments to the constituent body, and acquaint them with this circumstance?

'With great esteem,
'My dear Mr. Pugstyles,
'Etc., etc'

'Then you will not resign, under any circumstances?' asked the spokesman.

Mr. Gregsbury smiled, and shook his head.

'Then, good morning, sir,' said Pugstyles, angrily.

'Heaven bless you!' said Mr. Gregsbury. And the deputation, with many growls and scowls, filed off as quickly as the narrowness of the staircase would allow of their getting down.

The last man being gone, Mr. Gregsbury rubbed his hands and chuckled, as merry fellows will, when then think they have said or done a more than commonly good thing; he was so engrossed in this self-congratulation, that he did not observe that Nicholas had been left behind in the shadow of the window-curtains, until that young gentleman, fearing he might otherwise overhear some soliloquy intended to have no listeners, coughed twice or thrice, to attract the member's notice.

'What's that?' said Mr. Gregsbury, in sharp accents.

Nicholas stepped forward and bowed.

'What do you do here, sir?' asked Mr. Gregsbury; 'a spy upon my privacy! A concealed voter! You have heard my answer, sir. Pray follow the deputation.'

'I should have done so, if I had belonged to it, but I do not,' said Nicholas.

'Then how came you here, sir?' was the natural inquiry of Mr. Gregsbury, M.P. 'And where the devil have you come from, sir?' was the question which followed it.

'I brought this card from the General Agency Office, sir,' said Nicholas, 'wishing to offer myself as your secretary, and understanding that you stood in need of one.'

'That's all you have come for, is it?' said Mr. Gregsbury, eyeing him in some doubt.

Nicholas replied in the affirmative.

'You have no connection with any of those rascally papers, have you?' said Mr. Gregsbury. 'You didn't get into the room to hear what was going forward, and put it in print, eh?'

'I have no connection, I am sorry to say, with anything at present,' rejoined Nicholas,—politely enough, but quite at his ease.

'Oh!' said Mr. Gregsbury. 'How did you find your way up here, then?'

Nicholas related how he had been forced up by the deputation.

'That was the way, was it?' said Mr. Gregsbury. 'Sit down.'

Nicholas took a chair, and Mr. Gregsbury stared at him for a long time, as if to make certain, before he asked any further questions, that there were no objections to his outward appearance.

'You want to be my secretary, do you?' he said at length.

'I wish to be employed in that capacity, sir,' replied Nicholas.

'Well,' said Mr. Gregsbury; 'now what can you do?'

'I suppose,' replied Nicholas, smiling, 'that I can do what usually falls to the lot of other secretaries.'

'What's that?' inquired Mr. Gregsbury.

'What is it?' replied Nicholas.

'Ah! What is it?' retorted the member, looking shrewdly at him, with his head on one side.

'A secretary's duties are rather difficult to define, perhaps,' said Nicholas, considering. 'They include, I presume, correspondence?'

'Good,' interposed Mr. Gregsbury.

'The arrangement of papers and documents?'

'Very good.'

'Occasionally, perhaps, the writing from your dictation; and possibly, sir,'—said Nicholas, with a half-smile, 'the copying of your speech for some public journal, when you have made one of more than usual importance.'

'Certainly,' rejoined Mr. Gregsbury. 'What else?'

'Really, said Nicholas, after a moment's reflection, 'I am not able, at this instant, to recapitulate any other duty of a secretary, beyond the general one of making himself as agreeable and useful to his employer as he can, consistently with his own respectability, and without overstepping that line of duties which he undertakes to perform, and which the designation of his office is usually understood to imply.'

Mr. Gregsbury looked fixedly at Nicholas for a short time, and then glancing warily round the room, said in a suppressed voice—

'This is all very well, Mr.—what is your name?'

'Nickleby.'

'This is all very well, Mr. Nickleby, and very proper, so far as it goes—so far as it goes, but it doesn't go far enough. There are other duties, Mr. Nickleby, which a secretary to a parliamentary gentleman must never lose sight of. I should require to be crammed, sir.'

'I beg your pardon,' interposed Nicholas, doubtful whether he had heard aright.

'—To be crammed, sir,' repeated Mr. Gregsbury.

'May I beg your pardon again, if I inquire what you mean, sir?' said Nicholas.

'My meaning, sir, is perfectly plain,' replied Mr. Gregsbury, with a solemn aspect. 'My secretary would have to make himself master of the foreign policy of the world, as it is mirrored in the newspapers; to run his eye over all accounts of public meetings, all leading articles, and accounts of the proceedings of public bodies; and to make notes of anything which it appeared to him might be made a point of, in any little speech upon the question of some petition lying on the table, or anything of that kind. Do you understand?'

'I think I do, sir,' replied Nicholas.

'Then,' said Mr. Gregsbury, 'it would be necessary for him to make himself acquainted, from day to day, with newspaper paragraphs on passing events; such as "Mysterious disappearance, and supposed suicide of a pot-boy," or anything of that sort, upon which I might found a question to the Secretary of State for the

Home Department. Then, he would have to copy the question, and as much as I remembered of the answer (including a little compliment about independence and good sense) ; and to send the manuscript in a frank to the local paper, with perhaps half a dozen lines of leader, to the effect, that I was always to be found in my place in Parliament, and never shrunk from the responsible and arduous duties, and so forth. You see?'

Nicholas bowed.

'Besides which,' continued Mr. Gregsbury, 'I should expect him, now and then, to go through a few figures in the printed tables, and to pick out a few results, so that I might come out pretty well on timber duty questions, and finance questions, and so on; and I should like him to get up a few little arguments about the disastrous effects of a return to cash payments and a metallic currency, with a touch now and then about the exportation of bullion, and the Emperor of Russia, and bank-notes, and all that kind of thing, which it 's only necessary to talk fluently about, because nobody understands it. Do you take me?'

'I think I understand,' said Nicholas.

'With regard to such questions as are not political,' continued Mr. Gregsbury, warming; 'and which one can't be expected to care a curse about, beyond the natural care of not allowing inferior people to be as well off as ourselves—else where are our privileges?— I should wish my secretary to get together a few little flourishing speeches, of a patriotic cast. For instance, if any preposterous bill were brought forward, for giving poor grubbing devils of authors a right to their own property, I should like to say, that I for one would never consent to opposing an insurmountable bar to the diffusion of literature among *the people,*—

you understand?—that the creations of the pocket, being man's, might belong to one man, or one family; but that the creations of the brain, being God's, ought as a matter of course to belong to the people at large —and if I was pleasantly disposed, I should like to make a joke about posterity, and say that those who wrote for posterity should be content to be rewarded by the approbation *of* posterity; it might take with the house, and could never do me any harm, because posterity can't be expected to know anything about me or my jokes either—do you see?'

'I see that, sir,' replied Nicholas.

'You must always bear in mind, in such cases as this, where our interests are not affected,' said Mr. Gregsbury, 'to put it very strong about the people, because it comes out very well at election-time; and you could be as funny as you liked about the authors; because I believe the greater part of them live in lodgings, and are not voters. This is a hasty outline of the chief things you'd have to do, except waiting in the lobby every night, in case I forgot anything, and should want fresh cramming; and, now and then, during great debates, sitting in the front row of the gallery, and saying to the people about—"You see that gentleman, with his hand to his face, and his arm twisted round the pillar—that's Mr. Gregsbury—the celebrated Mr. Gregsbury"—with any other little eulogium that might strike you at the moment. And for salary,' said Mr. Gregsbury, winding up with great rapidity; for he was out of breath—'And for salary, I don't mind saying at once in round numbers, to prevent any dissatisfaction—though it's more than I've been accustomed to give—fifteen shillings a week, and find yourself. There!'

With this handsome offer, Mr. Gregsbury once

more threw himself back in his chair, and looked like a man who had been most profligately liberal, but is determined not to repent of it notwithstanding.

'Fifteen shillings a week is not much,' said Nicholas, mildly.

'Not much! Fifteen shillings a week not much, young man?' cried Mr. Gregsbury. 'Fifteen shillings a—'

'Pray do not suppose that I quarrel with the sum, sir,' replied Nicholas; 'for I am not ashamed to con-fess, that whatever it may be in itself, to me it is a great deal. But the duties and responsibilities make the recompense small, and they are so very heavy that I fear to undertake them.'

'Do you decline to undertake them, sir?' inquired Mr. Gregsbury, with his hand on the bell-rope.

'I fear they are too great for my powers, however good my will may be, sir,' replied Nicholas.

'That is as much as to say that you had rather not accept the place, and that you consider fifteen shillings a week too little,' said Mr. Gregsbury, ringing. 'Do you decline it, sir?'

'I have no alternative but to do so,' replied Nicholas.

'Door, Matthews!' said Mr. Gregsbury, as the boy appeared.

'I am sorry I have troubled you unnecessarily, sir,' said Nicholas.

'I am sorry you have,' rejoined Mr. Gregsbury, turning his back upon him. 'Door, Matthews!'

'Good morning, sir,' said Nicholas.

'Door, Matthews!' cried Mr. Gregsbury.

The boy beckoned Nicholas, and tumbling lazily downstairs before him, opened the door, and ushered him into the street. With a sad and pensive air, he retraced his steps homeward.

Smike had scraped a meal together from the rem-

nant of last night's supper, and was anxiously awaiting his return. The occurrences of the morning had
not improved Nicholas's appetite, and, by him, the
dinner remained untasted. He was sitting in a
thoughtful attitude, with the plate which the poor fellow had assiduously filled with the choicest morsels,
untouched, by his side, when Newman Noggs looked
into the room.

'Come back?' asked Newman.

'Yes,' replied Nicholas, 'tired to death; and, what is
worse, might have remained at home for all the good
I have done.'

'Couldn't expect to do much in one morning,' said
Newman.

'May be so, but I am sanguine, and did expect,' said
Nicholas, 'and am proportionately disappointed.'
Saying which, he gave Newman an account of his
proceedings.

'If I could do anything,' said Nicholas, 'anything
however slight, until Ralph Nickleby returns, and I
have eased my mind by confronting him, I should feel
happier. I should think it no disgrace to work,
Heaven knows. Lying indolently here, like a half-
tamed sullen beast, distracts me.'

'I don't know,' said Newman; 'small things offer—
they would pay the rent, and more—but you wouldn't
like them; no, you could hardly be expected to undergo it—no, no.'

'What could I hardly be expected to undergo?'
asked Nicholas, raising his eyes. 'Show me, in this
wide waste of London, any honest means by which
I could even defray the weekly hire of this poor room,
and see if I shrink from resorting to them! Undergo! I have undergone too much, my friend, to feel
pride or squeamishness now. Except—' added Nicholas, hastily, after a short silence, 'except such

squeamishness as is common honesty, and so much pride as constitutes self-repect. I see little to choose, between assistant to a brutal pedagogue, and toad-eater to a mean and ignorant upstart, be he member or no member.'

'I hardly know whether I should tell you what I heard this morning, or not,' said Newman.

'Has it reference to what you said just now?' asked Nicholas.

'It has.'

'Then in Heaven's name, my good friend, tell it me,' said Nicholas. 'For God's sake consider my deplorable condition; and, while I promise to take no step without taking counsel with you, give me, at least, a vote in my own behalf.'

Moved by this entreaty, Newman stammered forth a variety of most unaccountable and entangled sentences, the upshot of which, was, that Mrs. Kenwigs had examined him, at great length that morning, touching the origin of his acquaintance with, and the whole life, adventures, and pedigree of, Nicholas; that Newman had parried these questions as long as he could, but being, at length, hard pressed and driven into a corner, had gone so far as to admit, that Nicholas was a tutor of great accomplishments, involved in some misfortunes which he was not at liberty to explain, and bearing the name of Johnson. That Mrs. Kenwigs, impelled by gratitude, or ambition, or maternal pride, or maternal love, or all four powerful motives conjointly, had taken secret conference with Mr. Kenwigs, and had finally returned to propose that Mr. Johnson should instruct the four Miss Kenwigses in the French language as spoken by natives, at the weekly stipend of five shillings, current coin of the realm; being at the rate of one shilling per week, per each Miss Kenwigs, and one shilling over, until such

NICHOLAS ENGAGED AS TUTOR IN A PRIVATE FAMILY.

time as the baby might be able to take it out in grammar.

'Which, unless I am very much mistaken,' observed Mrs. Kenwigs in making the proposition, 'will not be very long; for such clever children, Mr. Noggs, never were born into this world, I do believe.'

'There,' said Newman, 'that's all. It's beneath you, I know; but I thought that perhaps you might—'

'Might!' cried Nicholas, with great alacrity; 'of course I shall. I accept the offer at once. Tell the worthy mother so, without delay, my dear fellow; and that I am ready to begin whenever she pleases.'

Newman hastened, with joyful steps, to inform Mrs. Kenwigs of his friend's acquiescence, and soon returning, brought back word that they would be happy to see him in the first floor as soon as convenient; that Mrs. Kenwigs had, upon the instant, sent out to secure a second-hand French grammar and dialogues, which had long been fluttering in the six-penny box at the book-stall round the corner; and that the family, highly excited at the prospect of this addition to their gentility, wished the initiatory lesson to come off immediately.

And here it may be observed, that Nicholas was not, in the ordinary sense of the word, a young man of high spirit. He would resent an affront to himself, or interpose to redress a wrong offered to another, as boldly and freely as any knight that ever set lance in rest; but he lacked that peculiar excess of coolness and great-minded selfishness, which invariably distinguish gentlemen of high spirit. In truth, for our own part, we are disposed to look upon such gentlemen as being rather incumbrances than otherwise in rising families: happening to be acquainted with several whose spirit prevents their settling down to any grovelling occupation, and only displays itself in a tendency to cultivate mustachios, and look fierce; and although mustachios and ferocity are both very pretty things in their way, and very much to be commended, we confess to a desire to see them bred at the owner's proper cost, rather than at the expense of low-spirited people.

Nicholas, therefore, not being a high-spirited young man according to common parlance, and deeming it a greater degradation to borrow, for the supply of his necessities, from Newman Noggs, than to teach French to the little Kenwigses for five shillings a week, accepted the offer, with the alacrity described, and betook himself to the first floor with all convenient speed.

Here, he was received by Mrs. Kenwigs with a genteel air, kindly intended to assure him of her protection and support; and here, too, he found Mr. Lillyvick and Miss Petowker; the four Miss Kenwigses on their form of audience; and the baby in a dwarf porter's chair with a deal tray before it, amusing himself with a toy horse without a head; the said horse being composed of a small wooden cylinder, not unlike an Italian iron, supported on four crooked pegs, and painted in ingenious resemblance of red wafers set in blacking.

'How do you do, Mr. Johnson?' said Mrs. Kenwigs. 'Uncle—Mr. Johnson.'

'How do you do, sir?' said Mr. Lillyvick—rather sharply; for he had not known what Nicholas was, on the previous night, and it was rather an aggravating circumstance if a tax-collector had been too polite to a teacher.

'Mr. Johnson is engaged as private master to the children, uncle,' said Mrs. Kenwigs.

'So you said just now, my dear,' replied Mr. Lillyvick.

'But I hope,' said Mrs. Kenwigs, drawing herself up, 'that that will not make them proud; but that they will bless their own good fortune, which has born them superior to common people's children. Do you hear, Morleena?'

'Yes, ma,' replied Miss Kenwigs.

'And when you go out in the streets, or elsewhere, I desire that you don't boast of it to the other children,' said Mrs. Kenwigs; 'and that if you must say anything about it, you don't say no more than "We've got a private master comes to teach us at home, but we ain't proud, because ma says it's sinful." Do you hear, Morleena?'

'Yes, ma,' replied Miss Kenwigs again.

'Then mind you recollect, and do as I tell you,' said Mrs. Kenwigs. 'Shall Mr. Johnson begin, uncle?'

'I am ready to hear, if Mr. Johnson is ready to commence, my dear,' said the collector, assuming the air of a profound critic. 'What sort of language do you consider French, sir?'

'How do you mean?' asked Nicholas.

'Do you consider it a good language, sir?' said the collector; 'a pretty language, a sensible language?'

'A pretty language, certainly,' replied Nicholas; 'and as it has a name for everything, and admits of elegant conversation about everything, I presume it is a sensible one.'

'I don't know,' said Mr. Lillyvick, doubtfully. 'Do you call it a cheerful language, now?'

'Yes,' replied Nicholas, 'I should say it was, certainly.'

'It's very much changed since my time, then,' said the collector, 'very much.'

'Was it a dismal one in your time?' asked Nicholas, scarcely able to repress a smile.

'Very,' replied Mr. Lillyvick, with some vehemence

of manner. 'It's the war time that I speak of; the last war. It may be a cheerful language. I should be sorry to contradict anybody; but I can only say that I've heard the French prisoners, who were natives, and ought to know how to speak it, talking in such a dismal manner, that it made one miserable to hear them. Ay, that I have, fifty times, sir—fifty times!'

Mr. Lillyvick was waxing so cross, that Mrs. Kenwigs thought it expedient to motion to Nicholas not to say anything; and it was not until Miss Petowker had practised several blandishments, to soften the excellent old gentleman, that he deigned to break silence, by asking—

'What's the water in French, sir?'

'*L'Eau*,' replied Nicholas.

'Ah!' said Mr. Lillyvick, shaking his head mournfully, 'I thought as much. Lo, eh? I don't think anything of that language—nothing at all.'

'I suppose the children may begin, uncle?' said Mrs. Kenwigs.

'Oh yes; they may begin, my dear,' replied the collector, discontentedly. 'I have no wish to prevent them.'

This permission being conceded, the four Miss Kenwigses sat in a row, with their tails all one way, and Morleena at the top: while Nicholas, taking the book, began his preliminary explanations. Miss Petowker and Mrs. Kenwigs looked on, in silent admiration, broken only by the whispered assurances of the latter, that Morleena would have it all by heart in no time; and Mr. Lillyvick regarded the group with frowning and attentive eyes, lying in wait for something upon which he could open a fresh discussion on the language.

CHAPTER XVII

FOLLOWS THE FORTUNES OF MISS NICKLEBY

IT was with a heavy heart, and many sad forebodings which no effort could banish, that Kate Nickleby, on the morning appointed for the commencement of her engagement with Madame Mantalini, left the city when its clocks yet wanted a quarter of an hour of eight, and threaded her way alone, amid the noise and bustle of the streets, towards the west end of London.

At this early hour many sickly girls, whose business, like that of the poor worm, is to produce, with patient toil, the finery that bedecks the thoughtless and luxurious, traverse our streets, making towards the scene of their daily labour, and catching, as if by stealth, in their hurried walk, the only gasp of wholesome air and glimpse of sunlight which cheers their monotonous existence during the long train of hours that make a working day. As she drew nigh to the more fashionable quarter of the town, Kate marked many of this class as they passed by, hurrying like herself to their painful occupation, and saw, in their unhealthy looks and feeble gait, but too clear an evidence that her misgivings were not wholly groundless.

She arrived at Madame Mantalini's some minutes before the appointed hour, and after walking a few times up and down, in the hope that some other female might arrive and spare her the embarrassment of stating her business to the servant, knocked timidly at the door: which, after some delay, was opened by the footman, who had been putting on his striped jacket as he came upstairs, and was now intent on fastening his apron.

'Is Madame Mantalini in?' faltered Kate.

'Not often out at this time, miss,' replied the man in a tone which rendered 'Miss' something more offensive than 'My dear.'

'Can I see her?' asked Kate.

'Eh?' replied the man, holding the door in his hand, and honouring the inquirer with a stare and a broad grin, 'Lord, no.'

'I came by her own appointment,' said Kate; 'I am —I am—to be employed here.'

'Oh! you should have rung the workers' bell,' said the footman, touching the handle of one in the doorpost. 'Let me see, though, I forgot—Miss Nickleby, is it?'

'Yes,' replied Kate.

'You 're to walk upstairs then, please,' said the man. 'Madame Mantalini wants to see you—this way— take care of these things on the floor.'

Cautioning her, in these terms, not to trip over a heterogeneous litter of pastrycook's trays, lamps, waiters full of glasses, and piles of rout seats which were strewn about the hall, plainly bespeaking a late party on the previous night, the man led the way to the second story, and ushered Kate into a back room, communicating by folding-doors with the apartment in which she had first seen the mistress of the establishment.

'If you 'll wait here a minute,' said the man, 'I 'll tell her presently.' Having made this promise with much affability, he retired and left Kate alone.

There was not much to amuse in the room; of which the most attractive feature was, a half-length portrait in oil, of Mr. Mantalini, whom the artist had depicted scratching his head in an easy manner, and thus displaying to advantage a diamond ring, the gift of Madame Mantalini before her marriage. There was, however, the sound of voices in conversation in the next room; and as the conversation was loud and the partition thin, Kate could not help discovering that they belonged to Mr. and Mrs. Mantalini.

'If you will be odiously, demnebly outri*g*eously jealous, my soul,' said Mr. Mantalini, 'you will be very miserable—horrid miserable—demnition miserable.' And then, there was a sound as though Mr. Mantalini were sipping his coffee.

'I *am* miserable,' returned Madame Mantalini, evidently pouting.

'Then you are an ungrateful, unworthy, demd unthankful little fairy,' said Mr. Mantalini.

'I am not,' returned Madame, with a sob.

'Do not put itself out of humour,' said Mr. Mantalini, breaking an egg. 'It is a pretty, bewitching little demd countenance, and it should not be out of humour, for it spoils its loveliness, and makes it cross and gloomy like a frightful, naughty, demd hobgoblin.'

'I am not to be brought round in that way, always,' rejoined Madame, sulkily.

'It shall be brought round in any way it likes best, and not brought round at all if it likes that better,' retorted Mr. Mantalini, with his egg-spoon in his mouth.

'It's very easy to talk,' said Mrs. Mantalini.

'Not so easy when one is eating a demnition egg,' replied Mr. Mantalini; 'for the yolk runs down the waistcoat, and yolk of egg does not match any waistcoat but a yellow waistcoat, demmit.'

'You were flirting with her during the whole night,' said Madame Mantalini, apparently desirous to lead the conversation back to the point from which it had strayed.

'No, no, my life.'

'You were,' said Madame; 'I had my eye upon you all the time.'

'Bless the little winking twinkling eye; was it on me all the time!' cried Mantalini, in a sort of lazy rapture. 'Oh, demmit!'

'And I say once more,' resumed Madame, 'that you ought not to waltz with anybody but your own wife; and I will not bear it, Mantalini, if I take poison first.'

'She will not take poison and have horrid pains, will she?' said Mantalini; who, by the altered sound of his voice, seemed to have moved his chair, and taken up his position nearer to his wife. 'She will not take poison, because she had a demd fine husband who might have married two countesses and a dowager—'

'Two countesses,' interposed Madame. 'You told me one before!'

'Two!' cried Mantalini. 'Two demd fine women, real countesses and splendid fortunes, demmit.'

'And why didn't you?' asked Madame, playfully.

'Why didn't I!' replied her husband. 'Had I not seen, at a morning concert, the demdest little fascinator in all the world, and while that little fascinator is my wife, may not all the countesses and dowagers in England be—'

Mr. Mantalini did not finish the sentence, but he gave Madame Mantalini a very loud kiss, which Madame Mantalini returned; after which, there seemed to be some more kissing mixed up with the progress of the breakfast.

'And what about the cash, my existence's jewel?' said Mantalini, when these endearments ceased. 'How much have we in hand?'

'Very little indeed,' replied Madame.

'We must have some more,' said Mantalini; 'we

must have some discount out of old Nickleby to carry on the war with, demmit.'

'You can't want any more just now,' said Madame coaxingly.

'My life and soul,' returned her husband, 'there is a horse for sale at Scrubbs's, which it would be a sin and a crime to lose—going, my senses' joy, for nothing.'

'For nothing,' cried Madame, 'I am glad of that.'

'For actually nothing,' replied Mantalini. 'A hundred guineas down will buy him; mane, and crest, and legs, and tail, all of the demdest beauty. I will ride him in the park before the very chariots of the rejected countesses. The demd old dowager will faint with grief and rage; the other two will say, "He is married, he has made away with himself, it is a demd thing, it is all up!" They will hate each other demnebly, and wish you dead and buried. Ha! ha! Demmit.'

Madame Mantalini's prudence, if she had any, was not proof against these triumphal pictures; after a little jingling of keys, she observed that she would see what her desk contained, and rising for that purpose, opened the folding-door, and walked into the room where Kate was seated.

'Dear me, child!' exclaimed Madame Mantalini, recoiling in surprise. 'How came you here?'

'Child!' cried Mantalini, hurrying in. 'How came —eh!—oh!—demmit, how d' ye do?'

'I have been waiting here some time, ma'am,' said Kate, addressing Madame Mantalini. 'The servant must have forgotten to let you know that I was here, I think.'

'You really must see to that man,' said Madame, turning to her husband. 'He forgets everything.'

'I will twist his demd nose off his countenance for

leaving such a very pretty creature all alone by herself,' said her husband.

'Mantalini,' cried Madame, 'you forget yourself.'

'I don't forget *you,* my soul, and never shall, and never can,' said Mantalini, kissing his wife's hand, and grimacing aside, to Miss Nickleby, who turned away.

Appeased by this compliment, the lady of the business took some papers from her desk which she handed over to Mr. Mantalini, who received them with great delight. She then requested Kate to follow her, and after several feints on the part of Mr. Mantalini to attract the young lady's attention, they went away: leaving that gentleman extended at full length on the sofa, with his heels in the air and a newspaper in his hand.

Madame Mantalini led the way down a flight of stairs, and through a passage, to a large room at the back of the premises where were a number of young women employed in sewing, cutting out, making up, altering, and various other processes known only to those who are cunning in the arts of millinery and dress-making. It was a close room with a skylight, and as dull and quiet as a room need be.

On Madame Mantalini calling aloud for Miss Knag, a short, bustling, over-dressed female, full of importance, presented herself, and all the young ladies suspending their operations for the moment, whispered to each other sundry criticisms upon the make and texture of Miss Nickleby's dress, her complexion, cast of features, and personal appearance, with as much good-breeding as could have been displayed by the very best society in a crowded ball-room.

'Oh, Miss Knag,' said Madame Mantalini, 'this is the young person I spoke to you about.'

Miss Knag bestowed a reverential smile upon Madame Mantalini, which she dexterously transformed into a gracious one for Kate, and said that certainly, although it was a great deal of trouble to have young people who were wholly unused to the business, still, she was sure the young person would try to do her best—impressed with which conviction she (Miss Knag) felt an interest in her, already.

'I think that, for the present at all events, it will be better for Miss Nickleby to come into the showroom with you, and try things on for people,' said Madame Mantalini. 'She will not be able for the present to be of much use in any other way; and her appearance will—'

'Suit very well with mine, Madame Mantalini,' interrupted Miss Knag. 'So it will; and to be sure I might have known that you would not be long in finding that out; for you have so much taste in all those matters, that really, as I often say, to the young ladies, I do not know how, when, or where, you possibly could have acquired all you know—hem—Miss Nickleby and I are quite a pair, Madame Mantalini, only I am a little darker than Miss Nickleby, and—hem—I think my foot may be a little smaller. Miss Nickleby, I am sure, will not be offended at my saying that, when she hears that our family always have been celebrated for small feet ever since—hem—ever since our family had any feet at all, indeed, I think. I had an uncle once, Madame Mantalini, who lived in Cheltenham, and had a most excellent business as a tobacconist—hem—who had such small feet, that they were no bigger than those which are usually joined to wooden legs—the most symmetrical feet, Madame Mantalini, that even you can imagine.'

'They must have had something the appearance of club feet, Miss Knag,' said Madame.

'Well now, that is so like you,' returned Miss Knag. 'Ha! ha! ha! Of club feet! Oh very good! As I often remark to the young ladies, "Well I must say, and I do not care who knows it, of all the ready humour—hem—I ever heard anywhere"—and I have heard a good deal; for when my dear brother was alive (I kept house for him, Miss Nickleby), we had to supper once a week two or three young men, highly celebrated in those days for their humour, Madame Mantalini—"Of all the ready humour," I say to the young ladies, "*I* ever heard, Madame Mantalini's is the most remarkable—hem. It is so gentle, so sarcastic, and yet so good-natured (as I was observing to Miss Simmonds only this morning), that how, or when, or by what means she acquired it, is to me a mystery indeed."'

Here Miss Knag paused to take breath, and while she pauses it may be observed—not that she was marvellously loquacious and marvellously deferential to Madame Mantalini, since these are facts which require no comment; but that every now and then, she was accustomed, in the torrent of her discourse, to introduce a loud, shrill, clear, 'hem!' the import and meaning of which, was variously interpreted by her acquaintance; some holding that Miss Knag dealt in exaggeration, and introduced the monosyllable, when any fresh invention was in course of coinage in her brain; others, that when she wanted a word, she threw it in to gain time, and prevent anybody else from striking into the conversation. It may be further remarked, that Miss Knag still aimed at youth, although she had shot beyond it, years ago; and that she was weak and vain, and one of those people who are best described by the axiom, that you may trust them as far as you can see them, and no farther.

'You'll take care that Miss Nickleby understands

her hours, and so forth,' said Madame Mantalini;
'and so I 'll leave her with you. You 'll not forget
my directions, Miss Knag?'

Miss Knag of course replied, that to forget anything Madame Mantalini had directed, was a moral
impossibility; and that lady, dispensing a general
good morning among her assistants, sailed away.

'Charming creature, isn't she, Miss Nickleby?' said
Miss Knag, rubbing her hands together.

'I have seen very little of her,' said Kate. 'I hardly
know yet.'

'Have you seen Mr. Mantalini?' inquired Miss
Knag.

'Yes; I have seen him twice.'

'Isn't _he_ a charming creature?'

'Indeed he does not strike me as being so, by any
means,' replied Kate.

'No, my dear!' cried Miss Knag, elevating her
hands. 'Why, goodness gracious mercy, where 's
your taste? Such a fine tall, full-whiskered dashing
gentlemanly man, with such teeth and hair, and—hem
—well now, you _do_ astonish me.'

'I dare say I am very foolish,' replied Kate, laying
aside her bonnet; 'but as my opinion is of very little
importance to him or any one else, I do not regret
having formed it, and shall be slow to change it, I
think.'

'He is a very fine man, don't you think so?' asked
one of the young ladies.

'Indeed he may be, for anything I could say to the
contrary,' replied Kate.

'And drives very beautiful horses, doesn't he?' inquired another.

'I dare say he may, but I never saw them,' answered
Kate.

'Never saw them!' interposed Miss Knag. 'Oh,

well! There it is at once you know; how can you possibly pronounce an opinion about a gentleman—hem—if you don't see him as he turns out altogether?'

There was so much of the world—even of the little world of the country girl—in this idea of the old milliner, that Kate, who was anxious, for every reason, to change the subject, made no further remark, and left Miss Knag in possession of the field.

After a short silence, during which most of the young people made a closer inspection of Kate's appearance, and compared notes respecting it, one of them offered to help her off with her shawl, and the offer being accepted, inquired whether she did not find black very uncomfortable wear.

'I do indeed,' replied Kate, with a bitter sigh.

'So dusty and hot,' observed the same speaker, adjusting her dress for her.

Kate might have said, that mourning is sometimes the coldest wear which mortals can assume; that it not only chills the breasts of those it clothes, but extending its influence to summer friends, freezes up their sources of good-will and kindness, and withering all the buds of promise they once so liberally put forth, leaves nothing but bared and rotten hearts exposed. There are few who have lost a friend or relative constituting in life their sole dependence, who have not keenly felt this chilling influence of their sable garb. She had felt it acutely, and feeling it at the moment, could not quite restrain her tears.

'I am very sorry to have wounded you by my thoughtless speech,' said her companion. 'I did not think of it. You are in mourning for some near relation?'

'For my father,' answered Kate.

'For what relation, Miss Simmonds?' asked Miss Knag in an audible voice.

'Her father,' replied the other softly.

'Her father, eh?' said Miss Knag without the slightest depression of her voice. 'Ah! A long illness, Miss Simmonds?'

'Hush,' replied the girl; 'I don't know.'

'Our misfortune was very sudden,' said Kate turning away, 'or I might perhaps, at a time like this, be enabled to support it better.'

There had existed not a little desire in the room, according to invariable custom, when any new 'young person' came, to know who Kate was, and what she was, and all about her; but, although it might have been very naturally increased by her appearance and emotion, the knowledge that it pained her to be questioned, was sufficient to repress even this curiosity; and Miss Knag, finding it hopeless to attempt extracting any further particulars just then, reluctantly commanded silence, and bade the work proceed.

In silence, then, the tasks were plied until half-past one, when a baked leg of mutton, with potatoes to correspond, was served in the kitchen. The meal over, and the young ladies having enjoyed the additional relaxation of washing their hands, the work began again, and was again performed in silence, until the noise of carriages rattling through the streets, and of loud double knocks at doors, gave token that the day's work of the more fortunate members of society was proceeding in its turn.

One of these double knocks at Madame Mantalini's door, announced the equipage of some great lady— or rather rich one, for there is occasionally a distinction between riches and greatness—who had come with her daughter to approve of some court-dresses which had been a long time preparing, and upon whom Kate was deputed to wait, accompanied by

Miss Knag, and officered of course by Madame Mantalini.

Kate's part in the pageant was humble enough, her duties being limited to holding articles of costume until Miss Knag was ready to try them on, and now and then tying a string, or fastening a hook-and-eye. She might, not unreasonably, have supposed herself beneath the reach of any arrogance, or bad humour; but it happened that the lady and daughter were both out of temper that day, and the poor girl came in for her share of their revilings. She was awkward—her hands were cold—dirty—coarse—she could do nothing right; they wondered how Madame Mantalini could have such people about her; requested that they might see some other young woman the next time they came; and so forth.

So common an occurrence would be hardly deserving of mention, but for its effect. Kate shed many bitter tears when these people were gone, and felt, for the first time, humbled by her occupation. She had, it is true, quailed at the prospect of drudgery and hard service; but she had felt no degradation in working for her bread, until she found herself exposed to insolence and pride. Philosophy would have taught her that the degradation was on the side of those who had sunk so low as to display such passions habitually, and without cause: but she was too young for such consolation, and her honest feeling was hurt. May not the complaint, that common people are above their station, often take its rise in the fact of *un*common people being below theirs?'

In such scenes and occupations the time wore on, until nine o'clock, when Kate, jaded and dispirited with the occurrences of the day, hastened from the confinement of the work-room, to join her mother at the street corner, and walk home:—the more sadly, from having to disguise her real feelings, and feign to participate in all the sanguine visions of her companion.

'Bless my soul, Kate,' said Mrs. Nickleby; 'I've been thinking all day, what a delightful thing it would be for Madame Mantalini to take you into partnership—such a likely thing too, you know! Why, your poor dear papa's cousin's sister-in-law— a Miss Browndock—was taken into partnership by a lady that kept a school at Hammersmith, and made her fortune in no time at all. I forget, by the bye, whether that Miss Browndock was the same lady that got the ten thousand pounds prize in the lottery, but I think she was; indeed, now I come to think of it, I am sure she was. "Mantalini and Nickleby," how well it would sound!—and if Nicholas has any good fortune, you might have Doctor Nickleby, the headmaster of Westminster School, living in the same street.'

'Dear Nicholas!' cried Kate, taking from her reticule her brother's letter from Dotheboys Hall. 'In all our misfortunes, how happy it makes me, mamma, to hear he is doing well, and to find him writing in such good spirits! It consoles me for all we may undergo, to think that he is comfortable and happy.'

Poor Kate! she little thought how weak her consolation was, and how soon she would be undeceived.

CHAPTER XVIII

MISS KNAG, AFTER DOTING ON KATE NICKLEBY FOR
THREE WHOLE DAYS, MAKES UP HER MIND TO HATE
HER FOR EVERMORE. THE CAUSES WHICH LEAD
MISS KNAG TO FORM THIS RESOLUTION

THERE are many lives of much pain, hardship, and suffering, which, having no stirring interest for any but those who lead them, are disregarded by persons who do not want thought or feeling, but who pamper their compassion and need high stimulants to rouse it. There are not a few among the disciples of charity who require, in their vocation, scarcely less excitement than the votaries of pleasure in theirs; and hence it is that diseased sympathy and compassion are every day expended on out-of-the-way objects, when only too many demands upon the legitimate exercise of the same virtues in a healthy state, are constantly within the sight and hearing of the most unobservant person alive. In short, charity must have its romance, as the novelist or playwright must have his. A thief in fustian is a vulgar character, scarcely to be thought of by persons of refinement; but dress him in green velvet, with a high-crowned hat, and change the scene of his operations, from a thickly peopled city, to a mountain road, and you shall find in him the very soul of poetry and adventure. So it is with the one great cardinal virtue, which, properly nourished and exercised, leads to, if it does not necessarily include, all the others. It must have its romance; and the less of real, hard, struggling work-a-day life there is in that romance, the better.

The life to which poor Kate Nickleby was devoted,

in consequence of the unforeseen train of circumstances already developed in this narrative, was a hard one; but lest the very dulness, unhealthy confinement, and bodily fatigue, which made up its sum and substance, should deprive it of any interest with the mass of the charitable and sympathetic, I would rather keep Miss Nickleby herself in view just now, than chill them, in the outset, by a minute and lengthened description of the establishment presided over by Madame Mantalini.

'Well, now, indeed Madame Mantalini,' said Miss Knag, as Kate was taking her weary way homewards on the first night of her noviciate; 'that Miss Nickleby is a very creditable young person—a very creditable young person indeed — hem — upon my word, Madame Mantalini, it does very extraordinary credit even to your discrimination that you should have found such a very excellent, very well behaved, very— hem—very unassuming young woman to assist in the fitting on. I have seen some young women when they had the opportunity of displaying before their betters, behave in such a—oh, dear—well—but you 're always right, Madame Mantalini, always; and as I very often tell the young ladies, how you do contrive to be always right, when so many people are so often wrong, is to me a mystery indeed.'

'Beyond putting a very excellent client out of humour, Miss Nickleby has not done anything very remarkable to-day—that I am aware of, at least,' said Madame Mantalini in reply.

'Oh, dear!' said Miss Knag; 'but you must allow a great deal for inexperience, you know.'

'And youth?' inquired Madame.

'Oh, I say nothing about that, Madame Mantalini,' replied Miss Knag, reddening; 'because if youth were any excuse, you wouldn't have—'

'Quite so good a forewoman as I have, I suppose,' suggested Madame.

'Well, I never did know anybody like you, Madame Mantalini,' rejoined Miss Knag most complacently, 'and that's the fact, for you know what one's going to say, before it has time to rise to one's lips. Oh, very good! Ha, ha, ha!'

'For myself,' observed Madame Mantalini, glancing with affected carelessness at her assistant, and laughing heartily in her sleeve, 'I consider Miss Nickleby the most awkward girl I ever saw in my life.'

'Poor dear thing,' said Miss Knag, 'it's not her fault. If it was, we might hope to cure it; but as it's her misfortune, Madame Mantalini, why really you know, as the man said about the blind horse, we ought to respect it.'

'Her uncle told me she had been considered pretty,' remarked Madame Mantalini. 'I think her one of the most ordinary girls I ever met with.'

'Ordinary!' cried Miss Knag with a countenance beaming delight; 'and awkward! Well, all I can say is, Madame Mantalini, that I quite love the poor girl; and that if she was twice as indifferent-looking, and twice as awkward as she is, I should be only so much the more her friend, and that's the truth of it.'

In fact, Miss Knag had conceived an incipient affection for Kate Nickleby, after witnessing her failure that morning, and this short conversation with her superior increased the favourable prepossession to a most surprising extent; which was the more remarkable, as when she first scanned that young lady's face and figure, she had entertained certain inward misgivings that they would never agree.

'But now,' said Miss Knag, glancing at the reflection of herself in a mirror at no great distance, 'I love her—I quite love her—I declare I do!'

Of such a highly disinterested quality was this devoted friendship, and so superior was it to the little weaknesses of flattery or ill nature, that the kind-hearted Miss Knag candidly informed Kate Nickleby, next day, that she saw she would never do for the business, but that she need not give herself the slightest uneasiness on this account, for that she (Miss Knag) by increased exertions on her own part, would keep her as much as possible in the background, and that all she would have to do, would be to remain perfectly quiet before company, and to shrink from attracting notice by every means in her power. This last suggestion was so much in accordance with the timid girl's own feelings and wishes, that she readily promised implicit reliance on the excellent spinster's advice: without questioning, or indeed bestowing a moment's reflection upon, the motives that dictated it.

'I take quite a lively interest in you, my dear soul, upon my word,' said Miss Knag; 'a sister's interest, actually. It's the most singular circumstance I ever knew.'

Undoubtedly it was singular, that if Miss Knag did feel a strong interest in Kate Nickleby, it should not rather have been the interest of a maiden aunt or grandmother; that being the conclusion to which the difference in their respective ages would have naturally tended. But Miss Knag wore clothes of a very youthful pattern, and perhaps her feelings took the same shape.

'Bless you!' said Miss Knag, bestowing a kiss upon Kate at the conclusion of the second day's work, 'how very awkward you have been all day.'

'I fear your kind and open communication, which

has rendered me more painfully conscious of my own defects, has not improved me,' sighed Kate.

'No, no, I dare say not,' rejoined Miss Knag, in a most uncommon flow of good humour. 'But how much better that you should know it at first, and so be able to go on, straight and comfortable! Which way are you walking, my love?'

'Towards the City,' replied Kate.

'The City!' cried Miss Knag, regarding herself with great favour in the glass as she tied her bonnet. 'Goodness gracious me! now do you really live in the City?'

'Is it so very unusual for anybody to live there?' asked Kate, half smiling.

'I couldn't have believed it possible that any young woman could have lived there, under any circumstances whatever, for three days together,' replied Miss Knag.

'Reduced—I should say poor people,' answered Kate, correcting herself hastily, for she was afraid of appearing proud, 'must live where they can.'

'Ah! very true, so they must; very proper indeed!' rejoined Miss Knag with that sort of half-sigh, which, accompanied by two or three slight nods of the head, is pity's small change in general society; 'and that 's what I very often tell my brother, when our servants go away ill, one after another, and he thinks the back-kitchen 's rather too damp for 'em to sleep in. These sort of people, I tell him, are glad to sleep anywhere! Heaven suits the back to the burden. What a nice thing it is to think that it should be so, isn't it?'

'Very,' replied Kate.

'I 'll walk with you part of the way, my dear,' said Miss Knag, 'for you must go very near our house; and as it 's quite dark, and our last servant went to the hospital a week ago, with Saint Anthony's fire in her face, I shall be glad of your company.'

Kate would willingly have excused herself from this flattering companionship; but Miss Knag adjusted her bonnet to her entire satisfaction, took her arm with an air which plainly showed how much she felt the compliment she was conferring, and they were in the street, before she could say another word.

'I fear,' said Kate, hesitating, 'that mamma—my mother, I mean—is waiting for me.'

'You needn't make the least apology, my dear,' said Miss Knag, smiling sweetly as she spoke; 'I dare say she is a very respectable old person, and I shall be quite—hem—quite pleased to know her.'

As poor Mrs. Nickleby was cooling—not her heels alone, but her limbs generally, at the street corner, Kate had no alternative but to make her known to Miss Knag, who, doing the last new carriage customer at second-hand, acknowledged the introduction with condescending politeness. The three then walked away, arm in arm: with Miss Knag in the middle, in a special state of amiability.

'I have taken such a fancy to your daughter, Mrs. Nickleby, you can't think,' said Miss Knag, after she had proceeded a little distance in dignified silence.

'I am delighted to hear it,' said Mrs. Nickleby; 'though it is nothing new to me, that even strangers should like Kate.'

'Hem!' cried Miss Knag.

'You will like her better when you know how good she is,' said Mrs. Nickleby. 'It is a great blessing to me, in my misfortunes, to have a child, who knows neither pride nor vanity, and whose bringing-up might very well have excused a little of both at first. You don't know what it is to lose a husband, Miss Knag.'

As Miss Knag had never yet known what it was to gain one, it followed, very nearly as a matter of course, that she didn't know what it was to lose one; so she said, in some haste, 'No, indeed I don't,' and said it with an air intending to signify that she should like to catch herself marrying anybody—no no, she knew better than that.

'Kate has improved even in this little time, I have no doubt,' said Mrs. Nickleby, glancing proudly at her daughter.

'Oh! of course,' said Miss Knag.

'And will improve still more,' added Mrs. Nickleby.

'That she will, I 'll be bound,' replied Miss Knag, squeezing Kate's arm in her own, to point the joke.

'She always was clever,' said poor Mrs. Nickleby, brightening up, 'always, from a baby. I recollect when she was only two years and a half old, that a gentleman who used to visit very much at our house —Mr. Watkins, you know, Kate, my dear, that your poor papa went bail for, who afterwards ran away to the United States, and sent us a pair of snow-shoes, with such an affectionate letter that it made your poor dear father cry for a week. You remember the letter? In which he said that he was very sorry he couldn't repay the fifty pounds just then, because his capital was all out at interest, and he was very busy making his fortune, but that he didn't forget you were his god-daughter, and he should take it very unkind if we didn't buy you a silver coral and put it down to his old account? Dear me, yes, my dear, how stupid you are! and spoke so affectionately of the old port wine that he used to drink a bottle and a half of every time he came. You must re-member, Kate?'

'Yes, yes, mamma; what of him?'

'Why, that Mr. Watkins, my dear,' said Mrs. Nickleby slowly, as if she were making a tremendous effort to recollect something of paramount importance; 'that Mr. Watkins—he wasn't any relation, Miss Knag will understand, to the Watkins who kept the Old Boar in the village; by the bye, I don't remember whether it was the Old Boar or the George the Third, but it was one of the two, I know, and it's much the same—that Mr. Watkins said, when you were only two years and a half old, that you were one of the most astonishing children he ever saw. He did indeed, Miss Knag, and he wasn't at all fond of children, and couldn't have had the slightest motive for doing it. I know it was he who said so, because I recollect, as well as if it was only yesterday, his borrowing twenty pounds of her poor dear papa the very moment afterwards.'

Having quoted this extraordinary and most disinterested testimony to her daughter's excellence, Mrs. Nickleby stopped to breathe; and Miss Knag, finding that the discourse was turning upon family greatness, lost no time in striking in, with a small reminiscence on her own account.

'Don't talk of lending money, Mrs. Nickleby,' said Miss Knag, 'or you'll drive me crazy, perfectly crazy. My mamma—hem—was the most lovely and beautiful creature, with the most striking and exquisite—hem—the most exquisite nose that ever was put upon a human face, I do believe, Mrs. Nickleby' (here Miss Knag rubbed her own nose sympathetically); 'the most delightful and accomplished woman, perhaps, that ever was seen; but she had that one failing of lending money, and carried it to such an extent that she lent—hem—oh! thousands of pounds, all our little fortunes, and what's more, Mrs.

Nickleby, I don't think, if we were to live till—till —hem—till the very end of time, that we should ever get them back again. I don't indeed.'

After concluding this effort of invention without being interrupted, Miss Knag fell into many more recollections, no less interesting than true, the full tide of which, Mrs. Nickleby in vain attempting to stem, at length sailed smoothly down, by adding an under-current of her own recollections; and so both ladies went on talking together in perfect contentment; the only difference between them, being, that whereas Miss Knag addressed herself to Kate, and talked very loud, Mrs. Nickleby kept on in one unbroken monotonous flow, perfectly satisfied to be talking, and caring very little whether anybody listened or not.

In this manner they walked on, very amicably, until they arrived at Miss Knag's brother's, who was an ornamental stationer and small circulating library keeper, in a by-street off Tottenham Court Road; and who let out by the day, week, month, or year, the newest old novels, whereof the titles were displayed in pen-and-ink characters on a sheet of pasteboard, swinging at his door-post. As Miss Knag happened at the moment, to be in the middle of an account of her twenty-second offer from a gentleman of large property, she insisted upon their all going in to supper together; and in they went.

'Don't go away, Mortimer,' said Miss Knag as they entered the shop. 'It's only one of our young ladies and her mother. Mrs. and Miss Nickleby.'

'Oh, indeed!' said Mr. Mortimer Knag. 'Ah!'

Having given utterance to these ejaculations with a very profound and thoughtful air, Mr. Knag slowly snuffed two kitchen candles on the counter, and two more in the window, and then snuffed himself from a box in his waistcoat pocket.

There was something very impressive in the ghostly air with which all this was done; and as Mr. Knag was a tall lank gentleman of solemn features, wearing spectacles, and garnished with much less hair than a gentleman bordering on forty, or thereabouts, usually boasts, Mrs. Nickleby whispered her daughter that she thought he must be literary.

'Past ten,' said Mr. Knag, consulting his watch. 'Thomas, close the warehouse.'

Thomas was a boy nearly half as tall as a shutter, and the warehouse was a shop about the size of three hackney coaches.

'Ah!' said Mr. Knag once more, heaving a deep sigh as he restored to its parent shelf the book he had been reading. 'Well—yes—I believe supper is ready, sister.'

With another sigh Mr. Knag took up the kitchen candles from the counter, and preceded the ladies with mournful steps to a back-parlour, where a charwoman, employed in the absence of the sick servant, and remunerated with certain eighteenpences to be deducted from her wages due, was putting the supper out.

'Mrs. Blockson,' said Miss Knag reproachfully, 'how very often I have begged you not to come into the room with your bonnet on!'

'I can't help it, Miss Knag,' said the charwoman, bridling up on the shortest notice. 'There's been a deal o' cleaning to do in this house, and if you don't like it, I must trouble you to look out for somebody else, for it don't hardly pay me, and that's the truth, if I was to be hung this minute.'

'I don't want any remarks, if *you* please,' said Miss

Knag, with a strong emphasis on the personal pronoun. 'Is there any fire downstairs for some hot water presently?'

'No there is not, indeed, Miss Knag,' replied the substitute; 'and so I won't tell you no stories about it.'

'Then why isn't there?' said Miss Knag.

'Because there an't no coals left out, and if I could make coals I would, but as I can't I won't, and so I make bold to tell you, mem,' replied Mrs. Blockson.

'Will you hold your tongue—female?' said Mr. Montimer Knag, plunging violently into this dialogue.

'By your leave, Mr. Knag,' retorted the charwoman, turning sharp round. 'I'm only too glad not to speak in this house, excepting when and where I'm spoke to, sir; and with regard to being a female, sir, I should wish to know what you considered yourself?'

'A miserable wretch,' exclaimed Mr. Knag, striking his forehead. 'A miserable wretch.'

'I'm very glad to find that you don't call yourself out of your name, sir,' said Mrs. Blockson; 'and as I had two twin children the day before yesterday was only seven weeks, and my little Charley fell down an airy and put his elber out, last Monday, I shall take it as a favior if you'll send nine shillings, for one week's work, to my house, afore the clock strikes ten to-morrow.'

With these parting words, the good woman quitted the room with great ease of manner, leaving the door wide open; Mr. Knag, at the same moment, flung himself into the 'warehouse,' and groaned aloud.

'What is the matter with that gentleman, pray?'

inquired Mrs. Nickleby, greatly disturbed by the sound.

'Is he ill?' inquired Kate, really alarmed.

'Hush!' replied Miss Knag; 'a most melancholy history. He was once most devotedly attached to —hem—to Madame Mantalini.'

'Bless me!' exclaimed Mrs. Nickleby.

'Yes,' continued Miss Knag, 'and received great encouragement too, and confidently hoped to marry her. He has a most romantic heart, Mrs. Nickleby, as indeed—hem—as indeed all our family have, and the disappointment was a dreadful blow. He is a wonderfully accomplished man—most extraordinarily accomplished—reads—hem—reads every novel that comes out; I mean every novel that—hem —that has any fashion in it, of course. The fact is, that he did find so much in the books he read, applicable to his own misfortunes, and did find himself in every respect so much like the heroes—because of course he is conscious of his own superiority, as we all are, and very naturally—that he took to scorning everything, and became a genius; and I am quite sure that he is, at this very present moment, writing another book.'

'Another book!' repeated Kate, finding that a pause was left for somebody to say something.

'Yes,' said Miss Knag, nodding in great triumph; 'another book, in three volumes post octavo. Of course it's a great advantage to him, in all his little fashionable descriptions, to have the benefit of my— hem—of my experience, because, of course, few authors who write about such things can have such opportunities of knowing them as I have. He's so wrapped up in high life, that the least allusion to business or worldly matters—like that woman just now, for instance—quite distracts him; but, as I often say, I think his disappointment a great thing for him, because if he hadn't been disappointed, he couldn't have written about blighted hopes and all that; and the fact is, if it hadn't happened as it has, I don't believe his genius would ever have come out at all.'

How much more communicative Miss Knag might have become under more favourable circumstances, it is impossible to divine, but as the gloomy one was within earshot, and the fire wanted making up, her disclosures stopped here. To judge from all appearances, and the difficulty of making the water warm, the last servant could not have been much accustomed to any other fire than St. Anthony's; but a little brandy-and-water was made at last, and the guests, having been previously regaled with cold leg of mutton and bread and cheese, soon afterwards took leave; Kate amusing herself, all the way home, with the recollection of her last glimpse of Mr. Mortimer Knag deeply abstracted in the shop; and Mrs. Nickleby by debating within herself whether the dressmaking firm would ultimately become 'Mantalini, Knag, and Nickleby,' or 'Mantalini, Nickleby, and Knag.'

At this high point, Miss Knag's friendship remained, for three whole days, much to the wonderment of Madame Mantalini's young ladies, who had never beheld such constancy in that quarter before; but on the fourth, it received a check no less violent than sudden, which thus occurred.

It happened that an old lord of great family, who was going to marry a young lady of no family in particular, came with the young lady, and the young lady's sister, to witness the ceremony of trying on two nuptial bonnets which had been ordered the day before, and Madame Mantalini announcing the fact, in a shrill treble, through the speaking-pipe, which communicated with the work-room, Miss Knag darted hastily upstairs with a bonnet in each hand, and presented herself in the show-room, in a charming state of palpitation, intended to demonstrate her enthusiasm in the cause. The bonnets were no sooner fairly on, than Miss Knag and Madame Mantalini fell into convulsions of admiration.

'A most elegant appearance,' said Madame Mantalini.

'I never saw anything so exquisite in all my life,' said Miss Knag.

Now, the old lord, who was a *very* old lord, said nothing, but mumbled and chuckled in a state of great delight, no less with the nuptial bonnets and their wearers, than with his own address in getting such a fine woman for his wife; and the young lady, who was a very lively young lady, seeing the old lord in this rapturous condition, chased the old lord behind a cheval-glass, and then and there kissed him, while Madame Mantalini and the other young lady looked, discreetly, another way.

But, pending the salutation, Miss Knag, who was tinged with curiosity, stepped accidentally behind the glass, and encountered the lively young lady's eye just at the very moment when she kissed the old lord; upon which the young lady, in a pouting manner, murmured something about 'an old thing,' and 'great impertinence,' and finished by darting a look of displeasure at Miss Knag, and smiling contemptuously.

'Madame Mantalini,' said the young lady.

'Ma'am,' said Madame Mantalini.

'Pray have up that pretty young creature we saw yesterday.'

'Oh yes, do,' said the sister.

'Of all things in the world, Madame Mantalini,' said the lord's intended, throwing herself languidly on a sofa, 'I hate being waited upon by frights or elderly persons. Let me always see that young creature, I beg, whenever I come.'

'By all means,' said the old lord; 'the lovely young creature, by all means.'

'Everybody is talking about her,' said the young lady, in the same careless manner; 'and my lord, being a great admirer of beauty, must positively see her.'

'She *is* universally admired,' replied Madame Mantalini. 'Miss Knag, send up Miss Nickleby. You needn't return.'

'I beg your pardon, Madame Mantalini, what did you say last?' asked Miss Knag, trembling.

'You needn't return,' repeated the superior, sharply. Miss Knag vanished without another word, and in all reasonable time was replaced by Kate, who took off the new bonnets and put on the old ones: blushing very much to find that the old lord and the two young ladies were staring her out of countenance all the time.

'Why, how you colour, child!' said the lord's chosen bride.

'She is not quite so accustomed to her business, as she will be in a week or two,' interposed Madame Mantalini with a gracious smile.

'I am afraid you have been giving her some of your wicked looks, my lord,' said the intended.

'No, no, no,' replied the old lord, 'no, no, I'm going to be married, and lead a new life. Ha, ha, ha! a new life, a new life! ha, ha, ha!'

It was a satisfactory thing to hear that the old gentleman was going to lead a new life, for it was pretty evident that his old one would not last him much longer. The mere exertion of protracted chuckling reduced him to a fearful ebb of coughing and gasping; it was some minutes before he could find breath to remark that the girl was too pretty for a milliner.

'I hope you don't think good looks a disqualification for the business, my lord,' said Madame Mantalini, simpering.

'Not by any means,' replied the old lord, 'or you would have left it long ago.'

'You naughty creature,' said the lively lady, poking the peer with her parasol; 'I won't have you talk so. How dare you?'

This playful inquiry was accompanied with another poke, and another, and then the old lord caught the parasol, and wouldn't give it up again, which induced the other lady to come to the rescue, and some very pretty sportiveness ensued.

'You will see that those little alterations are made, Madame Mantalini,' said the lady. 'Nay, you bad man, you positively shall go first; I wouldn't leave you behind with that pretty girl, not for half a second. I know you too well. Jane, my dear, let him go first, and we shall be quite sure of him.'

The old lord, evidently much flattered by this suspicion, bestowed a grotesque leer upon Kate as he passed; and, receiving another tap with the parasol for his wickedness, tottered downstairs to the door, where his sprightly body was hoisted into the carriage by two stout footmen.

'Foh!' said Madame Mantalini, 'how he ever gets into a carriage without thinking of a hearse, I can't think. There, take the things away, my dear, take them away.'

Kate, who had remained during the whole scene

with her eyes modestly fixed upon the ground, was only too happy to avail herself of the permission to retire, and hasten joyfully downstairs to Miss Knag's dominion.

The circumstances of the little kingdom had greatly changed, however, during the short period of her absence. In place of Miss Knag being stationed in her accustomed seat, preserving all the dignity and greatness of Madame Mantalini's representative, that worthy soul was reposing on a large box, bathed in tears, while three or four of the young ladies in close attendance upon her, together with the presence of hartshorn, vinegar, and other restoratives, would have borne ample testimony, even without the derangement of the head-dress and front row of curls, to her having fainted desperately.

'Bless me!' said Kate, stepping hastily forward, 'what is the matter?'

This inquiry produced in Miss Knag violent symptoms of a relapse; and several young ladies, darting angry looks at Kate, applied more vinegar and hartshorn, and said it was 'a shame.'

'What is a shame?' demanded Kate. 'What is the matter? What has happened? tell me.'

'Matter!' cried Miss Knag, coming all at once bolt upright, to the great consternation of the assembled maidens; 'Matter! Fie upon you, you nasty creature!'

'Gracious!' cried Kate, almost paralysed by the violence with which the adjective had been jerked out from between Miss Knag's closed teeth; 'have *I* offended you?'

'*You* offended me!' retorted Miss Knag, '*You!* a chit, a child, an upstart nobody! Oh, indeed! Ha, ha!'

Now, it was evident, as Miss Knag laughed, that

something struck her as being exceedingly funny; and as the young ladies took their tone from Miss Knag—she being the chief—they all got up a laugh without a moment's delay, and nodded their heads a little, and smiled sarcastically to each other, as much as to say, how very good that was!

'Here she is,' continued Miss Knag, getting off the box, and introducing Kate with much ceremony and many low curtseys to the delighted throng; 'here she is—everybody is talking about her—the belle, ladies—the beauty, the—oh, you bold-faced thing!'

At this crisis, Miss Knag was unable to repress a virtuous shudder, which immediately communicated itself to all the young ladies; after which, Miss Knag laughed, and after that, cried.

'For fifteen years,' exclaimed Miss Knag, sobbing in a most affecting manner, 'for fifteen years have I been the credit and ornament of this room and the one upstairs. Thank God,' said Miss Knag, stamping first her right foot and then her left with remarkable energy, 'I have never in all that time, till now, been exposed to the arts, the vile arts, of a creature, who disgraces us with all her proceedings, and makes proper people blush for themselves. But I feel it, I do feel it, although I am disgusted.'

Miss Knag here relapsed into softness, and the young ladies renewing their attentions, murmured that she ought to be superior to such things, and that for their part they despised them, and considered them beneath their notice; in witness whereof, they called out, more emphatically than before, that it was a shame, and that they felt so angry, they did, they hardly knew what to do with themselves.

'Have I lived to this day to be called a fright!' cried Miss Knag, suddenly becoming convulsive, and making an effort to tear her front off.

'Oh no, no,' replied the chorus, 'pray don't say so; don't now!'

'Have I deserved to be called an elderly person?' screamed Miss Knag, wrestling with the supernumeraries.

'Don't think of such things, dear,' answered the chorus.

'I hate her,' cried Miss Knag; 'I detest and hate her. Never let her speak to me again; never let anybody who is a friend of mine speak to her; a slut, a hussy, an impudent artful hussy!' Having denounced the object of her wrath, in these terms, Miss Knag screamed once, hiccupped thrice, gurgled in her throat several times, slumbered, shivered, woke, came to, composed her headdress, and declared herself quite well again.

Poor Kate had regarded these proceedings, at first, in perfect bewilderment. She had then turned red and pale by turns, and once or twice essayed to speak; but, as the true motives of this altered behaviour developed themselves, she retired a few paces, and looked calmly on without deigning a reply. Nevertheless, although she walked proudly to her seat, and turned her back upon the group of little satellites who clustered round their ruling planet in the remotest corner of the room, she gave way, in secret, to some such bitter tears as would have gladdened Miss Knag's inmost soul, if she could have seen them fall.

CHAPTER XIX

DESCRIPTIVE OF A DINNER AT MR. RALPH NICKLEBY'S,
AND OF THE MANNER IN WHICH THE COMPANY
ENTERTAINED THEMSELVES, BEFORE DINNER, AT
DINNER, AND AFTER DINNER

THE bile and rancour of the worthy Miss Knag undergoing no diminution during the remainder of the week, but rather augmenting with every successive hour; and the honest ire of all the young ladies rising, or seeming to rise in exact proportion to the good spinster's indignation, and both waxing very hot every time Miss Nickleby was called upstairs; it will be readily imagined that that young lady's daily life was none of the most cheerful or enviable kind. She hailed the arrival of Saturday night, as a prisoner would a few delicious hours' respite from slow and wearing torture, and felt, that the poor pittance for her first week's labour would have been dearly and hardly earned, had its amount been trebled.

When she joined her mother, as usual, at the street corner, she was not a little surprised to find her in conversation with Mr. Ralph Nickleby; but her surprise was soon redoubled, no less by the matter of their conversation, than by the smoothed and altered manner of Mr. Nickleby himself.

'Ah! my dear!' said Ralph; 'we were at that moment talking about you.'

'Indeed!' replied Kate, shrinking, though she scarce knew why, from her uncle's cold glistening eye.

'That instant,' said Ralph. 'I was coming to call for you, making sure to catch you before you left; but your mother and I have been talking over family affairs, and the time has slipped away so rapidly—'

'Well, now, hasn't it?' interposed Mrs. Nickleby, quite insensible to the sarcastic tone of Ralph's last remark. 'Upon my word, I couldn't have believed it possible, that such a— Kate, my dear, you're to dine with your uncle at half-past six o'clock to-morrow.'

Triumphing in having been the first to communicate this extraordinary intelligence, Mrs. Nickleby nodded and smiled a great many times, to impress its full magnificence on Kate's wondering mind, and then flew off, at an acute angle, to a committee of ways and means.

'Let me see,' said the good lady. 'Your black silk frock will be quite dress enough, my dear, with that pretty little scarf, and a plain band in your hair, and a pair of black silk stock— Dear, dear,' cried Mrs. Nickleby, flying off at another angle, 'if I had but those unfortunate amethysts of mine—you recollect them, Kate, my love—how they used to sparkle, you know—but your papa, your poor dear papa—ah! there never was anything so cruelly sacrificed as those jewels were, never!' Overpowered by this agonising thought, Mrs. Nickleby shook her head, in a melancholy manner, and applied her handkerchief to her eyes.

'I don't want them, mamma, indeed,' said Kate. 'Forget that you ever had them.'

'Lord, Kate, my dear,' rejoined Mrs. Nickleby, pettishly, 'how like a child you talk! Four-and-twenty silver teaspoons, brother-in-law, two gravies, four salts, all the amethysts—necklace, brooch, and ear-rings—all made away with, at the same time, and I saying, almost on my bended knees, to that poor good soul, "Why don't you do something, Nicholas? Why don't you make some arrangement?" I am sure that anybody who was about us at that time, will do me the justice to own, that if I said that, once, I said it fifty times a day. Didn't I, Kate, my dear? Did I ever lose an opportunity of impressing it on your poor papa?'

'No, no, mamma, never,' replied Kate. And to do Mrs. Nickleby justice, she never had lost—and to do married ladies as a body justice, they seldom do lose—any occasion of inculcating similar golden precepts, whose only blemish is, the slight degree of vagueness and uncertainty in which they are usually enveloped.

'Ah!' said Mrs. Nickleby, with great fervour, 'if my advice had been taken at the beginning— Well, I have always done *my* duty, and that's some comfort.'

When she had arrived at this reflection, Mrs. Nickleby sighed, rubbed her hands, cast up her eyes, and finally assumed a look of meek composure; thus importing that she was a persecuted saint, but that she wouldn't trouble her hearers by mentioning a circumstance which must be so obvious to everybody.

'Now,' said Ralph, with a smile, which, in common with all other tokens of emotion, seemed to skulk under his face, rather than play boldly over it—'to return to the point from which we have strayed. I have a little party of—of—gentlemen with whom I am connected in business just now, at my house tomorrow; and your mother has promised that you shall keep house for me. I am not much used to parties; but this is one of business, and such fooleries are an important part of it sometimes. You don't mind obliging me?'

'Mind!' cried Mrs. Nickleby. 'My dear Kate, why—'

'Pray,' interrupted Ralph, motioning her to be silent. 'I spoke to my niece.'

'I shall be very glad, of course, uncle,' replied Kate; 'but I am afraid you will find me awkward and embarrassed.'

'Oh no,' said Ralph; 'come when you like, in a hackney coach—I 'll pay for it. Good night—a—a —God bless you.'

The blessing seemed to stick in Mr. Ralph Nickleby's throat, as if it were not used to the thoroughfare, and didn't know the way out. But it got out somehow, though awkwardly enough; and having disposed of it, he shook hands with his two relatives, and abruptly left them.

'What a very strongly marked countenance your uncle has!' said Mrs. Nickleby, quite struck with his parting look. 'I don't see the slightest resemblance to his poor brother.'

'Mamma!' said Kate reprovingly. 'To think of such a thing!'

'No,' said Mrs. Nickleby, musing. 'There certainly is none. But it 's a very honest face.'

The worthy matron made this remark with great emphasis and elocution, as if it comprised no small quantity of ingenuity and research; and, in truth, it was not unworthy of being classed among the extraordinary discoveries of the age. Kate looked up hastily, and as hastily looked down again.

'What has come over you, my dear, in the name of goodness?' asked Mrs. Nickleby, when they had walked on, for some time, in silence.

'I was only thinking, mamma,' answered Kate.

'Thinking!' repeated Mrs. Nickleby. 'Aye, and indeed plenty to think about, too. Your uncle has taken a strong fancy to you, that 's quite clear; and if some extraordinary good fortune doesn't come to

you, after this, I shall be a little surprised, that's
all.'

With this she launched out into sundry anecdotes
of young ladies, who had had thousand-pound notes
given them in reticules, by eccentric uncles; and of
young ladies who had accidentally met amiable gentlemen of enormous wealth at their uncles' houses,
and married them, after short but ardent courtships;
and Kate, listening first in apathy, and afterwards
in amusement, felt, as they walked home, something
of her mother's sanguine complexion gradually awakening in her own bosom, and began to think that her
prospects might be brightening, and that better days
might be dawning upon them.   Such is hope, Heav-
en's own gift to struggling mortals; pervading, like
some subtle essence from the skies, all things, both
good and bad; as universal as death, and more infec-
tious than disease!

The feeble winter's sun—and winter's suns in the
City are very feeble indeed—might have brightened
up, as he shone through the dim windows of the large
old house, on witnessing the unusual sight which one
half-furnished room displayed.   In a gloomy corner,
where, for years, had stood a silent dusty pile of mer-
chandise, sheltering its colony of mice, and frowning,
a dull and lifeless mass, upon the panelled room, save
when, responding to the roll of heavy waggons in the
street without, it quaked with sturdy tremblings and
caused the bright eyes of its tiny citizens to grow
brighter still with fear, and struck them motionless,
with attentive ear and palpitating heart, until the
alarm had passed away—in this dark corner, was
arranged, with scrupulous care, all Kate's little finery
for the day; each article of dress partaking of that
indescribable air of jauntiness and individuality which
empty garments—whether by association, or that they

become moulded, as it were, to the owner's form—will take, in eyes accustomed to, or picturing, the wearer's smartness. In place of a bale of musty goods, there lay the black silk dress: the neatest possible figure in itself. The small shoes, with toes delicately turned out, stood upon the very pressure of some old iron weight; and a pile of harsh discoloured leather had unconsciously given place to the very same little pair of black silk stockings, which had been the objects of Mrs. Nickleby's peculiar care. Rats and mice, and such small gear, had long ago been starved, or had emigrated to better quarters: and, in their stead, appeared gloves, bands, scarfs, hair-pins, and many other little devices, almost as ingenious in their way as rats and mice themselves, for the tantalisation of mankind. About and among them all, moved Kate herself, not the least beautiful or unwonted relief to the stern, old, gloomy building.

In good time, or in bad time, as the reader likes to take it—for Mrs. Nickleby's impatience went a great deal faster than the clocks at that end of the town, and Kate was dressed to the very last hairpin a full hour and a half before it was at all necessary to begin to think about it—in good time, or in bad time, the toilet was completed; and it being at length the hour agreed upon for starting, the milkman fetched a coach from the nearest stand, and Kate, with many adieux to her mother, and many kind messages to Miss La Creevy, who was to come to tea, seated herself in it, and went away in state, if ever anybody went away in state in a hackney coach yet. And the coach, and the coachman, and the horses, rattled, and jangled, and whipped, and cursed, and swore, and tumbled on together, until they came to Golden Square.

The coachman gave a tremendous double knock at the door, which was opened long before he had done, as quickly as if there had been a man behind it, with his hand tied to the latch. Kate, who had expected no more uncommon appearance than Newman Noggs in a clean shirt, was not a little astonished to see that the opener was a man in handsome livery, and that there were two or three others in the hall. There was no doubt about its being the right house, however, for there was the name upon the door; so she accepted the laced coat-sleeve which was tendered her, and entering the house, was ushered upstairs, into a back drawing-room, where she was left alone.

If she had been surprised at the apparition of the footman, she was perfectly absorbed in amazement at the richness and splendour of the furniture. The softest and most elegant carpets, the most exquisite pictures, the costliest mirrors; articles of richest ornament, quite dazzling from their beauty, and perplexing from the prodigality with which they were scattered around; encountered her on every side. The very staircase nearly down to the hall door, was crammed with beautiful and luxurious things, as though the house were brimful of riches, which, with a very trifling addition, would fairly run over into the street.

Presently, she heard a series of loud double knocks at the street-door, and after every knock some new voice in the next room; the tones of Mr. Ralph Nickleby were easily distinguishable at first, but by degrees they merged into the general buzz of conversation, and all she could ascertain was, that there were several gentlemen with no very musical voices, who talked very loud, laughed very heartily, and swore more than she would have thought quite necessary. But this was a question of taste.

At length, the door opened, and Ralph himself, divested of his boots, and ceremoniously embellished with black silks and shoes, presented his crafty face.

'I couldn't see you before, my dear,' he said, in a low tone, and pointing, as he spoke, to the next room. 'I was engaged in receiving them. Now—shall I take you in?'

'Pray, uncle,' said Kate, a little flurried, as people much more conversant with society often are, when they are about to enter a room full of strangers, and have had time to think of it previously, 'are there any ladies there?'

'No,' said Ralph, shortly, 'I don't know any.'

'Must I go in immediately?' asked Kate, drawing back a little.

'As you please,' said Ralph, shrugging his shoulders. 'They are all come, and dinner will be announced directly afterwards—that's all.'

Kate would have entreated a few minutes' respite, but reflecting that her uncle might consider the payment of the hackney-coach fare a sort of bargain for her punctuality, she suffered him to draw her arm through his, and to lead her away.

Seven or eight gentlemen were standing round the fire when they went in, and, as they were talking very loud, were not aware of their entrance until Mr. Ralph Nickleby, touching one on the coat-sleeve, said in a harsh emphatic voice, as if to attract general attention—

'Lord Frederick Verisopht, my niece, Miss Nickleby.'

The group dispersed, as if in great surprise, and the gentleman addressed, turning round, exhibited a suit of clothes of the most superlative cut, a pair of whiskers of similar quality, a moustache, a head of hair, and a young face.

'Eh?' said the gentleman. 'What—the—deyvle!'
With which broken ejaculations, he fixed his glass
in his eye, and stared at Miss Nickleby in great surprise.

'My niece, my lord,' said Ralph.

'Then my ears did not deceive me, and it's not
wa-a-x work,' said his lordship. 'How de do? I'm
very happy.' And then his lordship turned to another superlative gentleman, something older, something stouter, something redder in the face, and something longer upon town, and said in a loud whisper
that the girl was 'deyvlish pitty.'

'Introduce me, Nickleby,' said this second gentleman, who was lounging with his back to the fire, and
both elbows on the chimneypiece.

'Sir Mulberry Hawk,' said Ralph.

'Otherwise the most knowing card in the pa-ack,
Miss Nickleby,' said Lord Frederick Verisopht.

'Don't leave me out, Nickleby,' cried a sharp-faced
gentleman, who was sitting on a low chair with a
high back, reading the paper.

'Mr. Pyke,' said Ralph.

'Nor me, Nickleby,' cried a gentleman with a
flushed face and a flash air, from the elbow of Sir
Mulberry Hawk.

'Mr. Pluck,' said Ralph. Then wheeling about
again, towards a gentleman with the neck of a stork
and the legs of no animal in particular, Ralph introduced him as the Honourable Mr. Snobb; and a
white-headed person at the table as Colonel Chowser.
The colonel was in conversation with somebody, who
appeared to be a make-weight, and was not introduced
at all.

There were two circumstances which, in this early
stage of the party, struck home to Kate's bosom, and
brought the blood tingling to her face. One, was

the flippant contempt with which the guests evidently regarded her uncle, and the other, the easy insolence of their manner towards herself. That the first symptom was very likely to lead to the aggravation of the second, it needed no great penetration to foresee. And here Mr. Ralph Nickleby had reckoned without his host; for however fresh from the country a young lady (by nature) may be, and however unacquainted with conventional behaviour, the chances are, that she will have quite as strong an innate sense of the decencies and proprieties of life as if she had run the gauntlet of a dozen London seasons—possibly a stronger one, for such senses have been known to blunt in this improving process.

When Ralph had completed the ceremonial of introduction, he led his blushing niece to a seat. As he did so, he glanced warily round as though to assure himself of the impression which her unlooked-for appearance had created.

'An unexpected playsure, Nickleby,' said Lord Frederick Verisopht, taking his glass out of his right eye, where it had, until now, done duty on Kate, and fixing it in his left, to bring it to bear on Ralph.

'Designed to surprise you, Lord Frederick,' said Mr. Pluck.

'Not a bad idea,' said his lordship, 'and one that would almost warrant the addition of an extra two and a half per cent.'

'Nickleby,' said Sir Mulberry Hawk, in a thick coarse voice, 'take the hint, and tack it on to the other five-and-twenty, or whatever it is, and give me half for the advice.'

Sir Mulberry garnished this speech with a hoarse laugh, and terminated it with a pleasant oath regarding Mr. Nickleby's limbs, whereat Messrs. Pyke and Pluck laughed consumedly.

These gentlemen had not yet quite recovered the jest, when dinner was announced, and then they were thrown in fresh ecstasies by a similar cause; for Sir Mulberry Hawk, in an excess of humour, shot dexterously past Lord Frederick Verisopht, who was about to lead Kate downstairs, and drew her arm through his up to the elbow.

'No, damn it, Verisopht,' said Sir Mulberry, 'fair play 's a jewel, and Miss Nickleby and I settled the matter with our eyes, ten minutes ago.'

'Ha, ha, ha!' laughed the Honourable Mr. Snobb, 'very good, very good.'

Rendered additionally witty by this applause, Sir Mulberry Hawk leered upon his friends most facetiously, and led Kate downstairs with an air of familiarity, which roused in her gentle breast such burning indignation, as she felt it almost impossible to repress. Nor was the intensity of these feelings at all diminished, when she found herself placed at the top of the table, with Sir Mulberry Hawk and Lord Frederick Verisopht on either side.

'Oh, you 've found your way into our neighbourhood, have you?' said Sir Mulberry, as his lordship sat down.

'Of course,' replied Lord Frederick, fixing his eyes on Miss Nickleby, 'how can you a-ask me?'

'Well, you attend your dinner,' said Sir Mulberry, 'and don't mind Miss Nickleby and me, for we shall prove very indifferent company, I dare say.'

'I wish you 'd interfere here, Nickleby,' said Lord Frederick.

'What is the matter, my lord?' demanded Ralph from the bottom of the table, where he was supported by Messrs. Pyke and Pluck.

'This fellow, Hawk, is monopolising your niece,' said Lord Frederick.

'He has a tolerable share of everything that you lay claim to, my lord,' said Ralph, with a sneer.

'Gad, so he has,' replied the young man; 'deyvle take me if I know which is master in my house, he or I.'

'*I* know,' muttered Ralph.

'I think I shall cut him off with a shilling,' said the young nobleman, jocosely.

'No, no, curse it,' said Sir Mulberry. 'When you come to the shilling—the last shilling—I 'll cut you fast enough; but till then, I 'll never leave you—you may take your oath of it.'

This sally (which was strictly founded on fact), was received with a general roar, above which, was plainly distinguishable the laughter of Mr. Pyke and Mr. Pluck, who were, evidently, Sir Mulberry's toads in ordinary. Indeed, it was not difficult to see, that the majority of the company preyed upon the unfortunate young lord, who, weak and silly as he was, appeared by far the least vicious of the party. Sir Mulberry Hawk was remarkable for his tact in ruining, by himself and his creatures, young gentlemen of fortune—a genteel and elegant profession, of which he had undoubtedly gained the head. With all the boldness of an original genius, he had struck out an entirely new course of treatment quite opposed to the usual method; his custom being, when he had gained the ascendancy over those he took in hand, rather to keep them down than to give them their own way; and to exercise his vivacity upon them, openly, and without reserve. Thus, he made them butts, in a double sense, and while he emptied them with great address, caused them to ring with sundry well-administered taps, for the diversion of society.

The dinner was as remarkable for the splendour and completeness of its appointments as the mansion itself, and the company were remarkable for doing it ample justice, in which respect Messrs. Pyke and Pluck particularly signalised themselves; these two gentlemen eating of every dish, and drinking of every bottle, with a capacity and perseverance truly astonishing. They were remarkably fresh, too, notwithstanding their great exertions: for, on the appearance of the dessert, they broke out again, as if nothing serious had taken place since breakfast.

'Well,' said Lord Frederick, sipping his first glass of port, 'if this is a discounting dinner, all I have to say is, deyvle take me, if it wouldn't be a good pla-an to get discount every day.'

'You 'll have plenty of it, in your time,' returned Sir Mulberry Hawk; 'Nickleby will tell you that.'

'What do you say, Nickleby?' inquired the young man; 'am I to be a good customer?'

'It depends entirely on circumstances, my lord,' replied Ralph.

'On your lordship's circumstances,' interposed Colonel Chowser of the Militia—'and the race-courses.'

The gallant colonel glanced at Messrs. Pyke and Pluck as if he thought they ought to laugh at his joke; but those gentlemen, being only engaged to laugh for Sir Mulberry Hawk, were, to his signal discomfiture, as grave as a pair of undertakers. To add to his defeat, Sir Mulberry, considering any such efforts an invasion of his peculiar privilege, eyed the offender steadily, through his glass, as if astonished at his presumption, and audibly stated his impression that it was an 'infernal liberty,' which being a hint to Lord Frederick, he put up *his* glass, and surveyed the object of censure as if he were some extraordinary wild animal then exhibiting for the first time. As a matter of course, Messrs. Pyke and Pluck stared at

the individual whom Sir Mulberry Hawk stared at;
so, the poor colonel, to hide his confusion, was reduced to the necessity of holding his port before his
right eye and affecting to scrutinise its colour with
the most lively interest.

All this while, Kate had sat as silently as she could,
scarcely daring to raise her eyes, lest they should encounter the admiring gaze of Lord Frederick Verisopht, or, what was still more embarrassing, the bold
looks of his friend Sir Mulberry. The latter gentleman was obliging enough to direct general attention
towards her.

'Here is Miss Nickleby,' observed Sir Mulberry,
'wondering why the deuce somebody doesn't make
love to her.'

'No, indeed,' said Kate, looking hastily up, 'I—'
and then she stopped, feeling it would have been
better to have said nothing at all.

'I'll hold any man fifty pounds,' said Sir Mulberry, 'that Miss Nickleby can't look in my face, and tell
me she wasn't thinking so.'

'Done!' cried the noble gull. 'Within ten minutes.'

'Done!' responded Sir Mulberry. The money was
produced on both sides, and the Honourable Mr.
Snobbs was elected to the double office of stakeholder
and time-keeper.

'Pray,' said Kate, in great confusion, while these
preliminaries were in course of completion. 'Pray
do not make me the subject of any bets. Uncle, I
cannot really—'

'Why not, my dear?' replied Ralph, in whose grating voice, however, there was an unusual huskiness,
as though he spoke unwillingly, and would rather that
the proposition had not been broached. 'It is done in
a moment; there is nothing in it. If the gentlemen
insist on it—'

'*I* don't insist on it,' said Sir Mulberry, with a loud laugh. 'That is, I by no means insist upon Miss Nickleby's making the denial, for if she does, I lose; but I shall be glad to see her bright eyes, especially as she favours the mahogany so much.'

'So she does, and it's too ba-a-d of you, Miss Nickleby,' said the noble youth.

'Quite cruel,' said Mr. Pyke.

'Horrid cruel,' said Mr. Pluck.

'I don't care if I do lose,' said Sir Mulberry; 'for one tolerable look at Miss Nickleby's eyes is worth double the money.'

'More,' said Mr. Pyke.

'Far more,' said Mr. Pluck.

'How goes the enemy, Snobb?' asked Sir Mulberry Hawk.

'Four minutes gone.'

'Bravo!'

'Won't you ma-ake one effort for me, Miss Nickleby?' asked Lord Frederick, after a short interval.

'You needn't trouble yourself to inquire, my buck,' said Sir Mulberry; 'Miss Nickleby and I understand each other; she declares on my side, and shows her taste. You haven't a chance, old fellow. Time, Snobb?'

'Eight minutes gone.'

'Get the money ready,' said Sir Mulberry; 'you'll soon hand over.'

'Ha, ha, ha!' laughed Mr. Pyke.

Mr. Pluck, who always came second, and topped his companion if he could, screamed outright.

The poor girl, who was so overwhelmed with confusion that she scarcely knew what she did, had determined to remain perfectly quiet; but fearing that by so doing she might seem to countenance Sir Mulberry's boast, which had been uttered with great coarseness and vulgarity of manner, raised her eyes, and looked him in the face. There was something so odious, so insolent, so repulsive in the look which met her, that, without the power to stammer forth a syllable, she rose and hurried from the room. She restrained her tears by a great effort until she was alone upstairs, and then gave them vent.

'Capital!' said Sir Mulberry Hawk, putting the stakes in his pocket. 'That's a girl of spirit, and we'll drink her health.'

It is needless to say, that Pyke and Co. responded, with great warmth of manner, to this proposal, or that the toast was drunk with many little insinuations from the firm, relative to the completeness of Sir Mulberry's conquest. Ralph, who, while the attention of the other guests was attracted to the principals in the preceding scene, had eyed them like a wolf, appeared to breathe more freely now his niece was gone; the decanters passing quickly round, he leaned back in his chair, and turned his eyes from speaker to speaker, as they warmed with wine, with looks that seemed to search their hearts, and lay bare, for his distempered sport, every idle thought within them.

Meanwhile Kate, left wholly to herself, had, in some degree, recovered her composure. She had learnt from a female attendant, that her uncle wished to see her before she left, and had also gleaned the satisfactory intelligence that the gentlemen would take coffee at table. The prospect of seeing them no more, contributed greatly to calm her agitation, and, taking up a book, she composed herself to read.

She started sometimes, when the sudden opening of the dining-room door let loose a wild shout of noisy revelry, and more than once rose in great alarm, as a fancied footstep on the staircase impressed her with the fear that some stray member of the party was returning alone. Nothing occurring, however, to realise her apprehensions, she endeavoured to fix her attention more closely on her book, in which by degrees she became so much interested, that she had read on through several chapters without heed of time or place, when she was terrified by suddenly hearing her name pronounced by a man's voice close at her ear.

The book fell from her hand. Lounging on an ottoman close beside her, was Sir Mulberry Hawk, evidently the worse—if a man may be a ruffian at heart, he is never the better—for wine.

'What a delightful studiousness!' said this accomplished gentleman. 'Was it real, now, or only to display the eyelashes?'

Kate, looking anxiously towards the door, made no reply.

'I have looked at 'em for five minutes,' said Sir Mulberry. 'Upon my soul, they're perfect. Why did I speak, and destroy such a pretty little picture!'

'Do me the favour to be silent now, sir,' replied Kate.

'No, don't,' said Sir Mulberry, folding his crush hat to lay his elbow on, and bringing himself still closer to the young lady; 'upon my life, you oughtn't to. Such a devoted slave of yours, Miss Nickleby, it's an infernal thing to treat him so harshly, upon my soul it is.'

'I wish you to understand, sir,' said Kate, trembling in spite of herself, but speaking with great indignation, 'that your behaviour offends and disgusts me. If you have a spark of gentlemanly feeling remaining, you will leave me.'

'Now why,' said Sir Mulberry, 'why will you keep up this appearance of excessive rigour, my sweet creature? Now, be more natural—my dear Miss Nickleby, be more natural—do.'

Kate hastily rose; but as she rose, Sir Mulberry caught her dress, and forcibly detained her.

'Let me go, sir,' she cried, her heart swelling with anger. 'Do you hear? Instantly—this moment.'

'Sit down, sit down,' said Sir Mulberry; 'I want to talk to you.'

'Unhand me, sir, this instant,' cried Kate.

'Not for the world,' rejoined Sir Mulberry. Thus speaking, he leaned over, as if to replace her in her chair; but the young lady, making a violent effort to disengage herself, he lost his balance, and measured his length upon the ground. As Kate sprung forward to leave the room, Mr. Ralph Nickleby appeared in the doorway, and confronted her.

'What is this?' said Ralph.

'It is this, sir,' replied Kate, violently agitated: 'that beneath the roof where I, a helpless girl, your dead brother's child, should most have found protection, I have been exposed to insult which should make you shrink to look upon me. Let me pass you.'

Ralph *did* shrink, as the indignant girl fixed her kindling eye upon him; but he did not comply with her injunction, nevertheless: for he led her to a distant seat, and returning, and approaching Sir Mulberry Hawk, who had by this time risen, motioned towards the door.

'Your way lies there, sir,' said Ralph, in a suppressed voice, that some devil might have owned with pride.

'What do you mean by that?' demanded his friend, fiercely.

The swollen veins stood out like sinews on Ralph's wrinkled forehead, and the nerves about his mouth worked as though some unendurable emotion wrung them; but he smiled disdainfully, and again pointed to the door.

'Do you know me, you old madman?' asked Sir Mulberry.

'Well,' said Ralph. The fashionable vagabond for the moment quite quailed under the steady look of the older sinner, and walked towards the door, muttering as he went.

'You wanted the lord, did you?' he said, stopping short when he reached the door, as if a new light had broken in upon him, and confronting Ralph again. 'Damme, I was in the way, was I?'

Ralph smiled again, but made no answer.

'Who brought him to you first?' pursued Sir Mulberry; 'and how, without me, could you ever have wound him in your net as you have?'

'The net is a large one, and rather full,' said Ralph. 'Take care that it chokes nobody in the meshes.'

'You would sell your flesh and blood for money; yourself, if you had not already made a bargain with the devil,' retorted the other. 'Do you mean to tell me that your pretty niece was not brought here, as a decoy for the drunken boy downstairs?'

Although this hurried dialogue was carried on, in a suppressed tone on both sides, Ralph looked involuntarily round to ascertain that Kate had not moved her position so as to be within hearing. His adversary saw the advantage he had gained, and followed it up.

'Do you mean to tell me,' he asked again, 'that it is not so? Do you mean to say that if he had found his way up here instead of me, you wouldn't have been a little more blind, and a little more deaf, and a little less flourishing, than you have been? Come, Nickleby, answer me that.'

'I tell you this,' replied Ralph, 'that if I brought her here, as a matter of business—'

'Aye, that's the word,' interposed Sir Mulberry, with a laugh. 'You're coming to yourself again now.'

'—As a matter of business,' pursued Ralph, speaking slowly and firmly, as a man who has made up his mind to say no more, 'because I thought she might make some impression on the silly youth you have taken in hand and are lending good help to ruin, I knew—knowing him—that it would be long before he outraged her girl's feelings, and that unless he offended by mere puppyism and emptiness, he would, with a little management, respect the sex and conduct even of his usurer's niece. But if I thought to draw him on more gently by this device, I did not think of subjecting the girl to the licentiousness and brutality of so old a hand as you. And now we understand each other.'

'Especially as there was nothing to be got by it—eh?' sneered Sir Mulberry.

'Exactly so,' said Ralph. He had turned away, and looked over his shoulder to make this last reply. The eyes of the two worthies met, with an expression as if each rascal felt that there was no disguising himself from the other; and Sir Mulberry Hawk shrugged his shoulders and walked slowly out.

His friend closed the door, and looked restlessly towards the spot where his niece still remained in the attitude in which he had left her. She had flung herself heavily upon the couch, and with her head drooping over the cushion, and her face hidden in her hands, seemed to be still weeping in an agony of shame and grief.

Ralph would have walked into any poverty-stricken

debtor's house, and pointed him out to a bailiff, though in attendance upon a young child's death-bed, without the smallest concern, because it would have been a matter quite in the ordinary course of business, and the man would have been an offender against his only code of morality. But, here was a young girl, who had done no wrong save that of coming into the world alive; who had patiently yielded to all his wishes; who had tried hard to please him—above all, who didn't owe him money—and he felt awkward and nervous.

Ralph took a chair at some distance; then, another chair a little nearer; then, moved a little nearer still; then nearer again, and finally sat himself on the same sofa, and laid his hand on Kate's arm.

'Hush, my dear!' he said, as she drew it back, and her sobs burst out afresh. 'Hush, hush! Don't mind it now; don't think of it.'

'Oh, for pity's sake, let me go home,' cried Kate. 'Let me leave this house, and go home.'

'Yes, yes,' said Ralph. 'You shall. But you must dry your eyes first, and compose yourself. Let me raise your head. There—there.'

'Oh, uncle!' exclaimed Kate, clasping her hands. 'What have I done—what have I done—that you should subject me to this? If I had wronged you in thought, or word, or deed, it would have been most cruel to me, and the memory of one you must have loved in some old time; but—'

'Only listen to me for a moment,' interrupted Ralph, seriously alarmed by the violence of her emotions. 'I didn't know it would be so; it was impossible for me to foresee it. I did all I could. Come, let us walk about. You are faint with the closeness of the room, and the heat of these lamps. You will be better now, if you make the slightest effort.'

'I will do anything,' replied Kate, 'if you will only send me home.'

'Well, well, I will,' said Ralph; 'but you must get back your own looks; for those you have, will frighten them, and nobody must know of this but you and I. Now let us walk the other way. There. You look better even now.'

With such encouragements as these, Ralph Nickleby walked to and fro, with his niece leaning on his arm; actually trembling beneath her touch.

In the same manner, when he judged it prudent to allow her to depart, he supported her down stairs, after adjusting her shawl and performing such little offices, most probably for the first time in his life. Across the hall, and down the steps, Ralph led her too; nor did he withdraw his hand, until she was seated in the coach.

As the door of the vehicle was roughly closed, a comb fell from Kate's hair, close at her uncle's feet; and as he picked it up, and returned it into her hand, the light from a neighbouring lamp shone upon her face. The lock of hair that had escaped and curled loosely over her brow, the traces of tears yet scarcely dry, the flushed cheek, the look of sorrow, all fired some dormant train of recollection in the old man's breast; and the face of his dead brother seemed present before him, with the very look it bore on some occasion of boyish grief, of which every minutest circumstance flashed upon his mind, with the distinctness of a scene of yesterday.

Ralph Nickleby, who was proof against all appeals of blood and kindred—who was steeled against every tale of sorrow and distress—staggered while he looked, and went back into his house, as a man who had seen a spirit from some world beyond the grave.

CHAPTER XX

WHEREIN NICHOLAS AT LENGTH ENCOUNTERS HIS
UNCLE, TO WHOM HE EXPRESSES HIS SENTIMENTS
WITH MUCH CANDOUR.   HIS RESOLUTION

LITTLE Miss La Creevy trotted briskly through
divers streets at the west end of the town, early on
Monday morning—the day after the dinner—charged
with the important commission of acquainting
Madame Mantalini that Miss Nickleby was too un-
well to attend that day, but hoped to be enabled to
resume her duties on the morrow.   And as Miss La
Creevy walked along, revolving in her mind various
genteel forms and elegant turns of expression, with
a view to the selection of the very best in which to
couch her communication, she cogitated a good deal
upon the probable causes of her young friend's indisposition.

'I don't know what to make of it,' said Miss La
Creevy.   'Her eyes were decidedly red last night.
She said she had a head-ache; head-aches don't oc-
casion red eyes.   She must have been crying.'

Arriving at this conclusion, which, indeed, she had
established to her perfect satisfaction on the previous
evening, Miss La Creevy went on to consider—as
she had done nearly all night—what new cause of
unhappiness her young friend could possibly have
had.

'I can't think of anything,' said the little portrait-
painter.   'Nothing at all, unless it was the behaviour
of that old bear.   Cross to her, I suppose?   Unpleasant brute!'

Relieved by this expression of opinion, albeit it was
vented upon empty air, Miss La Creevy trotted on to

Madame Mantalini's; and being informed that the governing power was not yet out of bed, requested an interview with the second in command; whereupon Miss Knag appeared.

'So far as *I* am concerned,' said Miss Knag, when the message had been delivered, with many ornaments of speech; 'I could spare Miss Nickleby for evermore.'

'Oh, indeed, ma'am!' rejoined Miss La Creevy, highly offended. 'But, you see, you are not mistress of the business, and therefore it's of no great consequence.'

'Very good, ma'am,' said Miss Knag. 'Have you any further commands for me?'

'No, I have not, ma'am,' rejoined Miss La Creevy.

'Then good morning, ma'am,' said Miss Knag.

'Good morning to you, ma'am; and many obligations for your extreme politeness and good breeding,' rejoined Miss La Creevy.

Thus terminating the interview during which both ladies had trembled very much, and been marvellously polite—certain indications that they were within an inch of a very desperate quarrel—Miss La Creevy bounced out of the room, and into the street.

'I wonder who that is,' said the queer little soul. 'A nice person to know, I should think! I wish I had the painting of her: *I'd* do her justice.' So, feeling quite satisfied that she had said a very cutting thing at Miss Knag's expense, Miss La Creevy had a hearty laugh, and went home to breakfast, in great good-humour.

Here was one of the advantages of having lived alone so long! The little bustling, active, cheerful creature, existed entirely within herself, talked to herself, made a confidant of herself, was as sarcastic as she could be, on people who offended her, by herself; pleased herself, and did no harm. If she indulged in scandal, nobody's reputation suffered; and if she enjoyed a little bit of revenge, no living soul was one atom the worse. One of the many to whom, from straitened circumstances, a consequent inability to form the associations they would wish, and a disinclination to mix with the society they could obtain, London is as complete a solitude as the plains of Syria, the humble artist had pursued her lonely, but contented way for many years; and, until the peculiar misfortunes of the Nickleby family attracted her attention, had made no friends, though brimful of the friendliest feelings to all mankind. There are many warm hearts in the same solitary guise as poor little Miss La Creevy's.

However, that's neither here nor there, just now. She went home to breakfast, and had scarcely caught the full flavour of her first sip of tea, when the servant announced a gentleman, whereat Miss La Creevy, at once imagining a new sitter transfixed by admiration at the street-door case, was in unspeakable consternation at the presence of the tea-things.

'Here, take 'em away; run with 'em into the bedroom; anywhere,' said Miss La Creevy. 'Dear, dear; to think that I should be late on this particular morning, of all others, after being ready for three weeks by half-past eight o'clock, and not a soul coming near the place!'

'Don't let me put you out of the way,' said a voice Miss La Creevy knew. 'I told the servant not to mention my name because I wished to surprise you.'

'Mr. Nicholas!' cried Miss La Creevy, starting in great astonishment.

'You have not forgotten me, I see,' replied Nicholas, extending his hand.

'Why, I think I should even have known you if I

had met you in the street,' said Miss La Creevy, with a smile. 'Hannah, another cup and saucer. Now, I'll tell you what, young man; I'll trouble you not to repeat the impertinence you were guilty of, on the morning you went away.'

'You would not be very angry, would you?' asked Nicholas.

'Wouldn't I!' said Miss La Creevy. 'You had better try; that's all!'

Nicholas, with becoming gallantry, immediately took Miss La Creevy at her word, who uttered a faint scream and slapped his face; but it was not a very hard slap, and that's the truth.

'I never saw such a rude creature!' exclaimed Miss La Creevy.

'You told me to try,' said Nicholas.

'Well; but I was speaking ironically,' rejoined Miss La Creevy.

'Oh! that's another thing,' said Nicholas; 'you should have told me that, too.'

'I dare say you didn't know, indeed!' retorted Miss La Creevy. 'But, now I look at you again, you seem thinner than when I saw you last, and your face is haggard and pale. And how come you to have left Yorkshire?'

She stopped here; for there was so much heart in her altered tone and manner, that Nicholas was quite moved.

'I need look somewhat changed,' he said, after a short silence; 'for I have undergone some suffering, both of mind and body, since I left London. I have been very poor, too, and have even suffered from want.'

'Good Heaven, Mr. Nicholas!' exclaimed Miss La Creevy, 'what are you telling me!'

'Nothing which need distress you quite so much,' answered Nicholas, with a more sprightly air; 'neither did I come here, to bewail my lot, but on matter more to the purpose. I wish to meet my uncle face to face. I should tell you that first.'

'Then all I have to say about that is,' interposed Miss La Creevy, 'that I don't envy you your taste; and that sitting in the same room with his very boots, would put me out of humour for a fortnight.'

'In the main,' said Nicholas, 'there may be no great difference of opinion between you and me, so far; but you will understand, that I desire to confront him, to justify myself, and to cast his duplicity and malice in his throat.'

'That's quite another matter,' rejoined Miss La Creevy. 'Heaven forgive me; but I shouldn't cry my eyes quite out of my head, if they choked him. Well?'

'To this end, I called upon him this morning,' said Nicholas. 'He only returned to town on Saturday, and I knew nothing of his arrival until late last night.'

'And did you see him?' asked Miss La Creevy.

'No,' replied Nicholas. 'He had gone out.'

'Hah!' said Miss La Creevy; 'on some kind, charitable business, I dare say.'

'I have reason to believe,' pursued Nicholas, 'from what has been told me, by a friend of mine who is acquainted with his movements, that he intends seeing my mother and sister to-day, and giving them his version of the occurrences that have befallen me. I will meet him there.'

'That's right,' said Miss La Creevy, rubbing her hands. 'And yet, I don't know,' she added, 'there is much to be thought of—others to be considered.'

'I have considered others,' rejoined Nicholas; 'but as honesty and honour are both at issue, nothing shall deter me.'

'You should know best,' said Miss La Creevy.

'In this case I hope so,' answered Nicholas. 'And all I want you to do for me, is, to prepare them for my coming. They think me a long way off, and if I went wholly unexpected, I should frighten them. If you can spare time to tell them that you have seen me, and that I shall be with them in a quarter of an hour afterwards, you will do me a great service.'

'I wish I could do you, or any of you, a greater,' said Miss La Creevy; 'but the power to serve, is as seldom joined with the will, as the will is with the power, *I* think.'

Talking on very fast and very much, Miss La Creevy finished her breakfast with great expedition, put away the tea-caddy and hid the key under the fender, resumed her bonnet, and, taking Nicholas's arm, sallied forth at once to the City. Nicholas left her near the door of his mother's house, and promised to return within a quarter of an hour.

It so chanced that Ralph Nickleby, at length seeing fit, for his own purposes, to communicate the atrocities of which Nicholas had been guilty, had (instead of first proceeding to another quarter of the town on business, as Newman Noggs supposed he would) gone straight to his sister-in-law. Hence, when Miss La Creevy, admitted by a girl who was cleaning the house, made her way to the sitting-room, she found Mrs. Nickleby and Kate in tears, and Ralph just concluding his statement of his nephew's misdemeanours. Kate beckoned her not to retire, and Miss La Creevy took a seat in silence.

'You are here already, are you, my gentleman?'

thought the little woman. 'Then he shall announce himself, and see what effect that has on you.'

'This is pretty,' said Ralph, folding up Miss Squeers's note; 'very pretty. I recommended him—against all my previous conviction, for I knew he would never do any good—to a man with whom, behaving himself properly, he might have remained, in comfort, for years. What is the result? Conduct, for which he might hold up his hand at the Old Bailey.'

'I never will believe it,' said Kate, indignantly; 'never. It is some base conspiracy, which carries its own falsehood with it.'

'My dear,' said Ralph, 'you wrong the worthy man. These are not inventions. The man is assaulted, your brother is not to be found; this boy, of whom they speak, goes with him—remember, remember.'

'It is impossible,' said Kate. 'Nicholas!—and a thief, too! Mamma, how can you sit and hear such statements?'

Poor Mrs. Nickleby, who had, at no time, been remarkable for the possession of a very clear understanding, and who had been reduced by the late changes in her affairs to a most complicated state of perplexity, made no other reply to this earnest remonstrance than exclaiming from behind a mass of pocket-handkerchief, that she never could have believed it—thereby most ingeniously leaving her hearers to suppose that she did believe it.

'It would be my duty, if he came in my way, to deliver him up to justice,' said Ralph, 'my bounden duty; I should have no other course, as a man of the world and a man of business, to pursue. And yet,' said Ralph, speaking in a very marked manner, and looking furtively, but fixedly, at Kate, 'and yet

I would not. I would spare the feelings of his—of his sister. And his mother of course,' added Ralph, as though by an afterthought, and with far less emphasis.

Kate very well understood that this was held out as an additional inducement to her, to preserve the strictest silence regarding the events of the preceding night. She looked involuntarily towards Ralph as he ceased to speak, but he had turned his eyes another way, and seemed for the moment quite unconscious of her presence.

'Everything,' said Ralph, after a long silence, broken only by Mrs. Nickleby's sobs, 'everything combines to prove the truth of this letter, if indeed there were any possibility of disputing it. Do innocent men steal away from the sight of honest folks, and skulk in hiding-places, like outlaws? Do innocent men inveigle nameless vagabonds, and prowl with them about the country as idle robbers do? Assault, riot, theft, what do you call these?'

'A lie!' cried a voice, as the door was dashed open, and Nicholas came into the room.

In the first moment of surprise, and possibly of alarm, Ralph rose from his seat, and fell back a few paces, quite taken off his guard by this unexpected apparition. In another moment, he stood, fixed and immovable with folded arms, regarding his nephew with a scowl; while Kate and Miss La Creevy threw themselves between the two, to prevent the personal violence which the fierce excitement of Nicholas appeared to threaten.

'Dear Nicholas,' cried his sister, clinging to him. 'Be calm, consider—'

'Consider, Kate!' cried Nicholas, clasping her hand so tight, in the tumult of his anger, that she could scarcely bear the pain. 'When I consider all, and think of what has passed, I need be made of iron to stand before him.'

'Or bronze,' said Ralph, quietly; 'there is not hardihood enough in flesh and blood to face it out.'

'Oh dear, dear!' cried Mrs. Nickleby, 'that things should have come to such a pass as this!'

'Who speaks in a tone, as if I had done wrong, and brought disgrace on them?' said Nicholas, looking round.

'Your mother, sir,' replied Ralph, motioning towards her.

'Whose ears have been poisoned by you,' said Nicholas; 'by you—who, under pretence of deserving the thanks she poured upon you, heaped every insult, wrong, and indignity, upon my head. You, who sent me to a den where sordid cruelty, worthy of yourself, runs wanton, and youthful misery stalks precocious; where the lightness of childhood shrinks into the heaviness of age, and its every promise blights, and withers as it grows. I call Heaven to witness,' said Nicholas, looking eagerly round, 'that I have seen all this, and that he knows it.'

'Refute these calumnies,' said Kate, 'and be more patient, so that you may give them no advantage. Tell us what you really did, and show that they are untrue.'

'Of what do they—or of what does he—accuse me?' said Nicholas.

'First, of attacking your master, and being within an ace of qualifying yourself to be tried for murder,' interposed Ralph. 'I speak plainly, young man, bluster as you will.'

'I interfered,' said Nicholas, 'to save a miserable creature from the vilest cruelty. In so doing, I inflicted such punishment upon a wretch as he will not readily forget, though far less than he deserved from me. If the same scene were renewed before me now, I would take the same part; but I would strike harder and heavier, and brand him with such marks as he should carry to his grave, go to it when he would.'

'You hear?' said Ralph, turning to Mrs. Nickleby. 'Penitence, this!'

'Oh dear me!' cried Mrs. Nickleby, 'I don't know what to think, I really don't.'

'Do not speak just now, mamma, I entreat you,' said Kate. 'Dear Nicholas, I only tell you, that you may know what wickedness can prompt, but they accuse you of—a ring is missing, and they dare to say that—'

'The woman,' said Nicholas, haughtily, 'the wife of the fellow from whom these charges come, dropped —as I suppose—a worthless ring among some clothes of mine, early in the morning on which I left the house. At least, I know that she was in the bedroom where they lay, struggling with an unhappy child, and that I found it when I opened my bundle on the road. I returned it, at once, by coach, and they have it now.'

'I knew, I knew,' said Kate, looking towards her uncle. 'About this boy, love, in whose company they say you left?'

'The boy, a silly, helpless creature, from the brutality and hard usage, is with me now,' rejoined Nicholas.

'You hear?' said Ralph, appealing to the mother again, 'everything proved, even upon his own confession. Do you choose to restore that boy, sir?'

'No. I do not,' replied Nicholas.

'You do not?' sneered Ralph.

'No,' repeated Nicholas, 'not to the man with whom I found him. I would that I knew on whom he has the claim of birth: I might wring something from his sense of shame, if he were dead to every tie of nature.'

'Indeed!' sneered Ralph. 'Now, sir, will you hear a word or two from me?'

'You can speak when and what you please,' replied Nicholas, embracing his sister. 'I take little heed of what you say or threaten.'

'Mighty well, sir,' retorted Ralph; 'but perhaps it may concern others, who may think it worth their while to listen, and consider what I tell them. I will address your mother, sir, who knows the world.'

'Ah! and I only too dearly wish I didn't,' sobbed Mrs. Nickleby.

There really was no necessity for the good lady to be much distressed upon this particular head; the extent of her worldly knowledge being, to say the least, very questionable; and so Ralph seemed to think, for he smiled as she spoke. He then glanced steadily at her and Nicholas by turns, as he delivered himself in these words—

'Of what I have done, or what I meant to do, for you, ma'am, and my niece, I say not one syllable. I held out no promise, and leave you to judge for yourself. I hold out no threat now, but I say that this boy, headstrong, wilful, and disorderly as he is, should not have one penny of my money, or one crust of my bread, or one grasp of my hand, to save him from the loftiest gallows in all Europe. I will not meet him, come where he comes, or hear his name. I will not help him, or those who help him. With a full knowledge of what he brought upon you by so doing, he has come back in his selfish sloth, to be an aggravation to your wants, and a burden upon his sister's scanty wages. I regret to leave you, and more to leave her, now, but I will not encourage this compound of meanness and cruelty, and, as I will not ask you to renounce him, I see you no more.'

If Ralph had not known and felt his power in wounding those he hated, his glances at Nicholas would have shown it him, in all its force, as he proceeded in the above address. Innocent as the young man was, of all wrong, every artful insinuation stung, every well-considered sarcasm cut him to the quick; and when Ralph noted his pale face and quivering lip, he hugged himself to mark how well he had chosen the taunts best calculated to strike deep into a young and ardent spirit.

'I can't help it,' cried Mrs. Nickleby, 'I know you have been very good to us, and meant to do a good deal for my dear daughter. I am quite sure of that; I know you did, and it was very kind of you, having her at your house and all—and of course it would have been a great thing for her and for me too. But I can't, you know, brother-in-law, I can't renounce my own son, even if he has done all you say he has—it's not possible; I couldn't do it; so we must go to rack and ruin, Kate, my dear. I can bear it, I dare say.' Pouring forth these and a perfectly wonderful train of other disjointed expressions of regret, which no mortal power but Mrs. Nickleby's could ever have strung together, that lady wrung her hands, and her tears fell faster.

'Why do you say, "*if* Nicholas has done what they say he has," mamma?' asked Kate, with honest anger. 'You know he has not.'

'I don't know what to think, one way or other, my dear,' said Mrs. Nickleby; 'Nicholas is so violent, and your uncle has so much composure, that I can only hear what he says, and not what Nicholas does. Never mind, don't let us talk any more about it. We can go to the Workhouse, or the Refuge for the Destitute, or the Magdalen Hospital, I dare say; and the sooner we go the better.' With this extraordinary jumble of charitable institutions, Mrs. Nickleby again gave way to her tears.

'Stay,' said Nicholas, as Ralph turned to go. 'You need not leave this place, sir, for it will be relieved of my presence, in one minute, and it will be long, very long, before I darken these doors again.'

'Nicholas,' cried Kate, throwing herself on her brother's shoulder, 'do not say so. My dear brother, you will break my heart. Mamma, speak to him. Do not mind her. Nicholas; she does not mean it, you should know her better. Uncle, somebody, for Heaven's sake speak to him.'

'I never meant, Kate,' said Nicholas, tenderly, 'I never meant to stay among you; think better of me than to suppose it possible. I may turn my back on this town a few hours sooner than I intended, but what of that? We shall not forget each other apart, and better days will come when we shall part no more. Be a woman, Kate,' he whispered, proudly, 'and do not make me one, while *he* looks on.'

'No, no, I will not,' said Kate, eagerly, 'but you will not leave us. Oh! think of all the happy days we have had together, before these terrible misfortunes came upon us; of all the comfort and happiness of home, and the trials we have to bear now; of our having no protector under all the slights and wrongs that poverty so much favours, and you cannot leave us to bear them alone, without one hand to help us.'

'You will be helped when I am away,' replied Nicholas, hurriedly. 'I am no help to you, no protector; I should bring you nothing but sorrow, and want, and suffering. My own mother sees it, and her fondness and fears for you, point to the course that I should take. And so all good angels bless you, Kate, till I can carry you to some home of mine, where we may revive the happiness denied to us now, and talk of these trials as of things gone by. Do not keep me here, but let me go at once. There. Dear girl—dear girl.'

The grasp which had detained him, relaxed, and Kate swooned in his arms. Nicholas stooped over her, for a few seconds, and placing her gently in a chair, confided her to their honest friend.

'I need not entreat your sympathy,' he said, wringing her hand, 'for I know your nature. You will never forget them.'

He stepped up to Ralph, who remained in the same attitude which he had preserved throughout the interview, and moved not a finger.

'Whatever step you take, sir,' he said, in a voice inaudible beyond themselves, 'I shall keep a strict account of. I leave them to you, at your desire. There will be a day of reckoning sooner or later, and it will be a heavy one for you if they are wronged.'

Ralph did not allow a muscle of his face to indicate that he heard one word of this parting address. He hardly knew that it was concluded, and Mrs. Nickleby had scarcely made up her mind to detain her son by force if necessary, when Nicholas was gone.

As he hurried through the streets to his obscure lodging, seeking to keep pace, as it were, with the rapidity of the thoughts which crowded upon him, many doubts and hesitations arose in his mind, and almost tempted him to return. But what would they gain by this? Supposing he were to put Ralph Nickleby at defiance, and were even fortunate enough to obtain some small employment, his being with them could only render their present condition worse, and might greatly impair their future prospects; for his mother had spoken of some new kindnesses towards Kate which she had not denied. 'No.' thought Nicholas, 'I have acted for the best.'

But, before he had gone five hundred yards, some other and different feeling would come upon him, and then he would lag again, and pulling his hat over his eyes, give way to the melancholy reflections which pressed thickly upon him. To have committed no fault, and yet to be so entirely alone in the world; to be separated from the only persons he loved, and to be proscribed like a criminal, when six months ago he had been surrounded by every comfort, and looked up to, as the chief hope of his family—this was hard to bear. He had not deserved it either. Well, there was comfort in that; and poor Nicholas would brighten up again, to be again depressed, as his quickly shifting thoughts presented every variety of light and shade before him.

Undergoing these alternations of hope and misgiving, which no one, placed in a situation of ordinary trial, can fail to have experienced, Nicholas at length reached his poor room, where, no longer borne up by the excitement which had hitherto sustained him, but depressed by the revulsion of feeling it left behind, he threw himself on the bed, and turning his face to the wall, gave free vent to the emotions he had so long stifled.

He had not heard anybody enter, and was unconscious of the presence of Smike, until, happening to raise his head, he saw him, standing at the upper end of the room, looking wistfully towards him. He withdrew his eyes when he saw that he was observed, and affected to be busied with some scanty preparations for dinner.

'Well, Smike,' said Nicholas, as cheerfully as he could speak, 'let me hear what new acquaintances you have made this morning, or what new wonder you have found out, in the compass of this street and the next one.'

'No,' said Smike, shaking his head mournfully; 'I must talk of something else to-day.'

'Of what you like,' replied Nicholas, good-humouredly.

'Of this,' said Smike. 'I know you are unhappy, and have got into great trouble by bringing me away. I ought to have known that, and stopped behind—I would, indeed, if I had thought it then. You—you —are not rich; you have not enough for yourself, and I should not be here. You grow,' said the lad, laying his hand timidly on that of Nicholas, 'you grow thinner every day; your cheek is paler, and your eye more sunk. Indeed I cannot bear to see you so, and think how I am burdening you. I tried to go away to-day, but the thought of your kind face drew me back. I could not leave you without a word.' The poor fellow could say no more, for his eyes filled with tears, and his voice was gone.

'The word which separates us,' said Nicholas, grasping him heartily by the shoulder, 'shall never be said by me, for you are my only comfort and stay. I would not lose you now, Smike, for all the world could give. The thought of you has upheld me through all I have endured to-day, and shall, through fifty times such trouble. Give me your hand. My heart is linked to yours. We will journey from this place together, before the week is out. What, if I am steeped in poverty? You lighten it, and we will be poor together.'

CHAPTER XXI

MADAME MANTALINI FINDS HERSELF IN A SITUATION
OF SOME DIFFICULTY, AND MISS NICKLEBY FINDS
HERSELF IN NO SITUATION AT ALL

THE agitation she had undergone, rendered Kate Nickleby unable to resume her duties at the dressmaker's for three days, at the expiration of which interval she betook herself at the accustomed hour, and with languid steps, to the temple of fashion where Madame Mantalini reigned paramount and supreme.

The ill-will of Miss Knag had lost nothing of its virulence, in the interval. The young ladies still scrupulously shrunk from all companionship with their denounced associate; and when that exemplary female arrived a few minutes afterwards, she was at no pains to conceal the displeasure with which she regarded Kate's return.

'Upon my word!' said Miss Knag, as the satellites flocked round, to relieve her of her bonnet and shawl; 'I should have thought some people would have had spirit enough to stop away altogether, when they know what an incumbrance their presence is to right-minded persons. But it's a queer world; oh! it's a queer world!'

Miss Knag, having passed this comment on the world, in the tone in which most people do pass comments on the world when they are out of temper, that is to say, as if they by no means belonged to it, concluded by heaving a sigh, wherewith she seemed meekly to compassionate the wickedness of mankind.

The attendants were not slow to echo the sigh, and Miss Knag was apparently on the eve of favouring them with some further moral reflections, when the voice of Madame Mantalini, conveyed through the speaking-tube, ordered Miss Nickleby upstairs to assist in the arrangement of the show-room; a distinction which caused Miss Knag to toss her head so much, and bite her lips so hard, that her powers of conversation were, for the time, annihilated.

'Well, Miss Nickleby, child,' said Madame Mantalini, when Kate presented herself; 'are you quite well again?'

'A great deal better, thank you,' replied Kate.

'I wish I could say the same,' remarked Madame Mantalini, seating herself with an air of weariness.

'Are you ill?' asked Kate. 'I am very sorry for that.'

'Not exactly ill, but worried, child—worried,' rejoined Madame.

'I am still more sorry to hear that,' said Kate, gently. 'Bodily illness is more easy to bear, than mental.'

'Ah! and it's much easier to talk than to bear either,' said Madame, rubbing her nose with much irritability of manner. 'There, get to your work, child, and put the things in order, do.'

While Kate was wondering within herself what these symptoms of unusual vexation portended, Mr. Mantalini put the tips of his whiskers, and, by degrees, his head, through the half-opened door, and cried in a soft voice—

'Is my life and soul there?'

'No,' replied his wife.

'How can it say so, when it is blooming in the front room like a little rose in a demnition flower-pot?' urged Mantalini. 'May its poppet come in and talk?'

'Certainly not,' replied Madame; 'you know I never allow you here. Go along!'

The poppet, however, encouraged perhaps by the relenting tone of this reply, ventured to rebel, and, stealing into the room, made towards Madame Mantalini on tiptoe, blowing her a kiss as he came along.

'Why will it vex itself, and twist its little face into bewitching nutcrackers?' said Mantalini, putting his left arm round the waist of his life and soul, and drawing her towards him with his right.

'Oh! I can't bear you,' replied his wife.

'Not—eh, not bear *me*!' exclaimed Mantalini. 'Fibs, fibs. It couldn't be. There's not a woman alive, that could tell me such a thing to my face—to my own face.' Mr. Mantalini stroked his chin as he said this, and glanced complacently at an opposite mirror.

'Such destructive extravagance,' reasoned his wife, in a low tone.

'All in its joy at having gained such a lovely creature, such a little Venus, such a demd enchanting, bewitching, engrossing, captivating little Venus,' said Mantalini.

'See what a situation you have placed me in!' urged Madame.

'No harm will come, no harm shall come, to its own darling,' rejoined Mr. Mantalini. 'It is all over; there will be nothing the matter; money shall be got in; and if it don't come in fast enough, old Nickleby shall stump up again, or have his jugular separated if he dares to vex and hurt the little—'

'Hush!' interposed Madame. 'Don't you see?'

Mr. Mantalini, who, in his eagerness to make up matters with his wife, had overlooked, or feigned to overlook, Miss Nickleby hitherto, took the hint, and laying his finger on his lip, sunk his voice still lower. There was, then, a great deal of whispering, during which Madame Mantalini appeared to make reference, more than once, to certain debts incurred by Mr. Mantalini previous to her coverture; and also to an unexpected outlay of money in payment of the aforesaid debts; and furthermore, to certain agreeable weaknesses on that gentleman's part, such as gaming, wasting, idling, and a tendency to horseflesh; each of which matters of accusation Mr. Mantalini disposed of, by one kiss or more, as its relative importance demanded. The upshot of it all, was, that Madame Mantalini was in raptures with him, and that they went upstairs to breakfast.

Kate busied herself in what she had to do, and was silently arranging the various articles of decoration in the best taste she could display, when she started to hear a strange man's voice in the room, and started again, to observe, on looking round, that a white hat, and a red handkerchief, and a broad round face, and a large head, and part of a green coat were in the room too.

'Don't alarm yourself, Miss,' said the proprietor of these appearances. 'I say; this here's the mantie-making consarn, an't it?'

'Yes,' rejoined Kate, greatly astonished. 'What did you want?'

The stranger answered not; but, first looking back, as though to beckon to some unseen person outside, came, very deliberately, into the room and was closely followed by a little man in brown, very much the worse for wear, who brought with him a mingled fumigation of stale tobacco and fresh onions. The clothes of this gentleman were much bespeckled with flue; and his shoes, stockings, and nether garments, from his heels to the waist buttons of his coat inclusive, were profusely embroidered with splashes of mud, caught a fortnight previously—before the setting-in of the fine weather.

THE PROFESSIONAL GENTLEMAN AT MADAME MANTALINI'S.

Kate's very natural impression was, that these engaging individuals had called with the view of possessing themselves, unlawfully, of any portable articles that chanced to strike their fancy. She did not attempt to disguise her apprehensions, and made a move towards the door.

'Wait a minnit,' said the man in the green coat, closing it softly, and standing with his back against it. 'This is a unpleasant bisness. Vere's your governor?'

'My what—did you say?' asked Kate, trembling; for she thought 'governor' might be slang for watch or money.

'Mr. Muntlehiney,' said the man. 'Wot's come on him? Is he at home?'

'He is above-stairs, I believe,' replied Kate, a little reassured by this inquiry. 'Do you want him?'

'No,' replied the visitor. 'I don't ezactly want him, if it's made a favour on. You can jist give him that 'ere card, and tell him if he wants to speak to *me,* and save trouble, here I am; that's all.'

With these words, the stranger put a thick square card into Kate's hand, and, turning to his friend, remarked, with an easy air, 'that the rooms was a good high pitch'; to which the friend assented, adding, by way of illustration, 'that there was lots of room for a little boy to grow up a man in either on 'em, vithout much fear of his ever bringing his head into contract vith the ceiling.'

After ringing the bell which would summon Madame Mantalini, Kate glanced at the card, and saw that it displayed the name of 'Scaley,' together with some other information to which she had not had time to refer, when her attention was attracted by Mr. Scaley himself, who, walking up to one of the cheval glasses, gave it a hard poke in the centre with his stick, as coolly as if it had been made of cast iron.

'Good plate this here, Tix,' said Mr. Scaley to his friend.

'Ah!' rejoined Mr. Tix, placing the marks of his four fingers, and a duplicate impression of his thumb on a piece of sky-blue silk; 'and this here article warn't made for nothing, mind you.'

From the silk, Mr. Tix transferred his admiration to some elegant articles of wearing apparel, while Mr. Scaley adjusted his neckcloth, at leisure, before the glass, and afterwards, aided by its reflection, proceeded to the minute consideration of a pimple on his chin; in which absorbing occupation he was yet engaged, when Madame Mantalini entering the room, uttered an exclamation of surprise which roused him.

'Oh! Is this the missis?' inquired Scaley.

'It is Madame Mantalini,' said Kate.

'Then,' said Mr. Scaley, producing a small document from his pocket and unfolding it very slowly, 'this is a writ of execution, and if it's not conwenient to settle we'll go over the house at wunst please, and take the inwentory.'

Poor Madame Mantalini wrung her hands for grief, and rung the bell for her husband; which done, she fell into a chair and a fainting fit, simultaneously. The professional gentlemen, however, were not at all discomposed by this event, for Mr. Scaley, leaning upon a stand on which a handsome dress was displayed (so that his shoulders appeared above it, in nearly the same manner as the shoulders of the lady for whom it was designed would have done if she had had it on), pushed his hat on one side and scratched his head with perfect unconcern, while his friend Mr. Tix, taking that opportunity for a general survey of the apartment preparatory to entering on business, stood with his inventory-book under his arm, and his hat in his hand, mentally occupied in putting a price upon every object within his range of vision.

Such was the posture of affairs when Mr. Mantalini hurried in; and as that distinguished specimen had had a pretty extensive intercourse with Mr. Scaley's fraternity in his bachelor days, and was, besides, very far from being taken by surprise on the present agitating occasion, merely shrugged his shoulders, thrust his hands down to the bottom of his pockets, elevated his eyebrows, whistled a bar or two, swore an oath or two, and, sitting astride upon a chair, put the best face upon the matter with great composure and decency.

'What's the demd total?' was the first question he asked.

'Fifteen hundred and twenty-seven pound, four and ninepence ha'penny,' replied Mr. Scaley, without moving a limb.

'The halfpenny be demd,' said Mr. Mantalini, impatiently.

'By all means if you vish it,' retorted Mr. Scaley; 'and the ninepence.'

'It don't matter to us if the fifteen hundred and twenty-seven pound went along with it, that I know on,' observed Mr. Tix.

'Not a button,' said Scaley.

'Well'; said the same gentleman, after a pause. 'Wot's to be done—anything? Is it only a small crack, or a out-and-out smash? A break-up of the constitootion is it—werry good. Then, Mr. Tom Tix, esk-vire, you must inform your angel wife and lovely family as you won't sleep at home for three nights to come, along of being in possession here. Wot's the good of the lady a fretting herself?' continued Mr. Scaley, as Madame Mantalini sobbed. 'A good half of wot 's here, isn't paid for, I des-say, and wot a consolation oughtn't that to be to her feelings!'

With these remarks, combining great pleasantry with sound moral encouragement under difficulties, Mr. Scaley proceeded to take the inventory, in which delicate task he was materially assisted by the uncommon tact and experience of Mr. Tix, the broker.

'My cup of happiness's sweetener,' said Mantalini, approaching his wife with a penitent air; 'will you listen to me for two minutes?'

'Oh! don't speak to me,' replied his wife, sobbing. 'You have ruined me, and that 's enough.'

Mr. Mantalini, who had doubtless well considered his part, no sooner heard these words pronounced in a tone of grief and severity, than he recoiled several paces, assumed an expression of consuming mental agony, rushed headlong from the room, and was, soon afterwards, heard to slam the door of an upstairs dressing-room with great violence.

'Miss Nickleby,' cried Madame Mantalini, when this sound met her ear, 'make haste for Heaven's sake, he will destroy himself! I spoke unkindly to him, and he cannot bear it from me. Alfred, my darling Alfred.'

With such exclamations, she hurried upstairs, followed by Kate, who, although she did not quite participate in the fond wife's apprehensions, was a little flurried, nevertheless. The dressing-room door being hastily flung open, Mr. Mantalini was disclosed to view, with his shirt-collar symmetrically thrown back: putting a fine edge to a breakfast knife by means of his razor strop.

'Ah!' cried Mr. Mantalini. 'Interrupted!' and whisk went the breakfast knife into Mr. Mantalini's dressing-gown pocket, while Mr. Mantalini's eyes rolled wildly, and his hair floating in wild disorder, mingled with his whiskers.

'Alfred,' cried his wife, flinging her arms about him, 'I didn't mean to say it, I didn't mean to say it!'

'Ruined!' cried Mr. Mantalini. 'Have I brought ruin upon the best and purest creature that ever blessed a demnition vagabond! Demmit, let me go.' At this crisis of his ravings Mr. Mantalini made a pluck at the breakfast knife, and being restrained by his wife's grasp, attempted to dash his head against the wall—taking very good care to be at least six feet from it.

'Compose yourself, my own angel,' said Madame. 'It was nobody's fault; it was mine as much as yours, we shall do very well yet. Come, Alfred, come.'

Mr. Mantalini did not think proper to come to, all at once; but, after calling several times for poison, and requesting some lady or gentleman to blow his brains out, gentler feelings came upon him, and he wept pathetically. In this softened frame of mind he did not oppose the capture of the knife—which, to tell the truth, he was rather glad to be rid of, as an inconvenient and dangerous article for a skirt pocket —and finally he suffered himself to be led away, by his affectionate partner.

After a delay of two or three hours, the young ladies were informed that their services would be dispensed with, until further notice, and at the expiration of two days, the name of Mantalini appeared in the list of bankrupts: Miss Nickleby received an intimation per post, on the same morning, that the business would be, in future, carried on under the name of Miss Knag, and that her assistance would no longer be required—a piece of intelligence with which Mrs. Nickleby was no sooner made acquainted, than that good lady declared she had expected it all along, and cited divers unknown occasions on which she had prophesied to that precise effect.

'And I say again,' remarked Mrs. Nickleby (who, it is scarcely necessary to observe, had never said so before), 'I say again, that a milliner's and dressmaker's is the very last description of business, Kate, that you should have thought of attaching yourself to. I don't make it a reproach to you, my love; but still I will say, that if you had consulted your own mother—'

'Well, well, mamma,' said Kate, mildly; 'what would you recommend now?'

'Recommend!' cried Mrs. Nickleby, 'isn't it obvious, my dear, that of all occupations in this world for a young lady situated as you are, that of companion to some amiable lady is the very thing for which your education, and manners, and personal appearance, and everything else, exactly qualify you? Did you never hear your poor dear papa speak of the young lady who was the daughter of the old lady who boarded in the same house that he boarded in once, when he was a bachelor—what was her name again? I know it began with a B, and ended with a g, but whether it was Waters or—no it couldn't have been that, either; but whatever her name was, don't you know that that young lady went as companion to a married lady who died soon afterwards, and that she married the husband, and had one of the finest little boys that the medical man had ever seen—all within eighteen months.'

Kate knew, perfectly well, that this torrent of favourable recollection was occasioned by some opening, real or imaginary, which her mother had discovered, in the companionship walk of life. She therefore waited, very patiently, until all reminiscences and anecdotes, bearing or not bearing upon the subject, had been exhausted, and at last ventured to inquire what discovery had been made. The truth then came out. Mrs. Nickleby had, that morning, had a yesterday's newspaper of the very first respectability from the public-house where the porter came from; and in this yesterday's newspaper was an advertisement, couched in the purest and most grammatical English, announcing that a married lady was in want of a genteel young person as companion, and that the married lady's name and address were to be known, on application at a certain library at the west end of the town, therein mentioned.

'And I say,' exclaimed Mrs. Nickleby, laying the paper down in triumph, 'that if your uncle don't object, it's well worth the trial.'

Kate was too sick at heart, after the rough jostling she had already had with the world, and really cared too little at the moment what fate was reserved for her, to make any objection. Mr. Ralph Nickleby offered none, but, on the contrary, highly approved of the suggestion; neither did he express any great surprise at Madame Mantalini's sudden failure, indeed it would have been strange if he had, inasmuch as it had been procured and brought about, chiefly by himself. So, the name and address were obtained without loss of time, and Miss Nickleby and her mamma went off in quest of Mrs. Wititterly, of Cadogan Place, Sloane Street, that same forenoon.

Cadogan Place is the one slight bond that joins two great extremes; it is the connecting link between the aristocratic pavements of Belgrave Square, and the barbarism of Chelsea. It is in Sloane Street, but not of it. The people in Cadogan Place look down upon Sloane Street, and think Brompton low. They affect fashion too, and wonder where the New Road is. Not that they claim to be on precisely the same footing as the high folks of Belgrave Square and Grosvenor Place, but that they stand, with reference to them, rather in the light of those illegitimate children of the great who are content to boast of their connections, although their connections disavow them. Wearing as much as they can of the airs and semblances of loftiest rank, the people of Cadogan Place have the realities of middle station. It is the conductor which communicates to the inhabitants of regions beyond its limit, the shock of pride of birth and rank, which it has not within itself, but derives from a fountain-head beyond; or, like the ligament which unites the Siamese twins, it contains something of the life and essence of two distinct bodies, and yet belongs to neither.

Upon this doubtful ground, lived Mrs. Wititterly, and at Mrs. Wititterly's door Kate Nickleby knocked with trembling hand. The door was opened by a big footman with his head floured, or chalked, or painted in some way (it didn't look genuine powder), and the big footman, receiving the card of introduction, gave it to a little page; so little, indeed, that his body would not hold, in ordinary array, the number of small buttons which are indispensable to a page's costume, and they were consequently obliged to be stuck on four abreast. This young gentleman took the card upstairs on a salver, and pending his return, Kate and her mother were shown into a dining-room of rather dirty and shabby aspect, and so comfortably arranged as to be adapted to almost any purpose rather than eating and drinking.

Now, in the ordinary course of things, and according to all authentic descriptions of high life, as set forth in books, Mrs. Wititterly ought to have been in her *boudoir*; but whether it was that Mr. Wititterly was at that moment shaving himself in the *boudoir*

or what not, certain it is that Mrs. Wititterly gave
audience in the drawing-room, where was everything
proper and necessary, including curtains and furniture coverings of a roseate hue, to shed a delicate
bloom on Mrs. Wititterly's complexion, and a little
dog to snap at strangers' legs for Mrs. Wititterly's
amusement, and the aforementioned page, to hand
chocolate for Mrs. Wititterly's refreshment.

The lady had an air of sweet insipidity, and a face
of engaging paleness; there was a faded look about
her, and about the furniture, and about the house.
She was reclining on a sofa in such a very unstudied
attitude, that she might have been taken for an actress
all ready for the first scene in a ballet, and only waiting for the drop-curtain to go up.

'Place chairs.'

The page placed them.

'Leave the room, Alphonse.'

The page left it; but if ever an Alphonse carried
plain Bill in his face and figure, that page was the
boy.

'I have ventured to call, ma'am,' said Kate, after
a few seconds of awkward silence, 'from having seen
your advertisement.'

'Yes,' replied Mrs. Wititterly, 'one of my people
put it in the paper. Yes.'

'I thought, perhaps,' said Kate, modestly, 'that if
you had not already made a final choice, you would
forgive my troubling you with an application.'

'Yes,' drawled Mrs. Wititterly again.

'If you have already made a selection—'

'Oh dear no,' interrupted the lady, 'I am not so
easily suited. I really don't know what to say. You
have never been a companion before, have you?'

Mrs. Nickleby, who had been eagerly watching her
opportunity, came dexterously in, before Kate could

reply. 'Not to any stranger, ma'am,' said the good lady; 'but she has been a companion to me for some years. I am her mother, ma'am.'

'Oh!' said Mrs. Wititterly, 'I apprehend you.'

'I assure you, ma'am,' said Mrs. Nickleby, 'that I very little thought, at one time, that it would be necessary for my daughter to go out into the world at all, for her poor dear papa was an independent gentleman, and would have been at this moment if he had but listened in time to my constant entreaties and—'

'Dear mamma,' said Kate, in a low voice.

'My dear Kate, if you will allow me to speak,' said Mrs. Nickleby, 'I shall take the liberty of explaining to this lady—'

'I think it is almost unnecessary, mamma.'

And notwithstanding all the frowns and winks with which Mrs. Nickleby intimated that she was going to say something which would clench the business at once, Kate maintained her point by an expressive look, and for once Mrs. Nickleby was stopped upon the very brink of an oration.

'What are your accomplishments?' asked Mrs. Wititterly, with her eyes shut.

Kate blushed as she mentioned her principal acquirements, and Mrs. Nickleby checked them all off, one by one, on her fingers; having calculated the number before she came out. Luckily the two calculations agreed, so Mrs. Nickleby had no excuse for talking.

'You are a good temper?' asked Mrs. Wititterly, opening her eyes for an instant, and shutting them again.

'I hope so,' rejoined Kate.

'And have a highly respectable reference for everything, have you?'

Kate replied that she had, and laid her uncle's card upon the table.

'Have the goodness to draw your chair a little nearer, and let me look at you,' said Mrs. Wititterly; 'I am so very near-sighted that I can't quite discern your features.'

Kate complied, though not without some embarrassment, with this request, and Mrs. Wititterly took a languid survey of her countenance, which lasted some two or three minutes.

'I like your appearance,' said that lady, ringing a little bell. 'Alphonse, request your master to come here.'

The page disappeared on this errand, and after a short interval, during which not a word was spoken on either side, opened the door for an important gentleman of about eight-and-thirty, of rather plebeian countenance, and with a very light head of hair, who leant over Mrs. Wititterly for a little time, and conversed with her in whispers.

'Oh!' he said, turning round, 'yes. This is a most important matter. Mrs. Wititterly is of a very excitable nature; very delicate, very fragile; a hothouse plant, an exotic.'

'Oh! Henry, my dear,' interposed Mrs. Wititterly.

'You are, my love, you know you are; one breath—,' said Mr. W., blowing an imaginary feather away. 'Pho! you 're gone!'

The lady sighed.

'Your soul is too large for your body,' said Mr. Wititterly. 'Your intellect wears you out; all the medical men say so; you know that there is not a physician who is not proud of being called in to you. What is their unanimous declaration? "My dear doctor," said I to Sir Tumley Snuffim, in this very room, the very last time he came. "My dear doctor, what is my wife's complaint? Tell me all. I can bear it. Is it nerves?" "My dear fellow," he said, "be proud of that woman; make much of her; she is an ornament to the fashionable world, and to you. Her complaint is soul. It swells, expands, dilates—the blood fires, the pulse quickens, the excitement increases—Whew!" ' Here Mr. Wititterly who, in the ardour of his description, had flourished his right hand to within something less than an inch of Mrs. Nickleby's bonnet, drew it hastily back again, and blew his nose as fiercely as if it had been done by some violent machinery.

'You make me out worse than I am, Henry,' said Mrs. Wititterly, with a faint smile.

'I do not, Julia, I do not,' said Mr. W. 'The society in which you move—necessarily move, from your station, connection, and endowments—is one vortex and whirlpool of the most frightful excitement. Bless my heart and body, can I ever forget the night you danced with the baronet's nephew at the election ball, at Exeter? It was tremendous.'

'I always suffer for these triumphs afterwards,' said Mrs. Wititterly.

'And for that very reason,' rejoined her husband, 'you must have a companion, in whom there is great gentleness, great sweetness, excessive sympathy, and perfect repose.'

Here, both Mr. and Mrs. Wititterly, who had talked rather at the Nicklebys than to each other, left off speaking, and looked at their two hearers, with an expression of countenance which seemed to say, 'What do you think of all this!'

'Mrs. Wititterly,' said her husband, addressing himself to Mrs. Nickleby, 'is sought after and courted by glittering crowds and brilliant circles. She is excited by the opera, the drama, the fine arts, the—the —the—'

'The nobility, my love,' interposed Mrs. Wititterly.

'The nobility, of course,' said Mr. Wititterly. 'And the military. She forms and expresses an immense variety of opinions on an immense variety of subjects. If some people in public life were acquainted with Mrs. Wititterly's real opinion of them, they would not hold their heads, perhaps, quite as high as they do.'

'Hush, Henry,' said the lady; 'this is scarcely fair.'

'I mention no names, Julia,' replied Mr. Wititterly; 'and nobody is injured. I merely mention the circumstance to show that you are no ordinary person, that there is a constant friction perpetually going on between your mind and your body; and that you must be soothed and tended. Now let me hear, dispassionately and calmly, what are this young lady's qualifications for the office.'

In obedience to this request, the qualifications were all gone through again, with the addition of many interruptions and cross-questionings from Mr. Wititterly. It was finally arranged that inquiries should be made, and a decisive answer addressed to Miss Nickleby under cover to her uncle, within two days. These conditions agreed upon, the page showed them down, as far as the staircase window; and the big footman, relieving guard at that point, piloted them in perfect safety to the street-door.

'They are very distinguished people, evidently,' said Mrs. Nickleby, as she took her daughter's arm. 'What a superior person Mrs. Wititterly is!'

'Do you think so, mamma?' was all Kate's reply.

'Why, who can help thinking so, Kate, my love?'

rejoined her mother. 'She is pale though, and looks much exhausted. I hope she may not be wearing herself out, but I am very much afraid.'

These considerations led the deep-sighted lady into a calculation of the probable duration of Mrs. Wititterly's life, and the chances of the disconsolate widower bestowing his hand on her daughter. Before reaching home, she had freed Mrs. Wititterly's soul from all bodily restraint; married Kate with great splendour at St. George's, Hanover Square; and only left undecided the minor question, whether a splendid French-polished mahogany bedstead should be erected for herself in the two-pair back of the house in Cadogan Place, or in the three-pair front: between which apartments she could not quite balance the advantages, and therefore adjusted the question at last, by determining to leave it to the decision of her son-in-law.

The inquiries were made. The answer—not to Kate's very great joy—was favourable; and at the expiration of a week she betook herself, with all her moveables and valuables, to Mrs. Wititterly's mansion, where for the present we will leave her.

CHAPTER XXII

NICHOLAS, ACCOMPANIED BY SMIKE, SALLIES FORTH TO SEEK HIS FORTUNE. HE ENCOUNTERS MR. VINCENT CRUMMLES; AND WHO HE WAS, IS HEREIN MADE MANIFEST

THE whole capital which Nicholas found himself entitled to, either in possession, reversion, remainder, or expectancy, after paying his rent and settling with the broker from whom he had hired his poor furni-

ture, did not exceed, by more than a few half-pence,
the sum of twenty shillings. And yet he hailed the
morning on which he had resolved to quit London,
with a light heart, and sprang from his bed with an
elasticity of spirit which is happily the lot of young
persons, or the world would never be stocked with old
ones.

It was a cold, dry, foggy morning in early spring.
A few meagre shadows flitted to and fro in the misty
streets, and occasionally there loomed through the dull
vapour, the heavy outline of some hackney-coach
wending homewards, which, drawing slowly nearer,
rolled jangling by, scattering the thin crust of frost
from its whitened roof and soon was lost again in
the cloud. At intervals were heard the tread of slip-
shod feet, and the chilly cry of the poor sweep as he
crept, shivering, to his early toil; the heavy footfall
of the official watcher of the night, pacing slowly up
and down and cursing the tardy hours that still inter-
vened between him and sleep; the rumbling of ponderous carts and waggons; the roll of the lighter
vehicles which carried buyers and sellers to the different markets; the sound of ineffectual knocking at
the doors of heavy sleepers—all these noises fell upon
the ear from time to time, but all seemed muffled by
the fog, and to be rendered almost as indistinct to the
ear as was every object to the sight. The sluggish
darkness thickened as the day came on; and those
who had the courage to rise and peep at the gloomy
street from their curtained windows crept back to bed
again, and coiled themselves up to sleep.

Before even these indications of approaching morning were rife in busy London, Nicholas had made his
way alone to the City, and stood beneath the windows
of his mother's house. It was dull and bare to see,
but it had light and life for him; for there was at

least one heart within its old walls to which insult or dishonour would bring the same blood rushing, that flowed in his own veins.

He crossed the road, and raised his eyes to the window of the room where he knew his sister slept. It was closed and dark. 'Poor girl,' thought Nicholas, 'she little thinks who lingers here!'

He looked again, and felt, for the moment, almost vexed that Kate was not there to exchange one word at parting. 'Good God!' he thought, suddenly correcting himself, 'what a boy I am!'

'It is better as it is,' said Nicholas, after he had lounged on, a few paces, and returned to the same spot. 'When I left them before, and could have said good-bye a thousand times if I had chosen, I spared them the pain of leave-taking, and why not now?' As he spoke, some fancied motion of the curtain almost persuaded him, for the instant, that Kate was at the window, and by one of those strange contradictions of feeling which are common to us all, he shrunk involuntarily into a doorway, that she might not see him. He smiled at his own weakness; said 'God bless them!' and walked away with a lighter step.

Smike was anxiously expecting him when he reached his old lodgings, and so was Newman, who had expended a day's income in a can of rum and milk to prepare them for the journey. They had tied up the luggage, Smike shouldered it, and away they went, with Newman Noggs in company; for he had insisted on walking as far as he could with them, overnight.

'Which way?' asked Newman, wistfully.

'To Kingston first,' replied Nicholas.

'And where afterwards?' asked Newman. 'Why won't you tell me?'

'Because I scarcely know myself, good friend,' rejoined Nicholas, laying his hand upon his shoulder; 'and if I did, I have neither plan nor prospect yet, and might shift my quarters a hundred times before you could possibly communicate with me.'

'I am afraid you have some deep scheme in your head,' said Newman, doubtfully.

'So deep,' replied his young friend, 'that even I can't fathom it. Whatever I resolve upon, depend upon it I will write you soon.'

'You won't forget?' said Newman.

'I am not very likely to,' rejoined Nicholas. 'I have not so many friends that I shall grow confused among the number, and forget my best one.'

Occupied in such discourse, they walked on for a couple of hours, as they might have done for a couple of days if Nicholas had not sat himself down on a stone by the wayside, and resolutely declared his intention of not moving another step until Newman Noggs turned back. Having pleaded ineffectually first for another half-mile, and afterwards for another quarter, Newman was fain to comply, and to shape his course towards Golden Square, after interchanging many hearty and affectionate farewells, and many times turning back to wave his hat to the two wayfarers when they had become mere specks in the distance.

'Now listen to me, Smike,' said Nicholas, as they trudged with stout hearts onwards. 'We are bound for Portsmouth.'

Smike nodded his head and smiled, but expressed no other emotion; for whether they had been bound for Portsmouth or Port Royal would have been alike to him, so they had been bound together.

'I don't know much of these matters,' resumed Nicholas; 'but Portsmouth is a sea-port town, and if no other employment is to be obtained, I should think we might get on board some ship. I am young and active, and could be useful in many ways. So could you.'

'I hope so,' replied Smike. 'When I was at that —you know where I mean?'

'Yes, I know,' said Nicholas. 'You needn't name the place.'

'Well, when I was there,' resumed Smike; his eyes sparkling at the prospect of displaying his abilities; 'I could milk a cow, and groom a horse, with anybody.'

'Ha!' said Nicholas, gravely. 'I am afraid they don't keep many animals of either kind on board ship, Smike, and even when they have horses, that they are not very particular about rubbing them down; still you can learn to do something else, you know. Where there's a will, there's a way.'

'And I am very willing,' said Smike, brightening up again.

'God knows you are,' rejoined Nicholas; 'and if you fail, it shall go hard but I'll do enough for us both.'

'Do we go all the way, to-day?' asked Smike, after a short silence.

'That would be too severe a trial, even for your willing legs,' said Nicholas, with a good-humoured smile. 'No. Godalming is some thirty and odd miles from London—as I found from a map I borrowed—and I purpose to rest there. We must push on again to-morrow, for we are not rich enough to loiter. Let me relieve you of that bundle! Come!'

'No, no,' rejoined Smike, falling back a few steps. 'Don't ask me to give it up to you.'

'Why not?' asked Nicholas.

'Let me do something for you, at least,' said Smike.

'You will never let me serve you as I ought. You will never know how I think, day and night, of ways to please you.'

'You are a foolish fellow to say it, for I know it well, and see it, or I should be a blind and senseless beast,' rejoined Nicholas. 'Let me ask you a question while I think of it, and there is no one by,' he added, looking him steadily in the face. 'Have you a good memory?'

'I don't know,' said Smike, shaking his head sorrowfully. 'I think I had once; but it's all gone now—all gone.'

'Why do you think you had once?' asked Nicholas, turning quickly upon him as though the answer in some way helped out the purport of his question.

'Because I could remember, when I was a child,' said Smike, 'but that is very, very long ago, or at least it seems so. I was always confused and giddy at that place you took me from; and could never remember, and sometimes couldn't even understand, what they said to me. I—let me see—let me see!'

'You are wandering now,' said Nicholas, touching him on the arm.

'No,' replied his companion, with a vacant look. 'I was only thinking how—' He shivered involuntarily as he spoke.

'Think no more of that place, for it is all over,' retorted Nicholas, fixing his eye full upon that of his companion, which was fast settling into an unmeaning stupefied gaze, once habitual to him, and common even then. 'What of the first day you went to Yorkshire?'

'Eh!' cried the lad.

'That was before you began to lose your recollection, you know,' said Nicholas quietly. 'Was the weather hot or cold?'

'Wet,' replied the boy. 'Very wet. I have always said, when it has rained hard, that it was like the night I came: and they used to crowd round and laugh to see me cry when the rain fell heavily. It was like a child, they said, and that made me think of it more. I turned cold all over sometimes, for I could see myself as I was then, coming in at the very same door.'

'As you were then,' repeated Nicholas, with assumed carelessness; 'how was that?'

'Such a little creature,' said Smike, 'that they might have had pity and mercy upon me, only to remember it.'

'You didn't find your way there, alone!' remarked Nicholas.

'No,' rejoined Smike, 'oh no.'

'Who was with you?'

'A man—a dark, withered man. I have heard them say so, at the school, and I remembered that before. I was glad to leave him, I was afraid of him; but they made me more afraid of them, and used me harder too.'

'Look at me,' said Nicholas, wishing to attract his full attention. 'There; don't turn away. Do you remember no woman, no kind woman, who hung over you once, and kissed your lips, and called you her child?'

'No,' said the poor creature, shaking his head, 'no, never.'

'Nor any house but that house in Yorkshire?'

'No,' rejoined the youth, with a melancholy look; 'a room—I remember I slept in a room, a large lonesome room at the top of a house, where there was a trap-door in the ceiling. I have covered my head with the clothes often, not to see it, for it frightened me: a young child with no one near at night: and I used to wonder what was on the other side. There was a clock too, an old clock, in one corner. I remember that. I have never forgotten that room; for when I have terrible dreams, it comes back, just as it was. I see things and people in it that I had never seen then, but there is the room just as it used to be; *that* never changes.'

'Will you let me take the bundle now?' asked Nicholas, abruptly changing the theme.

'No,' said Smike, 'no. Come, let us walk on.'

He quickened his pace as he said this, apparently under the impression that they had been standing still, during the whole of the previous dialogue. Nicholas marked him closely, and every word of this conversation remained upon his memory.

It was, by this time, within an hour of noon, and although a dense vapour still enveloped the city they had left, as if the very breath of its busy people hung over their schemes of gain and profit and found greater attraction there than in the quiet region above, in the open country it was clear and fair. Occasionally, in some low spots they came upon patches of mist which the sun had not yet driven from their strongholds; but these were soon passed, and as they laboured up the hills beyond, it was pleasant to look down, and see how the sluggish mass rolled heavily off, before the cheering influence of day. A broad, fine, honest sun lighted up the green pastures and dimpled water with the semblance of summer, while it left the travellers all the invigorating freshness of that early time of year. The ground seemed elastic under their feet; the sheep-bells were music to their ears; and exhilarated by exercise, and stimulated by hope, they pushed onward with the strength of lions.

The day wore on, and all these bright colours subsided, and assumed a quieter tint, like young hopes softened down by time, or youthful features by degrees resolving into the calm and serenity of age. But they were scarcely less beautiful in their slow decline, than they had been in their prime; for nature gives to every time and season some beauties of its own; and from morning to night, as from the cradle to the grave, is but a succession of changes so gentle and easy, that we can scarcely mark their progress.

To Godalming they came at last, and here they bargained for two humble beds, and slept soundly. In the morning they were astir, though not quite so early as the sun, and again afoot; if not with all the freshness of yesterday, still, with enough of hope and spirit to bear them cheerily on.

It was a harder day's journey than yesterday's, for there were long and weary hills to climb; and in journeys, as in life, it is a great deal easier to go down hill than up. However, they kept on, with unabated perseverance, and the hill has not yet lifted its face to heaven that perseverance will not gain the summit of at last.

They walked upon the rim of the Devil's Punch Bowl; and Smike listened with greedy interest as Nicholas read the inscription upon the stone which, reared upon that wild spot, tells of a murder committed there by night. The grass on which they stood, had once been dyed with gore; and the blood of the murdered man had run down, drop by drop, into the hollow which gives the place its name. 'The Devil's Bowl,' thought Nicholas, as he looked into the void, 'never held fitter liquor than that!'

Onward they kept, with steady purpose, and entered at length upon a wide and spacious tract of downs, with every variety of little hill and plain to change their verdant surface. Here, there shot up, almost perpendicularly, into the sky, a height so steep, as to be hardly accessible to any but the sheep and goats that fed upon its sides, and there, stood a mound of green, sloping and tapering off so delicately, and merging so gently into the level ground, that you could scarce define its limits. Hills swelling above each other; and undulations, shapely and uncouth, smooth and rugged, graceful and grotesque, thrown negligently side by side, bounded the view in each direction; while frequently, with unexpected noise, there uprose from the ground, a flight of crows, who, cawing and wheeling round the nearest hills, as if uncertain of their course, suddenly poised themselves upon the wing and skimmed down the long vista of some opening valley, with the speed of light itself.

By degrees, the prospect receded more and more on either hand, and as they had been shut out from rich and extensive scenery, so they emerged once again upon the open country. The knowledge that they were drawing near their place of destination, gave them fresh courage to proceed; but the way had been difficult, and they had loitered on the road, and Smike was tired. Thus, twilight had already closed in, when they turned off the path to the door of a roadside inn, yet twelve miles short of Portsmouth.

'Twelve miles,' said Nicholas, leaning with both hands on his stick, and looking doubtfully at Smike.

'Twelve long miles,' repeated the landlord.

'Is it a good road?' inquired Nicholas.

'Very bad,' said the landlord. As of course, being a landlord, he would say.

'I want to get on', observed Nicholas, hesitating. 'I scarcely know what to do.'

'Don't let me influence you,' rejoined the landlord. '*I* wouldn't go on if it was me.'

'Wouldn't you?' asked Nicholas, with the same uncertainty.

'Not if I knew when I was well off,' said the landlord. And having said it he pulled up his apron, put his hands into his pockets, and, taking a step or two outside the door, looked down the dark road with an assumption of great indifference.

A glance at the toil-worn face of Smike determined Nicholas, so without any further consideration he made up his mind to stay where he was.

The landlord led them into the kitchen, and as there was a good fire he remarked that it was very cold. If there had happened to be a bad one he would have observed that it was very warm.

'What can you give us for supper?' was Nicholas's natural question.

'Why—what would you like?' was the landlord's no less natural answer.

Nicholas suggested cold meat, but there was no cold meat—poached eggs, but there were no eggs— mutton chops, but there wasn't a mutton chop within three miles, though there had been more last week than they knew what to do with, and would be an extraordinary supply the day after to-morrow.

'Then,' said Nicholas, 'I must leave it entirely to you, as I would have done, at first, if you had allowed me.'

'Why, then I'll tell you what,' rejoined the landlord. 'There's a gentleman in the parlour that's ordered a hot beef-steak pudding and potatoes, at nine. There's more of it than he can manage, and I have very little doubt that if I ask leave, you can sup with him. I'll do that, in a minute.'

'No, no,' said Nicholas, detaining him. 'I would rather not. I—at least—pshaw! why cannot I speak out? Here; you see that I am travelling in a very humble manner, and have made my way hither on foot. It is more than probable, I think, that the gentleman may not relish my company; and although I am the dusty figure you see, I am too proud to thrust myself into his.'

'Lord love you,' said the landlord, 'it's only Mr. Crummles; *he* isn't particular.'

'Is he not?' asked Nicholas, on whose mind, to tell the truth, the prospect of the savoury pudding was making some impression.

'Not he,' replied the landlord. 'He'll like your way of talking, I know. But we'll soon see all about that. Just wait a minute.'

The landlord hurried into the parlour, without staying for further permission, nor did Nicholas strive to prevent him: wisely considering that supper, under the circumstances, was too serious a matter to trifle with. It was not long before the host returned, in a condition of much excitement.

'All right,' he said in a low voice. 'I knew he would. You'll see something rather worth seeing, in there. Ecod, how they are a going of it!'

There was no time to inquire to what this exclamation, which was delivered in a very rapturous tone, referred; for he had already thrown open the door of the room; into which Nicholas, followed by Smike with the bundle on his shoulder (he carried it about with him as vigilantly as if it had been a sack of gold), straightway repaired.

Nicholas was prepared for something odd, but not for something quite so odd as the sight he encountered. At the upper end of the room, were a couple of boys, one of them very tall and the other very short, both dressed as sailors—or at least as theatrical sailors, with belts, buckles, pigtails, and pistols complete—fighting what is called in playbills a terrific combat, with two of those short broadswords with basket hilts which are commonly used at our minor theatres. The short boy had gained a great advantage over the tall boy, who was reduced to mortal strait, and both were overlooked by a large heavy man, perched against the corner of a table, who emphatically adjured them to strike a little more fire out of the swords, and they couldn't fail to bring the house down, on the very first night.

'Mr. Vincent Crummles,' said the landlord with an air of great deference. 'This is the young gentleman.'

Mr. Vincent Crummles received Nicholas with an inclination of the head, something between the courtesy of a Roman emperor and the nod of a pot companion; and bade the landlord shut the door and begone.

'There's a picture,' said Mr. Crummles, motioning Nicholas not to advance and spoil it. 'The little 'un has him; if the big 'un doesn't knock under, in three seconds, he's a dead man. Do that again, boys.'

The two combatants went to work afresh, and chopped away until the swords emitted a shower of sparks: to the great satisfaction of Mr. Crummles, who appeared to consider this a very great point indeed. The engagement commenced with about two hundred chops administered by the short sailor and the tall sailor alternately, without producing any particular result, until the short sailor was chopped down on one knee; but this was nothing to him, for he worked himself about on the one knee with the assistance of his left hand, and fought most desperately until the tall sailor chopped his sword out of his grasp. Now, the inference was, that the short sailor, reduced to this extremity, would give in at once and cry quarter, but, instead of that, he all of a sudden drew a large pistol from his belt and presented it at the face of the tall sailor, who was so overcome at this (not expecting it) that he let the short sailor pick up his sword and begin again. Then, the chopping recommenced, and a variety of fancy chops were administered on both sides; such as chops dealt with the left hand, and under the leg, and over the right shoulder, and over the left; and when the short sailor made a vigorous cut at the tall sailor's legs, which would have shaved them clean off if it had taken effect, the tall sailor jumped over the short sailor's sword, wherefore to balance the matter, and make it all fair, the tall sailor administered the same cut, and the short sailor jumped over *his* sword. After this, there was a good deal of dodging about, and hitching up of the inexpressibles in the absence of braces, and then the short sailor (who was the moral character evidently, for he always had the best of it) made a violent demonstration and closed with the tall sailor, who, after a few unavailing struggles, went down, and expired in great torture as the short sailor put his foot upon his breast, and bored a hole in him through and through.

'That 'll be a double *encore* if you take care, boys,' said Mr. Crummles. 'You had better get your wind now and change your clothes.'

Having addressed these words to the combatants, he saluted Nicholas, who then observed that the face of Mr. Crummles was quite proportionate in size to his body; that he had a very full under-lip, a hoarse voice, as though he were in the habit of shouting very much, and very short black hair, shaved off nearly to the crown of his head—to admit (as he afterwards learnt) of his more easily wearing character wigs of any shape or pattern.

'What do you think of that, sir?' inquired Mr. Crummles.

'Very good, indeed—capital,' answered Nicholas.

'You won't see such boys as those very often, I think,' said Mr. Crummles.

Nicholas assented—observing, that if they were a little better match—

'Match!' cried Mr. Crummles.

'I mean if they were a little more of a size,' said Nicholas, explaining himself.

'Size!' repeated Mr. Crummles; 'why it's the essence of the combat that there should be a foot or two between them. How are you to get up the sympathies of the audience in a legitimate manner, if there isn't a little man contending against a big one—unless there's at least five to one, and we haven't hands enough for that business in our company.'

'I see,' replied Nicholas. 'I beg your pardon. That didn't occur to me, I confess.'

'It's the main point,' said Mr. Crummles. 'I open at Portsmouth the day after to-morrow. If you're going there, look into the theatre, and see how that'll tell.'

Nicholas promised to do so, if he could, and drawing a chair near the fire, fell into conversation with the manager at once. He was very talkative and communicative, stimulated perhaps, not only by his natural disposition, but by the spirits and water he sipped very plentifully, or the snuff he took in large quantities from a piece of whitey-brown paper in his waistcoat pocket. He laid open his affairs without the smallest reserve, and descanted at some length upon the merits of his company, and the acquirements of his family; of both of which, the two broadsword boys formed an honourable portion. There was to be a gathering, it seemed, of the different ladies and gentlemen at Portsmouth on the morrow, whither the father and sons were proceeding (not for the regular season, but in the course of a wandering speculation), after fulfilling an engagement at Guildford with the greatest applause.

'You are going that way?' asked the manager.

'Ye-yes,' said Nicholas. 'Yes, I am.'

'Do you know the town at all?' inquired the manager, who seemed to consider himself entitled to the same degree of confidence as he had himself exhibited.

'No,' replied Nicholas.

'Never there?'

'Never.'

Mr. Vincent Crummles gave a short dry cough, as much as to say, 'If you won't be communicative, you won't'; and took so many pinches of snuff from the piece of paper, one after another, that Nicholas quite wondered where it all went to.

While he was thus engaged, Mr. Crummles looked, from time to time, with great interest at Smike, with whom he had appeared considerably struck from the first. He had now fallen asleep, and was nodding in his chair.

'Excuse my saying so,' said the manager, leaning over to Nicholas, and sinking his voice, 'but what a capital countenance your friend has got!'

'Poor fellow!' said Nicholas, with a half-smile, 'I wish it were a little more plump, and less haggard.'

'Plump!' exclaimed the manager, quite horrified, 'you 'd spoil it for ever.'

'Do you think so?'

'Think so, sir! Why, as he is now,' said the manager, striking his knee emphatically; 'without a pad upon his body, and hardly a touch of paint upon his face, he 'd make such an actor for the starved business as was never seen in this country. Only let him be tolerably well up in the Apothecary in Romeo and Juliet with the slightest possible dab of red on the tip of his nose, and he'd be certain of three rounds the moment he put his head out of the practicable door in the front grooves O. P.'

'You view him with a professional eye,' said Nicholas, laughing.

'And well I may,' rejoined the manager, 'I never saw a young fellow so regularly cut out for that line, since I've been in the profession. And I played the heavy children when I was eighteen months old.'

The appearance of the beef-steak pudding, which came in simultaneously with the junior Vincent Crummleses, turned the conversation to other matters, and indeed, for a time, stopped it altogether. These two young gentlemen wielded their knives and forks with scarcely less address than their broadswords, and as the whole party were quite as sharp-set as either class of weapons, there was no time for talking until the supper had been disposed of.

The Master Crummleses had no sooner swallowed the last procurable morsel of food, than they evinced, by various half-suppressed yawns and stretchings of their limbs, an obvious inclination to retire for the night, which Smike had betrayed still more strongly: he having, in the course of the meal, fallen asleep several times while in the very act of eating. Nicholas therefore proposed that they should break up at once, but the manager would by no means hear of it; vowing that he had promised himself the pleasure of inviting his new acquaintance to share a bowl of punch, and that if he declined, he should deem it very unhandsome behaviour.

'Let them go,' said Mr. Vincent Crummles, 'and we'll have it snugly and cosily together by the fire.'

Nicholas was not much disposed to sleep—being in truth too anxious—so, after a little demur, he accepted the offer, and having exchanged a shake of the hand with the young Crummleses, and the manager having on his part bestowed a most affectionate benediction on Smike, he sat himself down opposite to that gentleman by the fireside to assist in emptying the bowl, which soon afterwards appeared, steaming in a manner which was quite exhilarating to behold, and sending forth a most grateful and inviting fragrance.

But, despite the punch and the manager, who told a variety of stories, and smoked tobacco from a pipe, and inhaled it in the shape of snuff, with a most astonishing power, Nicholas was absent and dispirited. His thoughts were in his old home, and when they reverted to his present condition, the uncertainty of the morrow cast a gloom upon him, which his utmost efforts were unable to dispel. His attention wandered; although he heard the manager's voice, he was deaf to what he said; and when Mr. Vincent Crummles concluded the history of some long adventure with a loud laugh, and an inquiry what Nicholas would have done under the same circumstances, he was obliged to make the best apology in his power, and to confess his entire ignorance of all he had been talking about.

'Why, so I saw,' observed Mr. Crummles. 'You 're uneasy in your mind. What 's the matter?'

Nicholas could not refrain from smiling at the abruptness of the question; but, thinking it scarcely worth while to parry it, owned that he was under some apprehensions lest he might not succeed in the object which had brought him to that part of the country.

'And what 's that? asked the manager.

'Getting something to do which will keep me and my poor fellow-traveller in the common necessaries of life,' said Nicholas. 'That's the truth. You guessed it long ago, I dare say, so I may as well have the credit of telling it you with a good grace.'

'What's to be got to do at Portsmouth more than anywhere else?' asked Mr. Vincent Crummles, melting the sealing-wax on the stem of his pipe in the candle, and rolling it out afresh with his little finger.

'There are many vessels leaving the port, I suppose,' replied Nicholas. 'I shall try for a berth in some ship or other. There is meat and drink there, at all events.'

'Salt meat and new rum; pease-pudding and chaff-biscuits,' said the manager, taking a whiff at his pipe to keep it alight, and returning to his work of embellishment.

'One may do worse than that,' said Nicholas. 'I can rough it, I believe, as well as most young men of my age and previous habits.'

'You need be able to,' said the manager, 'if you go on board ship; but you won't.'

'Why not?'

'Because there's not a skipper or mate that would think you worth your salt, when he could get a practised hand,' replied the manager; 'and they as plentiful there, as the oysters in the streets.'

'What do you mean?' asked Nicholas, alarmed by this prediction, and the confident tone in which it had been uttered. 'Men are not born able seamen. They must be reared, I suppose?'

Mr. Vincent Crummles nodded his head. 'They must; but not at your age, or from young gentlemen like you.'

There was a pause. The contenance of Nicholas fell, and he gazed ruefully at the fire.

'Does no other profession occur to you, which a young man of your figure and address could take up easily, and see the world to advantage in?' asked the manager.

'No,' said Nicholas, shaking his head.

'Why, then, I'll tell you one,' said Mr. Crummles, throwing his pipe into the fire, and raising his voice. 'The stage.'

'The stage!' cried Nicholas, in a voice almost as loud.

'The theatrical profession,' said Mr. Vincent Crummles. 'I am in the theatrical profession myself, my wife is in the theatrical profession, my children are in the theatrical profession. I had a dog that lived and died in it from a puppy; and my chaise-pony goes on, in Timon the Tartar. I'll bring you out, and your friend too. Say the word. I want a novelty.'

'I don't know anything about it,' rejoined Nicholas, whose breath had been almost taken away, by this sudden proposal. 'I never acted a part in my life, except at school.'

'There's genteel comedy in your walk and manner, juvenile tragedy in your eye, and touch-and-go farce in your laugh,' said Mr. Vincent Crummles. 'You'll do as well as if you had thought of nothing else but the lamps, from your birth downwards.'

Nicholas thought of the small amount of small change that would remain in his pocket after paying the tavern bill: and he hesitated.

'You can be useful to us in a hundred ways,' said Mr. Crummles. 'Think what capital bills a man of your education could write for the shop windows.'

'Well, I think I could manage that department,' said Nicholas.

'To be sure you could,' replied Mr. Crummles.

' "For further particulars see small hand-bills"—we might have half a volume in every one of 'em. Pieces too; why, you could write us a piece to bring out the whole strength of the company, whenever we wanted one.'

'I am not quite so confident about that,' replied Nicholas. 'But I dare say I could scribble something now and then, that would suit you.'

'We'll have a new show-piece out directly,' said the manager. 'Let me see—peculiar resources of this establishment—new and splendid scenery—you must manage to introduce a real pump and two washing-tubs.'

'Into the piece?' said Nicholas.

'Yes,' replied the manager. 'I bought 'em cheap, at a sale the other day, and they'll come in admirably. That's the London plan. They look up some dresses, and properties, and have a piece written to fit 'em. Most of the theatres keep an author on purpose.'

'Indeed!' cried Nicholas.

'Oh yes,' said the manager; 'a common thing. It'll look very well in the bills in separate lines —Real pump!—Splendid tubs!—Great attraction! You don't happen to be anything of an artist, do you.'

'That is not one of my accomplishments,' rejoined Nicholas.

'Ah! Then it can't be helped,' said the manager. 'If you had been, we might have had a large woodcut of the last scene for the posters, showing the whole depth of the stage, with the pump and tubs in the middle; but however, if you're not, it can't be helped.'

'What should I get for all this?' inquired Nicholas, after a few moments' reflection. 'Could I live by it?'

'Live by it!' said the manager. 'Like a prince!

With your own salary, and your friend's, and your writings, you 'd make—ah! you 'd make a pound a week!'

'You don't say so!'

'I do indeed, and if we had a run of good houses, nearly double the money.'

Nicholas shrugged his shoulders; but sheer destitution was before him; and if he could summon fortitude to undergo the extremes of want and hardship, for what had he rescued his helpless charge if it were only to bear as hard a fate as that from which he had wrested him? It was easy to think of seventy miles as nothing, when he was in the same town with the man who had treated him so ill and roused his bitterest thoughts; but now, it seemed far enough. What if he went abroad, and his mother or Kate were to die the while?

Without more deliberation, he hastily declared that it was a bargain, and gave Mr. Vincent Crummels his hand upon it.

CHAPTER XXIII

TREATS OF THE COMPANY OF MR. VINCENT CRUM-
MLES, AND OF HIS AFFAIRS, DOMESTIC AND THE-
ATRICAL

As Mr. Crummles had a strange four-legged animal in the inn stables, which he called a pony, and a vehicle of unknown design, on which he bestowed the appellation of a four-wheeled phaeton, Nicholas proceeded on his journey next morning with greater ease than he had expected: the manager and himself occupying the front seat: and the Master Crummleses and Smike being packed together behind, in company with a wicker basket defended from wet by a stout oilskin, in which were the broadswords, pistols, pigtails, nautical costumes, and other professional necessaries of the aforesaid young gentlemen.

The pony took his time upon the road, and—possibly in consequence of his theatrical education—evinced, every now and then, a strong inclination to lie down. However, Mr. Vincent Crummles kept him up pretty well, by jerking the rein, and plying the whip; and when these means failed, and the animal came to a stand, the elder Master Crummles got out and kicked him. By dint of these encouragements, he was persuaded to move from time to time, and they jogged on (as Mr. Crummles truly observed) very comfortably for all parties.

'He's a good pony at bottom,' said Mr. Crummles, turning to Nicholas.

He might have been at bottom, but he certainly was not at top, seeing that his coat was of the roughest and most ill-favoured kind. So, Nicholas merely observed that he shouldn't wonder if he was.

'Many and many is the circuit this pony has gone,' said Mr. Crummles, flicking him skilfully on the eyelid for old acquaintance' sake. 'He is quite one of us. His mother was on the stage.'

'Was she?' rejoined Nicholas.

'She ate apple-pie at a circus for upwards of fourteen years,' said the manager; 'fired pistols, and went to bed in a night-cap; and, in short, took the low comedy entirely. His father was a dancer.'

'Was he at all distinguished?'

'Not very,' said the manager. 'He was rather a low sort of pony. The fact is, he had been originally jobbed out by the day, and he never quite got over his old habits. He was clever in melodrama too, but too broad—too broad. When the mother died, he took the port-wine business.'

'The port-wine business!' cried Nicholas.

'Drinking port-wine with the clown,' said the manager; 'but he was greedy, and one night bit off the bowl of the glass, and choked himself, so his vulgarity was the death of him at last.'

The descendant of this ill-starred animal requiring increased attention from Mr. Crummles as he progressed in his day's work, that gentleman had very little time for conversation. Nicholas was thus left at leisure to entertain himself with his own thoughts, until they arrived at the drawbridge at Portsmouth, when Mr. Crummles pulled up.

'We'll get down here,' said the manager, 'and the boys will take him round to the stable, and call at my lodgings with the luggage. You had better let yours be taken there, for the present.'

Thanking Mr. Vincent Crummles for his obliging offer, Nicholas jumped out, and, giving Smike his arm, accompanied the manager up High Street on their way to the theatre; feeling nervous and uncomfortable enough at the prospect of an immediate introduction to a scene so new to him.

They passed a great many bills, pasted against the walls and displayed in windows, wherein the names of Mr. Vincent Crummles, Mrs. Vincent Crummles, Master Crummles, Master P. Crummles, and Miss Crummles, were printed in very large letters, and everything else in very small ones; and, turning at length into an entry, in which was a strong smell of orange-peel and lamp-oil, with an undercurrent of sawdust, groped their way through a dark passage, and, descending a step or two, threaded a little maze of canvas screens and paint-pots, and emerged upon the stage of the Portsmouth Theatre.

'Here we are,' said Mr. Crummles.

It was not very light, but Nicholas found himself close to the first entrance on the prompt side, among bare walls, dusty scenes, mildewed clouds, heavily daubed draperies, and dirty floors. He looked about him; ceiling, pit, boxes, gallery, orchestra, fittings, and decorations of every kind,—all looked coarse, cold, gloomy, and wretched.

'Is this a theatre?' whispered Smike, in amazement; 'I thought it was a blaze of light and finery.'

'Why, so it is,' replied Nicholas, hardly less surprised; 'but not by day, Smike—not by day.'

The manager's voice recalled him from a more careful inspection of the building, to the opposite side of the proscenium, where, at a small mahogany table with rickety legs and of an oblong shape, sat a stout, portly female, apparently between forty and fifty, in a tarnished silk cloak, with her bonnet dangling by the strings in her hand, and her hair (of which she had a great quantity) braided in a large festoon over each temple.

'Mr. Johnson,' said the manager (for Nicholas had given the name which Newman Noggs had bestowed upon him in his conversation with Mrs. Kenwigs), 'let me introduce Mrs. Vincent Crummles.'

'I am glad to see you, sir,' said Mrs. Vincent Crummles, in a sepulchral voice. 'I am very glad to see you, and still more happy to hail you as a promising member of our corps.'

The lady shook Nicholas by the hand as she addressed him in these terms; he saw it was a large one, but had not expected quite such an iron grip as that with which she honoured him.

'And this,' said the lady, crossing to Smike, as

tragic actresses cross when they obey a stage direction, 'and this is the other. You too, are welcome, sir.'

'He 'll do, I think, my dear?' said the manager, taking a pinch of snuff.

'He is admirable,' replied the lady. 'An acquisition, indeed.'

As Mrs. Vincent Crummles recrossed back to the table, there bounded on to the stage from some mysterious inlet, a little girl in a dirty white frock with tucks up to the knees, short trousers, sandaled shoes, white spencer, pink gauze bonnet, green veil and curl-papers; who turned a pirouette, cut twice in the air, turned another pirouette, then, looking off at the opposite wing, shrieked, bounded forward to within six inches of the footlights, and fell into a beautiful attitude of terror, as a shabby gentleman in an old pair of buff slippers came in at one powerful slide, and chattering his teeth, fiercely brandished a walking stick.

'They are going through the Indian Savage and the Maiden,' said Mrs. Crummles.

'Oh!' said the manager, 'the little ballet interlude. Very good, go on. A little this way, if you please, Mr. Johnson. That 'll do. Now!'

The manager clapped his hands as a signal to proceed, and the savage, becoming ferocious, made a slide towards the maiden; but the maiden avoided him in six twirls, and came down, at the end of the last one, upon the very points of her toes. This seemed to make some impression upon the savage; for, after a little more ferocity and chasing of the maiden into corners, he began to relent, and stroked his face several times with his right thumb and four fingers, thereby intimating that he was struck with admiration of the maiden's beauty. Acting upon the impulse of this passion, he (the savage) began to hit himself severe thumps in the chest, and to exhibit other indications of being desperately in love, which being rather a prosy proceeding, was very likely the cause of the maiden's falling asleep; whether it was or no, asleep she did fall, sound as a church, on a sloping bank, and the savage perceiving it, leant his left ear on his left hand, and nodded sideways, to intimate to all whom it might concern that she *was* asleep, and no shamming. Being left to himself, the savage had a dance, all alone. Just as he left off, the maiden woke up, rubbed her eyes, got off the bank, and had a dance all alone too—such a dance that the savage looked on in ecstasy all the while, and when it was done, plucked from a neighbouring tree some botanical curiosity, resembling a small pickled cabbage, and offered it to the maiden, who at first wouldn't have it, but on the savage shedding tears relented. Then the savage jumped for joy; then the maiden jumped for rapture at the sweet smell of the pickled cabbage. Then the savage and the maiden danced violently together, and, finally, the savage dropped down on one knee, and the maiden stood on one leg upon his other knee; thus concluding the ballet, and leaving the spectators in a state of pleasing uncertainty, whether she would ultimately marry the savage, or return to her friends.

'Very well indeed,' said Mr. Crummles; 'bravo!'

'Bravo!' cried Nicholas, resolved to make the best of everything. 'Beautiful!'

'This, sir,' said Mr. Vincent Crummles, bringing the maiden forward, 'this is the infant phenomenon —Miss Ninetta Crummles.'

'Your daughter?' inquired Nicholas.

'My daughter—my daughter,' replied Mr. Vincent Crummles; 'the idol of every place we go into, sir.

We have had complimentary letters about this girl, sir, from the nobility and gentry of almost every town in England.'

'I am not surprised at that,' said Nicholas; 'she must be quite a natural genius.'

'Quite a—!' Mr. Crummles stopped: language was not powerful enough to describe the infant phenomenon. I 'll tell you what, sir,' he said; 'the talent of this child is not to be imagined. She must be seen, sir—seen—to be ever so faintly appreciated. There; go to your mother, my dear.'

'May I ask how old she is?' inquired Nicholas.

'You may, sir,' replied Mr. Crummles, looking steadily in his questioner's face, as some men do when they have doubts about being implicitly believed in what they are going to say. 'She is ten years of age, sir.'

'Not more!'

'Not a day.'

'Dear me!' said Nicholas, 'it 's extraordinary.'

It was; for the infant phenomenon, though of short stature, had a comparatively aged countenance, and had moreover been precisely the same age—not perhaps to the full extent of the memory of the oldest inhabitant, but certainly for five good years. But she had been kept up late every night, and put upon an unlimited allowance of gin-and-water from infancy, to prevent her growing tall, and perhaps this system of training had produced in the infant phenomenon these additional phenomena.

While this short dialogue was going on, the gentleman who had enacted the savage, came up, with his walking shoes on his feet, and his slippers in his hand, to within a few paces, as if desirous to join in the conversation. Deeming this a good opportunity, he put in his word.

'Talent there, sir!' said the savage, nodding towards Miss Crummles.

Nicholas assented.

'Ah!' said the actor, setting his teeth together, and drawing in his breath with a hissing sound, 'she oughtn't to be in the provinces, she oughtn't.'

'What do you mean?' asked the manager.

'I mean to say,' replied the other, warmly, 'that she is too good for country boards, and that she ought to be in one of the large houses in London, or nowhere; and I tell you more, without mincing the matter, that if it wasn't for envy and jealousy in some quarter that you know of, she would be. Perhaps you 'll introduce me here, Mr. Crummles.'

'Mr. Folair,' said the manager, presenting him to Nicholas.

'Happy to know you, sir.' Mr. Folair touched the brim of his hat with his forefinger, and then shook hands. 'A recruit, sir, I understand?'

'An unworthy one,' replied Nicholas.

'Did you ever see such a set-out as that?' whispered the actor, drawing him away, as Crummles left them to speak to his wife.

'As what?'

Mr. Folair made a funny face from his pantomime collection, and pointed over his shoulder.

'You don't mean the infant phenomenon?'

'Infant humbug, sir,' replied Mr. Folair. 'There isn't a female child of common sharpness in a charity school, that couldn't do better than that. She may thank her stars she was born a manager's daughter.'

'You seem to take it to heart,' observed Nicholas, with a smile.

'Yes, by Jove, and well I may,' said Mr. Folair, drawing his arm through his, and walking him up and down the stage. 'Isn't it enough to make a man crusty to see that little sprawler put up in the best business every night, and actually keeping money out of the house, by being forced down the people's throats, while other people are passed over? Isn't it extraordinary to see a man's confounded family conceit blinding him, even to his own interest? Why I *know* of fifteen-and-sixpence that came to Southampton one night last month, to see me dance the Highland Fling; and what's the consequence? I've never been put up in it since—never once—while the "infant phenomenon" has been grinning through artificial flowers at five people and a baby in the pit, and two boys in the gallery, every night.'

'If I may judge from what I have seen of you,' said Nicholas, 'you must be a valuable member of the company.'

'Oh!' replied Mr. Folair, beating his slippers together, to knock the dust out; 'I *can* come it pretty well—nobody better, perhaps, in my own line—but having such business as one gets here, is like putting lead on one's feet instead of chalk, and dancing in fetters without the credit of it. Holloa, old fellow, how are you?'

The gentleman addressed in these latter words, was a dark complexioned man, inclining indeed to sallow, with long thick black hair, and very evident indications (although he was close shaved) of a stiff beard, and whiskers of the same deep shade. His age did not appear to exceed thirty, though many at first sight would have considered him much older, as his face was long, and very pale, from the constant application of stage paint. He wore a checked shirt, an old green coat with new gilt buttons, a neckerchief of broad red and green stripes, and full blue trousers; he carried, too, a common ash walking-stick, apparently more for show than use, as he flourished it about, with the hooked end downwards, except when he raised it for a few seconds, and throwing himself into a fencing attitude, made a pass or two at the side-scenes, or at any other object, animate or inanimate, that chanced to afford him a pretty good mark at the moment.

'Well, Tommy,' said this gentleman, making a thrust at his friend, who parried it dexterously with his slipper, 'what's the news?'

'A new appearance, that's all,' replied Mr. Folair, looking at Nicholas.

'Do the honours, Tommy, do the honours,' said the other gentleman, tapping him reproachfully on the crown of the hat with his stick.

'This is Mr. Lenville, who does our first tragedy, Mr. Johnson,' said the pantomimist.

'Except when old bricks and mortar takes it into his head to do it himself, you should add, Tommy,' remarked Mr. Lenville. 'You know who bricks and mortar is, I suppose, sir?'

'I do not, indeed,' replied Nicholas.

'We call Crummles that, because his style of acting is rather in the heavy and ponderous way,' said Mr. Lenville. 'I mustn't be cracking jokes though, for I've got a part of twelve lengths here, which I must be up in to-morrow night, and I haven't had time to look at it yet; I'm a confounded quick study, that's one comfort.'

Consoling himself with this reflection, Mr. Lenville drew from his coat-pocket a greasy and crumpled manuscript, and, having made another pass at his friend, proceeded to walk to and fro, conning it to himself and indulging occasionally in such appropriate action as his imagination and the text suggested.

A pretty general muster of the company had by

this time taken place; for besides Mr. Lenville and his friend Tommy, there were present, a slim young gentleman with weak eyes, who played the low-spirited lovers and sang tenor songs, and who had come arm-in-arm with the comic countryman—a man with a turned-up nose, large mouth, broad face, and staring eyes. Making himself very amiable to the infant phenomenon, was an inebriated elderly gentleman in the last depths of shabbiness, who played the calm and virtuous old men; and paying especial court to Mrs. Crummles was another elderly gentleman, a shade more respectable, who played the irascible old men—those funny fellows who have nephews in the army, and perpetually run about with sticks to compel them to marry heiresses. Besides these, there was a roving-looking person in a rough great-coat, who strode up and down in front of the lamps, flourishing a dress-cane, and rattling away, in an undertone, with great vivacity for the amusement of an ideal audience. He was not quite so young as he had been, and his figure was rather running to seed; but there was an air of exaggerated gentility about him, which bespoke the hero of swaggering comedy. There was, also, a little group of three or four young men, with lantern jaws and thick eye-brows, who were conversing in one corner; but they seemed to be of secondary importance, and laughed and talked together without attracting any attention.

The ladies were gathered in a little knot by themselves round the rickety table before mentioned. There was Miss Snevellicci—who could do anything, from a medley dance to Lady Macbeth, and also always played some part in blue silk knee-smalls at her benefit—glancing from the depths of her coal-scuttle straw bonnet, at Nicholas, and affecting to be absorbed in the recital of a diverting story to her friend Miss Ledrook, who had brought her work, and was making up a ruff in the most natural manner possible. There was Miss Belvawney—who seldom aspired to speaking parts, and usually went on as a page in white silk hose, to stand with one leg bent, and contemplate the audience, or to go in and out after Mr. Crummles in stately tragedy—twisting up the ringlets of the beautiful Miss Bravassa, who had once had her likeness taken 'in character' by an engraver's apprentice, whereof impressions were hung up for sale in the pastry-cook's window, and the greengrocer's, and at the circulating library, and the box-office, whenever the announce bills came out for her annual night. There was Mrs. Lenville, in a very limp bonnet and veil, decidedly in that way in which she would wish to be if she truly loved Mr. Lenville; there was Miss Gazingi, with an imitation ermine boa tied in a loose knot round her neck, flogging Mr. Crummles, junior, with both ends, in fun. Lastly, there was Mrs. Grudden in a brown cloth pelisse and a beaver bonnet, who assisted Mrs. Crummles in her domestic affairs, and took money at the doors, and dressed the ladies, and swept the house, and held prompt book when everybody else was on for the last scene, and acted any kind of part on any emergency without ever learning it, and was put down in the bills under any name or names whatever, that occurred to Mr. Crummles as looking well in print.

Mr. Folair having obligingly confided these particulars to Nicholas, left him to mingle with his fellows; the work of personal introduction was completed by Mr. Vincent Crummles, who publicly heralded the new actor as a prodigy of genius and learning.

'I beg your pardon,' said Miss Snevellicci, sidling towards Nicholas, 'but did you ever play at Canterbury?'

'I never did,' replied Nicholas.

'I recollect meeting a gentleman at Canterbury,' said Miss Snevellicci, 'only for a few moments, for I was leaving the company as he joined it, so like you that I felt almost certain it was the same.'

'I see you now, for the first time,' rejoined Nicholas with all due gallantry. 'I am sure I never saw you before; I couldn't have forgotten it.'

'Oh, I 'm sure it 's very flattering of you to say so,' retorted Miss Snevellicci with a graceful bend. 'Now I look at you again, I see that the gentleman at Canterbury hadn't the same eyes as you—you 'll think me very foolish for taking notice of such things, won't you?'

'Not at all,' said Nicholas. 'How can I feel otherwise than flattered by your notice in any way?'

'Oh! you men are such vain creatures!' cried Miss Snevillicci. Whereupon, she became charmingly confused, and, pulling out her pocket-handkerchief from a faded pink silk reticule with a gilt clasp, called to Miss Ledrook—

'Led, my dear,' said Miss Snevellicci.

'Well, what is the matter?' said Miss Ledrook.

'It 's not the same.'

'Not the same what?'

'Canterbury—you know what I mean. Come here! I want to speak to you.'

But Miss Ledrook wouldn't come to Miss Snevellicci, so Miss Snevellicci was obliged to go to Miss Ledrook, which she did, in a skipping manner that was quite fascinating; and Miss Ledrook evidently joked Miss Snevellicci about being struck with Nicholas; for, after some playful whispering, Miss Snevellicci hit Miss Ledrook very hard on the backs of her hands, and retired up, in a state of pleasing confusion.

'Ladies and gentlemen,' said Mr. Vincent Crummles, who had been writing on a piece of paper, 'we 'll call the Mortal Struggle to-morrow at ten; everybody for the procession. Intrigue, and Ways and Means, you 're all up in, so we shall only want one rehearsal. Everybody at ten, if you please.'

'Everybody at ten,' repeated Mrs. Grudden, looking about her.

'On Monday morning we shall read a new piece,' said Mr. Crummles; 'the name 's not known yet, but everybody will have a good part. Mr. Johnson will take care of that.'

'Hallo!' said Nicholas, starting, 'I—'

'On Monday morning,' repeated Mr. Crummles, raising his voice, to drown the unfortunate Mr. Johnson's remonstrance; 'that 'll do, ladies and gentlemen.'

The ladies and gentlemen required no second notice to quit; and, in a few minutes, the theatre was deserted, save by the Crummles family, Nicholas, and Smike.

'Upon my word,' said Nicholas, taking the manager aside, 'I don't think I can be ready by Monday.'

'Pooh, pooh,' replied Mr. Crummles.

'But really I can't,' returned Nicholas; 'my invention is not accustomed to these demands, or possibly I might produce—'

'Invention! what the devil 's that got to do with it!' cried the manager, hastily.

'Everything, my dear sir.'

'Nothing, my dear sir,' retorted the manager, with evident impatience. 'Do you understand French?'

'Perfectly well.'

'Very good,' said the manager, opening the table-drawer, and giving a roll of paper from it to Nicholas. 'There! Just turn that into English, and put your name on the title-page. Damn me,' said Mr. Crummles, angrily, 'if I haven't often said that I wouldn't have a man or woman in my company that wasn't master of the language, so that they might learn it from the original, and play it in English, and save all this trouble and expense.'

Nicholas smiled and pocketed the play.

'What are you going to do about your lodgings?' said Mr. Crummles.

Nicholas could not help thinking that, for the first week, it would be an uncommon convenience to have a turn-up bedstead in the pit, but he merely remarked that he had not turned his thoughts that way.

'Come home with me, then,' said Mr. Crummles, 'and my boys shall go with you after dinner, and show you the most likely place.'

The offer was not to be refused; Nicholas and Mr. Crummles gave Mrs. Crummles an arm each, and walked up the street in stately array. Smike, the boys, and the phenomenon, went home by a shorter cut, and Mrs. Grudden remained behind to take some cold Irish stew and a pint of porter in the box-office.

Mrs. Crummles trod the pavement as if she were going to immediate execution with an animating consciousness of innocence, and that heroic fortitude which virtue alone inspires. Mr. Crummles, on the other hand, assumed the look and gait of a hardened despot; but they both attracted some notice from many of the passers-by, and when they heard a whisper of 'Mr. and Mrs. Crummles!' or saw a little boy run back to stare them in the face, the severe expression of their countenances relaxed, for they felt it was popularity.

Mr. Crummles lived in Saint Thomas's Street, at the house of one Bulph, a pilot, who sported a boat-green door, with window-frames of the same colour, and had the little finger of a drowned man on his parlour mantel-shelf, with other maritime and natural curiosities. He displayed also a brass knocker, a brass plate, and a brass bell-handle, all very bright and shining; and had a mast, with a vane on the top of it, in his back-yard.

'You are welcome,' said Mrs. Crummles, turning round to Nicholas when they reached the bow-windowed front room on the first floor.

Nicholas bowed his acknowledgments, and was unfeignedly glad to see the cloth laid.

'We have but a shoulder of mutton with onion sauce,' said Mrs. Crummles, in the same charnel-house voice; 'but such as our dinner is, we beg you to partake of it.'

'You are very good,' replied Nicholas, 'I shall do it ample justice.'

'Vincent,' said Mrs. Crummles, 'what is the hour?'

'Five minutes past dinner-time,' said Mr. Crummles.

Mrs. Crummles rang the bell. 'Let the mutton and onion sauce appear.'

The slave who attended upon Mr. Bulph's lodgers, disappeared, and after a short interval re-appeared with the festive banquet. Nicholas and the infant phenomenon opposed each other at the pembroke-table, and Smike and the Master Crummleses dined on the sofa bedstead.

'Are they very theatrical people here?' asked Nicholas.

'No,' replied Mr. Crummles, shaking his head, 'far from it—far from it.'

'I pity them,' observed Mrs. Crummles.

'So do I,' said Nicholas; 'if they have no relish for theatrical entertainments, properly conducted.'

'Then they have none, sir,' rejoined Mr. Crummles. 'To the infant's benefit, last year, on which occasion she repeated three of her most popular characters, and also appeared in the Fairy Porcupine, as originally performed by her, there was a house of no more than four pound twelve.'

'Is it possible?' cried Nicholas.

'And two pound of that was trust, pa,' said the phenomenon.

'And two pound of that was trust,' repeated Mr. Crummles. 'Mrs. Crummles herself has played to mere handfuls.'

'But they are always a taking audience, Vincent,' said the manager's wife.

'Most audiences are, when they have good acting —real good acting—the regular thing,' replied Mr. Crummles, forcibly.

'Do you give lessons, ma'am?' inquired Nicholas.

'I do,' said Mrs. Crummles.

'There is no teaching here, I suppose?'

'There has been,' said Mrs. Crummles. 'I have received pupils here. I imparted tuition to the daughter of a dealer in ships' provisions; but it afterwards appeared that she was insane when she first came to me. It was very extraordinary that she should come, under such circumstances.'

Not feeling quite so sure of that, Nicholas thought it best to hold his peace.

'Let me see,' said the manager, cogitating after dinner. 'Would you like some nice little part with the infant?'

'You are very good,' replied Nicholas hastily; 'but I think perhaps it would be better if I had somebody of my own size at first, in case I should turn out awkward. I should feel more at home perhaps.'

'True,' said the manager. 'Perhaps you would. And you could play up to the infant, in time, you know.'

'Certainly,' replied Nicholas: devoutly hoping that it would be a very long time before he was honoured with this distinction.

'Then I 'll tell you what we 'll do,' said Mr. Crummles. 'You shall study Romeo when you 've done that piece—don't forget to throw the pump and tubs in by the bye—Juliet Miss Snevellicci, old Grudden the nurse.—Yes, that 'll do very well. Rover, too:—you might get up Rover while you were about it, and Cassio, and Jeremy Diddler. You can easily knock them off; one part helps the other so much. Here they are, cues and all.'

With these hasty general directions Mr. Crummles thrust a number of little books into the faltering hands of Nicholas, and bidding his eldest son go with him and show where the lodgings were to be had, shook him by the hand, and wished him good night.

There is no lack of comfortable furnished apartments in Portsmouth, and no difficulty in finding some that are proportionate to very slender finances; but the former were too good, and the latter too bad, and they went into so many houses, and came out unsuited, that Nicholas seriously began to think he should be obliged to ask permission to spend the night in the theatre, after all.

Eventually, however, they stumbled upon two small rooms up three pair of stairs, or rather two pair and a ladder, at a tobacconist's shop, on the Common Hard: a dirty street leading down to the dockyard. These Nicholas engaged, only too happy to have escaped any request for payment of a week's rent beforehand.

'There! Lay down our personal property, Smike,' he said, after showing young Crummles downstairs. 'We have fallen upon strange times, and Heaven only knows the end of them; but I am tired with the events of these three days, and will postpone reflection till to-morrow—if I can.'

CHAPTER XXIV

OF THE GREAT BESPEAK FOR MISS SNEVELLICCI, AND THE FIRST APPEARANCE OF NICHOLAS UPON ANY STAGE

NICHOLAS was up betimes in the morning; but he had scarcely begun to dress, notwithstanding, when he heard footsteps ascending the stairs, and was presently saluted by the voices of Mr. Folair the pantomimist, and Mr. Lenville the tragedian.

'House, house, house!' cried Mr. Folair.

'What, ho! within there!' said Mr. Lenville, in a deep voice.

'Confound these fellows!' thought Nicholas; 'they have come to breakfast, I suppose. I'll open the door directly, if you'll wait an instant.'

The gentlemen entreated him not to hurry himself; and, to beguile the interval, had a fencing bout with their walking-sticks on the very small landing-place: to the unspeakable discomposure of all the other lodgers downstairs.

'Here, come in,' said Nicholas, when he had completed his toilet. 'In the name of all that's horrible, don't make that noise outside.'

'An uncommon snug little box this,' said Mr. Lenville, stepping into the front room, and taking his hat off, before he could get in at all. 'Pernicious snug.'

'For a man at all particular in such matters, it might be a trifle too snug,' said Nicholas; 'for, although it is, undoubtedly, a great convenience to be able to reach anything you want from the ceiling or the floor, or either side of the room, without having to move from your chair, still these advantages can only be had in an apartment of the most limited size.'

'It isn't a bit too confined for a single man,' returned Mr. Lenville. 'That reminds me,—my wife, Mr. Johnson,—I hope she'll have some good part in this piece of yours?'

'I glanced at the French copy last night,' said Nicholas. 'It looks very good, I think.'

'What do you mean to do for me, old fellow?' asked Mr. Lenville, poking the struggling fire with his walking-stick, and afterwards wiping it on the skirt of his coat. 'Anything in the gruff and grumble way?'

'You turn your wife and child out of doors,' said Nicholas; 'and in a fit of rage and jealousy, stab your eldest son in the library.'

'Do I though!' exclaimed Mr. Lenville. 'That's very good business.'

'After which,' said Nicholas, 'you are troubled with remorse till the last act, and then you make up your mind to destroy yourself. But, just as you are raising the pistol to your head, a clock strikes—ten.'

'I see,' cried Mr. Lenville. 'Very good.'

'You pause,' said Nicholas; 'you recollect to have heard a clock strike ten in your infancy. The pistol falls from your hand—you are overcome—you burst into tears, and become a virtuous and exemplary character for ever afterwards.'

'Capital!' said Mr. Lenville: 'that's a sure card, a sure card. Get the curtain down with a touch of nature like that, and it'll be a triumphant success.'

'Is there anything good for me?' inquired Mr. Folair, anxiously.

'Let me see,' said Nicholas. 'You play the faithful and attached servant; you are turned out of doors with the wife and child.'

'Always coupled with that infernal phenomenon,' sighed Mr. Folair; 'and we go into poor lodgings, where I won't take any wages, and talk sentiment, I suppose?'

'Why—yes,' replied Nicholas; 'that is the course of the piece.'

'I must have a dance of some kind, you know,' said Mr. Folair. 'You'll have to introduce one for the phenomenon, so you'd better made a *pas de deux*, and save time.'

'There's nothing easier than that,' said Mr. Lenville, observing the disturbed look of the young dramatist.

'Upon my word I don't see how it's to be done,' rejoined Nicholas.

'Why, isn't it obvious?' reasoned Mr. Lenville. 'Gadzooks, who can help seeing the way to do it?— you astonish me! You get the distressed lady, and the little child, and the attached servant, into the poor lodgings, don't you?—Well, look here. The distressed lady sinks into a chair, and buries her face in her pocket-handkerchief—"What makes you weep, mamma?" says the child. "Don't weep, mamma, or you'll make me weep too!"—"And me!" says the faithful servant, rubbing his eyes with his arm. "What can we do to raise your spirits, dear mamma?" says the little child. "Aye, what *can* we do?" says the faithful servant. "Oh, Pierre!" says the distressed lady; "would that I could shake off these painful thoughts."—"Try, ma'am, try," says the faithful servant; "rouse yourself, ma'am; be amused."—"I will," says the lady, "I will learn to suffer with fortitude. Do you remember that dance, my honest friend, which, in happier days, you practised with this sweet angel? It never failed to calm my spirits then. Oh! let me see it once again before I die!"—There it is—cue for the band, *before I die*,—and off they go. That 's the regular thing; isn't it, Tommy?'

'That 's it,' replied Mr. Folair. 'The distressed lady, overpowered by old recollections, faints at the end of the dance, and you close in with a picture.'

Profiting by these and other lessons, which were the result of the personal experience of the two actors, Nicholas willingly gave them the best breakfast he could, and, when he at length got rid of them, applied himself to his task: by no means displeased to find that it was so much easier than he had at first supposed. He worked very hard all day, and did not leave his room until the evening, when he went down to the theatre, whither Smike had repaired before him to go on with another gentleman as a general rebellion.

Here all the people were so much changed that he scarcely knew them. False hair, false colour, false calves, false muscles—they had become different beings. Mr. Lenville was a blooming warrior of most exquisite proportions; Mr. Crummles, his large face shaded by a profusion of black hair, a Highland outlaw of most majestic bearing; one of the old gentlemen a gaoler, and the other a venerable patriarch; the comic countryman, a fighting-man of great valour, relieved by a touch of humour; each of the Master Crummleses a prince in his own right; and the low-spirited lover, a desponding captive. There was a gorgeous banquet ready spread for the third act, consisting of two pasteboard vases, one plate of biscuits, a black bottle, and a vinegar cruet; and, in short, everything was on a scale of the utmost splendour and preparation.

Nicholas was standing with his back to the curtain, now contemplating the first scene, which was a Gothic archway, about two feet shorter than Mr. Crummles, through which that gentleman was to make his first entrance, and now listening to a couple of people who were cracking nuts in the gallery, wondering whether they made the whole audience, when the manager himself walked familiarly up and accosted him.

'Been in front to-night?' said Mr. Crummles.

'No,' replied Nicholas, 'not yet. I am going to see the play.'

'We've had a pretty good Let,' said Mr. Crummles. 'Four front places in the centre, and the whole of the stage-box.'

'Oh, indeed!' said Nicholas; 'a family, I suppose?'

'Yes,' replied Mr. Crummles, 'yes. It's an affecting thing. There are six children, and they never come unless the phenomenon plays.'

It would have been difficult for any party, family or otherwise, to have visited the theatre on a night when the phenomenon did *not* play, inasmuch as she always sustained one, and not uncommonly two or three, characters, every night; but Nicholas, sympathising with the feelings of a father, refrained from hinting at this trifling circumstance, and Mr. Crummles continued to talk, uninterrupted by him.

'Six,' said that gentleman; 'Pa and Ma eight, aunt nine, governess ten, grandfather and grandmother twelve. Then, there's the footman, who stands outside, with a bag of oranges and a jug of toast-and-water, and sees the play for nothing through the little pane of glass in the box-door—it 's cheap at a guinea; they gain by taking a box.'

'I wonder you allow so many,' observed Nicholas.

'There 's no help for it,' replied Mr. Crummles; 'it 's always expected in the country. If there are six children, six people come to hold them in their laps. A family-box carries double always. Ring in the orchestra, Grudden!'

That useful lady did as she was requested, and shortly afterwards the tuning of three fiddles was heard. Which process having been protracted as long as it was supposed that the patience of the audience could possibly bear it, was put a stop to by another jerk of the bell, which, being the signal to begin in earnest, set the orchestra playing a variety of popular airs, with involuntary variations.

If Nicholas had been astonished at the alteration for the better which the gentlemen displayed, the transformation of the ladies was still more extraordinary. When, from a snug corner of the manager's box, he beheld Miss Snevellicci in all the glories of white muslin with a golden hem, and Mrs. Crummles in all the dignity of the outlaw's wife, and Miss Bravassa in all the sweetness of Miss Snevellicci's confidential friend, and Miss Belvawney in the white silks of a page doing duty everywhere and swearing to live and die in the service of everybody, he could scarcely contain his admiration, which testified itself in great applause, and the closest possible attention to the business of the scene. The plot was most interesting. It belonged to no particular age, people, or country, and was perhaps the more delightful on that account, as nobody's previous information could afford the remotest glimmering of what would ever come of it. An outlaw had been very successful in doing something somewhere, and came home, in triumph, to the sound of shouts and fiddles, to greet his wife—a lady of masculine mind, who talked a good deal about her father's bones, which it seemed were unburied, though whether from a peculiar taste on the part of the old gentleman himself, or the reprehensible neglect of his relations, did not appear. This outlaw's wife was, somehow or other, mixed up with a patriarch, living in a castle a long way off, and this patriarch was the father of several of the characters, but he didn't exactly know which, and was uncertain whether he had brought up the right ones in his castle, or the wrong ones; he rather inclined to the latter opinion, and, being uneasy, relieved his mind with a banquet, during which solemnity somebody in a cloak said 'Beware!' which somebody was known by nobody (except the audience) to be the outlaw himself, who had come there, for reasons unexplained, but possibly with an eye to the spoons. There was an agreeable little surprise in the way of certain love passages between the desponding captive and Miss Snevellicci, and the comic fighting-man and Miss Bravassa; besides which, Mr. Lenville had several very tragic scenes in the dark, while on throat-cutting expeditions, which were all baffled by the skill and bravery of the comic fighting-man (who overheard whatever was said all through the piece) and the intrepidity of Miss Snevellicci, who adopted tights, and therein repaired to the prison of her captive lover, with a small basket of refreshments and a dark lantern. At last, it came out that the patriarch was the man who had treated the bones of the outlaw's father-in-law with so much disrespect, for which cause and reason the outlaw's wife repaired to his castle to kill him, and so got into a dark room, where, after a good deal of groping in the dark, everybody got hold of everybody else, and took them for somebody besides, which occasioned a vast quantity of confusion, with some pistolling, loss of life, and torchlight; after which, the patriarch came forward, and observing, with a knowing look, that he knew all about his children now, and would tell them when they got inside, said that there could not be a more appropriate occasion for marrying the young people than that; and therefore he joined their hands, with the full consent of the indefatigable page, who (being the only other person surviving) pointed with his cap into the clouds, and his right hand to the ground; thereby invoking a blessing and giving the cue for the curtain to come down, which it did, amidst general applause.

'What did you think of that?' asked Mr. Crummles, when Nicholas went round to the stage again. Mr. Crummles was very red and hot, for your outlaws are desperate fellows to shout.

'I think it was very capital indeed,' replied Nicholas; 'Miss Snevellicci in particular was uncommonly good.'

'She's a genius,' said Mr. Crummles; 'quite a genius, that girl. By the bye, I've been thinking of bringing out that piece of yours on her bespeak night.'

'When?' asked Nicholas.

'The night of her bespeak. Her benefit night, when her friends and patrons bespeak the play,' said Mr. Crummles.

'Oh! I understand,' replied Nicholas.

'You see,' said Mr. Crummles, 'it's sure to go, on such an occasion, and even if it should not work up quite as well as we expect, why it will be her risk, you know, and not ours.'

'Yours, you mean,' said Nicholas.

'I said mine, didn't I?' returned Mr. Crummles. 'Next Monday week. What do you say? You'll have done it, and are sure to be up in the lover's part, long before that time.'

'I don't know about "long before,"' replied Nicholas; 'but *by* that time I think I can undertake to be ready.'

'Very good,' pursued Mr. Crummles, 'then we'll call that settled. Now, I want to ask you something else. There's a little—what shall I call it—a little canvassing takes place on these occasions.

'Among the patrons, I suppose?' said Nicholas.

'Among the patrons; and the fact is, that Snevellicci has had so many bespeaks in this place, that she wants an attraction. She had a bespeak when her mother-in-law died, and a bespeak when her uncle died; and Mrs. Crummles and myself have had bespeaks on the anniversary of the phenomenon's birthday, and our wedding-day, and occasions of that description, so that, in fact, there's some difficulty in getting a good one. Now, won't you help this poor girl, Mr. Johnson?' said Crummles, sitting himself down on a drum, and taking a great pinch of snuff, as he looked him steadily in the face.

'How do you mean?' rejoined Nicholas.

'Don't you think you could spare half an hour tomorrow morning, and call with her at the houses of one or two of the principal people?' murmured the manager in a persuasive tone.

'Oh dear me,' said Nicholas, with an air of very strong objection, 'I shouldn't like to do that.'

'The infant will accompany her,' said Mr. Crummles. 'The moment it was suggested to me, I gave permission for the infant to go. There will not be the smallest impropriety—Miss Snevellicci, sir, is the very soul of honour. It would be of material service—the gentleman from London—author of the new piece—actor in the new piece—first appearance on any boards—it would lead to a great bespeak, Mr. Johnson.'

'I am very sorry to throw a damp upon the prospects of anybody, and more especially a lady,' replied Nicholas; 'but really I must decidedly object to making one of the canvassing party.'

'What does Mr. Johnson say, Vincent?' inquired a voice close to his ear; and, looking round, he found Mrs. Crummles and Miss Snevellicci herself standing behind him.

'He has some objection, my dear,' replied Mr. Crummles, looking at Nicholas.

'Objection!' exclaimed Mrs. Crummles. 'Can it be possible?'

'Oh, I hope not!' cried Miss Snevellicci. 'You surely are not so cruel—oh, dear me!—Well, I—to think of that now, after all one's looking forward to it!'

'Mr. Johnson will not persist, my dear,' said Mrs. Crummles. 'Think better of him than to suppose it. Gallantry, humanity, all the best feelings of his nature, must be enlisted in this interesting cause.'

'Which moves even a manager,' said Mr. Crummles, smiling.

'And a manager's wife,' added Mrs. Crummles, in her accustomed tragedy tones. 'Come, come, you will relent, I know you will.'

'It is not in my nature,' said Nicholas, moved by these appeals, 'to resist any entreaty, unless it is to do something positively wrong; and, beyond a feeling of pride, I know nothing which should prevent my doing this. I know nobody here, and nobody knows me. So be it then. I yield.'

Miss Snevellicci was at once overwhelmed with blushes and expressions of gratitude, of which latter commodity neither Mr. nor Mrs. Crummles was by any means sparing. It was arranged that Nicholas should call upon her, at her lodgings, at eleven next morning, and soon after they parted: he to return home to his authorship: Miss Snevellicci to dress for the after-piece: and the disinterested manager and his wife to discuss the probable gains of the forthcoming bespeak, of which they were to have two-thirds of the profits by solemn entreaty of agreement.

At the stipulated hour next morning, Nicholas repaired to the lodgings of Miss Snevellicci, which were in a place called Lombard Street, at the house of a tailor. A strong smell of ironing pervaded the little passage; and the tailor's daughter, who opened the door, appeared in that flutter of spirits which is so often attendant upon the periodical getting up of a family's linen.

'Miss Snevellicci lives here, I believe?' said Nicholas, when the door was opened.

The tailor's daughter replied in the affirmative.

'Will you have the goodness to let her know that Mr. Johnson is here?' said Nicholas.

'Oh, if you please, you 're to come upstairs,' replied the tailor's daughter, with a smile.

Nicholas followed the young lady, and was shown into a small apartment on the first floor, communicating with a back-room; in which, as he judged from a certain half-subdued clinking sound, as of cups and saucers, Miss Snevellicci was then taking her breakfast in bed.

'You 're to wait, if you please,' said the tailor's daughter, after a short period of absence, during which the clinking in the back-room had ceased, and had been succeeded by whispering—'She won't be long.'

As she spoke she pulled up the window-blind, and having by this means (as she thought) diverted Mr.

Johnson's attention from the room to the street, caught up some articles which were airing on the fender, and had very much the appearance of stockings, and darted off.

As there were not many objects of interest outside the windows, Nicholas looked about the room with more curiosity than he might otherwise have bestowed upon it. On the sofa lay an old guitar, several thumbed pieces of music, and a scattered litter of curl-papers: together with a confused heap of playbills, and a pair of soiled white satin shoes with large blue rosettes. Hanging over the back of a chair was a half-finished muslin apron with little pockets ornamented with red ribbons, such as waiting-women wear on the stage, and (by consequence) are never seen with anywhere else. In one corner stood the diminutive pair of top-boots in which Miss Snevellicci was accustomed to enact the little jockey, and, folded on a chair hard by, was a small parcel, which bore a very suspicious resemblance to the companion smalls.

But the most interesting object of all, was, perhaps, the open scrap-book, displayed in the midst of some theatrical duodecimos that were strewn upon the table; and pasted into which scrap-book were various critical notices of Miss Snevellicci's acting, extracted from different provincial journals, together with one poetic address in her honour, commencing—

> Sing, God of Love, and tell me in what dearth
> Thrice-gifted Snevellicci came on earth,
> To thrill us with her smile, her tear, her eye,
> Sing, God of Love, and tell me quickly why.

Besides this effusion, there were innumerable complimentary allusions, also extracted from newspapers, such as—'We observe from an advertisement in another part of our paper of to-day, that the charming and highly-talented Miss Snevellicci takes her benefit on Wednesday, for which occasion she has put forth a bill of fare that might kindle exhilaration in the breast of a misanthrope. In the confidence that our fellow-townsmen have not lost that high appreciation of public utility and private worth, for which they have long been so pre-eminently distinguished, we predict that this charming actress will be greeted with a bumper.' 'To Correspondents.—J. S. is misinformed when he supposes that the highly-gifted and beautiful Miss Snevellicci, nightly captivating all hearts at our pretty and commodious little theatre, is *not* the same lady to whom the young gentleman of immense fortune, residing within a hundred miles of the good city of York, lately made honourable proposals. We have reason to know that Miss Snevellicci *is* the lady who was implicated in that mysterious and romantic affair, and whose conduct on that occasion did no less honour to her head and heart, than do her histrionic triumphs to her brilliant genius.' A copious assortment of such paragraphs as these, with long bills of benefits all ending with 'Come Early,' in large capitals, formed the principal contents of Miss Snevellicci's scrap-book.

Nicholas had read a great many of these scraps, and was absorbed in a circumstantial and melancholy account of the train of events which had led to Miss Snevellicci's spraining her ankle by slipping on a piece of orange-peel flung by a monster in human form, (so the paper said,) upon the stage at Winchester,—when that young lady herself, attired in the coal-scuttle bonnet and walking-dress complete, tripped into the room, with a thousand apologies for having detained him so long after the appointed time.

'But really,' said Miss Snevellicci, 'my darling Led,

who lives with me here, was taken so very ill in the
night that I thought she would have expired in my
arms.'

'Such a fate is almost to be envied,' returned Nicholas, 'but I am very sorry to hear it nevertheless.'

'What a creature you are to flatter!' said Miss Snevellicci, buttoning her glove in much confusion.

'If it be flattery to admire your charms and accomplishments,' rejoined Nicholas, laying his hand upon
the scrap-book, 'you have better specimens of it here.'

'Oh you cruel creature, to read such things as those!
I 'm almost ashamed to look you in the face afterwards, positively I am,' said Miss Snevellicci, seizing
the book and putting it away in a closet. 'How careless of Led! How could she be so naughty!'

'I thought you had kindly left it here, on purpose
for me to read,' said Nicholas. And really it did seem
possible.

'I wouldn't have had you see if for the world!' rejoined Miss Snevellicci. 'I never was so vexed—
never! But she is such a careless thing, there 's no
trusting her.'

The conversation was here interrupted by the entrance of the phenomenon, who had discreetly remained in the bedroom up to this moment, and now
presented herself, with much grace and lightness,
bearing in her hand a very little green parasol with
a broad fringe border, and no handle. After a few
words of course, they sallied into the street.

The phenomenon was rather a troublesome companion, for first the right sandal came down, and
then the left, and these mischances being repaired, one
leg of the little white trousers was discovered to be
longer than the other; besides these accidents, the
green parasol was dropped down an iron grating, and
only fished up again, with great difficulty and by dint

of much exertion. However, it was impossible to scold her, as she was the manager's daughter, so Nicholas took it all in perfect good humour, and walked on, with Miss Snevellicci, arm in arm on one side, and the offending infant on the other.

The first house to which they bent their steps, was situated in a terrace of respectable appearance. Miss Snevellicci's modest double-knock was answered by a foot-boy, who, in reply to her inquiry whether Mrs. Curdle was at home, opened his eyes very wide, grinned very much, and said he didn't know, but he 'd inquire. With this, he showed them into a parlour where he kept them waiting, until the two women-servants had repaired thither, under false pretences, to see the play-actors; and having compared notes with them in the passage, and joined in a vast quantity of whispering and giggling, he at length went up-stairs with Miss Snevellicci's name.

Now, Mrs. Curdle was supposed, by those who were best informed on such points, to possess quite the London taste in matters relating to literature and the drama; and as to Mr. Curdle, he had written a pamphlet of sixty-four pages, post octavo, on the character of the Nurse's deceased husband in Romeo and Juliet, with an inquiry whether he really had been a 'merry man' in his life-time, or whether it was merely his widow's affectionate partiality that induced her so to report him. He had likewise proved, that by altering the received mode of punctuation, any one of Shakespeare's plays could be made quite different, and the sense completely changed; it is needless to say, therefore, that he was a great critic, and a very profound and most original thinker.

'Well, Miss Snevellicci,' said Mrs. Curdle, entering the parlour, 'and how do *you* do?'

Miss Snevellicci made a graceful obeisance, and

hoped Mrs. Curdle was well, as also Mr. Curdle, who at the same time appeared. Mrs. Curdle was dressed in a morning wrapper, with a little cap stuck upon the top of her head. Mr. Curdle wore a loose robe on his back, and his right fore-finger on his forehead, after the portraits of Sterne, to whom somebody or other had once said he bore a striking resemblance.

'I ventured to call, for the purpose of asking whether you would put your name to my bespeak, ma'am,' said Miss Snevellicci, producing documents.

'Oh! I really don't know what to say,' replied Mrs. Curdle. 'It's not as if the theatre was in its high and palmy days—you needn't stand, Miss Snevellicci —the drama is gone, perfectly gone.'

'As an exquisite embodiment of the poet's visions, and a realisation of human intellectuality, gilding with refulgent light our dreamy moments, and laying open a new and magic world before the mental eye, the drama is gone, perfectly gone,' said Mr. Curdle.

'What man is there, now living, who can present before us all those changing and prismatic colours with which the character of Hamlet is invested?' exclaimed Mrs. Curdle.

'What man indeed—upon the stage,' said Mr. Curdle, with a small reservation in favour of himself. 'Hamlet! Pooh! ridiculous! Hamlet is gone, perfectly gone.'

Quite overcome by these dismal reflections, Mr. and Mrs. Curdle sighed, and sat for some short time without speaking. At length, the lady, turning, to Miss Snevellicci, inquired what play she proposed to have.

'Quite a new one,' said Miss Snevellicci, 'of which this gentleman is the author, and in which he plays; being his first appearance on any stage. Mr. Johnson is the gentleman's name.'

'I hope you have preserved the unities, sir?' said Mr. Curdle.

'The original piece is a French one,' said Nicholas. 'There is abundance of incident, sprightly dialogue, strongly-marked characters—'

'—All unavailing without a strict observance of the unities, sir,' returned Mr. Curdle. 'The unities of the drama, before everything.'

'Might I ask you,' said Nicholas, hesitating between the respect he ought to assume, and his love of the whimsical, 'might I ask you what the unities are?'

Mr. Curdle coughed and considered. 'The unities, sir,' he said, 'are a completeness—a kind of universal dovetailedness with regard to place and time—a sort of a general oneness, if I may be allowed to use so strong an expression. I take those to be the dramatic unities, so far as I have been enabled to bestow attention upon them, and I have read much upon the subject, and thought much. I find, running through the performances of this child,' said Mr. Curdle, turning to the phenomenon, 'a unity of feeling, a breadth, a light and shade, a warmth of colouring, a tone, a harmony, a glow, an artistical development of original conceptions, which I look for, in vain, among older performers. I don't know whether I make myself understood?'

'Perfectly,' replied Nicholas.

'Just so,' said Mr. Curdle, pulling up his neckcloth. 'That is my definition of the unities of the drama.'

Mrs. Curdle had sat listening to this lucid explanation with great complacency. It being finished, she inquired what Mr. Curdle thought, about putting down their names.

'I don't know, my dear; upon my word I don't know,' said Mr. Curdle. 'If we do, it must be dis-

tinctly understood that we do not pledge ourselves
to the quality of the performances. Let it go forth
to the world, that we do not give *them* the sanction of
our names, but that we confer the distinction merely
upon Miss Snevellicci. That being clearly stated, I
take it to be, as it were, a duty, that we should extend
our patronage to a degraded stage, even for the sake
of the associations with which it is entwined. Have
you got two-and-sixpence for half-a-crown, Miss
Snevellicci?' said Mr. Curdle, turning over four of
those pieces of money.

Miss Snevellicci felt in all the corners of the pink
reticule, but there was nothing in any of them. Nicholas murmured a jest about his being an author, and
thought it best not to go through the form of feeling
in his own pockets at all.

'Let me see,' said Mr. Curdle; 'twice four's eight—
four shillings a-piece to the boxes, Miss Snevellicci, is
exceedingly dear in the present state of the drama—
three half-crowns is seven-and-six; we shall not differ
about sixpence, I suppose? Sixpence will not part us,
Miss Snevellicci?'

Poor Miss Snevellicci took the three half-crowns,
with many smiles and bends, and Mrs. Curdle, adding
several supplementary directions relative to keeping
the places for them and dusting the seat, and sending
two clean bills as soon as they came out, rang the bell,
as a signal for breaking up the conference.'

'Odd people those,' said Nicholas, when they got
clear of the house.

'I assure you,' said Miss Snevellicci, taking his arm,
'that I think myself very lucky they did not owe all
the money instead of being sixpence short. Now, if
you were to succeed, they would give people to understand that they had always patronised you; and if you

were to fail, they would have been quite certain of that from the very beginning.'

At the next house they visited they were in great glory; for, there, resided the six children who were so enraptured with the public actions of the phenomenon, and who, being called down from the nursery to be treated with a private view of that young lady, proceeded to poke their fingers into her eyes, and tread upon her toes, and show her many other little attentions peculiar to their time of life.

'I shall certainly persuade Mr. Borum to take a private box,' said the lady of the house, after a most gracious reception. 'I shall only take two of the children, and will make up the rest of the party, of gentlemen—your admirers, Miss Snevellicci. Augustus, you naughty boy, leave the little girl alone.'

This was addressed to a young gentleman who was pinching the phenomenon behind, apparently with a view of ascertaining whether she was real.

'I am sure you must be very tired,' said the mamma, turning to Miss Snevellicci. 'I cannot think of allowing you to go, without first taking a glass of wine. Fie, Charlotte, I am ashamed of you! Miss Lane, my dear, pray see to the children.'

Miss Lane was the governess, and this entreaty was rendered necessary by the abrupt behaviour of the youngest Miss Borum, who, having filched the phenomenon's little green parasol, was now carrying it bodily off, while the distracted infant looked helplessly on.

'I am sure, where you ever learnt to act as you do,' said good-natured Mrs. Borum, turning again to Miss Snevellicci, 'I cannot understand (Emma, don't stare so); laughing in one piece, and crying in the next, and so natural in all—oh, dear!'

'I am very happy to hear you express so favourable an opinion,' said Miss Snevellicci. 'It's quite delightful to think you like it.'

'Like it!' cried Mrs. Borum. 'Who can help liking it! I would go to the play, twice a week if I could: I dote upon it. Only you're too affecting sometimes. You do put me in such a state; into such fits of crying! Goodness gracious me, Miss Lane, how can you let them torment that poor child so!'

The phenomenon was really in a fair way of being torn limb from limb; for two strong little boys, one holding on by each of her hands, were dragging her in different directions as a trial of strength. However, Miss Lane (who had herself been too much occupied in contemplating the grown-up actors, to pay the necessary attention to these proceedings) rescued the unhappy infant at this juncture, who, being recruited with a glass of wine, was shortly afterwards taken away by her friends, after sustaining no more serious damage than a flattening of the pink gauze bonnet, and a rather extensive creasing of the white frock and trousers.

It was a trying morning; for there were a great many calls to make, and everybody wanted a different thing. Some wanted tragedies, and others comedies; some objected to dancing; some wanted scarcely anything else. Some thought the comic singer decidedly low, and others hoped he would have more to do than he usually had. Some people wouldn't promise to go, because other people wouldn't promise to go; and other people wouldn't go at all, because other people went. At length, and by little and little, omitting something in this place, and adding something in that, Miss Snevellicci pledged herself to a bill of fare which was comprehensive enough, if it had no other merit (it included among other trifles, four pieces, divers songs, a few combats, and several dances); and they returned home, pretty well exhausted with the business of the day.

Nicholas worked away at the piece, which was speedily put into rehearsal, and then worked away at his own part, which he studied with great perseverance and acted—as the whole company said—to perfection. And at length the great day arrived. The crier was sent round, in the morning, to proclaim the entertainments with sound of bell in all the thoroughfares; and extra bills of three feet long by nine inches wide, were dispersed in all directions, flung down all the areas, thrust under all the knockers, and developed in all the shops. They were placarded on all the walls too, though not with complete success, for an illiterate person having undertaken this office during the indisposition of the regular bill-sticker, a part were posted sideways, and the remainder upside-down.

At half-past five, there was a rush of four people to the gallery-door; at a quarter before six, there were at least a dozen; at six o'clock the kicks were terrific; and when the elder Master Crummles opened the door, he was obliged to run behind it for his life. Fifteen shillings were taken by Mrs. Grudden in the first ten minutes.

Behind the scenes the same unwonted excitement prevailed. Miss Snevellicci was in such a perspiration that the paint would scarcely stay on her face. Mrs. Crummles was so nervous that she could hardly remember her part. Miss Bravassa's ringlets came out of curl with the heat and anxiety; even Mr. Crummles himself kept peeping through the hole in the curtain, and running back, every now and then, to announce that another man had come into the pit.

At last, the orchestra left off, and the curtain rose

upon the new piece. The first scene, in which there was nobody particular, passed off calmly enough, but when Miss Snevellicci went on in the second, accompanied by the phenomenon as child, what a roar of applause broke out! The people in the Borum box rose as one man, waving their hats and handkerchiefs, and uttering shouts of 'Bravo!' Mrs. Borum and the governess cast wreaths upon the stage, of which, some fluttered into the lamps, and one crowned the temples of a fat gentleman in the pit, who, looking eagerly towards the scene, remained unconscious of the honour; the tailor and his family kicked at the panels of the upper boxes till they threatened to come out altogether; the very ginger-beer boy remained transfixed in the centre of the house; a young officer, supposed to entertain a passion for Miss Snevellicci, stuck his glass in his eye as though to hide a tear. Again and again Miss Snevellicci curtseyed lower and lower, and again and again the applause came down, louder and louder. At length, when the phenomenon picked up one of the smoking wreaths and put it on, sideways, over Miss Snevellicci's eye, it reached its climax, and the play proceeded.

But when Nicholas came on for his crack scene with Mrs. Crummles, what a clapping of hands there was! When Mrs. Crummles (who was his unworthy mother) sneered, and called him 'presumptuous boy,' and he defied her, what a tumult of applause came on! When he quarrelled with the other gentlemen about the young lady, and producing a case of pistols, said, that if he *was* a gentleman, he would fight him in that drawing-room, until the furniture was sprinkled with the blood of one, if not of two—how boxes, pit, and gallery, joined in one most vigorous cheer! When he called his mother names, because she wouldn't give up the young lady's property, and she

THE GREAT BESPEAK FOR MISS SNEVELLICCI.

relenting, caused him to relent likewise, and fall down on one knee and ask her blessing, how the ladies in the audience sobbed! When he was hid behind the curtain in the dark, and the wicked relation poked a sharp sword in every direction, save where his legs were plainly visible, what a thrill of anxious fear ran through the house! His air, his figure, his walk, his look, everything he said or did, was the subject of commendation. There was a round of applause every time he spoke. And when, at last, in the pump-and-tub scene, Mrs. Grudden lighted the blue fire, and all the unemployed members of the company came in, and tumbled down in various directions—not because that had anything to do with the plot, but in order to finish off with a tableau—the audience (who had by this time increased considerably) gave vent to such a shout of enthusiasm, as had not been heard in those walls for many and many a day.

In short, the success both of new piece and new actor was complete, and when Miss Snevellicci was called for at the end of the play, Nicholas led her on, and divided the applause.

CHAPTER XXV

CONCERNING A YOUNG LADY FROM LONDON, WHO JOINS THE COMPANY, AND AN ELDERLY ADMIRER WHO FOLLOWS HER TRAIN; WITH AN AFFECTING CEREMONY CONSEQUENT ON THEIR ARRIVAL

THE new piece being a decided hit, was announced for every evening of performance until further notice, and the evenings when the theatre was closed, were reduced from three in the week to two. Nor were these the only tokens of extraordinary success; for, on the succeeding Saturday, Nicholas received, by favour of the indefatigable Mrs. Grudden, no less a sum than thirty shillings; besides which substantial reward, he enjoyed considerable fame and honour: having a presentation copy of Mr. Curdle's pamphlet forwarded to the theatre, with that gentleman's own autograph (in itself an inestimable treasure) on the fly-leaf, accompanied with a note, containing many expressions of approval, and an unsolicited assurance that Mr. Curdle would be very happy to read Shakespeare to him for three hours every morning before breakfast during his stay in the town.

'I 've got another novelty, Johnson,' said Mr. Crummles one morning in great glee.

'What 's that?' rejoined Nicholas. 'The pony?'

'No, no, we never come to the pony till everything else has failed,' said Mr. Crummles. 'I don't think we shall come to the pony at all, this season. No, no, not the pony.'

'A boy phenomenon, perhaps?' suggested Nicholas.

'There is only one phenomenon, sir,' replied Mr. Crummles impressively, 'and that 's a girl.'

'Very true,' said Nicholas. 'I beg your pardon. Then I don't know what it is, I am sure.'

'What should you say to a young lady from London?' inquired Mr. Crummles. 'Miss So-and-so, of the Theatre Royal, Drury Lane?'

'I should say she would look very well in the bills,' said Nicholas.

'You 're about right there,' said Mr. Crummles; 'and if you had said she would look very well upon the stage too, you wouldn't have been far out. Look here; what do you think of this?'

With this inquiry Mr. Crummles unfolded a red poster, and a blue poster, and a yellow poster, at the top of each of which public notification was inscribed in enormous characters 'First appearance of the un-rivalled Miss Petowker of the Theatre Royal, Drury Lane!'

'Dear me!' said Nicholas, 'I know that lady.'

'Then you are acquainted with as much talent as was ever compressed into one young person's body,' retorted Mr. Crummles, rolling up the bills again; 'that is, talent of a certain sort—of a certain sort. "The Blood Drinker,"' added Mr. Crummles with a prophetic sigh, ' "The Blood Drinker" will die with that girl; and she's the only sylph *I* ever saw, who could stand upon one leg, and play the tambourine on her other knee, *like* a sylph.'

'When does she come down?' asked Nicholas.

'We expect her to-day,' replied Mr. Crummles. 'She is an old friend of Mrs. Crummles's. Mrs. Crummles saw what she could do—always knew it from the first. She taught her, indeed, nearly all she knows. Mrs. Crummles was the original Blood Drinker.'

'Was she, indeed?'

'Yes. She was obliged to give it up though.'

'Did it disagree with her?' asked Nicholas.

'Not so much with her, as with her audiences,' replied Mr. Crummles. 'Nobody could stand it. It was too tremendous. You don't quite know what Mrs. Crummles is, yet.'

Nicholas ventured to insinuate that he thought he did.

'No, no, you don't,' said Mr. Crummles; 'you don't, indeed. *I* don't, and that's a fact. I don't think her country will, till she is dead. Some new proof of talent bursts from that astonishing woman every year of her life. Look at her, mother of six children, three of 'em alive, and all upon the stage!'

'Extraordinary!' cried Nicholas.

'Ah! extraordinary indeed,' rejoined Mr. Crummles, taking a complacent pinch of snuff, and shaking his head gravely. 'I pledge you my professional word I didn't even know she could dance, till her last benefit, and then she played Juliet, and Helen Macgregor, and did the skipping-rope hornpipe between the pieces. The very first time I saw that admirable woman, Johnson,' said Mr. Crummles, drawing a little nearer, and speaking in the tone of confidential friendship, 'she stood upon her head on the butt-end of a spear, surrounded with blazing fireworks.'

'You astonish me!' said Nicholas.

'*She* astonished *me!*' returned Mr. Crummles, with a very serious countenance. 'Such grace, coupled with such dignity! I adored her from that moment!'

The arrival of the gifted subject of these remarks put an abrupt termination to Mr. Crummles's eulogium. Almost immediately afterwards, Master Percy Crummles entered with a letter, which had arrived by the General Post, and was directed to his gracious mother; at sight of the superscription whereof, Mrs. Crummles exclaimed, 'From Henrietta Petowker, I do declare!' and instantly became absorbed in the contents.

'Is it—?' inquired Mr. Crummles, hesitating.

'Oh, yes, it's all right,' replied Mrs. Crummles, anticipating the question. 'What an excellent thing for her, to be sure!'

'It's the best thing altogether, that I ever heard of, I think,' said Mr. Crummles; and then Mr. Crummles, Mrs. Crummles, and Master Percy Crummles, all fell to laughing violently. Nicholas left them to enjoy their mirth together, and walked to his lodgings: wondering very much what mystery connected with Miss Petowker could provoke such merriment, and pondering still more on the extreme surprise with which that lady would regard his sudden enlistment in a profession of which she was such a distinguished and brilliant ornament.

But, in this latter respect he was mistaken; for— whether Mr. Vincent Crummles had paved the way, or Miss Petowker had some special reason for treating him with even more than her usual amiability— their meeting at the theatre next day was more like that of two dear friends who had been inseparable from infancy, than a recognition passing between a lady and gentleman who had only met some half dozen times, and then by mere chance. Nay, Miss Petowker even whispered that she had wholly dropped the Kenwigses in her conversations with the manager's family, and had represented herself as having encountered Mr. Johnson in the very first and most fashionable circles; and on Nicholas receiving this intelligence with unfeigned surprise, she added, with a sweet glance, that she had a claim on his good nature now, and might tax it before long.

Nicholas had the honour of playing in a slight piece with Miss Petowker that night, and could not but observe that the warmth of her reception was mainly attributable to a most persevering umbrella in the upper boxes; he saw, too, that the enchanting actress cast many sweet looks towards the quarter whence these sounds proceeded; and that every time she did so, the umbrella broke out afresh. Once, he thought that a peculiarly shaped hat in the same corner was not wholly unknown to him; but, being occupied with his share of the stage business, he bestowed no great attention upon this circumstance, and it had quite vanished from his memory by the time he reached home.

He had just sat down to supper with Smike, when one of the people of the house came outside the door,

and announced that a gentleman below-stairs wished
to speak to Mr. Johnson.

'Well, if he does, you must tell him to come up;
that's all I know,' replied Nicholas. 'One of our
hungry brethren, I suppose, Smike.'

His fellow-lodger looked at the cold meat in silent
calculation of the quantity that would be left for dinner next day, and put back a slice he had cut for himself, in order that the visitor's encroachments might
be less formidable in their effects.

'It is not anybody who has been here before,' said
Nicholas, 'for he is stumbling up every stair. Come
in, come in. In the name of wonder! Mr. Lillyvick?'

It was, indeed, the collector of water-rates who,
regarding Nicholas, with a fixed look and immovable
countenance, shook hands with most portentous
solemnity, and sat himself down in a seat by the chim-
ney-corner.

'Why, when did you come here?' asked Nicholas.

'This morning, sir,' replied Mr. Lillyvick.

'Oh! I see; then you were at the theatre to-night,
and it was your umb—'

'This umbrella,' said Mr. Lillyvick, producing a fat
green cotton one with a battered ferrule. 'What did
you think of that performance?'

'So far as I could judge, being on the stage,' replied
Nicholas, 'I thought it very agreeable.'

'Agreeable!' cried the collector. 'I mean to say,
sir, that it was delicious.'

Mr. Lillyvick bent forward to pronounce the last
word with greater emphasis; and having done so, drew
himself up, and frowned and nodded a great many
times.

'I say, delicious,' repeated Mr. Lillyvick. 'Absorbing, fairy-like, toomultuous,' and again Mr. Lilly-

vick drew himself up, and again he frowned and nodded.

'Ah!' said Nicholas, a little surprised at these symptoms of ecstatic approbation. 'Yes, she is a clever girl.'

'She is a divinity,' returned Mr. Lillyvick, giving a collector's double knock on the ground with the umbrella before-mentioned. 'I have known divine actresses before now, sir; I used to collect—at least I used to *call for*—and very often call for—the water-rate at the house of a divine actress, who lived in my beat for upwards of four year, but never—no, never, sir—of all divine creatures, actresses or no actresses, did I see a diviner one than is Henrietta Petowker.'

Nicholas had much ado to prevent himself from laughing; not trusting himself to speak, he merely nodded in accordance with Mr. Lillyvick's nods, and remained silent.

'Let me speak a word with you in private,' said Mr. Lillyvick.

Nicholas looked good-humouredly at Smike, who, taking the hint, disappeared.

'A bachelor is a miserable wretch, sir,' said Mr. Lillyvick.

'Is he?' asked Nicholas.

'He is,' rejoined the collector. 'I have lived in the world for nigh sixty year, and I ought to know what it is.'

'You *ought* to know, certainly,' thought Nicholas; 'but whether you do or not, is another question.'

'If a bachelor happens to have saved a little matter of money,' said Mr. Lillyvick, 'his sisters and brothers, and nephews and nieces, look *to* that money, and not to him; even if, by being a public character, he is the head of the family, or, as it may be, the main from which all the other little branches are turned on, they still wish him dead all the while, and get low-spirited every time they see him looking in good health, because they want to come into his little property. You see that?'

'Oh yes,' replied Nicholas: 'it's very true, no doubt.'

'The great reason for not being married,' resumed Mr. Lillyvick, 'is the expense; that's what's kept me off, or else—Lord!' said Mr. Lillyvick, snapping his fingers, 'I might have had fifty women.'

'Fine women?' asked Nicholas.

'Fine women, sir!' replied the collector; 'aye! not so fine as Henrietta Petowker, for she is an uncommon specimen, but such women as don't fall into every man's way, I can tell you. Now suppose a man can get a fortune *in* a wife instead of with her—eh?'

'Why, then, he's a lucky fellow,' replied Nicholas.

'That's what I say,' retorted the collector, patting him benignantly on the side of the head with his umbrella; 'just what I say. Henrietta Petowker, the talented Henrietta Petowker has a fortune in herself, and I am going to—'

'To make her Mrs. Lillyvick?' suggested Nicholas.

'No, sir, not to make her Mrs. Lillyvick,' replied the collector. 'Actresses, sir, always keep their maiden names—that's the regular thing—but I'm going to marry her; and the day after to-morrow, too.'

'I congratulate you, sir,' said Nicholas.

'Thank you, sir,' replied the collector, buttoning his waistcoat. 'I shall draw her salary, of course, and I hope after all that it's nearly as cheap to keep two as it is to keep one; that's a consolation.'

'Surely you don't want any consolation at such a moment?' observed Nicholas.

'No,' replied Mr. Lillyvick, shaking his head nervously: 'no—of course not.'

'But how come you both here, if you 're going to be married, Mr. Lillyvick?' asked Nicholas.

'Why, that 's what I came to explain to you,' replied the collector of water-rate. 'The fact is, we have thought it best to keep it secret from the family.'

'Family!' said Nicholas. 'What family?'

'The Kenwigses of course,' rejoined Mr. Lillyvick. 'If my niece and the children had known a word about it before I came away, they 'd have gone into fits at my feet, and never have come out of 'em till I took an oath not to marry anybody. Or they 'd have got out a commission of lunacy, or some dreadful thing,' said the collector, quite trembling as he spoke.

'To be sure,' said Nicholas. 'Yes; they would have been jealous, no doubt.'

'To prevent which,' said Mr. Lillyvick, 'Henrietta Petowker (it was settled between us) should come down here to her friends, the Crummleses, under pretence of this engagement, and I should go down to Guildford the day before, and join her on the coach there; which I did, and we came down from Guildford yesterday together. Now, for fear you should be writing to Mr. Noggs, and might say anything about us, we have thought it best to let you into the secret. We shall be married from the Crummleses' lodgings, and shall be delighted to see you, either before church or at breakfast-time, which you like. It won't be expensive, you know,' said the collector, highly anxious to prevent any misunderstanding on this point; 'just muffins and coffee, with perhaps a shrimp or something of that sort for a relish, you know.'

'Yes, yes, I understand,' replied Nicholas. 'Oh, I shall be most happy to come; it will give me the greatest pleasure. Where 's the lady stopping? With Mrs. Crummles?'

'Why, no,' said the collector; 'they couldn't very well dispose of her at night, and so she is staying with an acquaintance of hers, and another young lady; they both belong to the theatre.'

'Miss Snevellicci, I suppose?' said Nicholas.

'Yes, that 's the name.'

'And they 'll be bridesmaids, I presume?' said Nicholas.

'Why,' said the collector, with a rueful face, 'they *will* have four bridesmaids; I 'm afraid they 'll make it rather theatrical.'

'Oh no, not at all,' replied Nicholas, with an awkward attempt to convert a laugh into a cough. 'Who may the four be? Miss Snevellicci of course—Miss Ledrook—'

'The—the phenomenon,' groaned the collector.

'Ha, ha!' cried Nicholas. 'I beg your pardon, I don't know what I 'm laughing at—yes, that 'll be very pretty—the phenomenon—who else?'

'Some young woman or other,' replied the collector, rising; 'some other friend of Henrietta Petowker's. Well, you 'll be careful not to say anything about it, will you?'

'You may safely depend upon me,' replied Nicholas. 'Won't you take anything to eat or drink?'

'No,' said the collector; 'I haven't any appetite. I should think it was a very pleasant life, the married one, eh?'

'I have not the least doubt of it,' rejoined Nicholas.

'Yes,' said the collector; 'certainly. Oh yes. No doubt. Good night.'

With these words, Mr. Lillyvick, whose manner had exhibited through the whole of this interview a most extraordinary compound of precipitation, hesitation,

confidence and doubt, fondness, misgiving, meanness, and self-importance, turned his back upon the
room, and left Nicholas to enjoy a laugh by himself
if he felt so disposed.

Without stopping to inquire whether the interven-
ing day appeared to Nicholas to consist of the usual
number of hours of the ordinary length, it may be remarked that, to the parties more directly interested in
the forthcoming ceremony, it passed with great
rapidity, insomuch that when Miss Petowker awoke
on the succeeding morning in the chamber of Miss
Snevellicci, she declared that nothing should ever persuade her that that really was the day which was to
behold a change in her condition.

'I never will believe it,' said Miss Petowker; 'I cannot really. It's of no use talking, I never can make
up my mind to go through with such a trial!'

On hearing this, Miss Snevellicci and Miss Ledrook, who knew perfectly well that their fair friend's
mind had been made up for three or four years, at
any period of which time she would have cheerfully
undergone the desperate trial now approaching if she
could have found any eligible gentleman disposed for
the venture, began to preach comfort and firmness,
and to say how very proud she ought to feel that it
was in her power to confer lasting bliss on a deserving object, and how necessary it was for the happiness of mankind in general that women should possess
fortitude and resignation on such occasions; and that
although for their parts they held true happiness to
consist in a single life, which they would not willingly exchange—no, not for any worldy consideration—still (thank Heaven), if ever the time *should*
come, they hoped they knew their duty too well to
repine, but would the rather submit with meekness
and humility of spirit to a fate for which Providence

had clearly designed them with a view to the contentment and reward of their fellow-creatures.

'I might feel it was a great blow,' said Miss Snevellicci, 'to break up old associations and what-do-you-call-ems of that kind, but I would submit, my dear, I would indeed.'

'So would I,' said Miss Ledrook; 'I would rather court the yoke than shun it. I have broken hearts before now, and I 'm very sorry for it. It 's a terrible thing to reflect upon.'

'It is indeed,' said Miss Snevellicci. 'Now, Led, my dear, we must positively get her ready, or we shall be too late, we shall indeed.'

This pious reasoning, and perhaps the fear of being too late, supported the bride through the ceremony of robing, after which, strong tea and brandy were administered in alternate doses as a means of strengthening her feeble limbs and causing her to walk steadier.

'How do you feel now, my love?' inquired Miss Snevellicci.

'Oh, Lillyvick!' cried the bride. 'If you knew what I am undergoing for you!'

'Of course he knows it, love, and will never forget it,' said Miss Ledrook.

'Do you think he won't?' cried Miss Petowker, really showing great capability for the stage. 'Oh, do you think he won't? Do you think Lillyvick will always remember it—always, always, always?'

There is no knowing in what this burst of feeling might have ended, if Miss Snevellicci had not at that moment proclaimed the arrival of the fly, which so astounded the bride that she shook off divers alarming symptoms which were coming on very strong, and running to the glass adjusted her dress, and calmly declared that she was ready for the sacrifice.

She was accordingly supported into the coach, and there 'kept up' (as Miss Snevellicci said) with perpetual sniffs of *sal volatile* and sips of brandy and other gentle stimulants, until they reached the manager's door, which was already opened by the two Master Crummleses, who wore white cockades, and were decorated with the choicest and most resplendent waistcoats in the theatrical wardrobe. By the combined exertions of these young gentlemen and the bridesmaids, assisted by the coachman, Miss Petowker was at length supported in a condition of much exhaustion to the first floor, where she no sooner encountered the youthful bridegroom than she fainted with great decorum.

'Henrietta Petowker!' said the collector; 'cheer up, my lovely one.'

Miss Petowker grasped the collector's hand, but emotion choked her utterance.

'Is the sight of me so dreadful, Henrietta Petowker?' said the collector.

'Oh no, no, no,' rejoined the bride; 'but all the friends, the darling friends, of my youthful days—to leave them all—it is such a shock!'

With such expressions of sorrow, Miss Petowker went on to enumerate the dear friends of her youthful days one by one, and to call upon such of them as were present to come and embrace her. This done, she remembered that Mrs. Crummles had been more than a mother to her, and after that, that Mr. Crummles had been more than a father to her, and after that, that the Master Crummleses and Miss Ninetta Crummles had been more than brothers and sisters to her. These various remembrances being each accompanied with a series of hugs, occupied a long time, and they were obliged to drive to church very fast, for fear they should be too late.

The procession consisted of two flys; in the first of which were Miss Bravassa (the fourth bridesmaid), Mrs. Crummles, the collector, and Mr. Folair, who had been chosen as his second on the occasion. In the other were the bride, Mr. Crummles, Miss Snevellicci, Miss Ledrook, and the phenomenon. The costumes were beautiful. The bridesmaids were quite covered with artificial flowers, and the phenomenon, in particular, was rendered almost invisible by the portable arbour in which she was enshrined. Miss Ledrook, who was of a romantic turn, wore in her breast the miniature of some field officer unknown, which she had purchased, a great bargain, not very long before; the other ladies displayed several dazzling articles of imitative jewellery, almost equal to real; and Mrs. Crummles came out in a stern and gloomy majesty, which attracted the admiration of all beholders.

But, perhaps the appearance of Mr. Crummles was more striking and appropriate than that of any member of the party. This gentleman, who personated the bride's father, had, in pursuance of a happy and original conception, 'made up' for the part by arraying himself in a theatrical wig, of a style and pattern commonly known as a brown George, and moreover assuming a snuff-coloured suit, of the previous century, with grey silk stockings, and buckles to his shoes. The better to support his assumed character he had determined to be greatly overcome, and, consequently, when they entered the church, the sobs of the affectionate parent were so heartrending that the pew-opener suggested the propriety of his retiring to the vestry, and comforting himself with a glass of water before the ceremony began.

The procession up the aisle was beautiful. The bride, with the four bridesmaids, forming a group previously arranged and rehearsed; the collector, followed by his second, imitating his walk and gestures, to the indescribable amusement of some theatrical friends in the gallery; Mr. Crummles, with an infirm and feeble gait; Mrs. Crummles advancing with that stage walk, which consists of a stride and a stop alternately; it was the completest thing ever witnessed. The ceremony was very quickly disposed of, and all parties present having signed the register (for which purpose, when it came to his turn, Mr. Crummles carefully wiped and put on an immense pair of spectacles), they went back to breakfast in high spirits. And here they found Nicholas awaiting their arrival.

'Now then,' said Crummles, who had been assisting Mrs. Grudden in the preparations, which were on a more extensive scale than was quite agreeable to the collector. 'Breakfast, breakfast.'

No second invitation was required. The company crowded and squeezed themselves at the table as well as they could, and fell to, immediately: Miss Petowker blushing very much when anybody was looking, and eating very much when anybody was *not* looking; and Mr. Lillyvick going to work as though with the cool resolve, that since the good things must be paid for by him, he would leave as little as possible for the Crummleses to eat up afterwards.

'It's very soon done, sir, isn't it?' inquired Mr. Folair of the collector, leaning over the table to address him.

'The tying up, the fixing oneself with a wife,' replied Mr. Folair. 'It don't take long, does it?'

'No, sir,' replied Mr. Lillyvick, colouring. 'It does not take long. And what then, sir?'

'Oh! nothing,' said the actor. 'It don't take a man long to hang himself, either, eh? Ha, ha!'

Mr. Lillyvick laid down his knife and fork, and looked round the table with indignant astonishment.

'To hang himself!' repeated Mr. Lillyvick.

A profound silence came upon all, for Mr. Lillyvick was dignified beyond expression.

'To hang himself!' cried Mr. Lillyvick again. 'Is any parallel attempted to be drawn in this company between matrimony and hanging?'

'The noose, you know,' said Mr. Folair, a little crestfallen.

'The noose, sir?' retorted Mr. Lillyvick. 'Does any man dare to speak to me of a noose, and Henrietta Pe—'

'Lillyvick,' suggested Mr. Crummles.

'—and Henrietta Lillyvick in the same breath?' said the collector. 'In this house, in the presence of Mr. and Mrs. Crummles, who have brought up a talented and virtuous family, to be blessings and phenomenons, and what not, are we to hear talk of nooses?'

'Folair,' said Mr. Crummles, deeming it a matter of decency to be affected by this allusion to himself and partner, 'I'm astonished at you.'

'What are you going on in this way at me for?' urged the unfortunate actor. 'What have I done?'

'Done, sir!' cried Mr. Lillyvick, 'aimed a blow at the whole framework of society—'

'And the best and tenderest feelings,' added Crummles, relapsing into the old man.

'And the highest and most estimable of social ties,' said the collector. 'Noose! As if one was caught, trapped, into the married state, pinned by the leg, instead of going into it of one's own accord and glorying in the act!'

'I didn't mean to make it out, that you were caught

and trapped, and pinned by the leg,' replied the actor. 'I 'm sorry for it; I can't say any more.'

'So you ought to be, sir,' returned Mr. Lillyvick; 'and I am glad to hear that you have enough of feeling left to be so.'

The quarrel appearing to terminate with this reply, Mrs. Lillyvick considered that the fittest occasion (the attention of the company being no longer distracted) to burst into tears, and require the assistance of all four bridesmaids, which was immediately rendered, though not without some confusion, for the room being small and the table-cloth long, a whole detachment of plates were swept off the board at the very first move. Regardless of this circumstance, however, Mrs. Lillyvick refused to be comforted until the belligerents had passed their words that the dispute should be carried no further, which, after a sufficient show of reluctance, they did, and from that time Mr. Folair sat in moody silence, contenting himself with pinching Nicholas's leg when anything was said, and so expressing his contempt both for the speaker and the sentiments to which he gave utterance.

There were a great number of speeches made; some by Nicholas, and some by Crummles, and some by the collector; two by the Master Crummleses in returning thanks for themselves, and one by the phenomenon on behalf of the bridesmaids, at which Mrs. Crummles shed tears. There was some singing, too, from Miss Ledrook and Miss Bravassa, and very likely there might have been more, if the fly-driver, who stopped to drive the happy pair to the spot where they proposed to take steam-boat to Ryde, had not sent in a peremptory message intimating, that if they didn't come directly he should infallibly demand eighteen-pence over and above his agreement.

This desperate threat effectually broke up the party. After a most pathetic leave-taking, Mr. Lillyvick and his bride departed for Ryde, where they were to spend the next two days in profound retirement, and whither they were accompanied by the infant, who had been appointed travelling bridesmaid on Mr. Lillyvick's express stipulation: as the steamboat people, deceived by her size, would (he had previously ascertained) transport her at half-price.

As there was no performance that night, Mr. Crummles declared his intention of keeping it up till everything to drink was disposed of; but Nicholas having to play Romeo for the first time on the ensuing evening, contrived to slip away in the midst of a temporary confusion, occasioned by the unexpected development of strong symptoms of inebriety in the conduct of Mrs. Grudden.

To this act of desertion he was led, not only by his own inclinations, but by his anxiety on account of Smike, who, having to sustain the character of the Apothecary, had been as yet wholly unable to get any more of the part into his head than the general idea that he was very hungry, which—perhaps from old recollections—he had acquired with great aptitude.

'I don't know what's to be done, Smike,' said Nicholas, laying down the book. 'I am afraid you can't learn it, my poor fellow.'

'I am afraid not,' said Smike, shaking his head. 'I think if you—but that would give you so much trouble.'

'What?' inquired Nicholas. 'Never mind me.'

'I think,' said Smike, 'if you were to keep saying it to me in little bits, over and over again, I should be able to recollect it from hearing you.'

'Do you think so!' exclaimed Nicholas. 'Well said.

Let us see who tires first. Not I, Smike, trust me.
Now then. "Who calls so loud?'

' "Who calls so loud?" ' said Smike.

' "Who calls so loud?" ' repeated Nicholas.

' "Who calls so loud?" ' cried Smike.

Thus they continued to ask each other who called so
loud, over and over again; and when Smike had that
by heart, Nicholas went to another sentence, and then
to two at a time, and then to three, and so on, until at
midnight poor Smike found to his unspeakable joy
that he really began to remember something about the
text.

Early in the morning they went to it again, and
Smike, rendered more confident by the progress he
had already made, got on faster and with better heart.
As soon as he began to acquire the words pretty freely,
Nicholas showed him how he must come in with both
hands spread out upon his stomach, and how he must
occasionally rub it, in compliance with the established
form by which people on the stage always denote that
they want something to eat. After the morning's rehearsal they went to work again, nor did they stop,
except for a hasty dinner, until it was time to repair
to the theatre at night.

Never had master a more anxious, humble, docile
pupil. Never had pupil a more patient, unwearying,
considerate, kind-hearted master.

As soon as they were dressed, and at every interval
when he was not upon the stage, Nicholas renewed his
instructions. They prospered well. The Romeo was
received with hearty plaudits and unbounded favour,
and Smike was pronounced unanimously, alike by
audience and actors, the very prince and prodigy of
Apothecaries.

CHAPTER XXVI

IS FRAUGHT WITH SOME DANGER TO MISS NICKLEBY'S
PEACE OF MIND

THE place was a handsome suite of private apartments in Regent Street; the time was three o'clock in the afternoon to the dull and plodding, and the first hour of morning to the gay and spirited; the persons were Lord Frederick Verisopht, and his friend Sir Mulberry Hawk.

These distinguished gentlemen were reclining listlessly on a couple of sofas, with a table between them, on which were scattered in rich confusion the materials of an untasted breakfast. Newspapers lay strewn about the room, but these, like the meal, were neglected and unnoticed; not, however, because any flow of conversation prevented the attractions of the journals from being called into request, for not a word was exchanged between the two, nor was any sound uttered, save when one, in tossing about to find an easier resting-place for his aching head, uttered an exclamation of impatience, and seemed for the moment to communicate a new restlessness to his companion.

These appearances would in themselves have furnished a pretty strong clue to the extent of the debauch of the previous night, even if there had not been other indications of the amusements in which it had been passed. A couple of billiard balls all mud and dirt, two battered hats, a champagne bottle with a soiled glove twisted round the neck, to allow of its being grasped more surely in its capacity of an offensive weapon; a broken cane; a card-case without the top; an empty purse; a watch-guard snapped asunder;

a handful of silver, mingled with fragments of half-smoked cigars, and their stale and crumbled ashes; these, and many other tokens of riot and disorder, hinted very intelligibly at the nature of last night's gentlemanly frolics.

Lord Frederick Verisopht was the first to speak. Dropping his slippered foot on the ground, and, yawning heavily, he struggled into a sitting posture, and turned his dull languid eyes towards his friend, to whom he called in a drowsy voice.

'Hallo!' replied Sir Mulberry, turning round.

'Are we going to lie here all da-a-y?' said the lord.

'I don't know that we're fit for anything else,' replied Sir Mulberry; 'yet awhile, at least. I haven't a grain of life in me this morning.'

'Life!' cried Lord Frederick. 'I feel as if there would be nothing so snug and comfortable as to die at once.'

'Then why don't you die?' said Sir Mulberry.

With which inquiry he turned his face away, and seemed to occupy himself in an attempt to fall asleep.

His hopeful friend and pupil drew a chair to the breakfast-table, and essayed to eat; but, finding that impossible, lounged to the window, then loitered up and down the room with his hand to his fevered head, and finally threw himself again on his sofa, and roused his friend once more.

'What the devil's the matter?' groaned Sir Mulberry, sitting upright on the couch.

Although Sir Mulberry said this with sufficient ill-humour, he did not seem to feel himself quite at liberty to remain silent; for, after stretching himself very often, and declaring with a shiver that it was 'infernal cold,' he made an experiment at the breakfast-table, and proving more successful in it than his less-seasoned friend, remained there.

'Suppose,' said Sir Mulberry, pausing with a morsel on the point of his fork, 'Suppose we go back to the subject of little Nickleby, eh?'

'Which little Nickleby; the money-lender or the ga-a-l?' asked Lord Frederick.

'You take me, I see,' replied Sir Mulberry. 'The girl, of course.'

'You promised me you'd find her out,' said Lord Frederick.

'So I did,' rejoined his friend; 'but I have thought further of the matter since then. You distrust me in the business—you shall find her out yourself.'

'Na—ay,' remonstrated the other.

'But I say yes,' returned his friend. 'You shall find her out yourself. Don't think that I mean, when you can—I know as well as you that if I did, you could never get sight of her without me. No. I say you shall find her out—*shall*—and I'll put you in the way.'

'Now, curse me, if you ain't a real, deyvlish, downright, thorough-paced friend,' said the young lord, on whom this speech had produced a most reviving effect.

'I'll tell you how,' said Sir Mulberry. 'She was at that dinner as a bait for you.'

'No!' cried the young lord. 'What the dey—'

'As a bait for you,' repeated his friend; 'old Nickleby told me so himself.'

'What a fine old cock it is!' exclaimed Lord Frederick; 'a noble rascal!'

'Yes,' said Sir Mulberry, 'he knew she was a smart little creature—'

'Smart!' interposed the young lord. 'Upon my soul, Hawk, she's a perfect beauty—a—a picture, a statue, a—a—upon my soul she is!'

'Well,' replied Sir Mulberry, shrugging his shoulders and manifesting an indifference, whether he felt it or not; 'that's a matter of taste; if mine doesn't agree with yours, so much the better.'

'Confound it!' reasoned the lord, 'you were thick enough with her that day, anyhow. I could hardly get in a word.'

'Well enough for once, well enough for once,' replied Sir Mulberry; 'but not worth the trouble of being agreeable to again. If you seriously want to follow up the niece, tell the uncle that you must know where she lives and how she lives, and with whom, or you are no longer a customer of his. He'll tell you fast enough.'

'Why didn't you say this before?' asked Lord Frederick, 'instead of letting me go on burning, consuming, dragging out a miserable existence for an a-age!'

'I didn't know it, in the first place,' answered Sir Mulberry carelessly; 'and in the second, I didn't believe you were so very much in earnest.'

Now, the truth was, that in the interval which had elapsed since the dinner at Ralph Nickleby's, Sir Mulberry Hawk had been furtively trying by every means in his power to discover whence Kate had so suddenly appeared, and whither she had disappeared. Unassisted by Ralph, however, with whom he had held no communication since their angry parting on that occasion, all his efforts were wholly unavailing, and he had therefore arrived at the determination of communicating to the young lord the substance of the admission he had gleaned from that worthy. To this he was impelled by various considerations; among which the certainty of knowing whatever the weak young man knew was decidedly not the least, as the desire of encountering the usurer's niece again, and using his utmost arts to reduce her pride, and revenge himself for her contempt, was uppermost in his thoughts. It was a politic course of proceeding, and one which could not fail to redound to his advantage in every point of view, since the very circumstance of his having extorted from Ralph Nickleby his real design in introducing his niece to such society, coupled with his extreme disinterestedness in communicating it so freely to his friend, could not but advance his interests in that quarter, and greatly facilitate the passage of coin (pretty frequent and speedy already) from the pockets of Lord Frederick Verisopht to those of Sir Mulberry Hawk.

Thus reasoned Sir Mulberry, and in pursuance of this reasoning he and his friend soon afterwards repaired to Ralph Nickleby's, there to execute a plan of operations concerted by Sir Mulberry himself, avowedly to promote his friend's object, and really to attain his own.

They found Ralph at home, and alone. As he led them into the drawing-room, the recollection of the scene which had taken place there seemed to occur to him, for he cast a curious look at Sir Mulberry, who bestowed upon it no other acknowledgment than a careless smile.

They had a short conference upon some money matters then in progress, which were scarcely disposed of when the lordly dupe (in pursuance of his friend's instructions) requested with some embarrassment to speak to Ralph alone.

'Alone, eh?' cried Sir Mulberry, affecting surprise. 'Oh, very good. I 'll walk into the next room here. Don't keep me long, that 's all.'

So saying, Sir Mulberry took up his hat, and humming a fragment of a song disappeared through the door of communication between the two drawing-rooms, and closed it after him.

'Now, my lord,' said Ralph, 'what is it?'

'Nickleby,' said his client, throwing himself along the sofa on which he had been previously seated, so as to bring his lips nearer to the old man's ear, 'what a pretty creature your niece is!'

'Is she, my lord?' replied Ralph. 'Maybe—maybe. I don't trouble my head with such matters.'

'You know she's a deyvlish fine girl,' said the client. 'You must know that, Nickleby. Come, don't deny that.'

'Yes, I believe she is considered so,' replied Ralph. 'Indeed, I know she is. If I did not, you are an authority on such points, and your taste, my lord—on all points, indeed—is undeniable.'

Nobody but the young man to whom these words were addressed could have been deaf to the sneering tone in which they were spoken, or blind to the look of contempt by which they were accompanied. But Lord Frederick Verisopht was both, and took them to be complimentary.

'Well,' he said, 'p'raps you're a little right, and p'raps you're a little wrong—a little of both, Nickleby. I want to know where this beauty lives, that I may have another peep at her, Nickleby.'

'Really—' Ralph began in his usual tones.

'Don't talk so loud,' cried the other, achieving the great point of his lesson to a miracle. 'I don't want Hawk to hear.'

'You know he is your rival, do you?' said Ralph, looking sharply at him.

'He always is, d-a-amn him,' replied the client; 'and I want to steal a march upon him. Ha, ha, ha! He'll cut up so rough, Nickleby, at our talking together without him. Where does she live, Nickleby, that's all? Only tell me where she lives, Nickleby.'

'He bites,' thought Ralph. 'He bites.'

'Eh, Nickleby, eh?' pursued the client. 'Where does she live?'

'Really, my lord,' said Ralph, rubbing his hands slowly over each other, 'I must think before I tell you.'

'No, not a bit of it, Nickleby; you mustn't think at all. Where is it?'

'No good can come of your knowing,' replied Ralph. 'She has been virtuously and well brought up; to be sure she is handsome, poor, unprotected! Poor girl, poor girl.'

Ralph ran over this brief summary of Kate's condition as if it were merely passing through his own mind, and he had no intention to speak aloud; but the shrewd sly look which he directed at his companion as he delivered it, gave this poor assumption the lie.

'I tell you I only want to see her,' cried his client. 'A ma-an may look at a pretty woman without harm, mayn't he? Now, where *does* she live? You know you 're making a fortune out of me, Nickleby, and upon my soul nobody shall ever take me to anybody else, if you only tell me this.'

'As you promise that, my lord,' said Ralph, with feigned reluctance, 'and as I am most anxious to oblige you, and as there 's no harm in it—no harm— I 'll tell you. But you had better keep it to yourself, my lord; strictly to yourself.' Ralph pointed to the adjoining room as he spoke, and nodded expressively.

The young lord, feigning to be equally impressed with the necessity of this precaution, Ralph disclosed the present address and occupation of his niece, observing that from what he heard of the family they appeared very ambitious to have distinguished acquaintances, and that a lord could, doubtless, introduce himself with great ease, if he felt disposed.

'Your object being only to see her again,' said Ralph, 'you could effect it at any time you chose by that means.'

Lord Frederick acknowledged the hint with a great many squeezes of Ralph's hard, horny hand, and whispering that they would now do well to close the conversation, called to Sir Mulberry Hawk that he might come back.

'I thought you had gone to sleep,' said Sir Mulberry, reappearing with an ill-tempered air.

'Sorry to detain you,' replied the gull; 'but Nickleby has been so ama-azingly funny that I couldn't tear myself away.'

'No, no,' said Ralph; 'it was all his lordship. You know what a witty, humourous, elegant, accomplished man Lord Frederick is. Mind the step, my lord— Sir Mulberry, pray give way.'

With such courtesies as these, and many low bows, and the same cold sneer upon his face all the while, Ralph busied himself in showing his visitors downstairs, and otherwise than by the slightest possible motion about the corners of his mouth, returned no show of answer to the look of admiration with which Sir Mulberry Hawk seemed to compliment him on being such an accomplished and most consummate scoundrel.

There had been a ring at the bell a few moments before, which was answered by Newman Noggs just as they reached the hall. In the ordinary course of business Newman would have either admitted the new-comer in silence, or have requested him or her to stand aside while the gentlemen passed out. But he no sooner saw who it was, than as if for some private reason of his own, he boldly departed from the established custom of Ralph's mansion in business hours, and looking towards the respectable trio who were approaching, cried in a loud and sonorous voice: 'Mrs. Nickleby!'

'Mrs. Nickleby!' cried Sir Mulberry Hawk, as his friend looked back, and stared him in the face.

It was, indeed, that well-intentioned lady, who, having received an offer for the empty house in the city directed to the landlord, had brought it post-haste to Mr. Nickleby without delay.

'Nobody *you* know,' said Ralph. 'Step into the office, my—my—dear. I'll be with you directly.'

'Nobody I know!' cried Sir Mulberry Hawk, advancing to the astonished lady. 'Is this Mrs. Nickleby—the mother of Miss Nickleby—the delightful creature that I had the happiness of meeting in this house the very last time I dined here! But no'; said Sir Mulberry, stopping short. 'No, it can't be. There is the same cast of features, the same indescribable air of—But no, no. This lady is too young for that.'

'I think you can tell the gentleman, brother-in-law, if it concerns him to know,' said Mrs. Nickleby, acknowledging the compliment with a graceful bend, 'that Kate Nickleby is my daughter.'

'Her daughter, my lord!' cried Sir Mulberry, turning to his friend. 'This lady's daughter, my lord.'

'My lord!' thought Mrs. Nickleby. 'Well, I never did—!'

'This, then, my lord,' said Sir Mulberry, 'is the lady to whose obliging marriage we owe so much happiness. This lady is the mother of sweet Miss Nickleby. Do you observe the extraordinary likeness, my lord? Nickleby—introduce us.'

Ralph did so, in a kind of desperation.

'Upon my soul, it's a most delightful thing,' said Lord Frederick, pressing forward: 'How de do?'

Mrs. Nickleby was too much flurried by these uncommonly kind salutations, and her regrets at not having on her other bonnet, to make any immediate reply, so she merely continued to bend and smile, and betray great agitation.

'A—and how is Miss Nickleby?' said Lord Frederick. 'Well, I hope?'

'She is quite well, I'm obliged to you, my lord,' returned Mrs. Nickleby, recovering. 'Quite well. She wasn't well for some days after that day she dined here, and I can't help thinking, that she caught cold in that hackney-coach coming home. Hackney-coaches, my lord, are such nasty things, that it's almost better to walk at any time, for although I believe a hackney-coachman can be transported for life, if he has a broken window, still they are so reckless, that they nearly all have broken windows. I once had a swelled face for six weeks, my lord, from riding in a hackney-coach—I think it was a hackney-coach,' said Mrs. Nickleby reflecting, 'though I'm not quite certain, whether it wasn't a chariot; at all events I know it was a dark green, with a very long number, beginning with a nought and ending with a nine—no, beginning with a nine, and ending with a nought, that was it, and of course the stamp-office people would know at once whether it was a coach or a chariot if any inquiries were made there—however that was, there it was with a broken window, and there was I for six weeks with a swelled face—I think that was the very same hackney-coach, that we found out afterwards, had the top open all the time, and we should never even have known it, if they hadn't charged us a shilling an hour extra for having it open, which it seems is the law, or was then, and a most shameful law it appears to be—I don't understand the subject, but I should say the Corn Laws could be nothing to *that* act of Parliament.'

Having pretty well run herself out by this time, Mrs. Nickleby stopped as suddenly as she had started off, and repeated that Kate was quite well. 'Indeed,' said Mrs. Nickleby, 'I don't think she ever was better, since she had the hooping-cough, scarlet-fever and measles, all at the same time, and that's the fact.'

'Is that letter for me?' growled Ralph, pointing to the little packet Mrs. Nickleby held in her hand.

'For you, brother-in-law,' replied Mrs. Nickleby, 'and I walked all the way up here on purpose to give it you.'

'All the way up here!' cried Sir Mulberry, seizing upon the chance of discovering where Mrs. Nickleby had come from. 'What a confounded distance! How far do you call it now?'

'How far do I call it!' said Mrs. Nickleby. 'Let me see. It's just a mile, from our door to the Old Bailey.'

'No, no. Not so much as that,' urged Sir Mulberry.

'Oh! It is indeed,' said Mrs. Nickleby. 'I appeal to his lordship.'

'I should decidedly say it was a mile,' remarked Lord Frederick, with a solemn aspect.

'It must be; it can't be a yard less,' said Mrs. Nickleby. 'All down Newgate Street, all down Cheapside, all up Lombard Street, down Gracechurch Street, and along Thames Street, as far as Spigwiffin's Wharf. Oh! It's a mile.'

'Yes, on second thoughts I should say it was,' replied Sir Mulberry. 'But you don't surely mean to walk all the way back?'

'Oh, no,' rejoined Mrs. Nickleby. 'I shall go back

in an omnibus. I didn't travel about in omnibuses, when my poor dear Nicholas was alive, brother-in-law. But as it is, you know—'

'Yes, yes,' replied Ralph impatiently, 'and you had better get back before dark.'

'Thank you, brother-in-law, so I had,' returned Mrs. Nickleby. 'I think I had better say good-bye, at once.'

'Not stop and—rest?' said Ralph, who seldom offered refreshments unless something was to be got by it.

'Oh dear me no,' returned Mrs. Nickleby, glancing at the dial.

'Lord Frederick,' said Sir Mulberry, 'we are going Mrs. Nickleby's way. We'll see her safe to the omnibus?'

'By all means. Ye-es.'

'Oh! I really couldn't think of it!' said Mrs. Nickleby.

But Sir Mulberry Hawk and Lord Frederick were peremptory in their politeness, and leaving Ralph, who seemed to think, not unwisely, that he looked less ridiculous as a mere spectator, than he would have done if he had taken any part in these proceedings, they quitted the house with Mrs. Nickleby between them; that good lady in a perfect ecstasy of satisfaction, no less with the attentions shown her by two titled gentlemen, than with the conviction that Kate might now pick and choose, at least between two large fortunes, and most unexceptionable husbands.

As she was carried away for the moment by an irresistible train of thought, all connected with her daughter's future greatness, Sir Mulberry Hawk and his friend exchanged glances over the top of the bonnet which the poor lady so much regretted not having left at home, and proceeded to dilate with great rapture, but much respect, on the manifold perfections of Miss Nickleby.

'What a delight, what a comfort, what a happiness, this amiable creature must be to you,' said Sir Mulberry, throwing into his voice an indication of the warmest feeling.

'She is indeed, sir,' replied Mrs. Nickleby; 'she is the sweetest-tempered, kindest-hearted creature—and so clever!'

'She looks clayver,' said Lord Frederick Verisopht, with the air of a judge of cleverness.

'I assure you she is, my lord,' returned Mrs. Nickleby. 'When she was at school in Devonshire, she was universally allowed to be beyond all exception the very cleverest girl there, and there were a great many very clever ones too, and that's the truth—twenty-five young ladies, fifty guineas a-year without the et-ceteras, both the Miss Dowdles, the most accomplished, elegant, fascinating creatures— Oh dear me!' said Mrs. Nickleby, 'I never shall forget what pleasure she used to give me and her poor dear papa, when she was at that school, never—such a delightful letter every half-year, telling us that she was the first pupil in the whole establishment, and had made more progress than anybody else! I can scarcely bear to think of it even now. The girls wrote all the letters themselves,' added Mrs. Nickleby, 'and the writing-master touched them up afterwards with a magnifying glass and a silver pen; at least I think they wrote them, though Kate was never quite certain about that, because she didn't know the handwriting of hers again; but any way, I know it was a circular which they all copied, and of course it was a very gratifying thing—very gratifying.'

With similar recollections Mrs. Nickleby beguiled the tediousness of the way, until they reached the omnibus, which the extreme politeness of her new friends would not allow them to leave until it actually started, when they took their hats, as Mrs. Nickleby solemnly assured her hearers on many subsequent occasions, 'completely off,' and kissed their straw-coloured kid gloves till they were no longer visible.

Mrs. Nickleby leant back in the furthest corner of the conveyance, and, closing her eyes, resigned herself to a host of most pleasing meditations. Kate had never said a word about having met either of these gentlemen; 'that,' she thought, 'argues that she is strongly prepossessed in favour of one of them.' Then the question arose, which one could it be. The lord was the youngest, and his title was certainly the grandest; still Kate was not the girl to be swayed by such considerations as these. 'I will never put any constraint upon her inclinations,' said Mrs. Nickleby to herself; 'but upon my word I think there's no comparison between his lordship and Sir Mulberry. Sir Mulberry is such an attentive gentlemanly creature, so much manner, such a fine man, and has so much to say for himself. I hope it's Sir Mulberry; I think it must be Sir Mulberry!' And then her thoughts flew back to her old predictions, and the number of times she had said, that Kate with no fortune would marry better than other people's daughters with thousands; and, as she pictured with the brightness of a mother's fancy all the beauty and grace of the poor girl who had struggled so cheerfully with her new life of hardship and trial, her heart grew too full, and the tears trickled down her face.

Meanwhile, Ralph walked to and fro in his little back office, troubled in mind by what had just occurred. To say that Ralph loved or cared for—in the most ordinary acceptation of those terms—any one of God's creatures, would be the wildest fiction.

Still, there had somehow stolen upon him from time to time a thought of his niece which was tinged with compassion and pity; breaking through the dull cloud of dislike or indifference which darkened men and women in his eyes, there was, in her case, the faintest gleam of light—a most feeble and sickly ray at the best of times—but there it was, and it showed the poor girl in a better and purer aspect than any in which he had looked on human nature yet.

'I wish,' thought Ralph, 'I had never done this. And yet it will keep this boy to me, while there is money to be made. Selling a girl—throwing her in the way of temptation, and insult, and coarse speech. Nearly two thousand pounds profit from him already though. Pshaw! match-making mothers do the same thing every day.'

He sat down, and told the chances, for and against, on his fingers.

'If I had not put them in the right track to-day,' thought Ralph, 'this foolish woman would have done so. Well. If her daughter is as true to herself as she should be from what I have seen, what harm ensues? A little teasing, a little humbling, a few tears. Yes,' said Ralph, aloud, as he locked his iron safe. 'She must take her chance. She must take her chance.'

CHAPTER XXVII

MRS. NICKLEBY BECOMES ACQUAINTED WITH MESSRS. PYKE AND PLUCK, WHOSE AFFECTION AND INTEREST ARE BEYOND ALL BOUNDS

MRS. NICKLEBY had not felt so proud and important for many a day, as when, on reaching home, she gave herself wholly up to the pleasant visions which had accompanied her on her way thither. Lady Mulberry Hawk—that was the prevalent idea. Lady Mulberry Hawk!—On Tuesday last, at St. George's, Hanover Square, by the Right Reverend the Bishop of Llandaff, Sir Mulberry Hawk, of Mulberry Castle, North Wales, to Catherine, only daughter of the late Nicholas Nickleby, Esquire, of Devonshire. 'Upon my word!' cried Mrs. Nicholas Nickleby, 'it sounds very well.'

Having despatched the ceremony, with its attendant festivities, to the perfect satisfaction of her own mind, the sanguine mother pictured to her imagination a long train of honours and distinctions which could not fail to accompany Kate in her new and brilliant sphere. She would be presented at court, of course. On the anniversary of her birthday, which was upon the nineteenth of July ('at ten minutes past three o'clock in the morning,' thought Mrs. Nickleby in a parenthesis, 'for I recollect asking what o'clock it was,') Sir Mulberry would give a great feast to all his tenants, and would return them three and a half per cent. on the amount of their last half-year's rent, as would be fully described and recorded in the fashionable intelligence, to the immeasurable delight and admiration of all the readers thereof. Kate's picture, too, would be in at least half a dozen of the annuals, and on the opposite page would appear, in delicate type, 'Lines on contemplating the Portrait of Lady Mulberry Hawk. By Sir Dingleby Dabber.' Perhaps some one annual, of more comprehensive design than its fellows, might even contain a portrait of the mother of Lady Mulberry Hawk, with lines by the father of Sir Dingleby Dabber. More unlikely things had come to pass. Less interesting portraits had appeared. As this thought occurred to the good lady, her countenance unconsciously assumed that compound expression of simpering and sleepiness which, being common to all such portraits, is perhaps one reason why they are always so charming and agreeable.

With such triumphs of aërial architecture did Mrs. Nickleby occupy the whole evening after her accidental introduction to Ralph's titled friends; and dreams, no less prophetic and equally promising, haunted her sleep that night. She was preparing for her frugal dinner next day, still occupied with the same ideas—a little softened down perhaps by sleep and daylight—when the girl who attended her, partly for company, and partly to assist in the household affairs, rushed into the room in unwonted agitation, and announced that two gentlemen were waiting in the passage for permission to walk upstairs.

'Bless my heart!' cried Mrs. Nickleby, hastily arranging her cap and front, 'if it should be—dear me, standing in the passage all this time—why don't you go and ask them to walk up, you stupid thing?'

While the girl was gone on this errand, Mrs. Nickleby hastily swept into a cupboard all vestiges of eating and drinking; which she had scarcely done, and seated herself with looks as collected as she could assume, when two gentlemen, both perfect strangers, presented themselves.

'How do you *do?*' said one gentleman, laying great stress on the last word of the inquiry.

'*How* do you do?' said the other gentleman, altering the emphasis, as if to give variety to the salutation.

Mrs. Nickleby curtseyed and smiled, and curtseyed again, and remarked, rubbing her hands as she did so, that she hadn't the—really the honour to—'

'To know us,' said the first gentleman. 'The loss

has been ours, Mrs. Nickleby. Has the loss been ours, Pyke?'

'It has, Pluck,' answered the other gentleman.

'We have regretted it very often, I believe, Pyke?' said the first gentleman.

'Very often, Pluck,' answered the second.

'But now,' said the first gentleman, 'now we have the happiness we have pined and languished for. Have we pined and languished for this happiness, Pyke, or have we not?'

'You know we have, Pluck,' said Pyke, reproachfully.

'You hear him, ma'am?' said Mr. Pluck, looking round; 'you hear the unimpeachable testimony of my friend Pyke—that reminds me,—formalities, formalities, must not be neglected in civilised society. Pyke—Mrs. Nickleby.'

Mr. Pyke laid his hand upon his heart, and bowed low.

'Whether I shall introduce myself with the same formality,' said Mr. Pluck—'whether I shall say myself that my name is Pluck, or whether I shall ask my friend Pyke (who being now regularly introduced, is competent to the office) to state for me, Mrs. Nickleby, that my name is Pluck; whether I shall claim your acquaintance on the plain ground of the strong interest I take in your welfare, or whether I shall make myself known to you as the friend of Sir Mulberry Hawk—these, Mrs. Nickleby, are considerations which I leave to you to determine.'

'Any friend of Sir Mulberry Hawk's requires no better introduction to me,' observed Mrs. Nickleby, graciously.

'It is delightful to hear you say so,' said Mr. Pluck, drawing a chair close to Mrs. Nickleby, and seating himself. 'It is refreshing to know that you hold my

excellent friend, Sir Mulberry, in such high esteem.
A word in your ear, Mrs. Nickleby. When Sir Mulberry knows it, he will be a happy man—I say, Mrs.
Nickleby, a happy man. Pyke, be seated.'

'*My* good opinion,' said Mrs. Nickleby, and the
poor lady exulted in the idea that she was marvelously
sly: 'my good opinion can be of very little consequence
to a gentleman like Sir Mulberry.'

'Of little consequence!' exclaimed Mr. Pluck.
'Pyke, of what consequence to our friend, Sir Mulberry, is the good opinion of Mrs. Nickleby?'

'Of what consequence?' echoed Pyke.

'Aye,' repeated Pluck; 'is it of the greatest consequence?'

'Of the very greatest consequence,' replied Pyke.

'Mrs. Nickleby cannot be ignorant,' said Mr. Pluck,
'of the immense impression which that sweet girl
has—'

'Pluck!' said his friend, 'beware!'

'Pyke is right,' muttered Mr. Pluck, after a short
pause; 'I was not to mention it. Pyke is very right.
Thank you, Pyke.'

'Well now, really!' thought Mrs. Nickleby within
herself. 'Such delicacy as that, I never saw!'

Mr. Pluck, after feigning to be in a condition of
great embarrassment for some minutes, resumed the
conversation by entreating Mrs. Nickleby to take no
heed of what he had inadvertently said—to consider
him imprudent, rash, injudicious. The only stipulation he would make in his own favour was, that she
should give him credit for the best intentions.

'But when,' said Mr. Pluck, 'when I see so much
sweetness and beauty on the one hand, and so much
ardour and devotion on the other, I—pardon me,
Pyke, I didn't intend to resume that theme. Change
the subject, Pyke.'

'We promised Sir Mulberry and Lord Frederick,' said Pyke, 'that we'd call this morning and inquire whether you took any cold last night.'

'Not the least in the world last night, sir'; replied Mrs. Nickleby, 'with many thanks to his lordship and Sir Mulberry for doing me the honour to inquire; not the least—which is the more singular, as I really am very subject to colds, indeed—very subject. I had a cold once,' said Mrs. Nickleby, 'I think it was in the year eighteen hundred and seventeen; let me see, four and five are nine, and—yes, eighteen hundred and seventeen, that I thought I never should get rid of; actually and seriously, that I thought I never should get rid of. I was only cured at last by a remedy that I don't know whether you ever happened to hear of, Mr. Pluck. You have a gallon of water as hot as you can possibly bear it, with a pound of salt and sixpenn'orth of the finest bran, and sit with your head in it for twenty minutes every night just before going to bed; at least, I don't mean your head —your feet. It's a most extraordinary cure—a most extraordinary cure. I used it for the first time, I recollect, the day after Christmas Day, and by the middle of April following the cold was gone. It seems quite a miracle when you come to think of it, for I had it ever since the beginning of September.'

'What an afflicting calamity!' said Mr. Pyke.

'Perfectly horrid!' exclaimed Mr. Pluck.

'But it's worth the pain of hearing, only to know that Mrs. Nickleby recovered it, isn't it, Pluck?' cried Mr. Pyke.

'That is the circumstance which gives it such a thrilling interest,' replied Mr. Pluck.

'But come,' said Pyke, as if suddenly recollecting himself; 'we must not forget our mission in the pleasure of this interview. We come on a mission, Mrs. Nickleby.'

'On a mission,' exclaimed that good lady, to whose mind a definitive proposal of marriage for Kate at once presented itself in lively colours.

'From Sir Mulberry,' replied Pyke. 'You must be very dull here.'

'Rather dull, I confess,' said Mrs. Nickleby.

'We bring the compliments of Sir Mulberry Hawk, and a thousand entreaties that you 'll take a seat in a private box at the play to-night,' said Mr. Pluck.

'Oh dear!' said Mrs. Nickleby, 'I never go out at all, never.'

'And that is the very reason, my dear Mrs. Nickleby, why you should go out to-night,' retorted Mr. Pluck. 'Pyke, entreat Mrs. Nickleby.'

'Oh, pray do,' said Pyke.

'You positively must,' urged Pluck.

'You are very kind,' said Mrs. Nickleby, hesitating: 'but—'

'There 's not a but in the case, my dear Mrs. Nickleby,' remonstrated Mr. Pluck; 'not such a word in the vocabulary. Your brother-in-law joins us, Lord Frederick joins us, Sir Mulberry joins us, Pyke joins us—a refusal is out of the question. Sir Mulberry sends a carriage for you—twenty minutes before seven to the moment—you 'll not be so cruel as to disappoint the whole party, Mrs. Nickleby?'

'You are so very pressing, that I scarcely know what to say,' replied the worthy lady.

'Say nothing; not a word, not a word, my dearest madam,' urged Mr. Pluck. 'Mrs. Nickleby,' said that excellent gentleman, lowering his voice, 'there is the most trifling, the most excusable breach of confidence in what I am about to say; and yet if my friend Pyke there overheard it—such is that man's delicate sense of honour, Mrs. Nickleby—he'd have me out before dinner-time.'

Mrs. Nickleby cast an apprehensive glance at the warlike Pyke, who had walked to the window; and Mr. Pluck, squeezing her hand, went on—

'Your daughter has made a conquest—a conquest on which I may congratulate you. Sir Mulberry, my dear ma'am, Sir Mulberry is her devoted slave. Hem!'

'Hah!' cried Mr. Pyke, at this juncture, snatching something from the chimney-piece with a theatrical air. 'What is this! what do I behold!'

'What *do* you behold, my dear fellow?' asked Mr. Pluck.

'It is the face, the countenance, the expression,' cried Mr. Pyke, falling into his chair with a miniature in his hand; 'feebly portrayed, imperfectly caught, but still *the* face, *the* countenance, *the* expression.'

'I recognise it at this distance!' exclaimed Mr. Pluck, in a fit of enthusiasm. 'Is it not, my dear madam, the faint similitude of—'

'It is my daughter's portrait,' said Mrs. Nickleby, with great pride. And so it was. And little Miss La Creevy had brought it home for inspection only two nights before.

Mr. Pyke no sooner ascertained that he was quite right in his conjecture, than he launched into the most extravagant encomiums of the divine original; and in the warmth of his enthusiasm kissed the picture a thousand times, while Mr. Pluck pressed Mrs. Nickleby's hand to his heart, and congratulated her on the possession of such a daughter, with so much earnestness and affection, that the tears stood, or seemed to stand, in his eyes. Poor Mrs. Nickleby, who had listened in a state of enviable complacency at first, became at length quite overpowered by these tokens of regard for, and attachment to, the family; and even the servant girl, who had peeped in at the door, remained rooted to the spot in astonishment at the ecstasies of the two friendly visitors.

By degrees these raptures subsided, and Mrs. Nickleby went on to entertain her guests with a lament over her fallen fortunes, and a picturesque account of her old house in the country: comprising a full description of the different apartments, not forgetting the little store-room, and a lively recollection of how many steps you went down to get into the garden, and which way you turned when you came out at the parlour-door, and what capital fixtures there were in the kitchen. This last reflection naturally conducted her into the wash-house, where she stumbled upon the brewing utensils, among which she might have wandered for an hour, if the mere mention of those implements had not, by an association of ideas, instantly reminded Mr. Pyke that he was 'amazing thirsty.'

'And I 'll tell you what,' said Mr. Pyke; 'if you 'll send round to the public-house for a pot of mild half-and-half, positively and actually I 'll drink it.'

And positively and actually Mr. Pyke *did* drink it, and Mr. Pluck helped him, while Mrs. Nickleby looked on in divided admiration of the condescension of the two, and the aptitude with which they accommodated themselves to the pewter-pot; in explanation of which seeming marvel it may be here observed, that gentlemen who, like Messrs. Pyke and Pluck, live upon their wits (or not so much, perhaps, upon the presence of their own wits as upon the absence of wits in other people) are occasionally reduced to very narrow shifts and straits, and are at such periods accustomed to regale themselves in a very simple and primitive manner.

'At twenty minutes before seven, then,' said Mr. Pyke, rising, 'the coach will be here. One more look—one little look—at that sweet face. Ah! here it is. Unmoved, unchanged!' This by the way was a very remarkable circumstance, miniatures being liable to so many changes of expression. 'Oh, Pluck! Pluck!'

Mr. Pluck made no other reply than kissing Mrs. Nickleby's hand with a great show of feeling and attachment; Mr. Pyke having done the same, both gentlemen hastily withdrew.

Mrs. Nickleby was commonly in the habit of giving herself credit for a pretty tolerable share of penetration and acuteness, but she had never felt so satisfied with her own sharp-sightedness as she did that day. She had found it all out the night before. She had never seen Sir Mulberry and Kate together —never even heard Sir Mulberry's name—and yet hadn't she said to herself from the very first, that she saw how the case stood? and what a triumph it was, for there was now no doubt about it. If these flattering attentions to herself were not sufficient proofs, Sir Mulberry's confidential friend had suffered the secret to escape him in so many words. 'I am quite in love with that dear Mr. Pluck, I declare I am,' said Mrs. Nickleby.

There was one great source of uneasiness in the midst of this good fortune, and that was the having nobody by, to whom she could confide it. Once or twice she almost resolved to walk straight to Miss La Creevy's and tell it all to her. 'But I don't know,' thought Mrs. Nickleby; 'she is a very worthy person, but I am afraid too much beneath Sir Mulberry's station for us to make a companion of. Poor thing!' Acting upon this grave consideration she rejected the idea of taking the little portrait-painter into her confidence, and contented herself with holding out sundry vague and mysterious hopes of preferment to the servant-girl, who received these obscure hints of dawning greatness with much veneration and respect.

Punctual to its time came the promised vehicle, which was no hackney-coach, but a private chariot, having behind it a footman, whose legs, although somewhat large for his body, might, as mere abstract legs, have set themselves up for models at the Royal Academy. It was quite exhilarating to hear the clash and bustle with which he banged the door and jumped up behind after Mrs. Nickleby was in; and as that good lady was perfectly unconscious that he applied the gold-headed end of his long stick to his nose, and so telegraphed most disrespectfully to the coachman over her very head, she sat in a state of much stiffness and dignity, not a little proud of her position.

At the theatre entrance there was more banging and more bustle, and there were also Messrs. Pyke and Pluck waiting to escort her to her box; and so polite were they, that Mr. Pyke threatened with many oaths to 'smifligate' a very old man with a lantern who accidentally stumbled in her way—to the great terror of Mrs. Nickleby, who, conjecturing more from Mr. Pyke's excitement than any previous acquaintance with the etymology of the word, that smifligation and bloodshed must be in the main one and the same thing, was alarmed beyond expression, lest something should occur. Fortunately, however, Mr. Pyke confined himself to mere verbal smifligation, and they reached their box with no more serious interruption by the way, than a desire on the part of the same pugnacious gentleman to 'smash' the assistant box-keeper for happening to mistake the number.

Mrs. Nickleby had scarcely been put away behind the curtain of the box in an arm-chair, when Sir Mulberry and Lord Frederick Verisopht arrived, arrayed from the crowns of their heads to the tips of their gloves, and from the tips of their gloves to the toes of their boots, in the most elegant and costly manner. Sir Mulberry was a little hoarser than on the previous day, and Lord Frederick looked rather sleepy and queer: from which tokens, as well as from the circumstance of their both being to a trifling extent unsteady on their legs, Mrs. Nickleby justly concluded that they had taken dinner.

'We have been—we have been—toasting your lovely daughter, Mrs. Nickleby,' whispered Sir Mulberry, sitting down behind her.

'Oh, ho!' thought that knowing lady; 'wine in, truth out.—You are very kind, Sir Mulberry.'

'No, no, upon my soul!' replied Sir Mulberry Hawk. 'It's you that's kind, upon my soul it is. It was so kind of you to come to-night.'

'So very kind of you to invite me, you mean, Sir Mulberry,' replied Mrs. Nickleby, tossing her head, and looking prodigiously sly.

'I am so anxious to know you, so anxious to cultivate your good opinion, so desirous that there should be a delicious kind of harmonious family understanding between us,' said Sir Mulberry, 'that you mustn't think I 'm disinterested in what I do. I 'm infernal selfish; I am—upon my soul I am.'

'I am sure you can't be selfish, Sir Mulberry,' replied Mrs. Nickleby, 'you have much too open and generous a countenance for that.'

'What an extraordinary observer you are!' said Sir Mulberry Hawk.

'Oh no, indeed, I don't see very far into things, Sir Mulberry,' replied Mrs. Nickleby, in a tone of voice which left the baronet to infer that she saw very far indeed.

'I am quite afraid of you,' said the baronet. 'Upon my soul,' repeated Sir Mulberry, looking round to his companions; 'I am afraid of Mrs. Nickleby. She is so immensely sharp.'

Messrs. Pyke and Pluck shook their heads mysteriously and observed together that they had found that out long ago; upon which Mrs. Nickleby tittered, and Sir Mulberry laughed, and Pyke and Pluck roared.

'But where's my brother-in-law, Sir Mulberry?' inquired Mrs. Nickleby. 'I shouldn't be here without him. I hope he's coming.'

'Pyke,' said Sir Mulberry, taking out his toothpick and lolling back in his chair, as if he were too lazy to invent a reply to this question. 'Where's Ralph Nickleby?'

'Pluck,' said Pyke, imitating the baronet's action, and turning the lie over to his friend, 'where's Ralph Nickleby?'

Mr. Pluck was about to return some evasive reply, when the bustle caused by a party entering the next box seemed to attract the attention of all four gentlemen, who exchanged glances of much meaning. The new party beginning to converse together, Sir Mulberry suddenly assumed the character of a most attentive listener, and implored his friends not to breathe—not to breathe.

'Why not?' said Mrs. Nickleby. 'What is the matter?'

'Hush!' replied Sir Mulberry, laying his hand on

her arm. 'Lord Frederick, do you recognise the tone of that voice?'

'Devvle take me if I didn't think it was the voice of Miss Nickleby.'

'Lor, my lord!' cried Miss Nickleby's mamma, thrusting her head round the curtain. 'Why actually—Kate, my dear, Kate.'

'*You* here, mamma! Is it possible!'

'Possible, my dear? Yes.'

'Why who—who on earth is that you have with you, mamma?' said Kate, shrinking back as she caught sight of a man smiling and kissing his hand.

'Who do you suppose, my dear?' replied Mrs. Nickleby, bending towards Mrs. Wititterly, and speaking a little louder for that lady's edification. 'There's Mr. Pyke, Mr. Pluck, Sir Mulberry Hawk, and Lord Frederick Verisopht.'

'Gracious Heaven!' thought Kate hurriedly. 'How comes she in such society!'

Now, Kate thought thus *so* hurriedly and the surprise was so great, and moreover brought back so forcibly the recollection of what had passed at Ralph's delectable dinner, that she turned extremely pale and appeared greatly agitated, which symptoms being observed by Mrs. Nickleby, were at once set down by that acute lady as being caused and occasioned by violent love. But, although she was in no small degree delighted by this discovery which reflected so much credit on her own quickness of perception, it did not lessen her motherly anxiety in Kate's behalf; and accordingly, with a vast quantity of trepidation, she quitted her own box to hasten into that of Mrs. Wititterly. Mrs. Wititterly, keenly alive to the glory of having a lord and a baronet among her visiting acquaintance, lost no time in signing to Mr. Wititterly to open the door, and thus it was that in less than thirty seconds Mrs. Nickleby's party had made an irruption into Mrs. Wititterly's box, which it filled to the very door, there being in fact only room for Messrs. Pyke and Pluck to get in their heads and waistcoats.

'My dear Kate,' said Mrs. Nickleby, kissing her daughter affectionately. 'How ill you looked a moment ago! You quite frightened me, I declare!'

'It was mere fancy, mamma—the—the reflection of the lights perhaps,' replied Kate, glancing nervously round, and finding it impossible to whisper any caution or explanation.

'Don't you see Sir Mulberry Hawk, my dear?'

Kate bowed slightly, and biting her lip turned her head towards the stage.

But Sir Mulberry Hawk was not to be so easily repulsed, for he advanced with extended hand; and Mrs. Nickleby officiously informing Kate of this circumstance, she was obliged to extend her own. Sir Mulberry detained it while he murmured a profusion of compliments, which Kate, remembering what had passed between them, rightly considered as so many aggravations of the insult he had already put upon her. Then followed the recognition of Lord Frederick Verisopht, and then the greeting of Mr. Pyke, and then that of Mr. Pluck, and finally, to complete the young lady's mortification, she was compelled at Mrs. Wititterly's request to perform the ceremony of introducing the odious persons, whom she regarded with the utmost indignation and abhorrence.

'Mrs. Wititterly is delighted,' said Mr. Wititterly, rubbing his hands; 'delighted, my lord, I am sure, with this opportunity of contracting an acquaintance which, I trust, my lord, we shall improve. Julia, my dear, you must not allow yourself to be too much excited, you must not. Indeed you must not. Mrs.

Wititterly is of a most excitable nature, Sir Mulberry. The snuff of a candle, the wick of a lamp, the bloom on a peach, the down on a butterfly. You might blow her away, my lord; you might blow her away.'

Sir Mulberry seemed to think that it would be a great convenience if the lady could be blown away. He said, however, that the delight was mutual, and Lord Frederick added that it was mutual, whereupon Messrs. Pyke and Pluck were heard to murmur from the distance that it was very mutual indeed.

'I take an interest, my lord,' said Mrs. Wititterly, with a faint smile, 'such an interest in the drama.'

'Ye—es. It's very interesting,' replied Lord Frederick.

'I'm always ill after Shakespeare,' said Mrs. Wititterly. 'I scarcely exist the next day; I find the reaction so very great after a tragedy, my lord, and Shakespeare is such a delicious creature.'

'Ye—es!' replied Lord Frederick. 'He was a clayver man.'

'Do you know, my lord,' said Mrs. Wititterly, after a long silence, 'I find I take so much more interest in his plays, after having been to that dear little dull house he was born in! Were you ever there, my lord?'

'No, nayver,' replied my lord.

'Then really you ought to go, my lord,' returned Mrs. Wititterly, in very languid and drawling accents. 'I don't know how it is, but after you've seen the place and written your name in the little book, somehow or other you seem to be inspired; it kindles up quite a fire within one.'

'Ye—es!' replied Lord Frederick, 'I shall certainly go there.'

'Julia, my life,' interposed Mr. Wititterly, 'you are

deceiving his lordship—unintentionally, my lord, she is deceiving you. It is your poetical temperament, my dear—your ethereal soul—your fervid imagination, which throws you into a glow of genius and excitement. There is nothing in the place, my dear—nothing, nothing.'

'I think there must be something in the place,' said Mrs. Nickleby, who had been listening in silence; 'for, soon after I was married, I went to Stratford with my poor dear Mr. Nickleby, in a post-chaise from Birmingham—was it a post-chaise though?' said Mrs. Nickleby, considering; 'yes, it must have been a post-chaise, because I recollect remarking at the time that the driver had a green shade over his left eye;—in a post-chaise from Birmingham, and after we had seen Shakespeare's tomb and birthplace, we went back to the inn there, where we slept that night, and I recollect that all night long I dreamt of nothing but a black gentleman, at full length, in plaster-of-Paris, with a lay-down collar tied with two tassels, leaning against a post and thinking; and when I woke in the morning and described him to Mr. Nickleby, he said it was Shakespeare just as he had been when he was alive, which was very curious indeed. Stratford—Stratford,' continued Mrs. Nickleby, considering. 'Yes, I am positive about that, because I recollect I was in the family way with my son Nicholas at the time, and I had been very much frightened by an Italian image boy that very morning. In fact, it was quite a mercy, ma'am,' added Mrs. Nickleby, in a whisper to Mrs. Wititterly, 'that my son didn't turn out to be a Shakespeare, and what a dreadful thing that would have been!'

When Mrs. Nickleby had brought this interesting anecdote to a close, Pyke and Pluck, ever zealous in their patron's cause, proposed the adjournment of a detachment of the party into the next box; and with so much skill were the preliminaries adjusted, that Kate, despite all she could say or do to the contrary, had no alternative but to suffer herself to be led away by Sir Mulberry Hawk. Her mother and Mr. Pluck accompanied them, but the worthy lady, pluming herself upon her discretion, took particular care not so much as to look at her daughter during the whole evening, and to seem wholly absorbed in the jokes and conversation of Mr. Pluck, who, having been appointed sentry over Mrs. Nickleby for that especial purpose, neglected, on his side, no possible opportunity of engrossing her attention.

Lord Frederick Verisopht remained in the next box to be talked to by Mrs. Wititterly, and Mr. Pyke was in attendance to throw in a word or two when necessary. As to Mr. Wititterly, he was sufficiently busy in the body of the house, informing such of his friends and acquaintances as happened to be there, that those two gentlemen upstairs, whom they had seen in conversation with Mrs. W., were the distinguished Lord Frederick Verisopht and his most intimate friend, the gay Sir Mulberry Hawk—a communication which inflamed several respectable housekeepers with the utmost jealousy and rage, and reduced sixteen unmarried daughters to the very brink of despair.

The evening came to an end at last, but Kate had yet to be handed downstairs by the detested Sir Mulberry; and so skilfully were the manœuvres of Messrs. Pyke and Pluck conducted, that she and the baronet were the last of the party, and were even—without an appearance of effort or design—left at some little distance behind.

'Don't hurry, don't hurry,' said Sir Mulberry, as Kate hastened on, and attempted to release her arm.

She made no reply, but still pressed forward.

'Nay, then—'coolly observed Sir Mulberry, stopping her outright.

'You had best not seek to detain me, sir!' said Kate, angrily.

'And why not?' retorted Sir Mulberry. 'My dear creature, now why do you keep up this show of displeasure?'

'*Show!*' repeated Kate, indignantly. 'How dare you presume to speak to me, sir—to address me—to come into my presence?'

'You look prettier in a passion, Miss Nickleby,' said Sir Mulberry Hawk, stooping down, the better to see her face.

'I hold you in the bitterest detestation and contempt, sir,' said Kate. 'If you find any attraction in looks of disgust and aversion, you—let me rejoin my friends, sir, instantly. Whatever considerations may have withheld me thus far, I will disregard them all, and take a course that even *you* might feel, if you do not immediately suffer me to proceed.'

Sir Mulberry smiled, and still looking in her face and retaining her arm, walked towards the door.

'If no regard for my sex or helpless situation will induce you to desist from this coarse and unmanly persecution,' said Kate, scarcely knowing, in the tumult of her passions, what she said, 'I have a brother who will resent it dearly, one day.'

'Upon my soul!' exclaimed Sir Mulberry, as though quietly communing with himself, and passing his arm round her waist as he spoke, 'she looks more beautiful, and I like her better, in this mood, than when her eyes are cast down. and she is in perfect repose.'

How Kate reached the lobby where her friends were waiting she never knew, but she hurried across it without at all regarding them, and disengaged herself suddenly from her companion, sprang into the coach, and throwing herself into its darkest corner burst into tears.

Messrs. Pyke and Pluck, knowing their cue, at once threw the party into great commotion by shouting for the carriages, and getting up a violent quarrel with sundry inoffensive bystanders; in the midst of which tumult they put the affrighted Mrs. Nickleby in her chariot, and having got her safely off, turned their thoughts to Mrs. Wititterly, whose attention also they had now effectually distracted from the young lady, by throwing her into a state of the utmost bewilderment and consternation. At length, the conveyance in which she had come rolled off too with its load, and the four worthies, being left alone under the portico, enjoyed a hearty laugh together.

'There,' said Sir Mulberry, turning to his noble friend. 'Didn't I tell you last night that if we could find where they were going by bribing a servant through my fellow, and then established ourselves close by with the mother, these people's house would be our own? Why here it is, done in four-and-twenty hours.'

'Ye—es,' replied the dupe. 'But I have been tied to the old woman all ni-ight.'

'Hear him!' said Sir Mulberry, turning to his two friends. 'Hear this discontented grumbler. Isn't it enough to make a man swear never to help him in his plots and schemes again? Isn't it an infernal shame?'

Pyke asked Pluck whether it was not an infernal shame, and Pluck asked Pyke; but neither answered.

'Isn't it the truth?' demanded Lord Frederick Verisopht. 'Wasn't it so?'

'Wasn t it so!' repeated Sir Mulberry. 'How would you have had it? How could we have got a general invitation at first sight—come when you like, go when you like, stop as long as you like, do what you like—if you, the lord, had not made yourself agreeable to the foolish mistress of the house? Do *I* care for this girl, except as your friend? Haven't I been sounding your praises in her ears, and bearing her pretty sulks and peevishness all night for you? What sort of stuff do you think I am made of? Would I do this for every man? Don't I deserve even gratitude in return?'

'You're a deyvlish good fellow,' said the poor young lord, taking his friend's arm. 'Upon my life, you 're a deyvlish good fellow, Hawk.'

'And I have done right, have I?' demanded Sir Mulberry.

'Quite ri-ight.'

'And like a poor, silly, good-natured, friendly dog as I am, eh?'

'Ye—es, ye—es; like a friend,' replied the other.

'Well then,' replied Sir Mulberry, 'I 'm satisfied. And now let 's go and have our revenge on the German baron and the Frenchman, who cleaned you out so handsomely last night.'

With these words the friendly creature took his companion's arm and led him away: turning half round as he did so, and bestowing a wink and a contemptuous smile on Messrs. Pyke and Pluck, who, cramming their handkerchiefs into their mouths to denote their silent enjoyment of the proceedings, followed their patron and his victim at a little distance.

CHAPTER XXVIII

MISS NICKLEBY, RENDERED DESPERATE BY THE PERSE-
CUTION OF SIR MULBERRY HAWK, AND THE COM-
PLICATED DIFFICULTIES AND DISTRESSES WHICH
SURROUND HER, APPEALS, AS A LAST RESOURCE, TO
HER UNCLE FOR PROTECTION

THE ensuing morning brought reflection with it, as morning usually does; but widely different was the train of thought it awakened in the different persons who had been so unexpectedly brought together on the preceding evening, by the active agency of Messrs. Pyke and Pluck.

The reflections of Sir Mulberry Hawk—if such a term can be applied to the thoughts of the systematic and calculating man of dissipation, whose joys, regrets, pains, and pleasures, are all of self, and who would seem to retain nothing of the intellectual faculty but the power to debase himself, and to degrade the very nature whose outward semblance he wears—the reflections of Sir Mulberry Hawk turned upon Kate Nickleby, and were, in brief, that she was undoubtedly handsome; that her coyness *must* be easily conquerable by a man of his address and experience, and that the pursuit was one which could not fail to redound to his credit, and greatly to enhance his reputation with the world. And lest this last consideration—no mean or secondary one with Sir Mulberry—should sound strangely in the ears of some, let it be remembered that most men live in a world of their own, and that in that limited circle alone are they ambitious for distinction and applause. Sir Mulberry's world was peopled with profligates, and he acted accordingly.

Thus, cases of injustice, and oppression, and tyranny, and the most extravagant bigotry, are in constant occurrence amongst us every day. It is the custom to trumpet forth much wonder and astonishment at the chief actors therein setting at defiance so completely the opinion of the world; but there is no greater fallacy; it is precisely because they do consult the opinion of their own little world that such things take place at all, and strike the great world dumb with amazement.

The reflections of Mrs. Nickleby were of the proudest and most complacent kind; under the influence of her very agreeable delusion she straightway sat down and indited a long letter to Kate, in which she expressed her entire approval of the admirable choice she had made, and extolled Sir Mulberry to the skies; asserting, for the more complete satisfaction of her daughter's feelings, that he was precisely the individual whom she (Mrs. Nickleby) would have chosen for her son-in-law, if she had had the picking and choosing from all mankind. The good lady then, with the preliminary observation that she might be fairly supposed not to have lived in the world so long without knowing its ways, communicated a great many subtle precepts applicable to the state of courtship, and confirmed in their wisdom by her own personal experience. Above all things she commended a strict maidenly reserve, as being not only a very laudable thing in itself, but as tending materially to strengthen and increase a lover's ardour. 'And I never,' added Mrs. Nickleby, 'was more delighted in my life than to observe last night, my dear, that your good sense had already told you this.' With which sentiment, and various hints of the pleasure she derived from the knowledge that her daughter inherited so large an instalment of her own excellent sense and discretion (to nearly the full measure of which she might hope, with care, to succeed in time), Mrs. Nickleby concluded a very long and rather illegible letter.

Poor Kate was well nigh distracted on the receipt of four closely-written and closely-crossed sides of congratulation on the very subject which had prevented her closing her eyes all night, and kept her weeping and watching in her chamber; still worse and more trying was the necessity of rendering herself agreeable to Mrs. Wititterly, who, being in low spirits after the fatigue of the preceding night, of course expected her companion (else wherefore had she board and salary?) to be in the best spirits possible. As to Mr. Wititterly, he went about all day in a tremor of delight at having shaken hands with a lord, and having actually asked him to come and see him in his own house. The lord himself, not being troubled to any inconvenient extent with the power of thinking, regaled himself with the conversation of Messrs. Pyke and Pluck, who sharpened their wit by a plentiful indulgence in various costly stimulants at his expense.

It was four in the afternoon—that is, the vulgar afternoon of the sun and the clock—and Mrs. Wititterly reclined, according to custom, on the drawing-room sofa, while Kate read aloud a new novel in three volumes, entitled 'The Lady Flabella,' which Alphonse the doubtful had procured from the library that very morning. And it was a production admirably suited to a lady labouring under Mrs. Wititterly's complaint, seeing that there was not a line in it, from beginning to end, which could, by the most remote contingency, awaken the smallest excitement in any person breathing.

Kate read on.

' "Cherizette," said the Lady Flabella, inserting her mouse-like feet in the blue satin slippers, which had unwittingly occasioned the half-playful half-angry altercation between herself and the youthful Colonel Befillaire, in the Duke of Mincefeuille's *salon de danse* on the previous night. "*Cherizette, ma chère, donnez-moi de l'eau de Cologne, s'il vous plaît, mon enfant.*"

' "*Merci*—thank you," said the Lady Flabella, as the lively but devoted Cherizette, plentifully besprinkled with the fragrant compound the Lady Flabella's *mouchoir* of the finest cambric, edged with richest lace, and emblazoned at the four corners with the Flabella crest, and gorgeous heraldic bearings of that noble family; "*Merci*—that will do."

'At this instant, while the Lady Flabella yet inhaled that delicious fragrance by holding the *mouchoir* to her exquisite, but thoughtfully-chiselled nose, the door of the *boudoir* (artfully concealed by rich hangings of silken damask, the hue of Italy's firmament) was thrown open, and with noiseless tread two valets de chambre, clad in sumptuous liveries of peach-blossom and gold, advanced into the room followed by a page in *bas de soie*—silk stockings—who, while they remained at some distance making the most graceful obeisances, advanced to the feet of his lovely mistress, and dropping on one knee presented, on a golden salver gorgeously chased, a scented *billet*.

'The Lady Flabella, with an agitation she could not repress, hastily tore off the *envelope* and broke the scented seal. It *was* from Befillaire—the young, the slim, the low-voiced—*her own* Befillaire.'

'Oh, charming!' interrupted Kate's patroness, who was sometimes taken literary. 'Poetic, really. Read that description again, Miss Nickleby.'

Kate complied.

'Sweet, indeed!' said Mrs. Wititterly, with a sigh. 'So voluptuous, is it not? So soft?'

'Yes, I think it is,' replied Kate, gently; 'very soft.'

'Close the book, Miss Nickleby,' said Mrs. Wititterly. 'I can hear nothing more to-day. I should be sorry to disturb the impression of that sweet description. Close the book.'

Kate complied, not unwillingly; and, as she did so, Mrs. Wititterly raising her glass with a languid hand, remarked, that she looked pale.

'It was the fright of that—that noise and confusion last night,' said Kate.

'How very odd!' exclaimed Mrs. Wititterly, with a look of surprise. And certainly, when one comes to think of it, it *was* very odd that anything should have disturbed a companion. A steam-engine, or other ingenious piece of mechanism out of order, would have been nothing to it.

'How did you come to know Lord Frederick, and those other delightful creatures, child?' asked Mrs. Wititterly, still eyeing Kate through her glass.

'I met them at my uncle's,' said Kate, vexed to feel that she was colouring deeply, but unable to keep down the blood which rushed to her face whenever she thought of that man.

'Have you known them long?'

'No,' rejoined Kate. 'Not long.'

'I was very glad of the opportunity which that respectable person, your mother, gave us of being known to them,' said Mrs. Wititterly, in a lofty manner. 'Some friends of ours were on the very point of introducing us, which makes it quite remarkable.'

This was said lest Miss Nickleby should grow conceited on the honour and dignity of having known four great people (for Pyke and Pluck were included among the delightful creatures), whom Mrs. Witit= terly did not know. But as the circumstance had made no impression one way or other upon Kate's mind, the force of the observation was quite lost upon her.

'They asked permission to call,' said Mrs. Wititter-ly. 'I gave it them of course.'

'Do you expect them to-day?' Kate ventured to in-quire.

Mrs. Wititterly's answer was lost in the noise of a tremendous rapping at the street-door, and, before it had ceased to vibrate, there drove up a handsome cab-riolet, out of which leaped Sir Mulberry Hawk and his friend Lord Frederick.

'They are here now,' said Kate, rising and hurrying away.

'Miss Nickleby!' cried Mrs. Wititterly, perfectly aghast at a companion's attempting to quit the room, without her permission first had and obtained. 'Pray don't think of going.'

'You are very good!' replied Kate. 'But—'

'For goodness' sake don't agitate me by making me speak so much,' said Mrs. Wititterly, with great sharpness. 'Dear me, Miss Nickleby, I beg—'

It was in vain for Kate to protest that she was un-well, for the footsteps of the knockers, whoever they were, were already on the stairs. She resumed her seat, and had scarcely done so, when the doubtful page darted into the room and announced, Mr. Pyke, and Mr. Pluck, and Lord Frederick Verisopht, and Sir Mulberry Hawk, all at one burst.

'The most extraordinary thing in the world,' said Mr. Pluck, saluting both ladies with the utmost cor-diality; 'the most extraordinary thing. As Lord Frederick and Sir Mulberry drove up to the door, Pyke and I had that instant knocked.'

'That instant knocked,' said Pyke.

'No matter how you came, so that you are here,' said Mrs. Wititterly, who, by dint of lying on the same sofa for three years and a half, had got up a little pantomime of graceful attitudes, and now threw herself into the most striking of the series, to astonish the visitors. 'I am delighted, I am sure.'

'And how is Miss Nickleby?' said Sir Mulberry Hawk, accosting Kate, in a low voice; not so low, however, but that it reached the ears of Mrs. Wititterly.

'Why, she complains of suffering from the fright of last night,' said the lady. 'I am sure I don't wonder at it, for my nerves are quite torn to pieces.'

'And yet you look,' observed Sir Mulberry, turning round; 'and yet you look—'

'Beyond everything,' said Mr. Pyke, coming to his patron's assistance. Of course Mr. Pluck said the same.

'I am afraid Sir Mulberry is a flatterer, my lord,' said Mrs. Wititterly, turning to that young gentleman, who had been sucking the head of his cane in silence, and staring at Kate.

'Oh, deyvlish!' replied my lord. Having given utterance to which remarkable sentiment, he occupied himself as before.

'Neither does Miss Nickleby look the worse,' said Sir Mulberry, bending his bold gaze upon her. 'She was always handsome, but upon my soul, ma'am, you seem to have imparted some of your own good looks to her besides.'

To judge from the glow which suffused the poor girl's countenance after this speech, Mrs. Wititterly might, with some show of reason, have been supposed to have imparted to it some of that artificial bloom which decorated her own. Mrs. Wititterly admitted, though not with the best grace in the world, that Kate *did* look pretty. She began to think too, that Sir Mulberry was not quite so agreeable a creature as she had at first supposed him; for, although a skilful flatterer is a most delightful companion if you can keep him all to yourself, his taste becomes very doubtful when he takes to complimenting other people.

'Pyke,' said the watchful Mr. Pluck, observing the effect which the praise of Miss Nickleby had produced.

'Well, Pluck,' said Pyke.

'Is there anybody,' demanded Mr. Pluck, mysteriously, 'anybody you know, whom Mrs. Wititterly's profile reminds you off?'

'Reminds me of?' answered Pyke. 'Of course there is.'

'Who do you mean?' said Pluck, in the same mysterious manner. 'The D. of B.?'

'The C. of B,' replied Pyke, with the faintest trace of a grin lingering in his countenance. 'The beautiful sister is the countess; not the duchess.'

'True,' said Pluck, 'the C. of B. The resemblance is wonderful!'

'Perfectly startling!' said Mr. Pyke.

Here was a state of things! Mrs. Wititterly was declared, upon the testimony of two veracious and competent witnesses, to be the very picture of a countess! This was one of the consequences of getting into good society. Why, she might have moved among grovelling people for twenty years, and never heard of it. How could she, indeed? what did *they* know about countesses?

The two gentlemen having by the greediness with which this little bait was swallowed, tested the extent of Mrs. Wititterly's appetite for adulation, proceeded to administer that commodity in very large doses, thus affording to Sir Mulberry Hawk an opportunity of pestering Miss Nickleby with questions and remarks, to which she was absolutely obliged to make some reply. Meanwhile, Lord Frederick enjoyed unmolested the full flavour of the gold knob at the top of his cane, as he would have done to the end of the interview if Mr. Wititterly had not come home, and caused the conversation to turn to his favourite topic.

'My lord,' said Mr. Wititterly, 'I am delighted—honoured—proud. Be seated again, my lord, pray. I am proud, indeed; most proud.'

It was to the secret annoyance of his wife that Mr. Wititterly said all this, for, although she was bursting with pride and arrogance, she would have had the illustrious guests believe that their visit was quite a common occurrence, and that they had lords and baronets to see them every day in the week. But Mr. Wititterly's feelings were beyond the power of suppression.

'It is an honour, indeed!' said Mr. Wititterly. 'Julia, my soul, you will suffer for this to-morrow.'

'Suffer!' cried Lord Frederick.

'The reaction, my lord, the reaction,' said Mr. Wititterly. 'This violent strain upon the nervous system over, my lord, what ensues? A sinking, a depression, a lowness, a lassitude, a debility. My lord, if Sir Tumley Snuffim was to see that delicate creature at this moment, he would not give a—a—*this* for her life.' In illustration of which remark, Mr. Wititterly took a pinch of snuff from his box, and jerked it lightly into the air as an emblem of instability.

'Not *that*,' said Mr. Wititterly, looking about him with a serious countenance. 'Sir Tumley Snuffim would not give that for Mrs. Wititterly's existence.'

Mr. Wititterly told this with a kind of sober exultation, as if it were no trifling distinction for a man to have a wife in such a desperate state, and Mrs. Wititterly sighed and looked on, as if she felt the honour, but had determined to bear it as meekly as might be.

'Mrs. Wititterly,' said her husband, 'is Sir Tumley Snuffim's favourite patient. I believe I may venture to say, that Mrs. Wititterly is the first person who took the new medicine which is supposed to have destroyed a family at Kensington Gravel Pits. I believe she was. If I am wrong, Julia, my dear, you will correct me.'

'I believe I was,' said Mrs. Wititterly, in a faint voice.

As there appeared to be some doubt in the mind of his patron how he could best join in this conversation, the indefatigable Mr. Pyke threw himself into the breach, and, by way of saying something to the point, inquired—with reference to the aforesaid medicine—whether it was nice?

'No, sir, it was not. It had not even that recommendation,' said Mr. W.

'Mrs. Wititterly is quite a martyr,' observed Pyke with a complimentary bow.

'I *think* I am,' said Mrs. Wititterly, smiling.

'I think you are, my dear Julia,' replied her husband, in a tone which seemed to say that he was not vain, but still must insist upon their privileges. 'If anybody, my lord,' added Mr. Wititterly, wheeling round to the nobleman, 'will produce to me a greater martyr, than Mrs. Wititterly, all I can say is, that I shall be glad to see that martyr, whether male or female—that 's all, my lord.'

Pyke and Pluck promptly remarked that certainly nothing could be fairer than that; and the call having been by this time protracted to a very great length, they obeyed Sir Mulberry's look, and rose to go. This brought Sir Mulberry himself and Lord Frederick on their legs also. Many protestations of friendship, and expressions anticipative of the pleasure which must inevitably flow from so happy an acquaintance, were exchanged, and the visitors departed, with renewed assurances that at all times and seasons the mansion of the Wititterlys would be honoured by receiving them beneath its roof.

That they came at all times and seasons—that they dined there one day, supped the next, dined again on the next, and were constantly to and fro on all—that they made parties to visit public places, and met by accident at lounges—that upon all these occasions Miss Nickleby was exposed to the constant and unremitting persecution of Sir Mulberry Hawk, who now began to feel his character, even in the estimation of his two dependents, involved in the successful reduction of her pride—that she had no intervals of peace or rest, except at those hours when she could sit in her solitary room, and weep over the trials of the day—all these were consequences naturally flowing from the well-laid plans of Sir Mulberry, and their able execution by the auxiliaries, Pyke and Pluck.

And thus for a fortnight matters went on. That any but the weakest and silliest of people could have seen in one interview that Lord Frederick Verisopht, though he was a lord, and Sir Mulberry Hawk, though he was a baronet, were not persons accustomed to be the best possible companions, and were certainly not calculated by habits, manners, tastes, or conversation, to shine with any very great lustre in the society of ladies, need scarcely be remarked. But with Mrs. Wititterly the two titles were all-sufficient; coarseness became humour, vulgarity softened itself down into the most charming eccentricity; insolence took the guise of an easy absence of reserve, attainable only by those who had had the good fortune to mix with high folks.

If the mistress put such a construction upon the behaviour of her new friends, what could the companion urge against them? If they accustomed themselves to very little restraint before the lady of the house, with how much more freedom could they address her paid dependent! Nor was even this the worst. As the odious Sir Mulberry Hawk attached himself to Kate with less and less of disguise, Mrs. Wititterly began to grow jealous of the superior attractions of Miss Nickleby. If this feeling had led to her banishment from the drawing-room when such company was there, Kate would have been only too happy and willing that it should have existed, but unfortunately for her she possessed that native grace and true gentility of manner, and those thousand nameless accomplishments which give to female society its greatest charm; if these be valuable anywhere, they were especially so where the lady of the house was a mere animated doll. The consequence was, that Kate had the double mortification of being an indispensable part of the circle when Sir Mulberry and his friends were there, and of being exposed, on that very account, to all Mrs. Wititterly's ill-humours and caprices when they were gone. She became utterly and completely miserable.

Mrs. Wititterly had never thrown off the mask with regard to Sir Mulberry, but when she was more than usually out of temper, attributed the circumstance, as ladies sometimes do, to nervous indisposition. However, as the dreadful idea that Lord Frederick Verisopht also was somewhat taken with Kate, and that she, Mrs. Wititterly, was quite a secondary person, dawned upon that lady's mind and gradually developed itself, she became possessed with a large quantity of highly proper and most virtuous indignation, and felt it her duty, as a married lady and a moral member of society, to mention the circumstance to 'the young person' without delay.

Accordingly Mrs. Wititterly broke ground next morning, during a pause in the novel-reading.

'Miss Nickleby,' said Mrs. Wititterly, 'I wish to speak to you very gravely. I am sorry to have to do it, upon my word I am very sorry, but you leave me no alternative, Miss Nickleby.' Here Mrs. Wititterly tossed her head—not passionately, only virtuously —and remarked, with some appearance of excitement, that she feared that palpitation of the heart was coming on again.

'Your behaviour, Miss Nickleby,' resumed the lady, 'is very far from pleasing me—very far. I am very anxious indeed that you should do well, but you may depend upon it, Miss Nickleby, you will not, if you go on as you do.'

'Ma'am!' exclaimed Kate, proudly.

'Don't agitate me by speaking in that way, Miss Nickleby, don't,' said Mrs. Wititterly, with some violence, 'or you 'll compel me to ring the bell.'

Kate looked at her, but said nothing.

'You needn't suppose,' resumed Mrs. Wititterly, 'that your looking at me in that way, Miss Nickleby, will prevent my saying what I am going to say, which I feel to be a religious duty. You needn't direct your glances towards me,' said Mrs. Wititterly, with a sudden burst of spite; 'I am not Sir Mulberry, no, nor Lord Frederick Verisopht, Miss Nickleby; nor am I Mr. Pyke, nor Mr. Pluck either.'

Kate looked at her again, but less steadily than before; and resting her elbow on the table, covered her eyes with her hand.

'If such things had been done when *I* was a young

girl,' said Mrs. Wititterly (this, by the way, must have been some little time before), 'I don't suppose anybody would have believed it.'

'I don't think they would,' murmured Kate. 'I do not think anybody would believe, without actually knowing it, what I seemed doomed to undergo!'

'Don't talk to me of being doomed to undergo, Miss Nickleby, if you please,' said Mrs. Wititterly, with a shrillness of tone quite surprising in so great an invalid. 'I will not be answered, Miss Nickleby. I am not accustomed to be answered, nor will I permit it for an instant. Do you hear?' she added, waiting with some apparent inconsistency *for* an answer.

'I do hear you, ma'am,' replied Kate, 'with surprise; with greater surprise than I can express.'

'I have always considered you a particularly well-behaved young person for your station in life,' said Mrs. Wititterly; 'and as you are a person of healthy appearance, and neat in your dress and so forth, I have taken an interest in you, as I do still, considering that I owe a sort of duty to that respectable old female, your mother. For these reasons, Miss Nickleby, I must tell you once for all, and begging you to mind what I say, that I must insist upon your immediately altering your very forward behaviour to the gentlemen who visit at this house. It really is not becoming,' said Mrs. Wititterly, closing her chaste eyes as she spoke; 'it is improper, quite improper.'

'Oh!' cried Kate, looking upwards and clasping her hands; 'is not this, is not this, too cruel, too hard to bear! Is it not enough that I should have suffered as I have, night and day; that I should almost have sunk in my own estimation from very shame of having been brought into contact with such people; but must I also be exposed to this unjust and most unfounded charge!'

'You will have the goodness to recollect, Miss Nickleby,' said Mrs. Wititterly, 'that when you use such terms as "unjust," and "unfounded," you charge me, in effect, with stating that which is untrue.'

'I do,' said Kate, with honest indignation. 'Whether you make this accusation of yourself, or at the prompting of others, is alike to me. I say it *is* vilely, grossly, wilfully untrue. Is it possible,' cried Kate, 'that any one of my own sex can have sat by, and not have seen the misery these men have caused me? Is it possible that you, ma'am, can have been present, and failed to mark the insulting freedom that their every look bespoke? Is it possible that you can have avoided seeing, that these libertines, in their utter disrespect for you, and utter disregard of all gentlemanly behaviour, and almost of decency, have had but one object in introducing themselves here, and that the furtherance of their designs upon a friendless, helpless girl, who, without this humiliating confession, might have hoped to receive from one so much her senior something like womanly aid and sympathy? I do not—I cannot believe it!'

If poor Kate had possessed the slightest knowledge of the world, she certainly would not have ventured, even in the excitement into which she had been lashed, upon such an injudicious speech as this. Its effect was precisely what a more experienced observer would have foreseen. Mrs. Wititterly received the attack upon her veracity with exemplary calmness, and listened with the most heroic fortitude to Kate's account of her own sufferings. But allusion being made to her being held in disregard by the gentlemen, she evinced violent emotion, and this blow was no sooner followed up by the remark concerning her seniority, than she fell back upon the sofa, uttering dismal screams.

'What is the matter?' cried Mr. Wititterly, bouncing into the room. 'Heavens, what do I see? Julia! Julia! look up, my life, look up!'

But Julia looked down most perseveringly, and screamed still louder; so Mr. Wititterly rang the bell, and danced in a frenzied manner round the sofa on which Mrs. Wititterly lay; uttering perpetual cries for Sir Tumley Snuffim, and never once leaving off to ask for any explanation of the scene before him.

'Run for Sir Tumley,' cried Mr. Wititterly, menacing the page with both fists. 'I knew it, Miss Nickleby,' he said, looking round with an air of melancholy triumph, 'that society has been too much for her. This is all soul, you know, every bit of it.' With this assurance Mr. Wititterly took up the prostrate form of Mrs. Wititterly, and carried her bodily off to bed.

Kate waited until Sir Tumley Snuffim had paid his visit and looked in with a report, that, through the special interposition of a merciful Providence (thus spake Sir Tumley), Mrs. Wititterly had gone to sleep. She then hastily attired herself for walking, and leaving word that she should return within a couple of hours, hurried away towards her uncle's house.

It had been a good day with Ralph Nickleby, quite a lucky day. As he walked to and fro in his little back-room with his hands clasped behind him, adding up in his own mind all the sums that had been, or would be, netted from the business done since morning, his mouth was drawn into a hard stern smile; while the firmness of the lines and curves that made it up, as well as the cunning glance of his cold bright eye, seemed to tell, that if any resolution or cunning would increase the profits, they would not fail to be exerted for the purpose.

'Very good!' said Ralph, in allusion, no doubt, to

some proceeding of the day. 'He defies the usurer, does he? Well, we shall see. "Honesty is the best policy," is it? We 'll try that too.'

He stopped and then walked on again.

'He is content,' said Ralph, relaxing into a smile, 'to set his known character and conduct against the power of money. Dross, as he calls it. Why, what a dull blockhead this fellow must be! Dross too, dross!—Who 's that?'

'Me,' said Newman Noggs, looking in. 'Your niece.'

'What of her?' asked Ralph sharply.

'She 's here.'

'Here?'

Newman jerked his head towards his little room, to signify that she was waiting there.

'What does she want?' asked Ralph.

'I don't know,' rejoined Newman. 'Shall I ask?' he added quickly.

'No,' replied Ralph. 'Show her in! Stay.' He hastily put away a padlocked cash-box that was on the table, and substituted in its stead an empty purse. 'There,' said Ralph. '*Now* she may come in.'

Newman, with a grim smile at this manœuvre, beckoned the young lady to advance, and having placed a chair for her, retired; looking stealthily over his shoulder at Ralph as he limped slowly out.

'Well,' said Ralph, roughly enough; but still with something more of kindness in his manner than he would have exhibited towards anybody else. 'Well, my—dear. What now?'

Kate raised her eyes, which were filled with tears; and with an effort to master her emotion strove to speak, but in vain. So drooping her head again, she remained silent. Her face was hidden from his view, but Ralph could see that she was weeping.

'I can guess the cause of this!' thought Ralph, after looking at her for some time in silence. 'I can—I can —guess the cause. Well! Well!' thought Ralph— for the moment quite disconcerted, as he watched the anguish of his beautiful niece. 'Where is the harm? Only a few tears; and it's an excellent lesson for her, an excellent lesson.'

'What is the matter?' asked Ralph, drawing a chair opposite, and sitting down.

He was rather taken aback by the sudden firmness with which Kate looked up and answered him.

'The matter which brings me to you, sir,' she said, 'is one which should call the blood up into your cheeks, and make you burn to hear, as it does me to tell. I have been wronged; my feelings have been outraged, insulted, wounded past all healing, and by your friends.'

'Friends!' cried Ralph, sternly. '*I* have no friends, girl.'

'By the men I saw here, then,' returned Kate, quickly. 'If they were no friends of yours, and you knew what they were,—oh, the more shame on you, uncle, for bringing me among them. To have subjected me to what I was exposed to here, through any misplaced confidence or imperfect knowledge of your guests, would have required some strong excuse; but if you did it—as I now believe you did—knowing them well, it was most dastardly and cruel.'

Ralph drew back in utter amazement at this plain speaking, and regarded Kate with the sternest look. But she met his gaze proudly and firmly, and although her face was very pale, it looked more noble and handsome, lighted up as it was, than it had ever appeared before.

'There is some of that boy's blood in you, I see,' said Ralph, speaking in his harshest tones, as something in the flashing eye reminded him of Nicholas at their last meeting.

'I hope there is!' replied Kate. 'I should be proud to know it. I am young, uncle, and all the difficulties and miseries of my situation have kept it down, but I have been roused to-day beyond all endurance, and come what may, *I will not*, as I am your brother's child, bear these insults longer.'

'What insults, girl?' demanded Ralph, sharply.

'Remember what took place here, and ask yourself,' replied Kate, colouring deeply. 'Uncle, you must— I am sure you will—release me from such vile and de-grading companionship as I am exposed to now. I do not mean,' said Kate, hurrying to the old man, and laying her arm upon his shoulder; 'I do not mean to be angry and violent—I beg your pardon if I have seemed so, dear uncle,—but you do not know what I have suffered, you do not indeed. You cannot tell what the heart of a young girl is—I have no right to expect you should; but when I tell you that I am wretched, and that my heart is breaking, I am sure you will help me. I am sure, I am sure you will!'

Ralph looked at her for an instant; then turned away his head, and beat his foot nervously upon the ground.

'I have gone on day after day,' said Kate, bending over him, and timidly placing her little hand in his, 'in the hope that this persecution would cease; I have gone on day after day, compelled to assume the ap-pearance of cheerfulness, when I was most unhappy. I have had no counsellor, no adviser, no one to protect me. Mamma supposes that these are honourable men, rich and distinguished, and how *can* I—how can I un-deceive her—when she is so happy in these little de-lusions, which are the only happiness she has? The lady with whom you placed me, is not the person to whom I could confide matters of so much delicacy, and I have come at last to you, the only friend I have at hand—almost the only friend I have at all—to intreat and implore you to assist me.'

'How can *I* assist you, child?' said Ralph, rising from his chair, and pacing up and down the room in his old attitude.

'You have influence with one of these men, I *know*,' rejoined Kate, emphatically. 'Would not a word from you induce them to desist from this unmanly course?'

'No,' said Ralph, suddenly turning; 'at least—that—I can't say it, if it would.'

'Can't say it!'

'No,' said Ralph, coming to a dead stop, and clasping his hands more tightly behind him. 'I can't say it.'

Kate fell back a step or two, and looked at him, as if in doubt whether she had heard aright.

'We are connected in business,' said Ralph, poising himself alternately on his toes and heels, and looking coolly in his niece's face, 'in business, and I can't afford to offend them. What is it after all? We have all our trials, and this is one of yours. Some girls would be proud to have such gallants at their feet.'

'Proud!' cried Kate.

'I don't say,' rejoined Ralph, raising his forefinger, 'but that you do right to despise them; no, you show your good sense in that, as indeed I knew from the first you would. Well. In all other respects you are comfortably bestowed. It's not much to bear. If this young lord does dog your footsteps, and whisper his drivelling inanities in your ears, what of it? It's a dishonourable passion. So be it; it won't last long. Some other novelty will spring up one day, and you will be released. In the mean time—'

'In the mean time,' interrupted Kate, with becoming pride and indignation, 'I am to be the scorn of my own sex, and the toy of the other; justly condemned by all women of right feeling, and despised by all honest and honourable men; sunken in my own esteem, and degraded in every eye that looks upon me. No, not if I work my fingers to the bone, not if I am driven to the roughest and hardest labour. Do not mistake me. I will not disgrace your recommendation. I will remain in the house in which it placed me, until I am entitled to leave it by the terms of my engagement; though, mind, I see these men no more! When I quit it, I will hide myself from them and you, and, striving to support my mother by hard service, I will live, at least, in peace, and trust in God to help me.'

With these words, she waved her hand, and quitted the room, leaving Ralph Nickleby motionless as a statue.

The surprise with which Kate, as she closed the room-door, beheld, close beside it, Newman Noggs standing bolt upright in a little niche in the wall like some scarecrow or Guy Faux laid up in winter quarters, almost occasioned her to call aloud. But, Newman laying his finger upon his lips, she had the presence of mind to refrain.

'Don't,' said Newman, gliding out of his recess, and accompanying her across the hall. 'Don't cry, don't cry.' Two very large tears, by the bye, were running down Newman's face as he spoke.

'I see how it is,' said poor Noggs, drawing from his pocket what seemed to be a very old duster, and wiping Kate's eyes with it, as gently as if she were an infant.

'You 're giving way now. Yes, yes, very good; that 's right, I like that. It was right not to give way before him. Yes, yes! Ha, ha, ha! Oh yes. Poor thing!'

With these disjointed exclamations, Newman wiped his own eyes with the afore-mentioned duster, and, limping to the street-door, opened it to let her out.

'Don't cry any more,' whispered Newman. 'I shall see you soon. Ha! ha! ha! And so shall somebody else too. Yes, yes. Ho! ho!'

'God bless you,' answered Kate, hurrying out, 'God bless you.

'Same to you,' rejoined Newman, opening the door again a little way, to say so. 'Ha, ha, ha! Ho! ho! ho!'

And Newman Noggs opened the door once again to nod cheerfully, and laugh—and shut it, to shake his head mournfully, and cry.

Ralph remained in the same attitude till he heard the noise of the closing door, when he shrugged his shoulders, and after a few turns about the room, hasty at first, but gradually becoming slower, as he relapsed into himself—sat down before his desk.

It is one of those problems of human nature, which may be noted down, but not solved—although Ralph felt no remorse at that moment for his conduct towards the innocent, true-hearted girl; although his libertine clients had done precisely what he had expected, precisely what he most wished, and precisely what would tend most to his advantage, still he hated them for doing it, from the very bottom of his soul.

'Ugh!' said Ralph, scowling round, and shaking his clenched hand as the faces of the two profligates rose up before his mind; 'you shall pay for this. Oh! you shall pay for this!'

As the usurer turned for consolation to his books and papers, a performance was going on outside his office-door, which would have occasioned him no small surprise, if he could by any means have become acquainted with it.

Newman Noggs was the sole actor. He stood at a little distance from the door, with his face towards it; and with the sleeves of his coat turned back at the wrists, was occupied in bestowing the most vigorous, scientific, and straightforward blows upon the empty air.

At first sight, this would have appeared merely a wise precaution in a man of sedentary habits, with the view of opening the chest and strengthening the muscles of the arms. But the intense eagerness and joy depicted in the face of Newman Noggs, which was suffused with perspiration; the surprising energy with which he directed a constant succession of blows towards a particular panel about five feet eight from the ground, and still worked away in the most untiring and persevering manner; would have sufficiently explained to the attentive observer, that his imagination was threshing to within an inch of his life, his body's most active employer, Mr. Ralph Nickleby.

CHAPTER XXIX

OF THE PROCEEDINGS OF NICHOLAS, AND CERTAIN INTERNAL DIVISIONS IN THE COMPANY OF MR. VINCENT CRUMMLES

THE unexpected success and favour with which his experiment at Portsmouth had been received, induced Mr. Crummles to prolong his stay in that town for a fortnight beyond the period he had originally assigned for the duration of his visit, during which time Nicholas personated a vast variety of characters with undiminished success, and attracted so many people to the theatre who had never been seen there before, that a benefit was considered by the manager a very promising speculation. Nicholas assenting to the terms proposed, the benefit was had, and by it he realised no less a sum than twenty pounds.

Possessed of this unexpected wealth, his first act was to enclose to honest John Browdie the amount of his friendly loan, which he accompanied with many expressions of gratitude and esteem, and many cordial wishes for his matrimonial happiness. To Newman Noggs he forwarded one half of the sum he had realised, entreating him to take an opportunity of handing it to Kate in secret, and conveying to her the warmest assurances of his love and affection. He made no mention of the way in which he had employed himself; merely informing Newman that a letter addressed to him under his assumed name at the Post Office, Portsmouth, would readily find him, and entreating that worthy friend to write full particulars of the situation of his mother and sister, and an account of all the grand things that Ralph Nickleby had done for them since his departure from London.

'You are out of spirits,' said Smike, on the night after the letter had been despatched.

'Not I!' rejoined Nicholas, with assumed gaiety, for the confession would have made the boy miserable all night; 'I was thinking about my sister, Smike.'

'Sister!'

'Aye.'

'Is she like you?' inquired Smike.

'Why, so they say,' replied Nicholas, laughing, 'only a great deal handsomer.'

'She must be *very* beautiful,' said Smike, after thinking a little while with his hands folded together, and his eyes bent upon his friend.

'Anybody who didn't know you as well as I do, my dear fellow, would say you were an accomplished courtier,' said Nicholas.

'I don't even know what that is,' replied Smike, shaking his head. 'Shall I ever see your sister?'

'To be sure,' cried Nicholas; 'we shall all be together one of these days—when we are rich, Smike.'

'How is it that you, who are so kind and good to me, have nobody to be kind to you?' asked Smike. 'I cannot make that out.'

'Why, it is a long story,' replied Nicholas, 'and one you would have some difficulty in comprehending, I fear. I have an enemy—you understand what that is?'

'Oh yes, I understand that,' said Smike.

'Well, it is owing to him,' returned Nicholas. 'He is rich, and not so easily punished as *your* old enemy, Mr. Squeers. He is my uncle, but he is a villain, and has done me wrong.'

'Has he though?' asked Smike, bending eagerly forward. 'What is his name? Tell me his name.'

'Ralph—Ralph Nickleby.'

'Ralph Nickleby,' repeated Smike. 'Ralph. I'll get that name by heart.'

He had muttered it over to himself some twenty times, when a loud knock at the door disturbed him from his occupation. Before he could open it, Mr. Folair, the pantomimist, thrust in his head.

Mr. Folair's head was usually decorated with a very round hat, unusually high in the crown, and curled up quite tight in the brims. On the present occasion he wore it very much on one side, with the back part forward in consequence of its being the least rusty;

round his neck he wore a flaming red worsted comforter, whereof the straggling ends peeped out beneath his threadbare Newmarket coat, which was very tight and buttoned all the way up. He carried in his hand one very dirty glove, and a cheap dress cane with a glass handle; in short, his whole appearance was unusually dashing, and demonstrated a far more scrupulous attention to his toilet, than he was in the habit of bestowing upon it.

'Good evening, sir,' said Mr. Folair, taking off the tall hat, and running his fingers through his hair. 'I bring a communication. Hem!'

'From whom and what about?' inquired Nicholas. 'You are unusually mysterious to-night.'

'Cold, perhaps,' returned Mr. Folair; 'cold, perhaps. That is the fault of my position—not of myself, Mr. Johnson. My position as a mutual friend requires it, sir.' Mr. Folair paused with a most impressive look, and diving into the hat before noticed, drew from thence a small piece of whitey-brown paper curiously folded, whence he brought forth a note which it had served to keep clean, and handing it over to Nicholas, said—

'Have the goodness to read that, sir.'

Nicholas, in a state of much amazement, took the note and broke the seal, glancing at Mr. Folair as he did so, who knitting his brow and pursing up his mouth with great dignity, was sitting with his eyes steadily fixed upon the ceiling.

It was directed to blank Johnson, Esq., by favour of Augustus Folair, Esq.; and the astonishment of Nicholas was in no degree lessened, when he found it to be couched in the following laconic terms:—

'Mr. Lenville presents his kind regards to Mr. Johnson, and will feel obliged if he will inform him at what hour to-morrow morning it will be most convenient to him to meet Mr. L. at the Theatre, for the purpose of having his nose pulled in the presence of the company.

'Mr. Lenville requests Mr. Johnson not to neglect making an appointment, as he has invited two or three professional friends to witness the ceremony, and cannot disappoint them upon any account whatever.'

'Portsmouth, Tuesday night.'

Indignant as he was at this impertinence, there was something so exquisitely absurd in such a cartel of defiance, that Nicholas was obliged to bite his lip and read the note over two or three times before he could muster sufficient gravity and sternness to address the hostile messenger, who had not taken his eyes from the ceiling, nor altered the expression of his face in the slightest degree.

'Do you know the contents of this note, sir?' he asked, at length.

'Yes,' rejoined Mr. Folair, looking round for an instant, and immediately carrying his eyes back again to the ceiling.

'And how dare you bring it here, sir?' asked Nicholas, tearing it into very little pieces, and jerking it in a shower towards the messenger. 'Had you no fear of being kicked downstairs, sir?'

Mr. Folair turned his head—now ornamented with several fragments of the note—towards Nicholas, and with the same imperturbable dignity, briefly replied 'No.'

'Then,' said Nicholas, taking up the tall hat and tossing it towards the door, 'you had better follow that article of your dress, sir, or you may find yourself very disagreeably deceived, and that within a dozen seconds.'

'I say, Johnson,' remonstrated Mr. Folair, suddenly losing all his dignity, 'none of that, you know. No tricks with a gentleman's wardrobe.'

'Leave the room,' returned Nicholas. 'How could you presume to come here on such an errand, you scoundrel?'

'Pooh! pooh!' said Mr. Folair, unwinding his comforter, and gradually getting himself out of it. 'There—that's enough.'

'Enough!' cried Nicholas, advancing towards him. 'Take yourself off, sir.'

'Pooh! pooh! I tell you,' returned Mr. Folair, waving his hand in deprecation of any further wrath; 'I wasn't in earnest. I only brought it in joke.'

'You had better be careful how you indulge in such jokes again,' said Nicholas, 'or you may find an allusion to pulling noses rather a dangerous reminder for the subject of your facetiousness. Was it written in joke, too, pray?'

'No, no, that's the best of it,' returned the actor; 'right down earnest—honour bright.'

Nicholas could not repress a smile at the odd figure before him, which, at all times more calculated to provoke mirth than anger, was especially so at that moment, when with one knee upon the ground, Mr. Folair twirled his old hat round upon his hand, and affected the extremest agony lest any of the nap should have been knocked off—an ornament which it is almost superfluous to say, it had not boasted for many months.

'Come, sir,' said Nicholas, laughing in spite of himself. 'Have the goodness to explain.'

'Why, I'll tell you how it is,' said Mr. Folair, sitting himself down in a chair with great coolness. 'Since you came here Lenville has done nothing but second business, and, instead of having a reception every night as he used to have, they have let him come on as if he was nobody.'

'What do you mean by a reception?' asked Nicholas.

'Jupiter!' exclaimed Mr. Folair, 'what an unsophisticated shepherd you are, Johnson! Why, applause from the house when you first come on. So he has gone on night after night, never getting a hand, and you getting a couple of rounds at least, and sometimes three, till at length he got quite desperate, and had half a mind last night to play Tybalt with a real sword, and pink you—not dangerously, but just enough to lay you up for a month or two.'

'Very considerate,' remarked Nicholas.

'Yes, I think it was under the circumstances; his professional reputation being at stake,' said Mr. Folair, quite seriously. 'But his heart failed him, and he cast about for some other way of annoying you, and making himself popular at the same time—for that's the point. Notoriety, notoriety, is the thing. Bless you, if he had pinked you,' said Mr. Folair, stopping to make a calculation in his mind, 'it would have been worth—ah, it would have been worth eight or ten shillings a week to him. All the town would have come to see the actor who nearly killed a man by mistake; I shouldn't wonder if it had got him an engagement in London. However, he was obliged to try some other mode of getting popular, and this one occurred to him. It's a clever idea, really. If you had shown the white feather, and let him pull your nose, he'd have got it into the paper; if you had sworn the peace against him, it would have been into the paper too, and he'd have been just as much talked about as you—don't you see?'

'Oh certainly,' rejoined Nicholas; 'but suppose I were to turn the tables, and pull *his* nose, what then? Would that make his fortune?'

'Why, I don't think it would,' replied Mr. Folair, scratching his head, 'because there wouldn't be any romance about it, and he wouldn't be favourably known. To tell you the truth though, he didn't calculate much upon that, for you 're always so mild spoken, and are so popular among the women, that we didn't suspect you of showing fight. If you did, however, he has a way of getting out of it easily, depend upon that.'

'Has he?' repeated Nicholas. 'We will try to-morrow morning. In the mean time, you can give whatever account of our interview you like best. Good night.'

As Mr. Folair was pretty well known among his fellow-actors for a man who delighted in mischief, and was by no means scrupulous, Nicholas had not much doubt that he had secretly prompted the tragedian in the course he had taken, and, moreover, that he would have carried his mission with a very high hand if he had not been disconcerted by the very unexpected demonstrations with which it had been received. It was not worth his while to be serious with him, however, so he dismissed the pantomimist, with a gentle hint that if he offended again it would be under the penalty of a broken head; and Mr. Folair, taking the caution in exceedingly good part, walked away to confer with his principal and give such an account of his proceedings as he might think best calculated to carry on the joke.

He had no doubt reported that Nicholas was in a state of extreme bodily fear; for when that young gentleman walked with much deliberation down to the theatre next morning at the usual hour, he found

all the company assembled in evident expectation, and
Mr. Lenville, with his severest stage face, sitting
majestically on a table, whistling defiance.

Now the ladies were on the side of Nicholas, and
the gentlemen (being jealous) were on the side of
the disappointed tragedian; so that the latter formed
a little group about the redoubtable Mr. Lenville, and
the former looked on at a little distance in some trepidation and anxiety. On Nicholas stopping to salute
them, Mr. Lenville laughed a scornful laugh, and
made some general remark touching the natural history of puppies.

'Oh!' said Nicholas, looking quietly round, 'are you
there?'

'Slave!' returned Mr. Lenville, flourishing his right
arm, and approaching Nicholas with a theatrical
stride. But somehow he appeared just at that
moment a little startled, as if Nicholas did not look
quite so frightened as he had expected, and came all
at once to an awkward halt, at which the assembled
ladies burst into a shrill laugh.

'Object of my scorn and hatred!' said Mr. Lenville, 'I hold ye in contempt.'

Nicholas laughed in very unexpected enjoyment of
this performance; and the ladies, by way of encouragement, laughed louder than before; whereat Mr.
Lenville assumed his bitterest smile, and expressed his
opinion that they were 'minions.'

'But they shall not protect ye!' said the tragedian,
taking an upward look at Nicholas, beginning at his
boots and ending at the crown of his head, and then a
downward one, beginning at the crown of his head,
and ending at his boots—which two looks, as everybody knows, express defiance on the stage. 'They
shall not protect ye—boy!'

Thus speaking, Mr. Lenville folded his arms, and

treated Nicholas to that expression of face with which, in melodramatic performances, he was in the habit of regarding the tyrannical kings when they said, 'Away with him to the deepest dungeon beneath the castle moat'; and which, accompanied with a little jingling of fetters, had been known to produce great effects in its time.

Whether it was the absence of the fetters or not, it made no very deep impression on Mr. Lenville's adversary, however, but rather seemed to increase the good-humour expressed in his countenance; in which stage of the contest, one or two gentlemen, who had come out expressly to witness the pulling of Nicholas's nose, grew impatient, murmuring that if it were to be done at all it had better be done at once, and that if Mr. Lenville didn't mean to do it he had better say so, and not keep them waiting there. Thus urged, the tragedian adjusted the cuff of his right coat sleeve for the performance of the operation, and walked in a very stately manner up to Nicholas, who suffered him to approach to within the requisite distance, and then, without the smallest discomposure, knocked him down.

Before the discomfited tragedian could raise his head from the boards, Mrs. Lenville (who, as has been before hinted, was in an interesting state) rushed from the rear rank of ladies, and uttering a piercing scream threw herself upon the body.

'Do you see this, monster? Do you see *this*?' cried Mr. Lenville, sitting up, and pointing to his prostrate lady, who was holding him very tight round the waist.

'Come,' said Nicholas, nodding his head, 'apologise for the insolent note you wrote to me last night, and waste no more time in talking.'

'Never!' cried Mr. Lenville.

'Yes—yes—yes!' screamed the wife. 'For my sake

—for mine, Lenville—forego all idle forms, unless you would see me a blighted corse at your feet.'

'This is affecting!' said Mr. Lenville, looking round him, and drawing the back of his hand across his eyes. 'The ties of nature are strong. The weak husband and the father—the father that is to be—relents. I apologise.'

'Humbly and submissively?' said Nicholas.

'Humbly and submissively,' returned the tragedian, scowling upward. 'But only to save her,—for a time will come—'

'Very good,' said Nicholas; 'I hope Mrs. Lenville may have a good one; and when it does come, and you are a father, you shall retract it if you have the courage. There. Be careful, sir, to what lengths your jealousy carries you another time; and be careful, also, before you venture too far, to ascertain your rival's temper.' With this parting advice Nicholas picked up Mr. Lenville's ash stick which had flown out of his hand, and breaking it in half, threw him the pieces and withdrew.

The profoundest deference was paid to Nicholas that night, and the people who had been most anxious to have his nose pulled in the morning, embraced occasions of taking him aside, and telling him with great feeling, how very friendly they took it that he should have treated that Lenville so properly, who was a most unbearable fellow, and on whom they had all, by a remarkable coincidence, at one time or other contemplated the infliction of condign punishment, which they had only been restrained from administering by considerations of mercy; indeed, to judge from the invariable termination of all these stories, there never was such a charitable and kind-hearted set of people as the male members of Mr. Crummles's company.

Nicholas bore his triumph, as he had his success in

the little world of the theatre, with the utmost moderation and good-humour. The crest-fallen Mr. Lenville made an expiring effort to obtain revenge by sending a boy into the gallery to hiss, but he fell a sacrifice to popular indignation, and was promptly turned out without having his money back.

'Well, Smike,' said Nicholas when the first piece was over, and he had almost finished dressing to go home, 'is there any letter yet?'

'Yes,' replied Smike, 'I got this one from the post-office.'

'From Newman Noggs,' said Nicholas, casting his eye upon the cramped direction; 'it's no easy matter to make his writing out. Let me see—let me see.'

By dint of poring over the letter for half an hour, he contrived to make himself master of the contents, which were certainly not of a nature to set his mind at ease. Newman took upon himself to send back the ten pounds, observing that he had ascertained that neither Mrs. Nickleby nor Kate was in actual want of money at the moment, and that a time might shortly come when Nicholas might want it more. He entreated him not to be alarmed at what he was about to say;—there was no bad news—they were in good health—but he thought circumstances might occur, or were occurring, which would render it absolutely necessary that Kate should have her brother's protection, and if so, Newman said, he would write to him to that effect, either by the next post or the next but one.

Nicholas read this passage very often, and the more he thought of it the more he began to fear some treachery upon the part of Ralph. Once or twice he felt tempted to repair to London at all hazards without an hour's delay, but a little reflection assured him that if such a step were necessary, Newman would have spoken out and told him so at once.

'At all events I should prepare them here for the possibility of my going away suddenly,' said Nicholas; 'I should lose no time in doing that.' As the thought occurred to him, he took up his hat and hurried to the green-room.

'Well, Mr. Johnson,' said Mrs. Crummles, who was seated there in full regal costume, with the phenomenon as the Maiden in her maternal arms, 'next week for Ryde, then for Winchester, then for—'

'I have some reason to fear,' interrupted Nicholas, 'that before you leave here my career with you will have closed.'

'Closed!' cried Mrs. Crummles, raising her hands in astonishment.

'Closed!' cried Miss Snevellicci, trembling so much in her tights that she actually laid her hand upon the shoulder of the manageress for support.

'Why he don't mean to say he's going!' exclaimed Mrs. Grudden, making her way towards Mrs. Crummles. 'Hoity toity! Nonsense.'

The phenomenon, being of an affectionate nature and moreover excitable, raised a loud cry, and Miss Belvawney and Miss Bravassa actually shed tears. Even the male performers stopped in their conversation, and echoed the word 'Going!' although some among them (and they had been the loudest in their congratulations that day) winked at each other as though they would not be sorry to lose such a favoured rival; an opinion, indeed, which the honest Mr. Folair, who was ready dressed for the savage, openly stated in so many words to a demon with whom he was sharing a pot of porter.

Nicholas briefly said that he feared it would be so,

although he could not yet speak with any degree of certainty; and getting away as soon as he could, went home to con Newman's letter once more, and speculate upon it afresh.

How trifling all that had been occupying his time and thoughts for many weeks seemed to him during that sleepless night, and how constantly and incessantly present to his imagination was the one idea that Kate in the midst of some great trouble and distress might even then be looking—and vainly too—for him!

CHAPTER XXX

FESTIVITIES ARE HELD IN HONOUR OF NICHOLAS, WHO SUDDENLY WITHDRAWS HIMSELF FROM THE SOCIETY OF MR. VINCENT CRUMMLES AND HIS THEATRICAL COMPANIONS

MR. VINCENT CRUMMLES was no sooner acquainted with the public announcement which Nicholas had made relative to the probability of his shortly ceasing to be a member of the company, than he evinced many tokens of grief and consternation; and, in the extremity of his despair, even held out certain vague promises of a speedy improvement not only in the amount of his regular salary, but also in the contingent emoluments appertaining to his authorship. Finding Nicholas bent upon quitting the society (for he had now determined that, even if no further tidings came from Newman, he would, at all hazards, ease his mind by repairing to London and ascertaining the exact position of his sister) Mr. Crummles was fain to content himself by calculating the chances of his coming back again, and taking prompt and energetic measures to make the most of him before he went away.

'Let me see,' said Mr. Crummles, taking off his outlaw's wig, the better to arrive at a cool-headed view of the whole case. 'Let me see. This is Wednesday night. We 'll have posters out the first thing in the morning, announcing positively your last appearance for to-morrow.'

'But perhaps it may not be my last appearance, you know,' said Nicholas. 'Unless I am summoned away, I should be sorry to inconvenience you by leaving before the end of the week.'

'So much the better,' returned Mr. Crummles. 'We can have positively your last appearance, on Thursday—re-engagement for one night more, on Friday—and, yielding to the wishes of numerous influential patrons, who were disappointed in obtaining seats, on Saturday. That ought to bring three very decent houses.'

'Then I am to make three last appearances, am I?' inquired Nicholas, smiling.

'Yes,' rejoined the manager, scratching his head with an air of some vexation; 'three is not enough, and it 's very bungling and irregular not to have more, but if we can't help it we can't, so there 's no use in talking. A novelty would be very desirable. You couldn't sing a comic song on the pony's back, could you?'

'No,' replied Nicholas, 'I couldn't indeed.'

'It has drawn money before now,' said Mr. Crummles, with a look of disappointment. 'What do you think of a brilliant display of fireworks?'

'That it would be rather expensive,' replied Nicholas, drily.

'Eighteenpence would do it,' said Mr. Crummles.

'You on the top of a pair of steps with the phenomenon in an attitude; "Farewell" on a transparency behind; and nine people at the wings with a squib in
each hand—all the dozen and a half going off at once
—it would be very grand—awful from the front,
quite awful.'

As Nicholas appeared by no means impressed with
the solemnity of the proposed effect, but, on the contrary, received the proposition in a most irreverent
manner, and laughed at it very heartily, Mr.
Crummles abandoned the project in its birth, and
gloomily observed that they must make up the best
bill they could with combats and hornpipes, and so
stick to the legitimate drama.

For the purpose of carrying this object into instant
execution, the manager at once repaired to a small
dressing-room, adjacent, where Mrs. Crummles was
then occupied in exchanging the habiliments of a
melodramatic empress for the ordinary attire of
matrons in the nineteenth century. And with the assistance of this lady, and the accomplished Mrs. Grudden (who had quite a genius for making out bills, being a great hand at throwing in the notes of admiration, and knowing from long experience exactly
where the largest capitals ought to go), he seriously
applied himself to the composition of the poster.

'Heigho!' sighed Nicholas, as he threw himself back
in the prompter's chair, after telegraphing the need-
ful directions to Smike, who had been playing a
meagre tailor in the interlude, with one skirt to his
coat, and a little pocket handkerchief with a large hole
in it, and a woollen nightcap, and a red nose, and other
distinctive marks peculiar to tailors on the stage.
'Heigho! I wish all this were over.'

'Over, Mr. Johnson!' repeated a female voice behind him, in a kind of plaintive surprise.

'It was an ungallant speech, certainly,' said Nicholas, looking up to see who the speaker was, and recognising Miss Snevellicci. 'I would not have made it if I had known you had been within hearing.'

'What a dear that Mr. Digby is!' said Miss Snevellicci, as the tailor went off on the opposite side, at the end of the piece with great applause. (Smike's theatrical name was Digby.)

'I 'll tell him presently, for his gratification, that you said so,' returned Nicholas.

'Oh you naughty thing!' rejoined Miss Snevellicci. 'I don't know though, that I should mind *his* knowing my opinion of him; with some other people, indeed, it might be—' Here Miss Snevellicci stopped, as though waiting to be questioned, but no questioning came, for Nicholas was thinking about more serious matters.

'How kind it is of you,' resumed Miss Snevellicci, after a short silence, 'to sit waiting here for him night after night, night after night, no matter how tired you are; and taking so much pains with him, and doing it all with as much delight and readiness as if you were coining gold by it!'

'He well deserves all the kindness I can show him, and a great deal more,' said Nicholas. 'He is the most grateful, single-hearted, affectionate creature, that ever breathed.'

'So odd, too,' remarked Miss Snevellicci, 'isn't he?'

'God help him, and those who have made him so; he is indeed,' rejoined Nicholas, shaking his head.

'He is such a devilish close chap,' said Mr. Folair, who had come up a little before, and now joined in the conversation. 'Nobody can ever get anything out of him.'

'What *should* they get out of him?' asked Nicholas, turning round with some abruptness.

'Zooks! what a fire-eater you are, Johnson!' returned Mr. Folair, pulling up the heel of his dancing shoe. 'I 'm only talking of the natural curiosity of the people here, to know what he has been about all his life.'

'Poor fellow! it is pretty plain, I should think, that he has not the intellect to have been about anything of much importance to them or anybody else,' said Nicholas.

'Ay,' rejoined the actor, contemplating the effect of his face in a lamp-reflector, 'but that involves the whole question, you know.'

'What question?' asked Nicholas.

'Why, the who he is and what he is, and how you two, who are so different, came to be such close companions,' replied Mr. Folair, delighted with the opportunity of saying something disagreeable. 'That 's in everybody's mouth.'

'The "everybody" of the theatre, I suppose?' said Nicholas, contemptuously.

'In it and out of it too,' replied the actor. 'Why, you know, Lenville says—'

'I thought I had silenced him effectually,' interrupted Nicholas, reddening.

'Perhaps you have,' rejoined the immovable Mr. Folair; 'if you have, he said this before he was silenced: Lenville says that you 're a regular stick of an actor, and that it 's only the mystery about you that has caused you to go down with the people here, and that Crummles keeps it up for his own sake; though Lenville says he don't believe there 's anything at all in it, except your having got into a scrape and run away from somewhere, for doing something or other.'

'Oh!' said Nicholas, forcing a smile.

'That 's a part of what he says,' added Mr. Folair.

'I mention it as the friend of both parties, and in strict confidence. *I* don't agree with him, you know. He says he takes Digby to be more knave than fool; and old Fluggers, who does the heavy business you know, *he* says that when he delivered messages at Covent Garden the season before last, there used to be a pickpocket hovering about the coach-stand who had exactly the face of Digby; though, as he very properly says, Digby may not be the same, but only his brother, or some near relation.'

'Oh!' cried Nicholas again.

'Yes,' said Mr. Folair, with undisturbed calmness, 'that's what they say. I thought I'd tell you, because really you ought to know. Oh! here's this blessed phenomenon at last. Ugh, you little imposition, I should like to—quite ready, my darling,—humbug—Ring up Mrs. G., and let the favourite wake 'em!'

Uttering in a loud voice such of the latter allusions as were complimentary to the unconscious phenomenon, and giving the rest in a confidential 'aside' to Nicholas, Mr. Folair followed the ascent of the curtain with his eyes, regarded with a sneer the reception of Miss Crummles as the Maiden, and, falling back a step or two to advance with the better effect, uttered a preliminary howl, and 'went on' chattering his teeth and brandishing his tin tomahawk as the Indian Savage.

'So these are some of the stories they invent about us, and bandy from mouth to mouth!' thought Nicholas. 'If a man would commit an inexpiable offence against any society, large or small, let him be successful. They will forgive him any crime but that.'

'You surely don't mind what that malicious creature says, Mr. Johnson?' observed Miss Snevellicci in her most winning tones.

'Not I,' replied Nicholas. 'If I were going to re-main here, I might think it worth my while to embroil myself. As it is, let them talk till they are hoarse. But here,' added Nicholas, as Smike approached, 'here comes the subject of a portion of their good-nature, so let he and I say good night together.'

'No, I will not let either of you say anything of the kind,' returned Miss Snevellicci. 'You must come home and see mamma, who only came to Portsmouth to-day, and is dying to behold you. Led, my dear, persuade Mr. Johnson.'

'Oh, I'm sure,' returned Miss Ledrook with con-siderable vivacity, 'if *you* can't persuade him—' Miss Ledrook said no more, but intimated, by a dexterous playfulness, that if Miss Snevellicci couldn't persuade him, nobody could.

'Mr. and Mrs. Lillyvick have taken lodgings in our house, and share our sitting-room for the present,' said Miss Snevellicci. 'Won't that induce you?'

'Surely,' returned Nicholas, 'I can require no pos-sible inducement beyond your invitation.'

'Oh no! I dare say,' rejoined Miss Snevellicci. And Miss Ledrook said, 'Upon my word!' Upon which Miss Snevellicci said that Miss Ledrook was a giddy thing; and Miss Ledrook said that Miss Snevel-licci needn't colour up quite so much; and Miss Snevellicci beat Miss Ledrook, and Miss Ledrook beat Miss Snevellicci.

'Come,' said Miss Ledrook, 'it's high time we were there, or we shall have poor Mrs. Snevellicci thinking that you have run away with her daughter, Mr. Johnson; and then we should have a pretty to-do.'

'My dear Led,' remonstrated Miss Snevellicci, 'how you do talk!'

Miss Ledrook made no answer, but taking Smike's arm in hers, left her friend and Nicholas to follow at their pleasure; which it pleased them, or rather pleased Nicholas, who had no great fancy for a *tête-à-tête* under the circumstances, to do at once.

There were not wanting matters of conversation when they reached the street, for it turned out that Miss Snevellicci had a small basket to carry home, and Miss Ledrook a small band-box, both containing such minor articles of theatrical costume as lady performers usually carried to and fro every evening. Nicholas would insist upon carrying the basket, and Miss Snevellicci would insist upon carrying it herself, which gave rise to a struggle, in which Nicholas captured the basket and the band-box likewise. Then Nicholas said, that he wondered what could possibly be inside the basket, and attempted to peep in, whereat Miss Snevellicci screamed, and declared that if she thought he had seen, she was sure she should faint away. This declaration was followed by a similar attempt on the band-box, and similar demonstrations on the part of Miss Ledrook, and then both ladies vowed that they wouldn't move a step further until Nicholas had promised that he wouldn't offer to peep again. At last Nicholas pledged himself to betray no further curiosity, and they walked on: both ladies giggling very much, and declaring that they never had seen such a wicked creature in all their born days—never.

Lightening the way with such pleasantry as this, they arrived at the tailor's house in no time; and here they made quite a little party, there being present besides Mr. Lillyvick and Mrs. Lillyvick, not only Miss Snevellicci's mamma, but her papa also. And an uncommonly fine man Miss Snevellicci's papa was, with a hook nose, and a white forehead, and curly black hair, and high cheek bones, and altogether quite a handsome face, only a little pimply as though with drinking. He had a very broad chest had Miss Snevellicci's papa, and he wore a threadbare blue dress coat buttoned with gilt buttons tight across it; and he no sooner saw Nicholas come into the room, than he whipped the two fore-fingers of his right hand in between the two centre buttons, and sticking his other arm gracefully a-kimbo, seemed to say, 'Now, here I am, my buck, and what have you got to say to me?'

Such was, and in such an attitude sat Miss Snevellicci's papa, who had been in the profession ever since he had first played the ten-year-old imps in the Christmas pantomimes; who could sing a little, dance a little, fence a little, act a little, and do everything a little, but not much; who had been sometimes in the ballet, and sometimes in the chorus, at every theatre in London; who was always selected in virtue of his figure to play the military visitors and the speechless noblemen; who always wore a smart dress, and came on arm-in-arm with a smart lady in short petticoats,— and always did it too with such an air that people in the pit had been several times known to cry out 'Bravo!' under the impression that he was somebody. Such was Miss Snevellicci's papa, upon whom some envious persons cast the imputation that he occasionally beat Miss Snevellicci's mamma, who was still a dancer, with a neat little figure and some remains of good looks, and who now sat, as she danced,—being rather too old for the full glare of the foot-lights,—in the back-ground.

To these good people Nicholas was presented with much formality. The introduction being completed, Miss Snevellicci's papa (who was scented with rum-and-water) said that he was delighted to make the acquaintance of a gentleman so highly talented; and furthermore remarked, that there hadn't been such a hit made—no, not since the first appearance of his friend Mr. Glavormelly, at the Coburg.

'You have seen him, sir?' said Miss Snevellicci's papa.

'No, really I never did,' replied Nicholas.

'You never saw my friend Glavormelly, sir!' said Miss Snevellicci's papa. 'Then you have never seen acting yet. If he had lived—'

'Oh, he is dead, is he?' interrupted Nicholas.

'He is,' said Mr. Snevellicci, 'but he isn't in Westminster Abbey, more's the shame. He was a— Well, no matter. He is gone to that bourne from whence no traveller returns. I hope he is appreciated *there.*'

So saying, Miss Snevellicci's papa rubbed the tip of his nose with a very yellow silk handkerchief, and gave the company to understand that these recollections overcame him.

'Well, Mr. Lillyvick,' said Nicholas, 'and how are you?'

'Quite well, sir,' replied the collector. 'There is nothing like the married state, sir, depend upon it.'

'Indeed?' said Nicholas, laughing.

'Nothing like it, sir,' replied Mr. Lillyvick solemnly. 'How do you think,' whispered the collector, drawing him aside, 'how do you think she looks to-night?'

'As handsome as ever,' replied Nicholas, glancing at the late Miss Petowker.

'Why, there's a air about her, sir,' whispered the collector, 'that I never saw in anybody. Look at her, now she moves to put the kettle on. There! Isn't it fascination, sir?'

'You 're a lucky man,' said Nicholas.

'Ha, ha, ha!' rejoined the collector. 'No. Do you think I am though, eh? Perhaps I may be, perhaps

I may be. I say, I couldn't have done much better if I had been a young man, could I? You couldn't have done much better yourself, could you—eh—could you?' With such inquiries, and many more such, Mr. Lillyvick jerked his elbow into Nicholas's side, and chuckled till his face became quite purple in the attempt to keep down his satisfaction.

By this time the cloth had been laid under the joint superintendence of all the ladies, upon two tables put together, one being high and narrow, and the other low and broad. There were oysters at the top, sausages at the bottom, a pair of snuffers in the centre, and baked potatoes wherever it was most convenient to put them. Two additional chairs were brought in from the bedroom; Miss Snevellicci sat at the head of the table, and Mr. Lillyvick at the foot; and Nicholas had not only the honour of sitting next Miss Snevellicci, but of having Miss Snevellicci's mamma on his right hand, and Miss Snevellicci's papa over the way. In short, he was the hero of the feast; and when the table was cleared and something warm introduced, Miss Snevellicci's papa got up and proposed his health in a speech containing such affecting allusions to his coming departure, that Miss Snevellicci wept, and was compelled to retire into the bedroom.

'Hush! Don't take any notice of it,' said Miss Ledrook, peeping in from the bedroom. 'Say, when she comes back, that she exerts herself too much.'

Miss Ledrook eked out this speech with so many mysterious nods and frowns before she shut the door again, that a profound silence came upon all the company, during which Miss Snevellicci's papa looked very big indeed—several sizes larger than life—at everybody in turn, but particularly at Nicholas, and kept on perpetually emptying his tumbler and filling it again, until the ladies returned in a cluster, with Miss Snevellicci among them.

'You needn't alarm yourself a bit, Mr. Snevellicci,' said Mrs. Lillyvick. 'She is only a little weak and nervous; she has been so ever since the morning.'

'Oh,' said Mr. Snevellicci, 'that's all, is it?'

'Oh yes, that's all. Don't make a fuss about it,' cried all the ladies together.

Now this was not exactly the kind of reply suited to Mr. Snevellicci's importance as a man and a father, so he picked out the unfortunate Mrs. Snevellicci, and asked her what the devil she meant by talking to him in that way.

'Dear me, my dear!' said Mrs. Snevellicci.

'Don't call me your dear, ma'am,' said Mr. Snevellicci, 'if you please.'

'Pray, pa, don't,' interposed Miss Snevellicci.

'Don't what, my child?'

'Talk in that way.'

'Why not?' said Mr. Snevellicci. 'I hope you don't suppose there's anybody here who is to prevent my talking as I like?'

'Nobody wants to, pa,' rejoined his daughter.

'Nobody would if they did want to,' said Mr. Snevellicci. 'I am not ashamed of myself. Snevellicci is my name. I'm to be found in Broad Court, Bow Street, when I'm in town. If I'm not at home, let any man ask for me at the stage door. Damme, they know me at the stage door I suppose? Most men have seen my portrait at the cigar shop round the corner. I've been mentioned in the newspapers before now, haven't I? Talk! I'll tell you what; if I found out that any man had been tampering with the affections of my daughter, I wouldn't talk. I'd astonish him without talking; that's my way.'

So saying, Mr. Snevellicci struck the palm of his

left hand three smart blows with his clenched fist; pulled a phantom nose with his right thumb and forefinger, and swallowed another glassful at a draught. 'That's my way,' repeated Mr. Snevellicci.

Most public characters have their failings; and the truth is that Mr. Snevellicci was a little addicted to drinking; or, if the whole truth must be told, that he was scarcely ever sober. He knew in his cups three distinct stages of intoxication,—the dignified—the quarrelsome—the amorous. When professionally engaged he never got beyond the dignified; in private circles he went through all three, passing from one to another with a rapidity of transition often rather perplexing to those who had not the honour of his acquaintance.

Thus Mr. Snevellicci had no sooner swallowed another glassful than he smiled upon all present in happy forgetfulness of having exhibited symptoms of pugnacity, and proposed 'The ladies! Bless their hearts!' in a most vivacious manner.

'I love 'em,' said Mr. Snevellicci, looking round the table, 'I love 'em, every one.'

'Not every one,' reasoned Mr. Lillyvick, mildly.

'Yes, every one,' repeated Mr. Snevellicci.

'That would include the married ladies, you know,' said Mr. Lillyvick.

'I love them too, sir,' said Mr. Snevellicci.

The collector looked into the surrounding faces with an aspect of grave astonishment, seeming to say, 'This is a nice man!' and appeared a little surprised that Mrs. Lillyvick's manner yielded no evidences of horror and indignation.

'One good turn deserves another,' said Mr. Snevellicci. 'I love them and they love me.' And as if this avowal were not made in sufficient disregard and defiance of all moral obligations, what did Mr. Snevellicci do? He winked—winked, openly and undisguisedly; winked with his right eye—upon Henrietta Lillyvick!

The collector fell back in his chair in the intensity of his astonishment. If anybody had winked at her as Henrietta Petowker, it would have been indecorous in the last degree; but as Mrs. Lillyvick! While he thought of it in a cold perspiration, and wondered whether it was possible that he could be dreaming, Mr. Snevellicci repeated the wink, and drinking to Mrs. Lillyvick in dumb show, actually blew her a kiss! Mr. Lillyvick left his chair, walked straight up to the other end of the table, and fell upon him—literally fell upon him—instantaneously. Mr. Lillyvick was no light weight, and consequently when he fell upon Mr. Snevellicci, Mr. Snevellicci fell under the table. Mr. Lillyvick followed him, and the ladies screamed.

'What is the matter with the men? Are they mad?' cried Nicholas, diving under the table, dragging up the collector by main force, and thrusting him, all doubled up, into a chair, as if he had been a stuffed figure. 'What do you mean to do? What do you want to do? What is the matter with you?'

While Nicholas raised up the collector, Smike had performed the same office for Mr. Snevellicci, who now regarded his late adversary in tipsy amazement.

'Look here, sir,' replied Mr. Lillyvick, pointing to his astonished wife, 'here is purity and elegance combined, whose feelings have been outraged—violated, sir!'

'Lor, what nonsense he talks!' exclaimed Mrs. Lillyvick in answer to the inquiring look of Nicholas. 'Nobody has said anything to me.'

'Said, Henrietta!' cried the collector. 'Didn't I

see him—' Mr. Lillyvick couldn't bring himself to utter the word, but he counterfeited the motion of the eye.

'Well!' cried Mrs. Lillyvick. 'Do you suppose nobody is ever to look at me? A pretty thing to be married indeed, if that was law!'

'You didn't mind it?' cried the collector.

'Mind it!' repeated Mrs. Lillyvick contemptuously. 'You ought to go down on your knees and beg everybody's pardon, that you ought.'

'Pardon, my dear?' said the dismayed collector.

'Yes, and mine first,' replied Mrs. Lillyvick. 'Do you suppose *I* ain't the best judge of what's proper and what's improper?'

'To be sure,' cried all the ladies. 'Do you suppose *we* shouldn't be the first to speak, if there was anything that ought to be taken notice of?'

'Do you suppose *they* don't know, sir?' said Miss Snevellicci's papa, pulling up his collar, and muttering something about a punching of heads, and being only withheld by considerations of age. With which Miss Snevellicci's papa looked steadily and sternly at Mr. Lillyvick for some seconds, and then rising deliberately from his chair, kissed the ladies all round, beginning with Mrs. Lillyvick.

The unhappy collector looked piteously at his wife, as if to see whether there was any one trait of Miss Petowker left in Mrs. Lillyvick, and finding too surely that there was not, begged pardon of all the company with great humility, and sat down such a crest-fallen, dispirited, disenchanted man, that despite all his selfishness and dotage, he was quite an object of compassion.

Miss Snevellicci's papa being greatly exalted by this triumph, and incontestable proof of his popularity with the fair sex, quickly grew convivial, not to say uproarious; volunteering more than one song of no inconsiderable length, and regaling the social circle between-whiles with recollections of divers splendid women who had been supposed to entertain a passion for himself, several of whom he toasted by name, taking occasion to remark at the same time that if he had been a little more alive to his own interest, he might have been rolling at that moment in his chariot-and-four. These reminiscences appeared to awaken no very torturing pangs in the breast of Mrs. Snevellicci, who was sufficiently occupied in descanting to Nicholas upon the manifold accomplishments and merits of her daughter. Nor was the young lady herself at all behindhand in displaying her choicest allurements; but these, heightened as they were by the artifices of Miss Ledrook, had no effect whatever in increasing the attentions of Nicholas, who, with the precedent of Miss Squeers still fresh in his memory, steadily resisted every fascination, and placed so strict a guard upon his behaviour that when he had taken his leave the ladies were unanimous in pronouncing him quite a monster of insensibility.

Next day the posters appeared in due course, and the public were informed, in all the colours of the rainbow, and in letters afflicted with every possible variation of spinal deformity, how that Mr. Johnson would have the honour of making his last appearance that evening, and how that an early application for places was requested, in consequence of the extraordinary overflow attendant on his performances. It being a remarkable fact in theatrical history, but one long since established beyond dispute, that it is a hopeless endeavour to attract people to a theatre unless they can be first brought to believe that they will never get into it.

Nicholas was somewhat at a loss, on entering the

theatre at night, to account for the unusual perturbation and excitement visible in the countenances of all the company, but he was not long in doubt as to the cause, for before he could make any inquiry respecting it Mr. Crummles approached, and in an agitated tone of voice, informed him that there was a London manager in the boxes.

'It's the phenomenon, depend upon it, sir,' said Crummles, dragging Nicholas to the little hole in the curtain that he might look through at the London manager. 'I have not the smallest doubt it's the fame of the phenomenon—that's the man, him in the great-coat and no shirt-collar. She shall have ten pound a week, Johnson; she shall not appear on the London boards for a farthing less. They shan't engage her either, unless they engage Mrs. Crummles too—twenty pound a week for the pair; or I'll tell you what, I'll throw in myself and the two boys, and they shall have the family for thirty. I can't say fairer than that. They must take us all, if none of us will go without the others. That's the way some of the London people do, and it always answers. Thirty pound a week. It's too cheap, Johnson. It's dirt cheap.'

Nicholas replied that it certainly was; and Mr. Vincent Crummles taking several huge pinches of snuff to compose his feelings, hurried away to tell Mrs. Crummles that he had quite settled the only terms that could be accepted, and had resolved not to abate one single farthing.

When everybody was dressed and the curtain went up, the excitement occasioned by the presence of the London manager increased a thousand-fold. Everybody happened to know that the London manager had come down specially to witness his or her performance, and all were in a flutter of anxiety and expectation. Some of those who were not on in the first scene, hurried to the wings, and there stretched their necks to have a peep at him; others stole up into the two little private boxes over the stage-doors, and from that position reconnoitred the London manager. Once the London manager was seen to smile. He smiled at the comic countryman's pretending to catch a blue-bottle, while Mrs. Crummles was making her greatest effect. 'Very good, my fine fellow,' said Mr. Crummles, shaking his fist at the comic country-man when he came off, 'you leave this company next Saturday night.'

In the same way, everybody who was on the stage beheld no audience but one individual; everybody played to the London manager. When Mr. Len-ville in a sudden burst of passion called the emperor a miscreant, and then biting his glove, said, 'But I must dissemble,' instead of looking gloomily at the boards and so waiting for his cue, as is proper in such cases, he kept his eye fixed upon the London man-ager. When Miss Bravassa sang her song at her lover, who according to custom stood ready to shake hands with her between the verses, they looked, not at each other, but at the London manager. Mr. Crummles died point blank at him; and when the two guards came in to take the body off after a very hard death, it was seen to open its eyes and glance at the London manager. At length the London manager was discovered to be asleep, and shortly after that he woke up and went away, whereupon all the company fell foul of the unhappy comic countryman, declaring that his buffoonery was the sole cause; and Mr. Crummles said, that he had put up with it a long time, but that he really couldn't stand it any longer, and therefore would feel obliged by his looking out for another engagement.

All this was the occasion of much amusement to Nicholas, whose only feeling upon the subject was one of sincere satisfaction that the great man went away before he appeared. He went through his part in the two last pieces as briskly as he could, and having been received with unbounded favour and un-precedented applause—so said the bills for next day, which had been printed an hour or two before—he took Smike's arm and walked home to bed.

With the post next morning came a letter from Newman Noggs, very inky, very short, very dirty, very small, and very mysterious, urging Nicholas to return to London instantly; not to lose an instant; to be there that night if possible.

'I will,' said Nicholas. 'Heaven knows I have remained here for the best, and sorely against my own will; but even now I may have dallied too long. What can have happened? Smike, my good fellow, here—take my purse. Put our things together, and pay what little debts we owe—quick, and we shall be in time for the morning coach. I will only tell them that we are going, and will return to you immediately.'

So saying, he took his hat, and hurrying away to the lodgings of Mr. Crummles, applied his hand to the knocker with such hearty good-will, that he awakened that gentleman, who was still in bed, and caused Mr. Bulph the pilot to take his morning's pipe very nearly out of his mouth in the extremity of his surprise.

The door being opened, Nicholas ran upstairs without any ceremony, and bursting into the darkened sitting-room on the one-pair front, found that the two Master Crummleses had sprung out of the sofa-bedstead and were putting on their clothes with great

THEATRICAL EMOTION OF MR. VINCENT CRUMMLES.

rapidity, under the impression that it was the middle of the night, and the next house was on fire.

Before he could undeceive them, Mr. Crummles came down in a flannel-gown and night-cap; and to him Nicholas briefly explained that circumstances had occurred which rendered it necessary for him to repair to London immediately.

'So good-bye,' said Nicholas; 'good-bye, good-bye.'

He was half way downstairs before Mr. Crummles had sufficiently recovered his surprise to gasp out something about the posters.

'I can't help it,' replied Nicholas. 'Set whatever I may have earned this week against them, or if that will not repay you, say at once what will. Quick, quick.'

'We'll cry quits about that,' returned Crummles. 'But can't we have one last night more?'

'Not an hour—not a minute,' replied Nicholas, impatiently.

'Won't you stop to say something to Mrs. Crummles?' asked the manager, following him down to the door.

'I couldn't stop if it were to prolong my life a score of years,' rejoined Nicholas. 'Here take my hand, and with it my hearty thanks. Oh! that I should have been fooling here!'

Accompanying these words with an impatient stamp upon the ground, he tore himself from the manager's detaining grasp, and darting rapidly down the street was out of sight in an instant.

'Dear me, dear me,' said Mr. Crummles, looking wistfully towards the point at which he had just disappeared; 'if he only acted like that, what a deal of money he'd draw! He should have kept upon this circuit; he'd have been very useful to me. But he don't know what's good for him. He is an impetuous youth. Young men are rash, very rash.'

Mr. Crummles being in a moralising mood, might possibly have moralised for some minutes longer if he had not mechanically put his hand towards his waistcoat pocket, where he was accustomed to keep his snuff. The absence of any pocket at all in the usual direction, suddenly recalled to his recollection the fact that he had no waistcoat on; and this leading him to a contemplation of the extreme scantiness of his attire, he shut the door abruptly, and retired upstairs with great precipitation.

Smike had made good speed while Nicholas was absent, and with his help everything was soon ready for their departure. They scarcely stopped to take a morsel of breakfast, and in less than half an hour arrived at the coach-office: quite out of breath with the haste they had made to reach it in time. There were yet a few minutes to spare, so, having secured the places, Nicholas hurried into a slop-seller's hard by, and bought Smike a great-coat. It would have been rather large for a substantial yeoman, but the shopman averring (and with considerable truth) that it was a most uncommon fit, Nicholas would have purchased it in his impatience if it had been twice the size.

As they hurried up to the coach, which was now in the open street and all ready for starting, Nicholas was not a little astonished to find himself suddenly clutched in a close and violent embrace, which nearly took him off his legs; nor was his amazement at all lessened by hearing the voice of Mr. Crummles exclaim, 'It is he—my friend, my friend!'

'Bless my heart,' cried Nicholas, struggling in the manager's arms, 'what are you about?'

The manager made no reply, but strained him to

his breast again, exclaiming as he did so, 'Farewell, my noble, my lion-hearted boy!'

In fact, Mr. Crummles, who could never lose any opportunity for professional display, had turned out for the express purpose of taking a public farewell of Nicholas; and to render it the more imposing, he was now, to that young gentleman's most profound annoyance, inflicting upon him a rapid succession of stage embraces, which, as everybody knows, are performed by the embracer's laying his or her chin on the shoulder of the object of affection, and looking over it. This Mr. Crummles did in the highest style of melodrama, pouring forth at the same time all the most dismal forms of farewell he could think of, out of the stock pieces. Nor was this all, for the elder Master Crummles was going through a similar ceremony with Smike; while Master Percy Crummles, with a very little second-hand camlet cloak, worn theatrically over his left shoulder, stood by, in the attitude of an attendant officer, waiting to convey the two victims to the scaffold.

The lookers-on laughed very heartily, and as it was as well to put a good face upon the matter, Nicholas laughed too when he had succeeded in disengaging himself; and rescuing the astonished Smike, climbed up to the coach roof after him, and kissed his hand in honour of the absent Mrs. Crummles as they rolled away.

CHAPTER XXXI

OF RALPH NICKLEBY AND NEWMAN NOGGS, AND SOME WISE PRECAUTIONS, THE SUCCESS OR FAILURE OF WHICH WILL APPEAR IN THE SEQUEL

IN blissful unconsciousness that his nephew was hastening at the utmost speed of four good horses towards his sphere of action, and that every passing minute diminished the distance between them, Ralph Nickleby sat that morning occupied in his customary avocations, and yet unable to prevent his thoughts wandering from time to time back to the interview which had taken place between himself and his niece on the previous day. At such intervals, after a few moments of abstraction, Ralph would mutter some peevish interjection, and apply himself with renewed steadiness of purpose to the ledger before him, but again and again the same train of thought came back despite all his efforts to prevent it, confusing him in his calculation, and utterly distracting his attention from the figures over which he bent. At length Ralph laid down his pen, and threw himself back in his chair as though he had made up his mind to allow the obtrusive current of reflection to take its own course, and, by giving it full scope, to rid himself of it effectually.

'I am not a man to be moved by a pretty face,' muttered Ralph sternly. 'There is a grinning skull beneath it, and men like me who look and work below the surface see that, and not its delicate covering. And yet I almost like the girl, or should if she had been less proudly and squeamishly brought up. If the boy were drowned or hanged, and the mother dead, this house should be her home. I wish they were, with all my soul.'

Notwithstanding the deadly hatred which Ralph felt towards Nicholas, and the bitter contempt with which he sneered at poor Mrs. Nickleby—notwithstanding the baseness with which he had behaved, and was then behaving, and would behave again if his interest prompted him, towards Kate herself—still there was, strange though it may seem, something humanising and even gentle in his thoughts at that moment. He thought of what his home might be if Kate were there; he placed her in the empty chair, looked upon her, heard her speak; he felt again upon his arm the gentle pressure of the trembling hand; he strewed his costly rooms with the hundred silent tokens of feminine presence and occupation; he came back again to the cold fireside and the silent dreary splendour; and in that one glimpse of a better nature, born as it was in selfish thoughts, the rich man felt himself friendless, childless, and alone. Gold, for the instant, lost its lustre in his eyes, for there were countless treasures of the heart which it could never purchase.

A very slight circumstance was sufficient to banish such reflections from the mind of such a man. As Ralph looked vacantly out across the yard towards the window of the other office, he became suddenly aware of the earnest observation of Newman Noggs, who, with his red nose almost touching the glass, feigned to be mending a pen with a rusty fragment of a knife, but was in reality staring at his employer with a countenance of the closest and most eager scrutiny.

Ralph exchanged his dreamy posture for his accustomed business attitude: the face of Newman disappeared, and the train of thought took to flight, all simultaneously and in an instant.

After a few minutes, Ralph rang his bell. Newman answered the summons, and Ralph raised his eyes stealthily to his face, as if he almost feared to read there, a knowledge of his recent thought.

There was not the smallest speculation, however, in the countenance of Newman Noggs. If it be possible to imagine a man, with two eyes in his head, and both wide open, looking in no direction whatever, and seeing nothing, Newman appeared to be that man while Ralph Nickleby regarded him.

'How now?' growled Ralph.

'Oh!' said Newman, throwing some intelligence into his eyes all at once, and dropping them on his master, 'I thought you rang.' With which laconic remark Newman turned round and hobbled away.

'Stop!' said Ralph.

Newman stopped; not at all disconcerted.

'I did ring.'

'I knew you did.'

'Then why do you offer to go if you know that?'

'I thought you rang to say you didn't ring,' replied Newman. 'You often do.'

'How dare you pry, and peer, and stare at me, sirrah?' demanded Ralph.

'Stare!' cried Newman, 'at *you!* Ha, ha!' which was all the explanation Newman deigned to offer.

'Be careful, sir,' said Ralph, looking steadily at him. 'Let me have no drunken fooling here. Do you see this parcel?'

'It's big enough,' rejoined Newman.

'Carry it into the City; to Cross, in Broad Street, and leave it there—quick. Do you hear?'

Newman gave a dogged kind of nod to express an

affirmative reply, and, leaving the room for a few seconds, returned with his hat. Having made various ineffectual attempts to fit the parcel (which was some two feet square) into the crown thereof, Newman took it under his arm, and after putting on his fingerless gloves with great precision and nicety, keeping his eyes fixed upon Mr. Ralph Nickleby all the time, he adjusted his hat upon his head with as much care, real or pretended, as if it were a brand-new one of the most expensive quality, and at last departed on his errand.

He executed his commission with great promptitude and despatch, only calling at one public-house for half a minute, and even that might be said to be in his way, for he went in at one door and came out at the other; but as he returned and had got so far homewards as the Strand, Newman began to loiter with the uncertain air of a man who has not quite made up his mind whether to halt or go straight forwards. After a very short consideration, the former inclination prevailed, and making towards the point he had had in his mind, Newman knocked a modest double-knock, or rather a nervous single one, at Miss La Creevy's door.

It was opened by a strange servant, on whom the odd figure of the visitor did not appear to make the most favourable impression possible, inasmuch as she no sooner saw him than she very nearly closed it, and placing herself in the narrow gap, inquired what he wanted. But Newman merely uttering the monosyllable 'Noggs,' as if it were some cabalistic word, at sound of which bolts would fly back and doors open, pushed briskly past and gained the door of Miss La Creevy's sitting-room, before the astonished servant could offer any opposition.

'Walk in if you please,' said Miss La Creevy in reply to the sound of Newman's knuckles; and in he
walked accordingly.

'Bless us!' cried Miss La Creevy, starting as Newman bolted in; 'what did you want, sir?'

'You have forgotten me,' said Newman, with an inclination of the head. 'I wonder at that. That nobody should remember me who knew me in other days,
is natural enough; but there are few people who, seeing me once, forget me *now*.' He glanced, as he
spoke, at his shabby clothes and paralytic limb, and
slightly shook his head.

'I did forget you, I declare,' said Miss La Creevy,
rising to receive Newman, who met her half-way,
'and I am ashamed of myself for doing so; for you
are a kind, good creature, Mr. Noggs. Sit down and
tell me all about Miss Nickleby. Poor dear thing!
I haven't seen her for this many a week.'

'How's that?' asked Newman.

'Why, the truth is, Mr. Noggs,' said Miss La
Creevy, 'that I have been out on a visit—the first visit
I have made for fifteen years.'

'That is a long time,' said Newman, sadly.

'So it is a very long time to look back upon in
years, though, somehow or other, thank Heaven, the
solitary days roll away peacefully and happily
enough,' replied the miniature-painter. 'I have a
brother, Mr. Noggs—the only relation I have—and
all that time I never saw him once. Not that we ever
quarrelled, but he was apprenticed down in the country, and he got married there, and new ties and affections springing up about him, he forgot a poor
little woman like me, as it was very reasonable he
should, you know. Don't suppose that I complain
about that, because I always said to myself, "It is
very natural; poor dear John is making his way in

the world, and has a wife to tell his cares and troubles to, and children now to play about him, so God bless him and them, and send we may all meet together one day where we shall part no more." But what do you think, Mr. Noggs,' said the miniature-painter, brightening up, and clapping her hands, 'of that very same brother coming up to London at last, and never resting till he found me out?—what do you think of his coming here and sitting down in that very chair, and crying like a child because he was so glad to see me?— what do you think of his insisting on taking me down all the way into the country to his own house (quite a sumptuous place, Mr. Noggs, with a large garden and I don't know how many fields, and a man in livery waiting at table, and cows and horses and pigs and I don't know what besides), and making me stay a whole month, and pressing me to stop there all my life——yes, all my life—and so did his wife, and so did the children—and there were four of them, and one, the eldest girl of all, they—they had named her after me eight good years before, they had indeed. I never was so happy; in all my life I never was!' The worthy soul hid her face in her handkerchief, and sobbed aloud; for it was the first opportunity she had had of unburdening her heart, and it would have its way.

'But bless my life,' said Miss La Creevy, wiping her eyes after a short pause, and cramming her handkerchief into her pocket with great bustle and despatch; 'what a foolish creature I must seem to you, Mr. Noggs! I shouldn't have said anything about it, only I wanted to explain to you how it was I hadn't seen Miss Nickleby.'

'Have you seen the old lady?' asked Newman.

'You mean Mrs. Nickleby?' said Miss La Creevy. 'Then I tell you what, Mr. Noggs, if you want to keep in the good books in that quarter, you had better not call her the old lady any more, for I suspect she wouldn't be best pleased to hear you. Yes, I went there the night before last, but she was quite on the high ropes about something, and was so grand and mysterious, that I couldn't make anything of her: so, to tell you the truth, I took it into my head to be grand too, and came away in state. I thought she would have come round again before this, but she hasn't been here.'

'About Miss Nickleby—' said Newman.

'Why, she was here twice while I was away,' returned Miss La Creevy. 'I was afraid she mightn't like to have me calling on her among those great folks in what 's-its-name Place, so I thought I 'd wait a day or two, and if I didn't see her, write.'

'Ah!' exclaimed Newman, cracking his fingers.

'However, I want to hear all the news about them from you,' said Miss La Creevy, 'How is the old rough and tough monster of Golden Square? Well, of course; such people always are. I don't mean how is he in health, but how is he going on: how is he behaving himself?'

'Damn him!' cried Newman, dashing his cherished hat on the floor; 'like a false hound.'

'Gracious, Mr. Noggs, you quite terrify me!' exclaimed Miss La Creevy, turning pale.

'I should have spoilt his features yesterday afternoon if I could have afforded it,' said Newman, moving restlessly about, and shaking his fist at a portrait of Mr. Canning over the mantel-piece. 'I was very near it. I was obliged to put my hands in my pockets, and keep 'em there very tight. I shall do it some day in that little back-parlour, I know I shall. I should have done it before now, if I hadn't been afraid of making bad worse. I shall double-lock my-

self in with him and have it out before I die, I'm
quite certain of it.'

'I shall scream if you don't compose yourself, Mr.
Noggs,' said Miss La Creevy; 'I'm sure I shan't be
able to help it.'

'Never mind,' rejoined Newman, darting violently to
and fro. 'He's coming up to-night: I wrote to tell
him. He little thinks I know; he little thinks I care.
Cunning scoundrel! he don't think that. Not he, not
he. Never mind, I'll thwart him—*I*, Newman
Noggs. Ho, ho, the rascal!'

Lashing himself up to an extravagant pitch of
fury, Newman Noggs jerked himself about the room
with the most eccentric motion ever beheld in a human
being: now sparring at the little miniatures on the
wall, and now giving himself violent thumps on the
head, as if to heighten the delusion, until he sank
down in his former seat quite breathless and exhausted.

'There,' said Newman, picking up his hat; 'that's
done me good. Now I'm better, and I'll tell you
all about it.'

It took some little time to reassure Miss La Creevy,
who had been almost frightened out of her senses
by this remarkable demonstration; but that done,
Newman faithfully related all that had passed in the
interview between Kate and her uncle, prefacing his
narrative with a statement of his previous suspicions
on the subject, and his reasons for forming them;
and concluding with a communication of the step he
had taken in secretly writing to Nicholas.

Though little Miss La Creevy's indignation was
not so singularly displayed as Newman's, it was
scarcely inferior in violence and intensity. Indeed
if Ralph Nickleby had happened to make his appearance in the room at that moment, there is some doubt
whether he would not have found Miss La Creevy

a more dangerous opponent than even Newman Noggs himself.

'God forgive me for saying so,' said Miss La Creevy, as a wind-up to all her expressions of anger, 'but I really feel as if I could stick this into him with pleasure.'

It was not a very awful weapon that Miss La Creevy held, it being in fact nothing more nor less than a black lead-pencil; but discovering her mistake, the little portrait-painter exchanged it for a mother-of-pearl fruit knife, wherewith, in proof of her desperate thoughts, she made a lunge as she spoke, which would have scarcely disturbed the crumb of a half-quartern loaf.

'She won't stop where she is, after to-night,' said Newman. 'That's a comfort.'

'Stop!' cried Miss La Creevy, 'she should have left there, weeks ago.'

'—If we had known of this,' rejoined Newman. 'But we didn't. Nobody could properly interfere but her mother or brother. The mother's weak— poor thing—weak. The dear young man will be here to-night.'

'Heart alive!' cried Miss La Creevy. 'He will do something desperate, Mr. Noggs, if you tell him all at once.'

Newman left off rubbing his hands, and assumed a thoughtful look.

'Depend upon it,' said Miss La Creevy, earnestly, 'if you are not very careful in breaking out the truth to him, he will do some violence upon his uncle or one of these men that will bring some terrible calamity upon his own head, and grief and sorrow to us all.'

'I never thought of that,' rejoined Newman, his countenance falling more and more. 'I came to ask you to receive his sister in case he brought her here, but—'

'But this is a matter of much greater importance,' interrupted Miss La Creevy; 'that you might have been sure of before you came, but the end of this, nobody can foresee, unless you are very guarded and careful.'

'What *can* I do?' cried Newman, scratching his head with an air of great vexation and perplexity. 'If he was to talk of pistolling 'em all, I should be obliged to say, "Certainly. Serve 'em right." '

Miss La Creevy could not suppress a small shriek on hearing this, and instantly set about extorting a solemn pledge from Newman that he would use his utmost endeavours to pacify the wrath of Nicholas; which, after some demur, was conceded. They then consulted together on the safest and surest mode of communicating to him the circumstances which had rendered his presence necessary.

'He must have time to cool before he can possibly do anything,' said Miss La Creevy. 'That is of the greatest consequence. He must not be told until late at night.'

'But he 'll be in town between six and seven this evening,' replied Newman. '*I* can't keep it from him when he asks me.'

'Then you must go out, Mr. Noggs,' said Miss La Creevy. 'You can easily have been kept away by business, and must not return till nearly midnight.'

'Then he 'll come straight here,' retorted Newman.

'So I suppose,' observed Miss La Creevy; 'but he won't find me at home, for I 'll go straight to the City the instant you leave, make up matters with Mrs. Nickleby, and take her away to the theatre, so that he may not even know where his sister lives.'

Upon further discussion, this appeared the safest and most feasible mode of proceeding that could possibly be adopted. Therefore it was finally determined that matters should be so arranged. Newman, after listening to many supplementary cautions and entreaties, took his leave of Miss La Creevy and trudged back to Golden Square, ruminating as he went upon a vast number of possibilities and impossibilities which crowded upon his brain, and arose out of the conversation that had just terminated.

CHAPTER XXXII

RELATING CHIEFLY TO SOME REMARKABLE CONVERSATION, AND SOME REMARKABLE PROCEEDINGS TO WHICH IT GIVES RISE

'LONDON at last!' cried Nicholas, throwing back his great-coat and rousing Smike from a long nap. 'It seemed to me as though we should never reach it.'

'And yet you came along at a tidy pace too,' observed the coachman, looking over his shoulder at Nicholas with no very pleasant expression of countenance.

'Ay, I know that,' was the reply; 'but I have been very anxious to be at my journey's end, and that makes the way seem long.'

'Well,' remarked the coachman, 'If the way seemed long with such cattle as you 've sat behind, you *must* have been most uncommon anxious'; and so saying, he let out his whip-lash and touched up a little boy on the calves of his legs by way of emphasis.

They rattled on through the noisy, bustling, crowded streets of London, now displaying long double rows of brightly-burning lamps, dotted here and there with the chemists' glaring lights, and illuminated besides with the brilliant flood that streamed from the windows of the shops, where sparkling jewellery, silks and velvets of the richest colours, the most inviting delicacies, and most sumptuous articles of luxurious ornament, succeeded each other in rich and glittering profusion. Streams of people apparently without end poured on and on, jostling each other in the crowd and hurrying forward, scarcely seeming to notice the riches that surrounded them on every side; while vehicles of all shapes and makes, mingled up together in one moving mass like running water, lent their ceaseless roar to swell the noise and tumult.

As they dashed by the quickly-changing and ever-varying objects, it was curious to observe in what a strange procession they passed before the eye. Emporiums of splendid dresses, the materials brought from every quarter of the world; tempting stores of everything to stimulate and pamper the sated appetite and give new relish to the oft-repeated feast; vessels of burnished gold and silver, wrought into every exquisite form of vase and dish, and goblet; guns, swords, pistols, and patent engines of destruction; screws and irons for the crooked, clothes for the newly-born, drugs for the sick, coffins for the dead, churchyards for the buried—all these jumbled each with the other and flocking side by side, seemed to flit by in motley dance like the fantastic groups of the old Dutch painter, and with the same stern moral for the unheeding restless crowd.

Nor were there wanting objects in the crowd itself to give new point and purpose to the shifting scene. The rags of the squalid ballad-singer fluttered in the rich light that showed the goldsmith's treasures; pale and pinched-up faces hovered about the windows where was tempting food; hungry eyes wandered over the profusion guarded by one thin sheet of brittle glass—an iron wall to them; half-naked shivering figures stopped to gaze at Chinese shawls and golden stuffs of India. There was a christening party at the largest coffin-maker's, and a funeral hatchment had stopped some great improvements in the bravest mansion. Life and death went hand in hand; wealth and poverty stood side by side; repletion and starvation laid them down together.

But it was London; and the old country lady inside, who had put her head out of the coach-window a mile or two on this side of Kingston, and had cried out to the driver that she was sure he must have passed it and forgotten to set her down, was satisfied at last.

Nicholas engaged beds for himself and Smike at the inn where the coach stopped, and repaired, without the delay of another moment, to the lodgings of Newman Noggs; for his anxiety and impatience had increased with every succeeding minute, and were almost beyond control.

There was a fire in Newman's garret, and a candle had been left burning; the floor was cleanly swept, the room was as comfortably arranged as such a room could be, and meat and drink were placed in order upon the table. Everything bespoke the affectionate care and attention of Newman Noggs, but Newman himself was not there.

'Do you know what time he will be home!' inquired Nicholas, tapping at the door of Newman's front neighbour.

'Ah, Mr. Johnson!' said Crowl, presenting himself. 'Welcome, sir.—How well you're looking! I never could have believed—'

'Pardon me,' interposed Nicholas. 'My question —I am extremely anxious to know.'

'Why, he has a troublesome affair of business,' replied Crowl, 'and will not be home before twelve o'clock. He was very unwilling to go, I can tell you, but there was no help for it. However, he left word that you were to make yourself comfortable till he came back, and that I was to entertain you, which I shall be very glad to do.'

In proof of his extreme readiness to exert himself for the general entertainment, Mr. Crowl drew a chair to the table as he spoke, and helping himself plentifully to the cold meat, invited Nicholas and Smike to follow his example.

Disappointed and uneasy, Nicholas could touch no food, so, after he had seen Smike comfortably established at the table, he walked out (despite a great many dissuasions uttered by Mr. Crowl with his mouth full), and left Smike to detain Newman in case he returned first.

As Miss La Creevy had anticipated, Nicholas betook himself straight to her house. Finding her from home, he debated within himself for some time whether he should go to his mother's residence and so compromise her with Ralph Nickleby. Fully persuaded, however, that Newman would not have solicited him to return unless there was some strong reason which required his presence at home, he resolved to go there, and hastened eastwards with all speed.

Mrs. Nickleby would not be at home, the girl said, until past twelve, or later. She believed Miss Nickleby was well, but she didn't live at home now, nor did she come home except very seldom. She couldn't say where she was stopping, but it was not at Madame Mantalini's. She was sure of that.

With his heart beating violently, and apprehending he knew not what disaster, Nicholas returned to where he had left Smike. Newman had not been home. He wouldn't be, till twelve o'clock; there was no chance of it. Was there no possibility of sending to fetch him if it were only for an instant, or forwarding to him one line of writing to which he might return a verbal reply? That was quite impracticable. He was not at Golden Square, and probably had been sent to execute some commission at a distance.

Nicholas tried to remain quietly where he was, but he felt so nervous and excited that he could not sit still. He seemed to be losing time unless he was moving. It was an absurd fancy, he knew, but he was wholly unable to resist it. So, he took up his hat and rambled out again.

He strolled westward this time, pacing the long streets with hurried footsteps, and agitated by a thousand misgivings and apprehensions which he could not overcome. He passed into Hyde Park, now silent and deserted, and increased his rate of walking as if in the hope of leaving his thoughts behind. They crowded upon him more thickly, however, now there were no passing objects to attract his attention; and the one idea was always uppermost, that some stroke of ill-fortune must have occurred so calamitous in its nature that all were fearful of disclosing it to him. The old question arose again and again—What could it be? Nicholas walked till he was weary, but was not one bit the wiser; and indeed he came out of the Park at last a great deal more confused and perplexed than he had gone into it.

He had taken scarcely anything to eat or drink since early in the morning, and felt quite worn out and exhausted. As he returned languidly towards the point from which he had started, along one of the thoroughfares which lie between Park Lane and Bond Street, he passed a handsome hotel, before which he stopped mechanically.

'An expensive place, I dare say,' thought Nicholas; 'but a pint of wine and a biscuit are no great debauch wherever they are had. And yet I don't know.'

He walked on a few steps, but looking wistfully down the long vista of gas-lamps before him, and thinking how long it would take to reach the end of it—and being besides in that kind of mood in which a man is most disposed to yield to his first impulse —and being, besides, strongly attracted to the hotel, in part by curiosity, and in part by some odd mixture of feelings which he would have been troubled to define—Nicholas turned back again, and walked into the coffee-room.

It was very handsomely furnished. The walls were ornamented with the choicest specimens of French paper, enriched with a gilded cornice of elegant design. The floor was covered with a rich carpet; and two superb mirrors, one above the chimney-piece and one at the opposite end of the room reaching from floor to ceiling, multiplied the other beauties and added new ones of their own to enhance the general effect. There was rather a noisy party of four gentlemen in a box by the fireplace, and only two other persons present—both elderly gentlemen, and both alone.

Observing all this in the first comprehensive glance with which a stranger surveys a place that is new to him, Nicholas sat himself down in the box next to the noisy party, with his back towards them, and postponing his order for a pint of claret until such time as the waiter and one of the elderly gentlemen should have settled a disputed question relative to the price of an item in the bill of fare, took up a newspaper and began to read.

He had not read twenty lines, and was in truth half-dozing, when he was startled by the mention of his sister's name. 'Little Kate Nickleby' were the words that caught his ear. He raised his head in amazement, and as he did so, saw by the reflection in the opposite glass, that two of the party behind him had risen and were standing before the fire. 'It must have come from one of them,' thought Nicholas. He waited to hear more with a countenance of some indignation, for the tone of speech had been anything but respectful, and the appearance of the individual whom he presumed to have been the speaker was coarse and swaggering.

This person—so Nicholas observed in the same glance at the mirror which had enabled him to see his face—was standing with his back to the fire conversing with a younger man, who stood with his back to the company, wore his hat, and was adjusting his shirt collar by the aid of the glass. They spoke in whispers, now and then bursting into a loud laugh, but Nicholas could catch no repetition of the words, nor anything sounding at all like the words, which had attracted his attention.

At length the two resumed their seats, and more wine being ordered, the party grew louder in their mirth. Still there was no reference made to anybody with whom he was acquainted, and Nicholas became persuaded that his excited fancy had either imagined the sounds altogether, or converted some other words into the name which had been so much in his thoughts. 'It is remarkable too,' thought Nicholas; 'if it had been "Kate" or "Kate Nickleby," I should not have been so much surprised; but "little Kate Nickleby"!'

NICHOLAS ATTRACTED BY THE MENTION OF HIS SISTER'S NAME.

The wine coming at the moment prevented his finishing the sentence. He swallowed a glassful and took up the paper again. At that instant—

'Little Kate Nickleby!' cried a voice behind him.

'I was right,' muttered Nicholas as the paper fell from his hand. 'And it was the man I supposed.'

'As there was a proper objection to drinking her in heel-taps,' said the voice, 'we 'll give her the first glass in the new magnum. Little Kate Nickleby!'

'Little Kate Nickleby,' cried the other three. And the glasses were set down empty.

Keenly alive to the tone and manner of this slight and careless mention of his sister's name in a public place, Nicholas fired at once; but he kept himself quiet by a great effort, and did not even turn his head.

'The jade!' said the same voice which had spoken before. 'She's a true Nickleby—a worthy imitator of her old uncle Ralph—she hangs back to be more sought after—so does he; nothing to be got out of Ralph unless you follow him up, and then the money comes doubly welcome, and the bargain doubly hard, for you 're impatient and he isn't. Oh! infernal cunning.'

'Infernal cunning,' echoed two voices.

Nicholas was in a perfect agony as the two elderly gentlemen opposite, rose one after the other and went away, lest they should be the means of his losing one word of what was said. But the conversation was suspended as they withdrew, and resumed with even greater freedom when they had left the room.

'I am afraid,' said the younger gentleman, 'that the old woman has grown jea-a-lous, and locked her up. Upon my soul it looks like it.'

'If they quarrel and little Nickleby goes home to her mother, so much the better,' said the first. 'I can do anything with the old lady. She'll believe anything I tell her.'

'Egad that's true,' returned the other voice. 'Ha, ha, ha! Poor deyvle!'

The laugh was taken up by the two voices which always came in together, and became general at Mrs. Nickleby's expense. Nicholas turned burning hot with rage, but he commanded himself for the moment, and waited to hear more.

What he heard need not be repeated here. Suffice it that as the wine went round he heard enough to acquaint him with the characters and designs of those whose conversation he overheard; to possess him with the full extent of Ralph's villainy, and the real reason of his own presence being required in London. He heard all this and more. He heard his sister's sufferings derided, and her virtuous conduct jeered at and brutally misconstrued; he heard her name bandied from mouth to mouth, and herself made the subject of coarse and insolent wagers, free speech, and licentious jesting.

The man who had spoken first, led the conversation and indeed almost engrossed it, being only stimulated from time to time by some slight observation from one or other of his companions. To him then Nicholas addressed himself when he was sufficiently composed to stand before the party, and force the words from his parched and scorching throat.

'Let me have a word with you sir,' said Nicholas.

'With me, sir?' retorted Sir Mulberry Hawk, eyeing him in disdainful surprise.

'I said with you,' replied Nicholas, speaking with great difficulty, for his passion choked him.

'A mysterious stranger, upon my soul!' exclaimed Sir Mulberry, raising his wine-glass to his lips, and looking round upon his friends.

'Will you step apart with me for a few minutes, or do you refuse?' said Nicholas sternly.

Sir Mulberry merely paused in the act of drinking, and bade him either name his business or leave the table.

Nicholas drew a card from his pocket, and threw it before him.

'There, sir,' said Nicholas; 'my business you will guess.'

A momentary expression of astonishment, not unmixed with some confusion, appeared in the face of Sir Mulberry as he read the name; but he subdued it in an instant, and tossing the card to Lord Frederick Verisopht, who sat opposite, drew a tooth-pick from a glass before him, and very leisurely applied it to his mouth.

'Your name and address?' said Nicholas, turning paler as his passion kindled.

'I shall give you neither,' replied Sir Mulberry.

'If there is a gentleman in this party,' said Nicholas, looking round and scarcely able to make his white lips form the words, 'he will acquaint me with the name and residence of this man.'

There was a dead silence.

'I am the brother of the young lady who has been the subject of conversation here,' said Nicholas. 'I denounce this person as a liar, and impeach him as a coward. If he has a friend here, he will save him the disgrace of the paltry attempt to conceal his name —an utterly useless one—for I will find it out, nor leave him until I have.'

Sir Mulberry looked at him contemptuously, and, addressing his companions, said—

'Let the fellow talk. I have nothing serious to say to boys of his station; and his pretty sister shall save him a broken head, if he talks till midnight.'

'You are a base and spiritless scoundrel!' said Nicholas, 'and shall be proclaimed so to the world. I *will* know you; I will follow you home if you walk the streets till morning.'

Sir Mulberry's hand involuntarily closed upon the decanter, and he seemed for an instant about to launch it at the head of his challenger. But he only filled his glass, and laughed in derision.

Nicholas sat himself down, directly opposite to the party, and, summoning the waiter, paid his bill.

'Do you know that person's name?' he inquired of the man in an audible voice, pointing out Sir Mulberry as he put the question.

Sir Mulberry laughed again, and the two voices which had always spoken together, echoed the laugh; but rather feebly.

'That gentleman, sir?' replied the waiter, who, no doubt, knew his cue, and answered with just as little respect, and just as much impertience as he could safely show: 'no, sir, I do not, sir.'

'Here, you sir!' cried Sir Mulberry, as the man was retiring. 'Do you know *that* person's name?'

'Name, sir? No, sir.'

'Then you 'll find it there,' said Sir Mulberry, throwing Nicholas's card towards him; 'and when you have made yourself master of it, put that piece of pasteboard in the fire.'

The man grinned, and, looking doubtfully at Nicholas, compromised the matter by sticking the card in the chimney-glass. Having done this, he retired.

Nicholas folded his arms, and, biting his lip, sat perfectly quiet; sufficiently expressing by his manner, however, a firm determination to carry his threat of following Sir Mulberry home, into steady execution.

It was evident from the tone in which the younger

member of the party appeared to remonstrate with
his friend, that he objected to this course of proceeding, and urged him to comply with the request which
Nicholas had made. Sir Mulberry, however, who
was not quite sober, and who was in a sullen and dogged state of obstinacy, soon silenced the representa-
tions of his weak young friend, and further seemed
—as if to save himself from a repetition of them—to
insist on being left alone. However this might have
been, the young gentleman and the two who had always spoke together, actually rose to go after a short
interval, and presently retired, leaving their friend
alone with Nicholas.

It will be very readily supposed that to one in the
condition of Nicholas the minutes appeared to move
with leaden wings indeed, and that their progress did
not seem the more rapid from the monotonous tick-
ing of a French clock, or the shrill sound of its little
bell which told the quarters. But there he sat; and
in his old seat on the opposite side of the room reclined Sir Mulberry Hawk, with his legs upon the
cushion, and his handkerchief thrown negligently
over his knees: finishing his magnum of claret with the
utmost coolness and indifference.

Thus they remained in perfect silence for upwards
of an hour—Nicholas would have thought for three
hours at least, but that the little bell had only gone
four times. Twice or thrice he looked angrily and
impatiently round; but there was Sir Mulberry in the
same attitude, putting his glass to his lips from time
to time, and looking vacantly at the wall, as if he
were wholly ignorant of the presence of any living
person.

At length he yawned, stretched himself and rose,
walked cooly to the glass, and, having surveyed himself therein, turned round and honoured Nicholas

with a long and contemptuous stare. Nicholas stared again with right goodwill; Sir Mulberry shrugged his shoulders, smiled slightly, rang the bell, and ordered the waiter to help him on with his great-coat.

The man did so, and held the door open.

'Don't wait,' said Sir Mulberry; and they were alone again.

Sir Mulberry took several turns up and down the room, whistling carelessly all the time: stopped to finish the last glass of claret which he had poured out a few minutes before, walked again, put on his hat, adjusted it by the glass, drew on his gloves, and, at last, walked slowly out. Nicholas, who had been fuming and chafing until he was nearly wild, darted from his seat, and followed him: so closely, that before the door had swung upon its hinges after Sir Mulberry's passing out, they stood side by side in the street together.

There was a private cabriolet in waiting; the groom opened the apron, and jumped out to the horse's head.

'Will you make yourself known to me?' asked Nicholas, in a suppressed voice.

'No,' replied the other fiercely, and confirming the refusal with an oath. 'No.'

'If you trust to your horse's speed, you will find yourself mistaken,' said Nicholas. 'I will accompany you. By Heaven I will, if I hang on to the foot-board!'

'You shall be horsewhipped if you do,' returned Sir Mulberry.

'You are a villain,' said Nicholas.

'You are an errand-boy for aught I know,' said Sir Mulberry Hawk.

'I am the son of a country gentleman,' returned Nicholas, 'your equal in birth and education, and your superior I trust in everything besides. I tell you again, Miss Nickleby is my sister. Will you or will you not answer for your unmanly and brutal conduct?'

'To a proper champion—yes. To you—no,' returned Sir Mulberry, taking the reins in his hand. 'Stand out of the way, dog. William, let go her head.'

'You had better not,' cried Nicholas, springing on the step as Sir Mulberry jumped in, and catching at the reins. 'He has no command over the horse, mind. You shall not go—you shall not, I swear—till you have told me who you are.'

The groom hesitated, for the mare, who was a high-spirited animal and throughbred, plunged so violently that he could not hold her.

'Leave go, I tell you!' thundered his master.

The man obeyed. The animal reared and plunged as though it would dash the carriage into a thousand pieces, but Nicholas, blind to all sense of danger, and conscious of nothing but his fury, still maintained his place and his hold upon the reins.

'Will you unclasp your hand?'

'Will you tell me who you are?'

'No!'

'No!'

In less time than the quickest tongue could tell it, these words were exchanged, and Sir Mulberry shortening his whip, applied it furiously to the head and shoulders of Nicholas. It was broken in the struggle; Nicholas gained the heavy handle, and with it laid open one side of his antagonist's face from his eye to his lip. He saw the gash; knew that the mare had darted off at a wild mad gallop; a hundred lights danced in his eyes, and he felt himself flung violently upon the ground.

He was giddy and sick, but staggered to his feet

directly, roused by the loud shouts of the men who were tearing up the street, and screaming to those ahead to clear the way. He was conscious of a torrent of people rushing quickly by—looking up, could discern the cabriolet whirled along the foot pavement with frightful rapidity—then heard a loud cry, the smashing of some heavy body, and the breaking of glass—and then the crowd closed in in the distance, and he could see or hear no more.

The general attention had been entirely directed from himself to the person in the carriage, and he was quite alone. Rightly judging that under such circumstances it would be madness to follow, he turned down a bye-street in search of the nearest coach-stand, finding after a minute or two that he was reeling like a drunken man, and aware for the first time of a stream of blood that was trickling down his face and breast.